SAGE was founded in 1965 by Sara Miller McCune to support the dissemination of usable knowledge by publishing innovative and high-quality research and teaching content. Today, we publish over 900 journals, including those of more than 400 learned societies, more than 800 new books per year, and a growing range of library products including archives, data, case studies, reports, and video. SAGE remains majority-owned by our founder, and after Sara's lifetime will become owned by a charitable trust that secures our continued independence.

Los Angeles | London | New Delhi | Singapore | Washington DC | Melbourne

CHARACTER STRENGTH DEVELOPMENT

Thank you for choosing a SAGE product!
If you have any comment, observation or feedback,
I would like to personally hear from you.

Please write to me at **contactceo@sagepub.in**

Vivek Mehra, Managing Director and CEO, SAGE India.

Bulk Sales

SAGE India offers special discounts
for purchase of books in bulk.
We also make available special imprints
and excerpts from our books on demand.

For orders and enquiries, write to us at

Marketing Department
SAGE Publications India Pvt Ltd
B1/I-1, Mohan Cooperative Industrial Area
Mathura Road, Post Bag 7
New Delhi 110044, India

E-mail us at **marketing@sagepub.in**

Subscribe to our mailing list
Write to **marketing@sagepub.in**

This book is also available as an e-book.

CHARACTER STRENGTH DEVELOPMENT

Perspectives from Positive Psychology

EDITED BY
Aneesh Kumar P.
Tony Sam George
Sudhesh N. T.

Los Angeles | London | New Delhi
Singapore | Washington DC | Melbourne

Copyright © Aneesh Kumar P., Tony Sam George, Sudhesh N.T., 2018

All rights reserved. No part of this book may be reproduced or utilized in any form or by any means, electronic or mechanical, including photocopying, recording, or by any information storage or retrieval system, without permission in writing from the publisher.

First published in 2018 by

SAGE Publications India Pvt Ltd
B1/I-1 Mohan Cooperative Industrial Area
Mathura Road, New Delhi 110 044, India
www.sagepub.in

SAGE Publications Inc
2455 Teller Road
Thousand Oaks, California 91320, USA

SAGE Publications Ltd
1 Oliver's Yard, 55 City Road
London EC1Y 1SP, United Kingdom

SAGE Publications Asia-Pacific Pte Ltd
3 Church Street
#10-04 Samsung Hub
Singapore 049483

Published by Vivek Mehra for SAGE Publications India Pvt Ltd, typeset in 10.5/13 pts Bembo by Zaza Eunice, Hosur, Tamil Nadu, India and printed at Chaman Enterprises, New Delhi.

Library of Congress Cataloging-in-Publication Data

Names: P., Aneesh Kumar | George, Tony Sam, editor. | T., Sudhesh N.
Title: Character strength development: perspectives from positive psychology/ edited by Aneesh Kumar P., Tony Sam George, Sudhesh N.T.
Description: Thousand Oaks: SAGE Publications India Pvt Ltd, 2018. | Includes bibliographical references and index.
Identifiers: LCCN 2018024803| ISBN 9789352807772 (print hb) | ISBN 9789352807789 (e-pub 2.0) | ISBN 9789352807796 (e-book)
Subjects: LCSH: Personality development. | Child psychology. | Adolescent psychology. | Positive psychology.
Classification: LCC BF723.P4 .C353 2018 | DDC 155.2/5—dc23 LC record available at https://lccn.loc.gov/2018024803

ISBN: 978-93-528-0777-2 (HB)

SAGE Team: Abhijit Baroi, Alekha Chandra Jena and Shaonli Deb

Contents

List of Tables	ix
List of Figures	xi
List of Abbreviations	xiii
Preface	xv

Chapter 1	Character Strengths in the Context of Positive Schooling by *Marco Weber*	1
Chapter 2	Eccomi Pronto: Developing Curricula to Promote Character Strength Development in Primary School Students Through Storytelling by *Jessica Bertolani and John C. Carey*	31
Chapter 3	Developing and Assessing Strategies to Foster Children's Character Strengths and Well-being by *Sarah Weissmeyer and Mark D. Holder*	44
Chapter 4	Considering Character Strength Development as an Approach to Addressing Disengagement in Secondary Schools by *Nick Holton*	79
Chapter 5	The Measurement of Character Strengths and Virtues by *Zohra Ihsan and Adrian Furnham*	92
Chapter 6	People's Theatre on Character Strengths Development with Youth by *Lui Ka Ki David*	113
Chapter 7	Resiliency, Positive Coping and Posttraumatic Growth in Survivors of Child Abuse and Neglect by *Jennifer M. Foster*	132

Chapter 8   *If the Character Is Lost....!* Strength and Value-based Solutions to Maintain the Character of the Victimized by *Santhosh Kareepadath Rajan and Ruopfuvinuo Pienyu*   151

Chapter 9   Children's Developing Emotional Competence in a Global Context by *Vaishali V. Raval and Jennifer H. Green*   160

Chapter 10   Self-compassion as a Foundation for the Development of Character Strengths in Young Adults by *Salome Divya Vijaykumar, Ranjitha Kumar, Avneet Kaur, Vibha Bhat, Ritu Verma and Anirudh Kedia*   179

Chapter 11   Nurturing Character Strength in Children: Agents of Socialization to Promote Well-being by *Bhagyalakshmi K. C. and Raseela K. N.*   204

Chapter 12   Scope for Character Strength Development in Organizations by *Vijayalaya Srinivas T., Vijaya R., Lijo Thomas and Hitankshi M. Trivedi*   232

Chapter 13   Heroes Begin Early: Parenting and the Development of Character Strengths by *Bishakha Majumdar and Sibnath Deb*   249

Chapter 14   The Popularization of Technology and Family: The Impacts of Family Atmosphere, Parent–Child Conflicts and Parenting Approaches on Adolescents' Digital Character by *Vincent Wan-ping Lee, Henry Wai-hang Ling and Johnson Chun-sing Cheung*   266

Chapter 15   Positivism in Relation to Signature Strengths in Educated Working Women and Housewives by *S. S. Nathawat and Tanya Tripathi*   292

Chapter 16   Character Strength Development: Does Family Matter? by *Padmakumari P. and Dolly Jose*   302

Chapter 17 Psychological Trauma and Posttraumatic
Growth: A Brief Introduction by *Rayees
Mohammad Bhat and Shoma Chakrawarty*   314

Chapter 18 Young Adults' Awareness and Commitment
to Use of Character Strengths:
An Examination of University
Students in Nairobi by *Beatrice
W. E. Churu and Sahaya G. Selvam*   337

Chapter 19 From Deficit to a Strength Model:
Character Strength Interventions for
Children with Disabilities
by *Jessline Williams and Aneesh Kumar P.*   353

Chapter 20 Character Strengths and Virtues:
Manifestation and Links with Positive
Youth Development in Greece
by *Sophie Leontopoulou*   368

About the Editors and Contributors   397
Index   406

List of Tables

1.1	VIA Classification of Six Core Virtues and 24 Character Strengths	3
1.2	Overview of Inputs, Processes and Outcomes Mentioned in the Present Chapter	15
5.1	Twenty-four Personal Strengths That Can Be Clustered into Six Core Virtues	95
5.2	Brief Descriptions of the Different Versions of the VIA-IS	99
5.3	Brief Descriptions of the Different Existing Measures of Character Strengths	103
5.4	The Corresponding Character Strengths to the Big Five Traits	104
5.5	Correlations of the VIA-IS's Scales with SWB (Subjective Well-being, N = 184), SWLS (Satisfaction with Life Scale, N = 635), PANAS (Positive = PA and Negative Affect = NA, N = 184), and Big Five Dimensions (N = Neuroticism, E = Extroversion, O = Openness, C = Conscientiousness, A = Agreeableness, N = 184)	105
14.1	Details of the Focus Group Interviews with the Types of Key Informants, Location and Number of People	275
14.2	The Coding Frame, with the Basic Themes, Organizing Themes and Reporting Themes Extracted from Data Analyses	276
14.3	Core Elements of Character Strengths-based Parent Training Programme Related to Technology	284
14.4	Basic Components in Parent Training Programmes	286

15.1a Means and SDs on WISDOM of Signature
       Strengths of Four Groups   296
15.1b ANOVA for Wisdom   296
15.2a Means and SDs on Courage of Signature
       Strengths of Four Groups   297
15.2b ANOVA for Courage   297
15.3a Means and SDs on Humanity of Signature
       Strengths of Four Groups   298
15.3b ANOVA for Humanity   298
15.4a Means and SDs on Justice of Signature
       Strengths of Four Groups   298
15.4b ANOVA for Justice   298
15.5a Means and SDs on Temperance of Signature
       Strengths of Four Groups   299
15.5b ANOVA for Temperance   299
15.6a Means and SDs on Transcendence of Signature
       Strengths of Four Groups   300
15.6b ANOVA for Transcendence   300

20.1   Means and Standard Deviations (SDs) for
       Character Strengths and Virtues and for Creativity,
       Optimism and Self-efficacy for the Total Sample,
       for Gender, Grade and SES   375
20.2   Correlations Between Character Strengths and
       Creativity, Optimism and Self-efficacy for
       the Total Sample   379
20.3   Correlations Between Virtues and Creativity,
       Optimism and Self-efficacy for the Total Sample   381
20.4   Hierarchical Regression Analyses for Virtues,
       Creativity and Optimism   387

List of Figures

2.1	Eccomi Pronto Logic Model	36
10.1	Self-compassion as a Foundation for the Development of Character Strengths	191
11.1	Socialization: Influencing Factors and Consequences	212
12.1	VBO Model of Ethical Decision-making	239
13.1	Classification of Character Strengths on the 'Heart vs. Mind' and 'Others vs. Self' Dimensions	252
17.1	A Model of Posttraumatic Growth	322
20.1	Gender (a), Grade (age, b) and SES (c) Differences in Character Strengths	384

List of Abbreviations

ACE	adverse childhood experiences
ACST	abbreviated character strengths test
ANOVAs	analyses of variance
CAN	child abuse and neglect
CASEL	collaborative for academic, social and emotional learning
CFIA	Canadian Food Inspection Agency
COR	conservation of resources
CSR	corporate social responsibility
CSRF	character strengths rating form
CSs	character strengths
CSV	character strengths and virtues
DPE	deliberate psychological education
EP	Eccomi Pronto
GPA	grade point average
ICAF	International Community Arts Festival
ICT	information and communication technology
MFY	making friends with yourself
NEF	New Economics Foundation
PA	public address
P-E	person–environment
PPI	positive psychology intervention
PTG	posttraumatic growth
PTSD	posttraumatic stress disorder
SDs	standard deviations

SEL	social–emotional learning
SES	socio-economic status
SIT	stress inoculation theory
SMEs	small and medium enterprises
SWB	subjective well-being
TF-CBT	trauma-focused cognitive behavioural therapy
UbD	understanding by design
VIA CSS	VIA children's strengths survey
VIA	values in action
VIA-IS	values in action inventory of strengths
VIA-RTO	values in action rising to the occasion inventory
VIA-Youth	values in action inventory of strengths for youth
WHO	World Health Organization
WOWs	walls of well-being

Preface

Research in the area of positive psychology has brought out the importance of human virtues such as resilience, happiness and coping. Research studies have highlighted that focusing on positive strengths and assets in human beings can foster well-being and coping among individuals. Character strengths, developmental assets and resilience research have been some of the major areas under the realm of positive psychology research. Character strengths are the positive assets or traits within individuals that are reflected through their behaviours, thoughts and actions (Park, Peterson, & Seligman, 2004). Research on character strengths has highlighted that both the individual and their environment play a crucial role in the development of character strengths (Hutchinson, Stuart, & Pretorius, 2010). The concept of character strengths has been applied and researched in various fields including education and schooling (Park & Peterson, 2008; Seligman, Ernst, Gillham, Reivich, & Linkins, 2009), counselling and psychotherapy (Uliaszek, Rashid, Williams, & Gulamani, 2016; Wong, 2006), and training and coaching (Linley & Harrington, 2006). The focus has also been on studying cultural differences and in connecting to values and moral development (Park, Peterson, & Seligman, 2006; Linley et al., 2007). The Values in Action (VIA) and related research by Seligman and his colleagues has been a major pathbreaking work in the area of character strength research. The VIA inventory and classification of character strengths involving multi-country studies has brought out evidence-based practices in the field (Peterson & Seligman, 2004). There are also researchers exploring character strengths from value-, ethics- and morality-based perspectives and understanding these strengths independent of VIA classification and measurement.

Development of character is as important as teaching academic skills (Seligman, Ernst, Gillham, Reivich, & Linkins, 2009). Contemporary research indicates that the social emotional learning of the child is very important not just for day-to-day management in classrooms but for later success in life. Character skills need not be taught to children as a separate subject, it can be taught to children through any subject they learn at school or at home. Teaching character to children can foster positive classroom environment and help build relationships (Park & Peterson, 2008). Students learn while they listen to each other's stories and reflect on their learning. It helps them to be more connected to the teachers and other students in the classrooms (Weber & Ruch, 2012). Teaching character to children when young is very important as they go on to become adults who shape our society in future years. Though the intellectual development of the child is important, it is also important that we develop future citizens who can interact with respect, kindness, integrity and honesty. Opportunities can be created in classrooms for children to develop hope, fairness, humour, appreciation and other character strengths. Educators, parents and others working with children can play a key role in fostering character strength development (McGovern & Miller, 2008; Peterson & Seligman, 2004). Psychologists and researchers in child development have found that character strengths enhance well-being and can be nurtured through systematic programmes.

This proposed edited book aims to document research- and evidence-based practices using character strengths. The book would provide a better understanding for professionals and researchers to connect the theoretical understanding about the concept of character strength. The arguments and discussions raised by the experts in their respective chapters would bring about new research ideas. The chapters in the book would act as a guide for practitioners, educators and policymakers to incorporate character strength-based approaches in their practice. The book would also be a document of reference for students and researchers. The idea underlying the book would be to understand the concept of character strengths and its development, and to bring out sustainable practices. The effort is to look at various aspects of character strength development and identify the best approaches to nurture them in children.

Aneesh Kumar P.
Tony Sam George
Sudhesh N. T.

REFERENCES

Hutchinson, A. M. K., Stuart, A. D., & Pretorius, H. G. (2010). Biological contributions to well-being: The relationships amongst temperament, character strengths and resilience. *SA Journal of Industrial Psychology, 36*(2), 1–10.

Linley, P. A., & Harrington, S. (2006). Strengths coaching: A potential-guided approach to coaching psychology. *International Coaching Psychology Review, 1*(1), 37–46.

Linley, P. A., Maltby, J., Wood, A. M., Joseph, S., Harrington, S., Peterson, C.,... & Seligman, M. E. (2007). Character strengths in the United Kingdom: The VIA inventory of strengths. *Personality and Individual Differences, 43*(2), 341–351.

McGovern, T. V., & Miller, S. L. (2008). Integrating teacher behaviors with character strengths and virtues for faculty development. *Teaching of Psychology, 35*(4), 278–285.

Park, N., & Peterson, C. (2008). Positive psychology and character strengths: Application to strengths-based school counseling. *Professional School Counseling, 12*(2), 85–92.

Park, N., Peterson, C., & Seligman, M. E. (2004). Strengths of character and well-being. *Journal of Social and Clinical Psychology, 23*(5), 603–619.

Park, N., Peterson, C., & Seligman, M. E. (2006). Character strengths in fifty-four nations and the fifty US states. *The Journal of Positive Psychology, 1*(3), 118–129.

Peterson, C., & Seligman, M. E. (2004). *Character strengths and virtues: A handbook and classification* (Vol. 1). New York: Oxford University Press.

Seligman, M. E., Ernst, R. M., Gillham, J., Reivich, K., & Linkins, M. (2009). Positive education: Positive psychology and classroom interventions. *Oxford Review Of Education, 35*(3), 293–311.

Uliaszek, A. A., Rashid, T., Williams, G. E., & Gulamani, T. (2016). Group therapy for university students: A randomized control trial of dialectical behavior therapy and positive psychotherapy. *Behaviour Research and Therapy, 77*, 78–85.

Weber, M., & Ruch, W. (2012). The role of a good character in 12-year-old school children: Do character strengths matter in the classroom? *Child Indicators Research, 5*(2), 317–334.

Wong, Y. J. (2006). Strength-Centered Therapy: A social constructionist, virtues-based psychotherapy. *Psychotherapy: Theory, Research, Practice, Training, 43*(2), 133.

Chapter 1

Character Strengths in the Context of Positive Schooling

Marco Weber

A CLASSIFICATION OF CHARACTER STRENGTHS

Character strengths as positive traits are the core concepts in this chapter. Therefore, an introduction of the values in action (VIA) classification of strengths by Peterson and Seligman (2004) will be presented here. The VIA Institute on Character was created to develop conceptual and empirical means addressing the question of how to define an individual's 'good character' and how to measure it (Peterson, 2006). Within this context, Peterson and Seligman (2004) started a project to identify a model helpful to describe the good character, which finally resulted in the VIA classification of strengths. In their approach, they focus on what is right about individuals with a special interest in specific traits (i.e., character strengths) and their contribution to optimal development and functioning (e.g., Park & Peterson, 2006a). According to Peterson and Seligman (2004), it is possible to distinguish three hierarchical levels describing the good character, namely *virtues* (i.e., abstract core characteristics, defined by philosophers and religious leaders) at the highest level, *character strengths* (i.e., manifest, assessable mechanisms and processes that lead to or exemplify the virtues) and *situational themes* (i.e., specific habits that help people in specific situations to use their character strengths) at the lowest level. As this chapter is about character strengths, only character strengths are of interest in the following discussion.

While identifying a first set of positive traits that might be appropriate to be included in such a classification of human strengths, diverse sources (e.g., psychiatric literature, texts on youth development, character education, religion, philosophy, also popular songs, greeting cards, bumper stickers, obituaries and testimonials, mottoes and credos, Tarot cards and the profiles of Pokémon characters) have been screened searching for possible candidates (Peterson, 2006). For the final decision on whether or not these candidates should be included in the VIA classification (Peterson & Seligman, 2004), several criteria were developed that character strengths need to satisfy to be distinguishable from common and broader personality traits. Among such criteria were, for example, (a) a character strength is trait-like and measurable (i.e., shows generality and stability and has been successfully measured by researchers as an individual difference), (b) is morally valued and widely recognized across cultures and (c) is fulfilling (e.g., it contributes to happiness broadly construed) (e.g., Peterson & Park, 2011; Peterson & Seligman, 2004). Table 1.1 presents the current VIA classification of strengths (Peterson & Seligman, 2004).

Table 1.1 shows the multidimensional set of 24 different character strengths in subgroups of three to five character strengths, which were classified under the virtues of wisdom and knowledge, courage, humanity, justice, temperance and transcendence (e.g., Dahlsgaard, Peterson, & Seligman, 2005; Peterson & Seligman, 2004). Character strengths as personality traits manifest in individuals' behaviours (e.g., helping others), thoughts (e.g., thinking of consequences before acting) and feelings (e.g., feeling strong enough to stand up for one's own opinion against others' opinions). Character strengths are seen as the inner determinants of a good life (e.g., satisfied, successful life) in addition to external factors such as a good education, stable social environment or financial security (e.g., Peterson, 2006). Furthermore, character strengths are seen and measured as unipolar constructs (as opposed to bipolar constructs), meaning, they exist from 'not at all existing' to 'highly existing' across individuals (e.g., from 'zero kindness' to 'high kindness'). That means, in the VIA approach 'zero kindness' is *not*

Table 1.1 VIA Classification of Six Core Virtues and 24 Character Strengths

Virtue I. Wisdom and knowledge: Cognitive character strengths that entail the acquisition and use of knowledge

1. Creativity: Thinking of novel and productive ways to do things
2. Curiosity: Taking an interest in all of ongoing experiences
3. Judgement: Thinking things through and examining them from all sides
4. Love of learning: Mastering new skills, topics and bodies of knowledge
5. Perspective: Being able to provide wise counsel to others

Virtue II. Courage: Emotional character strengths that involve the exercise of will to accomplish goals in the face of opposition, external or internal

6. Bravery: Not shrinking from threat, challenge, difficulty or pain
7. Perseverance: Finishing what one starts
8. Honesty: Speaking the truth and presenting oneself in a genuine way
9. Zest: Approaching life with excitement and energy

Virtue III. Humanity: Interpersonal character strengths that involve 'tending and befriending' others

10. Capacity to love and be loved (short: love): Valuing close relations with others
11. Kindness: Doing favours and good deeds for others
12. Social intelligence: Being aware of the motives and feelings of oneself and others

Virtue IV. Justice: Civic character strengths that underlie healthy community life

13. Teamwork: Working well as member of a group or team
14. Fairness: Treating all people the same according to notions of fairness and justice
15. Leadership: Organizing group activities and seeing that they happen

Virtue V. Temperance: Character strengths that protect against excess

16. Forgiveness: Forgiving those who have done wrong
17. Modesty: Letting one's accomplishments speak for themselves

(Continued)

Table 1.1 *(Continued)*

---

18. Prudence: Being careful about one's choices; not saying or doing things that might later be regretted
19. Self-regulation: Regulating what one feels and does

Virtue VI. Transcendence: Character strengths that forge connections to the larger universe and provide meaning

20. Appreciation of beauty and excellence (short: appreciation): Noticing and appreciating beauty, excellence and/or skilled performance in all domains of life
21. Gratitude: Being aware of and thankful for the good things that happen
22. Hope: Expecting the best and working to achieve it
23. Humour: Liking to laugh and joke; bringing smiles to other people
24. Spirituality: Having coherent beliefs about the higher purpose and meaning of life

---

Source: Peterson and Seligman (2004).

equal to 'unfriendliness' (which would be the opposite pole in a bipolar approach 'kindness *vs.* unfriendliness') (e.g., Peterson, 2006). Although 24 different character strengths are included in the VIA classification, individuals can be high on one strength but low on others (Peterson, 2006). Furthermore, character strengths are not seen as fixed or based in immutable biogenetic characteristics (Peterson, 2006), meaning that character strengths are postulated to be malleable, which is important for training and intervention purposes.

Park and Peterson (2006a) defined the good character as a core characteristic of moral competence of children and adolescents. Moral competence is seen as one crucial competence in positive youth development, defined as 'a youth's ability to assess and respond to the ethical, affective, or social-justice dimensions of a situation' (Catalano, Berglund, Ryan, Lonczak, & Hawkins, 2004, p. 105). Hence, a good character supports young people not only to know the good, but also to desire to do the good (cf. Park & Peterson, 2006a). As character strengths are postulated as positive, morally valued personality traits that contribute to individuals' fulfilments, they are clearly relevant characteristics in the context of schooling. But what role character strengths play in the context of *positive schooling*? Following a definition of positive schooling, an answer to this question is given.

A TENTATIVE DEFINITION OF POSITIVE SCHOOLING

Due to the huge amount of time students spend daily in school, the topic of *positive schooling* is among the relevant topics in young peoples' lives. Such a perspective with a focus on optimal functioning and well-being in schooling is strongly related to the assumption of the 'positive institution school'. Positive institutions are those which support, foster and cultivate positive experiences as well as the development and use of positive character traits (e.g., Seligman & Csikszentmihalyi, 2000). Taking this into account, the chapter at hand is aimed at describing positive schooling by considering latest theories and models of well-being broadly construed (cf. Jayawickreme, Forgeard, & Seligman, 2012; Seligman, 2011).

There is currently no commonly accepted 'final' definition of positive schooling; therefore, in this section I provide one possible view of what positive schooling could mean. The assumed key component of positive schooling is *flourishing*, which is seen as well-being broadly construed (e.g., Seligman, 2011). Furthermore, research on schooling has often focused only on one relevant group of individuals at school— the students—but it is proposed that models on schooling and, more importantly, on positive schooling should consider at least one further crucial group of individuals that are also relevant at school—the teachers (cf. Harzer, Weber, & Huebner, 2017). It should be noted that there are further groups of relevant people and roles involved in the complex system of schooling, such as principals, school psychologists, parents and other school personnel. But, within the scope of the present chapter, I mainly focus on the largest groups at school, the students and the teachers, as school serves as a major learning environment for students, and it is a major working environment for teachers.

Different criteria are needed to define positive schooling for the two groups. For instance, positive schooling could mean for students to experience positive school emotions before and after accomplishing their goals at school. Furthermore, positive schooling experiences from the perspective of teachers could mean being aware of substantial degrees of teaching self-efficacy, which leads them to high-quality instructional behaviours at class, which in turn could lead to the experience of positive emotions by themselves (but also by their students) during lessons (Harzer et al., 2017).

All of these exemplarily mentioned aspects are components of student- and teacher-related well-being, because they are related to individuals' functioning and flourishing. Seligman's (2011) theory of human flourishing and well-being offers a meaningful, theoretically guided perspective when defining positive schooling. Well-being is not seen as only being happy all the time. In accordance with Seligman (2011), well-being or flourishing is more broadly construed. He postulates well-being as a five-dimensional construct composed of *positive emotions and experiences* (e.g., hope, pride, satisfaction), *engagement* (e.g., using own strengths to reach a goal, flow experiences), *positive relationships*, *meaning* (e.g., using own strengths to serve others) and *accomplishments* (e.g., reaching goals, motivation for mastery). An extension of this approach took into consideration that well-being is not a static characteristic and might be adequately described in the theoretical framework of an 'engine model' of well-being (Jayawickreme et al., 2012). This approach differentiated between inputs, processes and outcomes of human well-being (cf. Jayawickreme et al., 2012). *Inputs* are resources that enable well-being and can be represented as exogenous and endogenous factors. Exogenous factors are, for example, individuals' income or education level. Endogenous factors are, for example, individuals' or communities' personalities, character strengths, values and so forth (cf. Jayawickreme et al., 2012). *Processes* are internal states or mechanisms that influence well-being such as emotions and cognitive evaluations of individuals. Such processes in turn lead individuals to specific, intrinsically valuable, voluntary behaviours that reflect the attainment of well-being (i.e., *outcomes*) (cf. Jayawickreme et al., 2012). Possible outcomes are, for example, engagement, meaningful activities and positive accomplishments (cf. Jayawickreme et al., 2012).

Recently, the *school-related engine model of well-being* has been presented that (a) includes student-level and teacher-level variables, (b) highlights that all inputs, processes and outcomes are reciprocally related within levels and (c) emphasizes the interactions between these two levels (cf. Harzer et al., 2017). On the *student level*, variables such as student–teacher relationships, parental involvement in schooling, peer relationships and perception of safety as well as teachers' organizational and instructional behaviours can be identified as *exogenous input variables* within this adapted engine model (Harzer et al., 2017). Personality variables such as self-esteem, hope, locus of control and character strengths are seen as *endogenous input variables* (Harzer et al., 2017). Students' cognitive evaluations such as academic self-efficacy, school and life satisfaction, and also their emotions at school are seen as *process variables* (Harzer et al., 2017). Finally, students' behaviours such as academic performance and school achievement, engagement at school, participation in structured extracurricular activities and problem behaviours (e.g., externalizing and internalizing behaviour) are identified as *outcome variables* (Harzer et al., 2017).

On the teacher level, *exogenous input variables* are variables such as the quality of interactions with principals, parental involvement, structural aspects (e.g., continuity of contact with students, administrative practices) and students' adaptive and maladaptive behaviours (Harzer et al., 2017). *Endogenous input variables* are variables such as teachers' character strengths, other personality traits and coping styles (Harzer et al., 2017). *Process variables* include, for example, teachers' job satisfaction, emotions and instructional self-efficacy (Harzer et al., 2017). Finally, *outcome variables* are, for example, teachers' attributions of student failures, instructional behaviour, emotional support provided to students and learning goals (Harzer et al., 2017). This adaptation of the engine model to the schooling context also considered the possible interaction between the student-level and teacher-level (Harzer et al., 2017). For instance, teachers' instructional behaviours as *teachers' output variable* may impact students' well-being, and would be described from the perspective of the students as an *exogenous input variable*. As another example, students' behaviours at class as students' *output variable* may serve as an *exogenous input variable* for teachers and so forth (Harzer et al., 2017).

It should be mentioned here that an understanding of 'schooling in general' needs to consider both deficit-oriented and well-being-oriented perspectives; however, the present chapter will primarily highlight the well-being-related results to complement the body of results in this field, which is often deficit-oriented. In doing so, the chapter at hand primarily focuses on *character strengths* in the context of positive schooling. Hence, the following section will summarize research findings that are related to students' and teachers' character strengths as endogenous input variables on the one hand, and on the other, their relations to students' and teachers' processes as well as outcome variables.

CHARACTER STRENGTHS AS ENDOGENOUS INPUT VARIABLES IN POSITIVE SCHOOLING

There is a steadily growing body of empirical research on the role of character strengths for a diverse set of relevant aspects (e.g., global life satisfaction, psychological well-being and job performance) in individuals' lives across different age groups. Among this variety of findings, also the role of character strengths in the context of schooling was of interest.

Although more research is needed on this topic, initial results highlight the significant role of character strengths in this important life domain. Currently available empirical studies focused on the relations between character strengths (as endogenous input factors), and further relevant aspects of positive schooling (e.g., processes like students' school satisfaction and academic self-efficacy as well as teachers' teaching self-efficacy and enjoyment at work). Furthermore, outcomes such as students' classroom behaviour and school achievement, and teachers' instructional behaviour were examined in relation to the character strengths of the respective group.

At the moment, there is no published research that comprehensively evaluates the full engine model of well-being within the context of schooling. However, it is important to understand the individual parts and mechanisms of such a complex model first (e.g., relations between input and process variables or relations between process and outcome variables) before studying the whole complexity of such a school-related engine model of well-being simultaneously in one study. Hence, the following results represent a sample of research findings examining the relations between inputs and processes, processes and outcomes, as well as inputs and outcomes for students and teachers, respectively (i.e., within-group relations). Additionally, and although such findings are quite rare at the moment, initial research findings will be presented representing between-group relations (i.e., teacher variables correlated with student variables), for instance, between teachers' output variables (e.g., teaching behaviour) and students' process variables (e.g., school satisfaction).

Results on Student Level

Across the globe young peoples' character strengths are associated with different aspects of positive functioning in life (e.g., Park & Peterson, 2006a; Ruch, Weber, Park, & Peterson, 2014; Van Eeden, Wissing, Dreyer, Park, & Peterson, 2008; Weber, Ruch, Littman-Ovadia, Lavy, & Gai, 2013). In the following, the relations between students' character strengths and school-relevant characteristics will be presented.

Relations Between Endogenous Input Variables and Process Variables

Different character strengths are predictive of different school-related variables (e.g., Park & Peterson, 2006a; Wagner & Ruch, 2015; Weber & Ruch, 2012a; Weber, Wagner, & Ruch, 2016). With respect to *cognitive processes*, the character strengths of love of learning, zest, gratitude, perseverance and curiosity are positively associated with satisfaction with school experiences (i.e., cognitive evaluations of the quality of schooling-related experiences; e.g., Huebner, 1994) (Weber & Ruch, 2012a). Furthermore, character strengths such as hope, love of learning, perseverance and prudence are positively associated with academic self-efficacy (Weber & Ruch, 2012a), that is, higher scores in the aforementioned character strengths are in line with higher degrees in students' beliefs in their capabilities to produce desired effects at school by their own actions (cf. Bandura, 1997). On a broader, more global level, character strengths are positively associated with global life satisfaction and general self-efficacy beliefs as well (e.g., Ruch et al., 2014; Weber et al., 2013).

With respect to *emotional processes*, the character strengths of zest, love of learning, perseverance and social intelligence are positively related to a set of several school-related positive affects like being active, happy, interested and proud at class (Weber et al., 2016). Further findings suggest that character strengths such as love of learning, perspective and zest are positively related to the academic emotion of joy to learn (i.e., enjoying learning new things at school) (Weber, 2018).

Relations Between Endogenous Input Variables and Outcome Variables

The complete set of 24 character strengths explains about 25 per cent of the variance in teacher-perceived students' positive classroom behaviour (e.g., being diligent, cooperative, orderly, interested; cf. Weber & Ruch, 2012a). The character strengths of gratitude, honesty, hope, love of learning, perseverance, prudence, self-regulation, social intelligence, teamwork and zest are among the most substantial correlates of positive classroom behaviour (e.g., Wagner & Ruch, 2015; Weber & Ruch, 2012a). Moreover, character strengths appear as buffer against negative classroom behaviour like a disruptive rule-breaking, class-clowning behaviour (e.g., finding rules stupid or laughing and poking fun at them) (Ruch, Platt, & Hofmann, 2014). Furthermore, Shoshani and Slone (2013) found that character strengths are positively associated with behavioural, cognitive, emotional and social adjustment at school. This means that character strengths play a relevant role for students' adequate and helpful/self-supportive behaviours in the classroom.

Specific subsets of character strengths, for example, character strengths of the mind or intellectual character strengths (e.g., perseverance, self-regulation and love of learning), are related to school success (e.g., Park & Peterson, 2006a; Shoshani & Slone, 2013; Weber & Ruch, 2012a). More specifically, character strengths such as love of learning, perseverance, perspective and prudence are in line with better performance and achievement at school (i.e., higher GPAs) (Wagner & Ruch, 2015; Weber, 2018). As already mentioned, specific character strengths (e.g., zest, love of learning) are strongly related to school-related positive affect (a process variable); on the other hand, this process variable is predictive of the outcome variable positive school functioning (i.e., being motivated, interested and engaged in school), which in turn is positively related to academic achievement (Weber et al., 2016).

Furthermore, as another outcome-related result, students who report higher scores in leadership, fairness, self-regulation, prudence and forgiveness are more popular at school (i.e., as rated by their homeroom teachers) (Park & Peterson, 2006a). Moreover, character strengths such as hope, zest and leadership are related to fewer internalizing behaviour (e.g., anxiety, depression) whereas perseverance, honesty, prudence and love buffer against externalizing behaviour (e.g., aggression, noncompliance) (Park & Peterson, 2006a), which is also relevant in the context of schooling. Although research on students' character strengths is in its beginnings, available findings suggest that character strengths as endogenous input variables matter in the context of schooling (e.g., Harzer & Weber, 2013; Harzer, Weber, & Huebner, 2017).

Results on Teacher Level

Research on the role of character strengths in teachers is also just in its beginnings. An examination of the character strengths profiles of different types of teachers (e.g., elementary, middle, high school) showed that the character strengths of curiosity, love of learning, love, fairness and leadership are among the five highest character strengths in this specific group of individuals (Harzer, 2011).

Relations Between Endogenous Input Variables and Process Variables

Also for teachers, results on relations between endogenous input variables and process variables will be grouped in those regarding cognitive processes and those regarding emotional processes. With respect to the *cognitive process* of evaluating life as being high in quality and therefore as being satisfying, studies found character strengths such as hope, zest and gratitude to be positively related to life satisfaction in pre- and in-service teachers (e.g., Chan, 2009; Gradišek, 2012). Character strengths were also found to be related to another cognitive process variable, that is, teaching self-efficacy (i.e., a teachers' belief to be able to teach students effectively). Results show that character strengths are generally positively correlated with personal teaching efficacy (Lim & Kim, 2014). The specific character strengths of leadership, zest, social intelligence and hope are substantially positively related to teachers' self-efficacy (Harzer, 2016).

Regarding *emotional processes*, character strengths such as zest, hope, bravery and teamwork are positively related to positive emotions and enjoyment at work (Chan, 2009; Harzer, 2016). Character strengths such as hope and zest are negatively related to negative emotions in pre-service (Chan, 2009) and in-service teachers (Chan, 2009; Harzer, 2016).

Relations Between Endogenous Input Variables and Outcome Variables

Some relevant outcomes have been already studied in relation to character strengths. For example, experiencing *meaning at work* (i.e., describing work as making meaning and experiencing work to be beneficial for some greater good; e.g., Steger, Dik, & Duffy, 2012) is in line with higher scores in the character strengths of gratitude, hope, leadership, spirituality and zest in teachers (Harzer, 2016). *Engagement at work* (i.e., being fully and positively absorbed at work) is positively related to the character strengths of perseverance, zest, leadership and hope (Harzer, 2016). Character strengths appear also as buffer against aspects of *burnout*. For instance, lower levels of emotional exhaustion are in line with higher levels of zest and hope, and lower levels in lack of accomplishment are associated with higher levels of teachers' zest, leadership, hope and social intelligence (Harzer, 2016).

There is also first evidence that teachers' character strengths are associated with their *instructional behaviour*. Harzer (2016) reports that, for example, a cognitive activating teaching style (i.e., encouraging students to use their own strategies while solving difficult exercises; cf. Kunter & Baumert, 2006) is in line with higher levels of teachers' leadership, love of learning, judgement and fairness. Teachers with higher degrees of self-regulation report more effective classroom management (i.e., managing lessons that are structured and not massively disturbed; cf. Kunter & Baumert, 2006). Furthermore, teachers with higher scores in perseverance and perspective seem to have a more adequate pace of teaching (i.e., teaching the material quickly, but without overcharging the students; cf. Kunter & Baumert, 2006). Teachers described themselves as more social supportive (e.g., being available if students want to talk about something; cf. Kunter & Baumert, 2006) when they possess higher degrees in the character strengths of leadership, love and social intelligence. Finally, teachers who report higher scores in establishing a positive error culture in class (e.g., being patient if a student makes a mistake; cf. Kunter & Baumert, 2006) report higher scores in the character strengths of fairness, forgiveness, curiosity, love and leadership (Harzer, 2016).

At the teacher level, such instructional behaviours of teachers are outcomes within the framework of the school-related engine model of well-being (cf. Harzer et al., 2017). However, from the perspective of students (i.e., at student level), such instructional behaviours are exogenous input variables that impact students' well-being at school. In a recent study, such exogenous inputs (i.e., student-perceived instructional behaviour of their teachers) are found as being related to students' process variables like satisfaction with school experiences as well as enjoyment at school, which in turn are predictive of school achievement as outcome variable (Weber & Dietel, 2018). Although research on teachers' character strengths in the complex context of schooling is still in its beginnings, initial results clearly demonstrate that those positive traits seem to play a relevant role for both teachers and students (e.g., Harzer, Weber, & Huebner, 2017).

In sum, the reported findings at both student level and teacher level demonstrate the relevant role of character strengths as endogenous input variables for several aspects in the schooling context. Character strengths appear as being relevant for cognitive and emotional processes at school. Furthermore, character strengths seem to be relevant for a diverse set of possible outcomes in the context of schooling.

CONCLUSIONS, IMPLICATIONS AND FUTURE DIRECTIONS

The primary goal of the chapter at hand was to present initial research findings on the role of character strengths in the context of positive schooling. In the framework of the *school-related engine model of well-being* (cf. Harzer et al., 2017), which is an extension of Jayawickreme et al.'s (2012) 'engine model of well-being', character strengths are seen as relevant *endogenous input factors*, which are associated with both schooling-relevant *processes* and *outcomes*. With their adapted model, Harzer et al. (2017) postulate the need to consider several groups of individuals when studying positive schooling (i.e., students but also teachers). As initial results are available at student level and at teacher level, research findings are presented that cover both groups of individuals. Table 1.2 summarizes the areas of research mentioned in this chapter.

At the moment, empirical research on the role of character strengths in the schooling context is quite in its beginnings, but nevertheless, the reported findings are encouraging at the same time. Findings in the areas already studied (see Table 1.2) build a meaningful basis for the current understanding of the role of character strengths in the context of positive schooling, but they are also relevant for future research endeavours. In the following, I will briefly summarize and conclude the most substantial findings. Furthermore, I will provide some implications of the results as well as ideas for future research that can be derived from the currently existing research base.

Conclusions

It is obvious that the components of a good character, which manifest in human character strengths (Peterson & Seligman, 2004), are positively linked to positive schooling and well-being broadly construed (cf. Harzer et al., 2017). Most character strengths of the full set of 24 character strengths appear as relevant in at least one of the different areas indicative for positive schooling. However, there are specific character strengths that appear more relevant than others in this context. For example, love of learning, perseverance, prudence and zest appear as especially relevant for students, because they are related to several of the student-related processes and outcomes mentioned in this chapter. On the other hand, character strengths such as hope, leadership and zest appear to be especially relevant for teachers. Although further character strengths for students (e.g., gratitude, honesty, hope, leadership, perspective, self-regulation and social intelligence) and teachers (e.g., curiosity, fairness, gratitude, love, love of learning, perseverance and social intelligence) appear as relevant as well, in the following, the most relevant character strengths will be focused on for some specific concluding remarks.

Relevant Character Strengths on Student Level

Love of learning is among the most relevant character strengths in the context of positive schooling. In accordance with Peterson and Seligman

Table 1.2 *Overview of Inputs, Processes and Outcomes Mentioned in the Present Chapter*

(1) Input variables
Endogenous: Character strengths (s, t)
Exogenous: Student-perceived instructional teacher behaviour (e.g., classroom management, cognitive activation, support and positive error culture) (s)

(2) Process variables
Satisfaction with school experiences (s)
Life satisfaction (t)
Academic self-efficacy (s)
Teaching self-efficacy (t)
Positive feelings/emotions at school (s)
Enjoyment to learn (s)
Enjoyment to work (t)

(3) Outcome variables
Positive classroom behaviour (s)
Disruptive class clown behaviour (s)
Internalizing/externalizing behaviour (s)
Popularity at class (s)
Positive school functioning (motivated, interested, engaged) (s)
Meaning at work (t)
Engagement at work (t)
Burnout (t)
Instructional behaviour (t)

Note: (s) = reported at student level; (t) = reported at teacher level.

(2004), students that report higher degrees in this character strength like learning new things everywhere and all the time. They like the lessons at school, and their love of learning can be directed to a specific field or topic (e.g., history, economics, languages, mathematics, royals and football), or directed to life in general (i.e., interested in a diverse set of topics). Generally speaking, students with higher degrees in love of learning have a desire to learn a lot about life and the world. Contrary to students with lower degrees in this character strength, students who love to learn experience learning not as a 'pain in the neck', but as a great chance to acquire new knowledge. Although there are hardly any people who do not like to learn about at least one topic in their lives, students with low levels of love of learning feel okay with their existing knowledge, and they do not desire learning any new things (cf. Peterson & Seligman, 2004). From this perspective, it makes sense that students possessing higher degrees of love of learning show higher levels of, for example, academic self-efficacy, enjoyment to learn and positive emotions at school, school satisfaction, positive classroom behaviour, positive school functioning (i.e., being motivated, interested and engaged at school) and school success/performance (e.g., Park & Peterson, 2006a; Wagner & Ruch, 2015; Weber, 2018; Weber & Ruch, 2012a; Weber et al., 2016). In more detail, students who love to attain new knowledge on a regular basis build knowledge-based resources, which on the other hand help them in challenging situations in schooling (i.e., higher levels of academic self-efficacy). Furthermore, when students love to learn, they very likely experience schooling as something positive in their lives, which should be in line with positive processes like good feelings at school and school satisfaction. Next, it appears meaningful that a characteristic like love of learning goes along with a positive, constructive classroom behaviour (e.g., being diligent, cooperative and reliable), because such a behaviour is quite supportive of acquiring new knowledge. Moreover, love of learning is in line with a motivated, interested and engaged manner in the schooling context, which is in turn easily linkable to higher performance and achievements at school.

As another character strength, students' *perseverance* emerged being especially relevant. Following Peterson and Seligman's definition (2004), students who show higher degrees of perseverance work diligently and hard to finish what they started, and those students feel good when they finish what they wanted to accomplish. Moreover, they are hardly ever distracted from the task they are working on. Although such students are determined to not give up easily, they are able to realize when a goal cannot be achieved, that is, they are flexible and realistic, and can adapt to situations without being a perfectionist. On the other hand, students who possess low levels of perseverance often begin tasks, but then hardly finish any of them; they give up quickly and often seek ways to get out of responsibilities (cf. Peterson & Seligman, 2004). Having this definition in mind, it is obvious why perseverant students show higher levels of, for example, academic self-efficacy, positive feelings at school, school satisfaction, positive classroom behaviour, lower levels of externalizing behaviour and school success/performance (e.g., Park & Peterson, 2006a; Wagner & Ruch, 2015; Weber 2018; Weber & Ruch, 2012a; Weber et al., 2016). Being perseverant supports students in solving challenges where others would give up, what in turn is very supportive for building higher levels of academic self-efficacy. Being able to solve and finish problems successfully is directly linked to positive feelings and school satisfaction. Furthermore, perseverant behaviour—contrary to impatient behaviour—is meaningfully linkable not only to positive classroom behaviour, but also to reduced externalizing problem behaviours (e.g., aggression and delinquency). Finally, these results are in line with a long history of research highlighting perseverance as a potent predictor of school success (e.g., De Raad & Schouwenburg, 1996; Hattie, 2009; Poffenberger & Carpenter, 1924). Perseverant students are students who finish the tasks that are needed to fully understand a topic at school and hence are more likely succeeding in corresponding tests compared to students who stop such tasks before fully finishing them (which results in a lack of knowledge).

As a third character strength, *prudence* contributed substantially to students' experiences of positive schooling. According to Peterson and Seligman (2004), prudent students always act carefully and their decisions are well thought out. Students who report higher levels of prudence do not say or do anything that they might regret later. Although prudent students do not actively search for dangerous physical activities (e.g., bungee jumping and cliff diving), this does not necessarily mean that they do not look for new experiences. Prudent students are perceived as being 'careful in a good way' (and not as being anxious!). They plan their goals on a long-term basis, and then pursue them in a responsible way. Such students do not act recklessly. On the contrary, students who possess low levels of prudence are perceived as careless and thoughtless in what they say and do (cf. Peterson & Seligman, 2004). From this perspective, it is meaningful that students possessing higher degrees of prudence show higher levels of, for example, academic self-efficacy, positive classroom behaviour, school performance, popularity at school and lower levels of externalizing behaviour (e.g., Park & Peterson, 2006a; Wagner & Ruch, 2015; Weber & Ruch, 2012a). Prudence appears as a meaningful correlate of academic self-efficacy, as prudent students make—in their thoughtful, careful style—relevant experiences that build up resources like self-efficacy, because those students more likely experience positive rather than negative consequences (i.e., successes vs. failures) as results of their actions. A positive conduct in the classroom is quite easily linkable to prudent students, because such students are not interested in disrupting the classwork (e.g., by externalized behaviours), which on the other hand leads to higher degrees in popularity.

Relevant Character Strengths on Teacher Level

The character strength of *hope* emerges as a relevant contributor to teachers' positive schooling experiences. In accordance with Peterson and Seligman (2004), individuals possessing hope have a positive attitude towards the future. Such teachers expect the best in the future, and they work hard in a goal-directed manner to achieve this. Furthermore, individuals possessing higher levels of the character strength of hope often know clearly what they want for their future, and they imagine their future accordingly; and even more important, if something does not work out as expected and planned, hopeful teachers try, despite such setbacks, to remain hopeful and to reach their goals by utilizing different paths. Individuals with lower levels of hope are often described as being hopeless. Such teachers often see their future as rather miserable, think that the future is difficult and that it is hard to have a good future (cf. Peterson & Seligman, 2004). This definition highlights that hope is a core character strength for a happy, satisfied life, something which has been demonstrated in several empirical studies throughout the lifespan (e.g., Park & Peterson, 2006a, b; Park, Peterson, & Seligman, 2004; Ruch et al., 2010; Ruch et al., 2014). Moreover, it appears meaningful why hopeful teachers show higher levels of, for example, life satisfaction, teaching self-efficacy, positive emotions, enjoyment, engagement and meaning at work, and lower levels of negative emotions and burnout symptoms at work (e.g., Chan, 2009; Gradišek, 2012; Harzer, 2016; Lim & Kim, 2014). For instance, hope is a personality characteristic that fosters the development of important resources like teaching self-efficacy, because teachers possessing hope will not give up after a teaching-related setback, but on the contrary, such teachers will continue and will succeed in another teaching-related situation, which in turn will strengthen context-specific self-efficacy beliefs. Hopeful teachers per se experience more positive feelings, less negative feelings and higher degrees of satisfaction than their colleagues with lower levels of hope, because they have a more positive view towards their future, and are not discouraged by setbacks which in turn may serve as a useful buffer against suffering from burnout-related symptoms.

As another example, the character strength of *leadership* contributes to teachers' positive schooling experiences. Following Peterson and Seligman (2004), individuals who possess leadership are able to manage tasks (e.g., organizing all the daily class businesses such as planning the lessons and tests and so on). Such teachers are able to motivate a group to successfully finish a task within a given time frame. Teachers who show leadership also manage to keep the 'peace' in a group as they convey a feeling of belonging to everyone in a group. Individuals with strong leadership are able to organize activities well and ensure that they are actually put into practice. On the other hand, individuals who show low degrees of leadership are not able to take responsibility for the group, and such teachers cannot establish a congenial climate in a group for all the members (e.g., Peterson & Seligman, 2004). Hence, leadership is a core character strength for teachers, as teachers always need to reach goals in mostly time-restricted situations (e.g., lessons), and teachers usually need to handle groups of quite diverse students. Having this definition in mind, it is obvious why teachers with higher levels of leadership show higher levels of, for example, teaching self-efficacy (e.g., being able to handle a diverse class), meaning and engagement at work (e.g., organize activities and put them into practice) as well as positive instructional behaviour at class (e.g., cognitive activating teaching style, social support and positive error culture) and lower levels of burnout symptoms like lack of accomplishment (e.g., Harzer, 2016; Lim & Kim, 2014). It appears that leadership is a supportive (e.g., for instructional behaviour) and protective resource (e.g., against burnout), especially for teachers, at the same time.

Zest as a Character Strength Relevant for Students and Teachers

Thinking within a framework of an 'engine' model, the character strength of *zest* emerges as being a very relevant 'fuel' for not only a good life in general (e.g., Gillham et al., 2011; Harzer, 2016; Park &

Peterson, 2006a, b; Park et al., 2004; Ruch et al., 2010; Ruch et al., 2014; Van Eeden et al., 2008; Weber & Ruch, 2012a, b; Weber et al., 2013), but also in the context of positive schooling. In both groups (i.e., students and teachers), zestful individuals report about characteristics which are indicative for positive schooling experiences. According to Peterson and Seligman (2004), individuals showing the character strength of zest are always full of energy. Adults as well as children and adolescents who report higher degrees of zest are enthusiastic about many different things and activities. Such individuals look positively forward to each new day. Zestful students and teachers always give 100 per cent, and they are fully engaged and committed to their tasks and goals. Furthermore, students and teachers showing the character strength of zest face life as an adventure and challenge, and such individuals feel generally alive and active, and are often described as cheerful people. On the contrary, students and teachers possessing lower levels of zest are often perceived as unmotivated and lazy (cf. Peterson & Seligman, 2004). It is obvious why zest is a core character strength in the context of schooling for both students and teachers. Schooling is a day-to-day challenge for both groups. Therefore, it appears meaningful that zestful students show higher levels of, for example, school satisfaction, positive emotions at school and enjoyment to learn, positive classroom behaviour and positive school functioning (e.g., Wagner & Ruch, 2015; Weber, 2018; Weber & Ruch, 2012a; Weber et al., 2016). Likewise, zestful teachers show higher levels of, for example, life satisfaction, teaching self-efficacy, positive emotions, and enjoyment, meaning and engagement at work as well as lower levels of burnout symptoms and negative emotions at work (e.g., Chan, 2009; Gradišek, 2012; Harzer, 2016; Lim & Kim, 2014).

Implications

From a theoretical point of view, the reported results highlight the importance of examining personality traits like character strengths (Peterson & Seligman, 2004) in the context of schooling in both students and teachers. There is a growing body of research highlighting that not only intellectual capabilities are important characteristics of students when investigating various aspects of positive schooling (e.g., school success and satisfaction at school). Research shows that also non-intellectual characteristics like students' character strengths are relevant for long-term successes, where teachers are seen as 'powerful agents' to help students develop such characteristics (e.g., Sokatch, 2017). Furthermore, regarding teachers, there is a growing body of research that underscores the relevant role of character strengths in the working context; such research mainly focuses on two aspects, namely, (a) the possession of character strengths and (b) the application of character strengths at work. With respect to the *possession* of character strengths, specific character strengths (e.g., zest, hope and gratitude) are associated with, for example, higher degrees of job satisfaction across various kinds of jobs (e.g., Peterson, Stephens, Park, Lee, & Seligman, 2010), and character strengths are positively linked to a healthier work behaviour (e.g., Gander, Proyer, Ruch, & Wyss, 2012) and effective coping with work-related stressors (Harzer & Ruch, 2015). With respect to the *application* of character strengths, research shows that employees who are able to actively use and apply their individual core character strengths (i.e., signature strengths) report higher levels of pleasure, engagement and meaning at work; they perceive their job as a calling, and thus they perform better at work (e.g., Harzer, Mubashar, & Dubreuil, 2017; Harzer & Ruch, 2012, 2013, 2014, 2016). Such findings regarding mixed groups of employees support the specific findings for teachers reported above; nevertheless, further studies are needed in the specific working context of teachers.

Having a *school-related engine model of well-being* in mind it appears meaningful that not only pure numbers (e.g., averaged grade levels) and countable outputs (e.g., number of taught classes, subjects or topics) (as examples for possible outcomes) matter, but also aspects such as teachers' positive emotions, job satisfaction and teaching self-efficacy (as examples of processes). The presented framework—the school-related engine model of well-being (Harzer et al., 2017)—which has been adapted from Jayawickreme et al. (2012) to the schooling sector might be a helpful model to design further empirical studies, which consider different groups of individuals and different types of variables (inputs, processes and outcomes) when studying character strengths' role in the context of positive schooling.

The results reported in the present chapter are relevant for several groups of individuals. Knowledge on such findings could be beneficial not only for policymakers, teachers and students, but also for parents and other schooling-related practitioners like school psychologists. In the following, some *practical implications* are discussed with respect to these different groups of individuals.

Although promising research findings are available, such topics are unfortunately underrepresented in policies that regulate schooling as well as actual teacher training programmes (pre- and in-service programmes) (e.g., Conoley, Conoley, Spaventa-Vancil, & Lee, 2014). A meaningful way of transferring such knowledge to schooling may be by implementing it in *pre-service training* of teachers. Future teachers need to learn about such relations between teachers' and students' character strengths and processes as well as outcomes included in a framework of positive schooling (cf. Harzer et al., 2017). However, reaching such a goal is only possible when teacher training curricula will be extended by adding these and related topics. Hence, policymakers should consider to foster and support such ideas, and subsequently modify relevant policies. When revisions of related policies are on the agenda, experts (i.e., positive psychologists with knowledge in this field of research) should serve as consultants and present relevant information and ideas. As teacher training mostly includes courses on psychological topics, an implementation of positive psychological topics would only be a minor revision of already existing curricula, but one that would have a noteworthy positive consequence for pre-service teacher training.

On the other hand, *in-service teachers* need to know about such relevant research findings as well. For instance, to transfer recent research findings to in-service teachers, workshops could be designed on this topic, which are presented by trained positive psychologists. Such workshops will then inform teachers about research findings and provide ideas for a practical implementation of this knowledge into their daily schooling lives. Furthermore, positive psychological coaches could support not only in-service teachers, but also school principals, who decide to implement this topic into their schools and classes. In more detail, knowledge on the findings reported in this chapter would help in-service teachers at least in two ways. First, on an individual level, teachers would profit from knowledge about the relations between character strengths and relevant processes and outcomes in the context of schooling. Such knowledge would support teachers to understand their own situation or the behaviours of their colleagues in a more nuanced way. For instance, when they or their colleagues show low level of positive emotions at school, they would have a scientifically proven answer on possible reasons (e.g., the possession or low levels of hope and zest). Such knowledge would be helpful to develop a deeper understanding for the own or others' situation. Second, as defined earlier, character strengths are personality traits showing different degrees of manifestation across individuals (e.g., one student is especially prudent, hopeful and kind, another is especially honest, socially intelligent and grateful, and another is especially creative, brave and perseverant, and so forth). This is relevant for a teachers' view of her/his students at class. That is, each single student has an individual character strengths profile (i.e., personality profile), which makes her/him a unique person. This uniqueness on the other hand is at the same time a challenge for teachers who have to interact with, for example, 30 of such unique students during class. It would be wrong to think about a group of 30 students as 'the students'. In most (if not all) cases, a general term like 'the students' does not cover reality appropriately. Knowledge on the character strengths provides teachers with the skills to recognize and value individuality and diversity. The results section of this chapter shows what specific character strengths are associated with specific processes and outcomes in schooling (e.g., school satisfaction, interest, enjoyment to learn and school achievement). For instance, when dealing with an 'unsatisfied' or 'unmotivated' student, teachers could consider that specific character strengths relevant in the schooling context (e.g., love of learning, perseverance and zest) might be underdeveloped in such a student.

From my perspective, *students* would enormously profit as well if topics like character strengths would be a more prominent topic on schools' agendas. First, far too often weaknesses and deficiencies (and not strengths) are at the centre of discussions between teachers and students when reflecting on students' performance (in such cases, mostly bad performances) at school. However, the awareness of the own character strengths would help students to realize that everyone has potential to succeed and, moreover, it would help students to feel proud about themselves. The reflective process of a student that 'I have my own character strengths profile, which makes me a unique individual that is worth being appreciated as it is' should have an enormous impact on the foundation of a positive self-concept very likely resulting in higher levels of self-esteem. Second, it might be important (also for students) to realize the relations between character strengths and processes (e.g., self-efficacy) and outcomes (e.g., engagement, grades) at school as this might foster self-efficacy because of the students' better understanding of such psychological mechanisms.

Also, *parents* need to know about the results presented in the chapter at hand. Such knowledge about the promising role of their children's character strengths for positive schooling might encourage parents to focus more on an adequate development of character strengths. A positive, supportive parenting style and positive role models might foster the development of children's character strengths (Park, 2004; Peterson, 2006). For instance, authoritative parents involve negotiation in daily parenting, and set limits, but give explanations for given rules and limits. Additionally, they encourage independence in their children, but offer support, when needed. It appears likely that an authoritative parenting style fosters and supports children to become friendly, cooperative, socially responsible and self-reliant individuals (e.g., Peterson, 2006)—all characteristics closely related to character strengths.

The actual development of character strengths is not fully investigated yet. Initial results on character strengths' heritability (Steger, Hicks, Kashdan, Krueger, & Bouchard, 2007) suggest not only a genetic influence on character strengths, but also much open space for environmental influences (e.g., non-shared environment, like friends or school, and also different parenting practices within the family) on the development of character strengths. With respect to parenting practices, Seligman (2002) states that whenever parents detect indicators of character strengths in their children they should foster those character strengths, instead of trying to reduce deficits or weaknesses in their children (Seligman, 2002). Seligman (2002) speculates that the first six years are very likely crucial in character shaping, and that newborns have some kind of a general capacity to build each of the character strengths, as individuals in this age are, for example, capable to learn each language as well (cf. Seligman, 2002). Hence, one important task of positive parenting might be supporting and fostering what is already good in their children.

Finally, *school psychologists* or other *educational practitioners* deal on a daily basis with both troubled students and troubled teachers; hence, this group of practitioners mostly acts in a deficit-focused way.

Exploring an extended list of relevant variables that are related to inputs, processes and outcomes in positive schooling might be helpful in getting a broader, more comprehensive view of possible intervention strategies. Knowledge about the role of character strengths appears useful for such a more comprehensive model approaching students' problems in the schooling context (in addition to aspects like students' intellectual capabilities, their peer and teacher relationships and so forth). Furthermore, when coaching teachers suffering from poor (mental) health conditions, school psychologists could use the knowledge presented in the chapter at hand as well, as it is obvious how beneficial such findings are to better understand and support teachers who are dissatisfied, not self-efficacious, unengaged or suffering from burnout symptoms.

Future Directions

Although the reported results appear quite promising as they tentatively support linkages among input, process and outcome variables in the schooling context, more research is needed to extend those initial findings. Hence, future research endeavours should focus on (but not limited to) the following aspects:

First, more basic research is needed to comprehensively understand the variables and relations postulated in the school-related engine model of well-being by Harzer et al. (2017). This model offers the possibility to study the interplay between different input, process and outcome variables in the complex context of schooling considering different groups of relevant individuals at school. Hence, more studies are needed that focus on both (a) the single relations between the specific components of the model and (b) the more complex relations between different components of the model and between different groups of individuals. More complex study designs considering the relations across different groups of individuals would help in unravelling the influences of teachers on students and vice versa.

Second, such research could be designed cross-sectionally; however, longitudinal studies are needed to address the complexities of the interrelations among inputs, processes and outcomes over time and across different groups of relevant individuals (i.e., students and teachers).

Cross-sectional results help determining whether an expected association between selected variables can be found empirically, but in a next step, longitudinal results can then validate assumed causalities in a statistically sound way.

Third, it is assumed that the development of character strengths is influenced by environmental influences (e.g., parents and peers), because they are defined as being learnable and trainable (cf. Peterson & Seligman, 2004), despite being partly influenced by human genes (Steger et al., 2007). Although some intervention programmes related to the topic character strengths already exist (e.g., Proctor et al., 2011; Quinlan, Swain, Cameron, & Vella-Brodrick, 2015; Seligman, Ernst, Gillham, Reivich, & Linkins, 2009; White & Waters, 2015), more experimental research designs and intervention research designs are needed to empirically test to what extent and how character strengths are malleable and trainable. Supporting results would help to detect relevant mechanisms that would be helpful for teachers, school psychologists and coaches counselling students or teachers who need help.

Finally, more cross-cultural and cross-national studies are needed to examine generalizability of results and to establish a solid foundation of empirical findings on this topic. Such cross-cultural and cross-national findings are needed for (a) detecting general mechanisms in the context of positive schooling and (b) detecting culture- and/or nation-specific mechanisms. Both aspects are crucial when it comes, for example, to an implementation of such research findings into policies and curricula that determine teacher training.

REFERENCES

Bandura, A. (1997). *Self-efficacy: The exercise of control.* New York, NY: Freeman.
Catalano, R. F., Berglund, M. L., Ryan, J. A. M., Lonczak, H. S., & Hawkins, J. D. (2004). Positive youth development in the United States: Research findings on evaluations of positive youth development programs. *The Annals of the American Academy of Political and Social Science, 591,* 98–124. doi:10.1177/0002716203260102
Chan, D. W. (2009). The hierarchy of strengths: Their relationships with subjective well-being among Chinese teachers in Hong Kong. *Teaching and Teacher Education, 25,* 867–875. doi:10.1016/j.tate.2009.01.010

Conoley, C. W., Conoley, J. C., Spaventa-Vancil, K. Z., & Lee, A. (2014). Positive psychology in schools: Good ideas are never enough. In M. J. Furlong, R. Gilman, & E. S. Huebner (Eds.), *Handbook of positive psychology in schools* (2nd ed., pp. 497–506). New York, NY: Routledge.

Dahlsgaard, K., Peterson, C., & Seligman, M. E. P. (2005). Shared virtue: The convergence of valued human strengths across culture and history. *Review of General Psychology, 9*, 203–213. doi:10.1037/1089-2680.9.3.203

De Raad, B., & Schouwenburg, H. C. (1996). Personality in learning and education: A review. *European Journal of Personality, 10*, 303–336. doi:10.1002/(SICI)1099-0984(199612)10:5<303::AID-PER262>3.0.CO;2-2

Gander, F., Proyer, R. T., Ruch, W., & Wyss, T. (2012). The good character at work: An initial study on the contribution of character strengths in identifying healthy and unhealthy work-related behavior and experience patterns. *International Archives of Occupational and Environmental Health, 85*, 895–904. doi:10.1007/s00420-012-0736-x

Gillham, J., Adams-Deutsch, Z., Werner, J., Reivich, K., Coulter-Heindl, V., Linkins, M.,... Seligman, M. E. P. (2011). Character strengths predict subjective well-being during adolescence. *Journal of Positive Psychology, 6*, 31–44. doi:10.1080/17439760.2010.536773

Gradišek, P. (2012). Character strengths and life satisfaction of Slovenian in-service and pre-service teachers. *Center for Educational Policies Studies Journal, 2*(3), 167–180.

Harzer, C. (2011). Profile verschiedener Berufe [Character strengths profiles of different vocations]. In D. Jungo, W. Ruch, & R. Zihlmann (Eds.), *Das VIA-IS (Values in Action Inventory of Strengths), ein Instrument zur Erfassung von Charakterstärken. Informationen und Interpretationshilfen für die Berufs-, Studien- und Laufbahnberatung* (2nd ed., pp. 40–44). Bern, Switzerland: SDBB Verlag.

Harzer, C. (2016, June). The relationships between character strengths and work-related outcomes in teachers. In M. Weber (Chair), *Character strengths and positive schooling: Focusing on teachers and students*. Symposium to be conducted at the 8th European Conference on Positive Psychology, Angers, France.

Harzer, C., Mubashar, T., & Dubreuil, P. (2017). Character strengths and strength-related person-job fit as predictors of work-related wellbeing, job performance, and workplace deviance. *Wirtschaftspsychologie, 19*(3), 23–38.

Harzer, C., & Ruch, W. (2012). When the job is a calling: The role of applying one's signature strengths at work. *The Journal of Positive Psychology, 7*, 362–371. doi:10.1080/17439760.2012.702784

———. (2013). The application of signature character strengths and positive experiences at work. *Journal of Happiness Studies, 14*, 965–983. doi:10.1007/s10902-012-9364-0

———. (2014). The role of character strengths for task performance, job dedication, interpersonal facilitation, and organizational support. *Human Performance, 27*, 183–205. doi:10.1080/08959285.2014.913592

Harzer, C., & Ruch, W. (2015). The relationships of character strengths with coping, work-related stress, and job satisfaction. *Frontiers in Psychology*, *6*, 165. doi:10.3389/fpsyg.2015.00165

———. (2016). Your strengths are calling: Preliminary results of a web-based strengths intervention to increase calling. *Journal of Happiness Studies*, *17*, 2237–2256. doi:10.1007/s10902-015-9692-y

Harzer, C., & Weber, M. (2013). Character strengths matter: A cross-national perspective on schooling. *Communiqué* (National Association of School Psychology), *42*(3), 10–11.

Harzer, C., Weber, M., & Huebner, E. S. (2017). School as a positive learning and working environment. In C. R. Snyder, S. J. Lopez, L. M. Edwards, & S. C. Marques (Eds.), *Oxford handbook of positive psychology* (3rd ed.). doi:10.1093/oxfordhb/9780199396511.013.45

Hattie, J. A. C. (2009). *Visible learning: A synthesis of over 800 meta-analyses relating to achievement*. New York, NY: Routledge.

Huebner, E. S. (1994). Preliminary development and validation of a multidimensional life satisfaction scale for children. *Psychological Assessment*, *6*, 149–158. doi:10.1037/1040-3590.6.2.149

Jayawickreme, E., Forgeard, M. J. C., & Seligman, M. E. P. (2012). The engine of well-being. *Review of General Psychology*, *16*, 327–342. doi:10.1037/a0027990

Kunter, M., & Baumert, J. (2006). Who is the expert? Construct and criteria validity of student and teacher ratings of instruction. *Learning Environments Research*, *9*, 231–251. doi:10.1007/s10984-006-9015-7

Lim, Y.-J., & Kim, M.-N. (2014). Relation of character strengths to personal teaching efficacy in Korean special education teachers. *International Journal of Special Education*, *29*(2), 53–58.

Park, N. (2004). Character strengths and positive youth development. *The Annals of the American Academy of Political and Social Science*, *591*, 40–54. doi:10.1177/0002716203260079

Park, N., & Peterson, C. (2006a). Moral competence and character strengths among adolescents: The development and validation of the Values in Action Inventory of Strengths for Youth. *Journal of Adolescence*, *29*, 891–909. doi:10.1016/j.adolescence.2006. 04.011

Park, N., & Peterson, C. (2006b). Character strengths and happiness among young children: Content analysis of parental descriptions. *Journal of Happiness Studies*, *7*, 323–341. doi:10.1007/s10902-005-3648-6

Park, N., Peterson, C., & Seligman, M. (2004). Strengths of character and well-being. *Journal of Social and Clinical Psychology*, *23*, 603–619. doi:10.1521/jscp.23.5.603.50748

Peterson, C. (2006). *A primer in positive psychology*. New York, NY: Oxford University Press.

Peterson, C., & Park, N. (2011). Character strengths and virtues: Their role in well-being. In S. I. Donaldson, M. Csikszentmihalyi, & J. Nakamura (Eds.), *Applied positive psychology: Improving everyday life, health, schools, work, and society* (pp. 49–62). New York, NY: Routledge.

Peterson, C., & Seligman, M. E. P. (2004). *Character strengths and virtues: A handbook and classification*. New York, NY: Oxford University Press.

Peterson, C., Stephens, J. P., Park, N., Lee, F., & Seligman, M. E. P. (2010). Strengths of character and work. In P. A. Linley, S. Harrington, & N. Garcea (Eds.), *Oxford handbook of positive psychology at work* (pp. 221–231). New York, NY: Oxford University Press.

Poffenberger, A. T., & Carpenter, F. L. (1924). Character traits in school success. *Journal of Experimental Psychology*, 7, 67–74. doi:10.1037/h0071997

Proctor, C., Tsukayama, E., Wood, A. M., Maltby, J., Fox Eades, J., & Linley, P. A. (2011). Strengths Gym: The impact of a character strengths-based intervention on the life satisfaction and well-being of adolescents. *Journal of Positive Psychology*, 6, 377–388. doi:10.1080/17439760.2011.594079

Quinlan, D. M., Swain, N., Cameron, C., & Vella-Brodrick, D. A. (2015). How 'other people matter' in a classroom-based strengths intervention: Exploring interpersonal strategies and classroom outcomes. *Journal of Positive Psychology*, 10, 77–89. doi:10.1080/17439760.2014.920407

Ruch, W., Platt, T., & Hofmann, J. (2014). The character strengths of class clowns. *Frontiers in Psychology*, 5, 1075. doi:10.3389/fpsyg.2014.01075

Ruch, W., Proyer, R. T., Harzer, C., Park, N., Peterson, C., & Seligman, M. E. P. (2010). Values in Action Inventory of Strengths (VIA-IS): Adaptation and validation of the German version and the development of a peer-rating form. *Journal of Individual Differences*, 31, 138–149. doi:10.1027/1614-0001/a000022

Ruch, W., Weber, M., Park, N., & Peterson, C. (2014). Character strengths in children and adolescents: Reliability and initial validity of the German Values in Action Inventory of Strengths for Youth (German VIA-Youth). *European Journal of Psychological Assessment*, 30, 57–64. doi:10.1027/1015-5759/a000169

Seligman, M. E. P. (2002). *Authentic happiness*. New York, NY: Free Press.

———. (2011). *Flourish: A visionary new understanding of happiness and well-being*. New York, NY: Free Press.

Seligman, M. E. P., & Csikszentmihalyi, M. (2000). Positive psychology: An introduction. *American Psychologist*, 55, 5–14. doi:10.1037//0003-066X.55.1.5

Seligman, M. E. P., Ernst, R. M., Gillham, J., Reivich, K., & Linkins, M. (2009). Positive education: Positive psychology and classroom interventions. *Oxford Review of Education*, 35, 293–311. doi:10.1080/03054980902934563

Shoshani, A., & Slone, M. (2013). Middle school transition from the strengths perspective: Young adolescents' character strengths, subjective well-being, and school adjustment. *Journal of Happiness Studies*, 14, 1163–1181. doi:10.1007/s10902-012-9374-y

Sokatch, A. (2017). Toward a research agenda: Building character strengths in school settings. *Journal of Youth and Adolescence*, 46, 1238–1239. doi:10.1007/s10964-017-0657-9

Steger, M. F., Dik, B. J., & Duffy, R. D. (2012). Measuring meaningful work: The Work and Meaning Inventory (WAMI). *Journal of Career Assessment*, 20, 322–337. doi:10.1177/1069072711436160

Steger, M. F., Hicks, B. M., Kashdan, T. B., Krueger, R. F., & Bouchard, T. J. J. (2007). Genetic and environmental influences on the positive traits of the values in action classification, and biometric covariance with normal personality. *Journal of Research in Personality, 41*, 524–539. doi:10.1016/j.jrp.2006.06.002

Van Eeden, C., Wissing, M. P., Dreyer, J., Park, N., & Peterson, C. (2008). Validation of the Values in Action Inventory of Strengths for Youth (VIA-Youth) among South African learners. *Journal of Psychology in Africa, 18*, 145–156.

Wagner, L., & Ruch, W. (2015). Good character at school: Positive classroom behavior mediates the link between character strengths and school achievement. *Frontiers in Psychology, 6*, 610. doi: 10.3389/fpsyg.2015.00610

Weber, M. (2018). The interplay between character strengths, school satisfaction, academic self-efficacy, enjoyment to learn, and school achievement in the context of a schooling-related engine model of well-being. [Manuscript submitted for publication]

Weber, M., & Dietel, L. (2018). On the relations between exogenous input factors and process as well as outcome variables in the context of the school-related engine model of well-being. [Unpublished raw data, Technical University of Darmstadt, Darmstadt, Germany]

Weber, M., & Ruch, W. (2012a). The role of a good character in 12-year-old school children: Do character strengths matter in the classroom? *Child Indicators Research, 5*, 317–334. doi:10.1007/s12187-011-9128-0

———. (2012b). The role of character strengths in adolescent romantic relationships: An initial study on partner selection and mates' life satisfaction. *Journal of Adolescence, 35*, 1537–1546. doi:10.1016/j.adolescence.2012.06.002

Weber, M., Ruch, W., Littman-Ovadia, H., Lavy, S., & Gai, O. (2013). Relationships among higher-order strengths-factors, subjective well-being, and general self-efficacy: The case of Israeli adolescents. *Personality and Individual Differences, 55*, 322–327. doi:10.1016/j.paid.2013.03.006

Weber, M., Wagner, L., & Ruch, W. (2016). Positive feelings at school: On the relationships between students' character strengths, school-related affect, and school functioning. *Journal of Happiness Studies, 17*, 341–355. doi:10.1007/s10902-014-9597-1

White, M. A., & Waters, L. E. (2015). A case study of 'The good school': Examples of the use of Peterson's strengths-based approach with students. *The Journal of Positive Psychology, 10*, 69–76. doi:10.1080/17439760.2014.920408

Chapter 2

Eccomi Pronto
Developing Curricula to Promote Character Strength Development in Primary School Students Through Storytelling

Jessica Bertolani and John C. Carey

INTRODUCTION

In this chapter, we describe a 'Eccomi Pronto' (EP) universal elementary school curriculum that we created to promote the development of self-direction in Italian schoolchildren. We also describe the lesson we learned from the process of developing EP and we make suggestions for educators who would like to develop similar story-based curricula to promote character strength development.

Educational research has consistently shown that narrowing down the scope of schooling gives rise to problems in children's development (see Greenberg et al., 2003; National Research Council, 2012). If schools focus narrowly on only academic learning, students may end up lacking character strength and social–emotional competence. In addition, educational research has consistently shown that non-academic skills are necessary for academic success (Durlak & Weissberg, 2010; Durlak et al., 2011; Hattie, Biggs, & Purdies, 1996; Masten & Coatsworth, 1998; Wang, Haertel, & Walberg, 1994). Heckman and Krueger's (2003) seminal analyses clearly indicate that the achievement gap between middle-class and low-income and minority students in the United States is attributable to differences in both cognitive (e.g., academic skills) and 'non-cognitive' skills (e.g., self-direction, social engagement, self-regulation and character strength). They concluded that school-based programmes that actively help students develop non-cognitive skills are instrumental in reducing the achievement gap.

Despite this broad consensus on the critical importance of character strength education, schools in many countries are still devoting limited time and curricular resources to systematically address the non-cognitive skill development of students; more investment is therefore needed in the development of purposeful, school-based interventions (Kim et al., 2015). We developed the EP curriculum to help address this issue.

The EP curriculum was developed through a partnership between the University of Verona and the University of Massachusetts, Amherst (Bertolani, Mortari, & Carey, 2014). The story-based curriculum units are designed to help students understand themselves, regulate their emotions and direct their behaviour. Sharing stories is a particularly powerful way for adults and children to build the type of relationship that promotes effective learning (Bianchi, 2008). A good teacher–student relationship is critically important for student learning. Students learn best when they perceive that their teacher knows, likes, respects and cares about them. Good stories evoke ideas and emotions in both adults and children. The collaborative dialogue between adults and children about the events and meaning of the story provide an opportunity for the development of caring and mutual understanding. EP supports educators in their efforts to provide character education in classrooms and serves a useful tool to connect parents with the school and develop a common understanding of students' character strength development.

EP has been implemented and evaluated in the primary schools in Trentino-Alto Adige (Bertolani, Mortari, & Carey, 2014). Bertolani et al. (2014) reported that EP was associated with a number of qualitative improvements in students' academic behaviour, including increased engagement, involvement, reading interest, reading comprehension, work conscientiousness, inquisitiveness and social support of classmates. Quantitative findings confirmed that implementation of the curriculum was associated with improvements in classroom climate and student engagement. EP has also been implemented and evaluated in a South Korean elementary school with similar results (Kim et al., 2015).

THE ECCOMI PRONTO CURRICULUM

The EP curriculum is aimed at early elementary school pupils, and is designed to promote the simultaneous development of self-direction and pre-literacy skills. School-based counsellors and teachers deliver the curriculum collaboratively, either in the classroom or in small groups. EP supplements direct skills-based reading instruction by getting students to focus on the structure of good stories; reinforcing their ability to remember and relate sequences of events; and helping them to make appropriate inferences about the characters' inner lives, thoughts and emotions, and the way these aspects affect behaviour.

Each EP story is based on key concepts from a research tradition in modern educational or developmental psychology related to the capacity to be an effective self-directed learner. The characters and events in the stories help students see how these concepts can be used to improve their lives. Each EP lesson is based on stories that a counsellor or a teacher reads to the students.

Each story has a lesson or a 'moral' but, unlike traditional children's stories, these lessons are based on sound psychological theory and research rather than on folk psychology. For example, the story related to goal setting includes two main characters, Becky and her sister Bertha; both want to become the most famous cow in the world. They engage in a contest to see who can jump over the moon first. The story describes how Bertha and Becky try to solve this problem in different ways. Bertha tries hard while Becky develops a plan with different goals for each day of the week. The story resolves with a lesson. Becky is successful because of the way she uses a systematic goal-setting process to solve the problem.

The 12 lessons all involve an introduction, the presentation of a story, a collective elaboration and processing of the story, and follow-up activities. The introduction is meant to establish the focus for the lesson and get the students familiar with the key concepts and skills of the session. The story describes an initial situation (i.e., the problem to be addressed); narrates a series of events (involving a set of characters who interact with each other, deal with the difficulties outlined in the story and eventually resolve the situation); and culminates in a solution that entails an explicit or implied lesson or moral. In the group discussion phase, a detailed protocol helps teachers lead the group's inquiry into the story. Finally, follow-up activities and projects are suggested that can be conducted in the classroom and/or at home to consolidate learning (Bertolani, Mortari, & Carey, 2014).

THE DEVELOPMENT OF ECCOMI PRONTO

In developing EP, we first reviewed the educational and developmental psychological research literatures to identify the constructs that would serve as the basis of curriculum units. To be considered, there needed to be empirical evidence that the construct was strongly related to student learning and achievement and that students' capabilities and behaviour as expressed in terms of the construct could be improved by short-term educational interventions (Squier, Nailor, & Carey, 2014). Twelve such constructs were identified: goal setting, causal attribution, help-seeking, possible selves, self-efficacy, use of self-talk to self-regulate behaviour, comfort with social difference, self-regulation of motivation, social skills for collaborative learning, social consciousness, learned optimism and intrinsic interests. Stories were written to draw on each construct at the appropriate cognitive and linguistic level for early elementary school children. Each story was intentionally constructed to provide children with the opportunity to internalize psychological concepts that promote optimal personal and social development. All the stories are rooted in a 'culture' of positive psychology that is based on the belief that all people are competent, active agents who are capable of directing their own lives, participating in productive nurturing relationships and contributing to the good of their communities.

Curriculum guides for teachers were written for each story. The guide included (a) an explanation of the construct upon which the story was based (including illustrations of the importance of the construct for students); (b) a script for introducing the story; (c) a detailed guide for processing the story, with specific procedures and questions; and (d) suggestions for follow-up activities (Bertolani, Mortari, & Carey, 2014). The guide for processing the story was designed to help teachers assist students to deepen their own self-knowledge and understanding and also to gain knowledge about the structure of stories (Weinstein & Alschuler, 1985) by asking students to recall the events of the story in proper sequence; to identify the initial situation of the story and how it changed; to identify how external events influenced the internal states of characters; to identify how the internal states of characters affected their behaviour; to identify how the behaviour of characters influenced the events of the story; to identify morals or lessons of the story; to compare and contrast themselves with the characters of the story; to find parallels between their own lives and the characters and events in the stories; and to evaluate the behaviour of characters in the story.

The general pedagogical approach and the related instructional methods for implementing EP in classrooms is based on the principles of Adlerian psychology (Adler, 1927). Adler maintained that all people are motivated by a desire to develop competence and to be able to master the challenges of like. He believed that all people have an innate desire to contribute to good of their group, community and larger society. Furthermore, he believed that children would develop optimally in environments (e.g., families and schools) that were both democratic and encouraging. EP lessons are conducted in a manner that is consistent with the democratic classroom practices advocated by Adlerian psychology. The teacher/counsellor sets clear rules for student behaviour and interaction and applies logical consequences when rules are violated. Students are encouraged to participate and put forward their ideas and guesses. Each individual student's contributions and strengths are acknowledged. Students are encouraged to help each other. This environment provides optimal support for student's risk-taking and their development of self-knowledge and self-direction.

EVALUATION OF ECCOMI PRONTO

In the early stages of EP's development, we created a Theory of Action and related Logic Model to document our expectations about how it would influence students' personal and academic development and to guide subsequent evaluations of its implementation. The Logic Model is summarized in Figure 2.1.

We hypothesized that participation in EP would result in increased student self-direction that would be manifested in enhanced engagement in academic learning activities. We further hypothesized that EP participation would also result in improved classroom climate and better teacher–student relationships, both of which would contribute to positive student engagement and enhance academic learning.

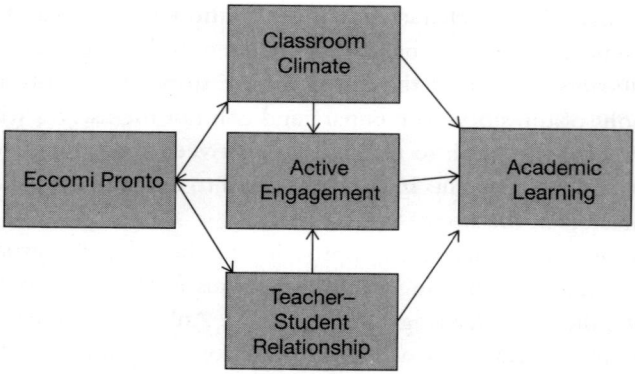

Figure 2.1 *Eccomi Pronto Logic Model*

Evaluation of educational programmes like EP is necessary for several reasons. Formative evaluations conducted with new programmes help to determine which facets of the programme are working as planned and which need to be modified. Summative evaluations of mature programmes help to establish that the programme is achieving its desired outcomes and is generating benefits for participating students.

We used a mixed methods approach in the initial formative evaluation that employed a single group, pre–post test design that used measures adapted from English language surveys, structured interviews and observations (Bertolani, Mortari, & Carey, 2014). The evaluation assessed whether there were EP-associated changes in students self-reported levels of engagement as measured by the Student Engagement Survey (based on Pintrich & DeGroot, 1990) and improvements in teacher-reported classroom climate as measured by the My Class Inventory (Sink & Spencer, 2007). In addition, the evaluation assessed EP-associated changes in students' behaviour as noted by teachers, parents and the students themselves, and teachers' views of the current strengths of EP and suggestions for improving its design and implementation. Pre–post comparisons found significant improvements in both student engagement and classroom climate. Parent, teacher and student comments corroborated these changes. Teachers indicated that the curriculum was effective and offered them new insights into working with students and individual learning needs. Teachers offered suggestions on improving EP that were incorporated in its next iteration.

DEVELOPING EFFECTIVE CURRICULA

Our process for developing EP was guided by two formal approaches to developing universal classroom curricula: Deliberate Psychological Education (DPE) (Mosher & Sprinthall, 1970) and Understanding by Design (UbD) (Wiggins & McTighe, 2005).

Deliberate Psychological Education

DPE as created to enable the use of psychological research-based constructs in the development of classroom curricula to promote students' development. Mosher and Sprinthall (1970) have described the foundation for DPE which rests upon the beliefs that self-understanding is an essential goal of education that is typically not addressed well through traditional classroom instruction. They suggested that a more experientially based instructional approach based on psychological theory and research was necessary to promote students' growth and development in the psychological and psychosocial realms. At the heart of this approach are curricular experiences that help students 'personalize' their new psychological knowledge—internalizing it by applying it to their own lives. These curricular experiences are designed to help students reflect on their own thoughts and feelings and to test their reflections through dialogue with other. DPE educators design curricula and use pedagogy that works within what Vygotsky (1978) would call the 'zone of proximal development' of the students (Faubert, Locke, Sprinthall, & Howland, 1996). Curricula and instruction are designed to provide scaffolding—eternal supports for students to help them understand and use psychological concepts that are just barely within their ability to grasp.

DPE has been used successfully to develop universal curricula to promote students' psychological development in a wide range of areas including abstract thinking, causal attributions, ego development, listening and communication skills, empathy, social role-taking, assertive communication skills and moral reasoning (Faubert et al., 1996; Kessler et al., 1986; Mosher & Sullivan, 1976; Schmidt, McAdams, & Foster, 2009; Sprinthall & Scott, 1989). Major strengths of DPE include the insurance that the curriculum is aligned with the research base and the insurance that students will internalize and apply learning through guided reflection and experiential exercises.

Understanding by Design

UbD was developed through an analysis of research the characteristics of effective curricula (Wiggins & McTighe, 2005). It is based on several fundamental principles including (a) learning is enhanced by purposefully made curricular planning; (b) curricula should focus on the development of deep understanding and the transfer of learning; (c) authentic performance is the best measure of student learning; (d) effective curriculum is planned backwards starting with the desired student behaviours and working back to the activities that will enable that behaviour; and (e) teachers need to monitor students' deep understanding, meaning making, application and transfer of learning.

Backwards design is a distinguishing concept of UbD that sets it apart from other approaches to curriculum design and development. UbD recommends a three-phase backwards design process for the development of new curricula (Wiggins & McTighe, 2005). Phase 1 requires that curriculum developers identify the desired results of the curriculum. Here the key questions are: What should students know, understand and be able to do as a consequence of the curricular experiences? And what are the most important enduring understandings and learning transfers that should result from the curricular experiences? Phase 2 requires that curriculum developers identify assessment evidence (quantitative and/or qualitative data) that they will use to know that students achieved the desired results of the curriculum. Finally, in Phase 3 curriculum developers attend to actually planning the curriculum by identifying learning experiences that will help students develop a deep, enduring understanding, apply their learning and develop the ability to transfer learning automatically. Learning materials are then developed and the resultant learning experiences are organized into a sequence that supports the development of understanding.

Eccomi Pronto

EP was developed in a manner consistent with both DPE and UbD. Consistent with DPE principles, EP was grounded in positive psychology research related to self-direction (Squier, Nailor, & Carey, 2014).

In addition, each curriculum unit emphasized learning activities that encouraged internalization and personalization of learning through reflection, application and dialogue. While the EP stories serve as important focal points for each curriculum unit, the power to create enduring learning actually resides in the group processing of the stories and the follow up activities that students do in school (individually and in groups) and at home. Finally, the EP curriculum places great emphasis on developmental appropriateness and working within students' zones of proximal development. Weinstein and Alschuler's (1985) self-knowledge development theory was used to design the complexity of the stories, the guides for processing the stories and the follow-up activities to ensure that they are at a challenging but achievable development level and that adequate scaffolding supports are built into the curriculum materials. In addition, teachers implementing EP learn the self-knowledge development model in order to help them provide needed scaffolding for all students.

UbD backwards design principles were also used in the development of EP. We started out by determining that the primary focus on EP would be on students' self-direction. We created a Theory of Action and a related Logic Model (see Figure 2.1) which indicated that, while we believed that becoming self-directed learners would ultimately result in gains in academic achievement, in the short-term, we expected that learning would be manifested in increased engagement in academic learning. We then determined that the primary evidence we would need to confirm EP*'s* success would be changes in students' engagement. We selected a standardized instrument that measures engagement and we also designed qualitative instruments to collect evidence for increased student engagement from teachers, parents and students. As noted earlier, both qualitative and quantitative formative evaluation procedures confirmed the effectiveness of EP and identify needed improvement in EP (Bertolani, Mortari, & Carey, 2014; Kim et al., 2015). Finally, we developed instructional materials (stories, teachers' guides, home activities and school activities) that focused on the development of deep understanding and transfer through guided reflection and group processing, and through activities that encourage application and transfer.

SUGGESTIONS FOR DEVELOPING CHARACTER STRENGTHS CURRICULA

Based on our own experiences developing EP, and on DPE and UbD curriculum design principles, we suggest the following process for developing new character strength curricula.

Step 1. Select an appropriate Character Strength Theoretical Model to serve as a theoretical framework for the curriculum. For EP, we chose Squier, Nailor and Carey's (2014) model because it identified self-directed learning-related constructs, which had been demonstrated by psychological research to be strongly related to academic achievement and able to be modified by organized school-based curricular experiences. Other appropriate models would include Peterson and Seligman's (2004) taxonomy of character strengths and virtues and McGrath's (2015) three-factor model of character strengths. Both models would provide excellent guidance on identifying the overall focus of the curriculum and the focus of specific lessons. McGrath's (2015) model offers the advantage of identifying clusters of related strengths that may represent a natural way to organize curricula.

Step 2. Develop a Theory of Action and a related Logic Model for the Curriculum. This step will explicitly identify the expected long-term benefits of the curriculum and the shorter-term changes that would be anticipated if the curriculum is effective.

Step 3. Determine what evidence you will use to know if the curriculum is effective. Select instruments and/or identify qualitative indicators that are aligned with the shorter-term changes you expect to see if the curriculum is working as expected.

Step 4. Develop the instructional materials and supports with an emphasis on personalization of transfer of learning. If you are developing a story-based curriculum, remember that although the stories are important focal points for the curriculum, the effectiveness of the curriculum in producing lasting behavioural change will be dependent on its ability to promote personalization and transfer of the learning through activities that involve personal reflection, dialogue and application.

Step 5. Evaluate the instructional materials and supports to ensure that they are developmentally appropriate and provide both challenge and scaffolding support in the students' zones of proximal development. Pre-implementation feedback from experienced educators, the use of formal development models (e.g., Weinstein & Alschuler, 1985) and formative evaluation results are useful ways to get this information.

Step 6. Conduct iterative series of formative evaluations to improve the design and implementation of the curriculum. Here simple, lower-cost (e.g., one group, pre-post) designs are preferable to complex, expensive designs. It is sufficient to only measure the expected short-term behaviour changes.

Step 7. Develop and test training materials for future users of the curriculum.

Step 8. Conduct a larger-scale summative evaluation of the curriculum with multiple sites, multiple implementers and an active control group. This evaluation is necessary to generate strong evidence of the effectiveness of the curriculum. Here, it is important to measure both the expected short-term behaviour changes and the expected long-term benefits associated with the curriculum.

CONCLUSION

It is important to recognize that the development and refinement of effective character strength curricula is a lengthy and time-consuming process. However, the benefits to students and society as a whole more than justify the investment. Attention to some simple curriculum design principles can result in more effective curricula.

REFERENCES

Adler, A. (1927). *Understanding human nature*. New York: Greenburg.
Bertolani, J., Mortari, L., & Carey, J. (2014). Formative evaluation of Eccomi Pronto ['Here I Am Ready']: A school counselor-led, research-based, preventative curriculum for Italian primary schools. *International Journal for the Advancement of Counselling*, 1–15. doi:10.1007/s10447-014-9209-0
Bianchi, E. (2008). *Il pane di ieri*. Torino: Giulio Einaudi Editore.
Durlak, J., & Weissberg, R. P. (2010). Social and emotional learning programs that work. In R. Slavin (Ed.), *Better evidence-based education: Social–emotional learning*. York, UK: Institute for Effective Education, University of York.
Durlak, J. A., Weissberg, R. P., Dymnicki, A. B., Taylor, R. D., & Schellimger, K. B. (2011). The impact of enhancing students' social and emotional learning: A meta-analysis of school-based universal interventions. *Child Development*, *82*(1), 405–432.
Faubert, M., Locke, D. C., Sprinthall, N. A., & Howland, W. H. (1996). Promoting cognitive and ego development of African–American rural youth: A program of deliberate psychological education. *Journal of Adolescence*, *19*, 533–543.
Greenberg, M. T., Weissberg, R. P., O'Brien, M. U., Zins, J. E., Fredericks, L., Resnik, H., & Elias, M. J. (2003). Enhancing school-based prevention and youth development through coordinated social, emotional, and academic learning. *American Psychologist*, *58*(6–7), 466–474.
Hattie, J., Biggs, J., & Purdie, N. (1996). Effects of learning skills interventions on student learning: A meta-analysis. *Review of Educational Research*, *66*, 99–130. doi:10.3102/00346543066002099
Heckman, J. J., & Krueger, A. B. (2003). *Inequality in America: What role for human capital policies?* Cambridge, MA: MIT Press.
Kessler, G. R., Ibrahim, F. A., & Kahn, H. (1986). Character development in adolescents. *Adolescence*, *21*(81), 1–9.
Kim, D. H., Lee, J. H., Hyun, J. H., Bertolani, J., Mortari, L., & Carey, J. C. (2015). Eccomi Pronto: Implementation of socio-emotional curriculum in a South Korean elementary school. *International Journal of Emotional Education*, *7*(2), 2–14.
Masten, A. S., & Coatsworth, J. D. (1998). The development of competence in favorable and unfavorable environments: Lessons from research on successful children. *American Psychologist*, *53*, 205–220. doi:10.1037//0003-066X.53.2.205
McGrath, R. (2015). Integrating psychological and cultural perspectives on virtue: The hierarchical structure of character strengths. *The Journal of Positive Psychology*, *10*(5), 407–424.
Mosher, L., & Sprinthall, N. A. (1970). Psychological education in secondary schools: A program to promote individual and human development. *American Psychologist*, *25*(10), 911–924.

Mosher, R. L., & Sullivan, P. R. (1976). A curriculum in moral education for adolescents. *Journal of Moral Education, 5*(2), 159–172.

National Research Council. (2012). *Education for life and work: Developing transferable knowledge and skills in the 21st century.* Washington, DC: The National Academies Press.

Peterson, C., & Seligman, M. E. P. (2004). *Character strengths and virtues: A handbook and classification.* Washington, DC: APA Press and Oxford University Press.

Pintrich, P. R., & Groot, E. V. D. (1990). Motivational and self-regulated learning components of classroom academic performance. *Journal of Educational Psychology, 82*(1), 33–40.

Schmidt, C. D., McAdams, C. R., & Foster, V., (2009). Promoting the moral reasoning of undergraduate business students through a deliberate psychological education-based classroom intervention. *Journal of Moral Education, 38*(3), 315–334.

Sink, C., & Spencer, L. (2007). Teacher version of the my class inventory-short form: An accountability tool for elementary school counselors. *Professional School Counseling, 11*(2), 129–139.

Sprinthall, N. A., & Scott, J. R. (1989). Promoting psychological development, math achievement, and success attribution of female students through deliberate psychological education. *Journal of Counseling Psychology, 36*(4), 440–446.

Squier, K., Nailor, P., & Carey, J. C. (2014). *Achieving excellence in school counseling through motivation, self-direction, self-knowledge and relationships.* Thousand Oaks, CA: Corwin.

Vygotsky, L. (1978). *Mind in society.* Cambridge, MA: Harvard University Press.

Wang, M. C., Haertel, G. D., & Walberg, H. J. (1994). What helps students learn? *Educational Leadership, 51*(4), 74–79.

Weinstein, G., & Alschuler, A. S. (1985). Educating and counseling for self-knowledge development. *Journal of Counselling and Development, 64*(1), 19–25.

Wiggins, G., & McTighe, J. (2005). *Understanding by design* (expanded 2nd ed.). Alexandria, VA: ASCD.

Chapter 3

Developing and Assessing Strategies to Foster Children's Character Strengths and Well-being

Sarah Weissmeyer and Mark D. Holder*

INTRODUCTION

Clinical psychology is rooted in the medical model of health and illness (Suls & Rothman, 2004). This model treats mental disorders as having physical causes such as brain injury or hormonal imbalance (Engel, 1989). The medical model has made invaluable contributions to the scientific study of the mind and behaviour. However, the theoretical magnification of people's flaws and disorders has led research to overlook their strengths and subjective well-being (SWB). Consequently, an increased focus on SWB and life satisfaction through the study of positive psychology is an important expansion to health-related research. Positive psychology focuses on 'what is right' with people and how their SWB can be promoted (Seligman, Steen, Park, & Peterson, 2005).

---

* The authors thank Holli-Anne Passmore for her help with an earlier version of this chapter.

This includes the study and fostering of character strengths (CSs) to achieve human flourishing.

To support the goals of positive psychology, Peterson and Seligman (2004) published the *Character Strengths and Virtues: A Handbook and Classification* (CSV), which serves as a complement to classification systems in abnormal psychology that are based on the traditional medical model. The classification system in the CSV is particularly valuable to positive psychology because it provides an empirical framework of understanding and measuring CSs from a cross-culturally relevant perspective. The CSV compared descriptions from interdisciplinary literature to identify, organize and condense 24 major CSs under six core virtues. These virtues reflect abstract ideals such as justice and humanity that are discussed most frequently in the studied literature. By providing a behavioural description of CSs that can be objectively measured, the CSV provides a reliable scientific foundation for CS studies and interventions (Peterson & Seligman, 2004). The scientific approach to studying and promoting CSs allows parents, educators and researchers to operate without being side-tracked by cultural, social or institutional bias. This is particularly important for CSs interventions designed to assist a variety of children from different cultural, social and religious backgrounds.

Nurturing children's CSs appears to be a fruitful investment in children, as many of the strengths presented in the CSV correlate with life satisfaction (Peterson & Seligman, 2004). However, two strengths—wisdom and knowledge—are not correlated with life satisfaction but are prioritized in education. Education needs to expand its focus to include values beyond fostering intellectual ability if its goal is to assist children in becoming independent adults who have the skills to enhance their own SWB.

This chapter addresses ways parents, educators and researchers can work together towards increasing children's SWB by nurturing CSs. To understand the relationship between CS and children's SWB, we first summarize the research regarding the correlates of strengths and SWB of children. We focus on research that investigates the CSs of hope, spirituality, appreciation of beauty and excellence, and kindness. This research helps identify approaches that may prove most fruitful to increase children's strengths. Second, we examine the empirical work on strategies designed to help children thrive by supporting their CSs. Third, we discuss the limitations of research aimed at understanding and promoting children's strengths. This includes the need for more cross-cultural research on a global level and the need for better metrics to assess children's strengths and SWB. Finally, we suggest future research that assesses the efficacy of programmes to enhance children's strengths. These proposed programmes include approaches, such as engagement in nature, which can be easily adopted by caregivers, parents and educators to enhance children's strengths. A fundamental part of character education is to explain to children the values underlying CSs. Caregivers and educators need to foster children's understanding of these strengths if they wish their children to use them regularly and independently. Children need to be engaged in CSs through conversations and activities. The CS interventions discussed below show that this can be achieved by employing culturally sensitive and age-appropriate activities and programmes. To appreciate and utilize CS interventions, it is important that caregivers and educators familiarize themselves with the most recent literature and research which we introduce in the following sections.

THE CORRELATES OF CSS AND SWB OF CHILDREN

SWB, as used in positive psychology, refers to more than simply the absence of negative cognitions and emotion; it encompasses additional evaluations people make of their own lives (Diener, 2006). SWB includes high levels of life satisfaction and positive affect, and low but appropriate levels of negative affect (Ryan & Deci, 2001). Although the term 'happiness' is used interchangeably with SWB in positive psychology, it more precisely refers to the positive affect component of SWB. Life satisfaction is one of the most frequently assessed components of SWB (Ryan & Deci, 2001). The CSs of hope, zest, love, gratitude and curiosity are particularly predictive of life satisfaction in adults (Park, Perterson, & Seligman, 2004; Peterson, Ruch, Beermann, Park, & Seligman, 2007). Similar positive correlations between life satisfaction and zest, hope, love and kindness have been found with samples from various countries including Croatia, Singapore, Switzerland and Japan (Brdar & Kashdan, 2010; Lee, Foo, Adams, Morgan, & Frewen,

2015; Martinez-Marti & Ruch, 2014; Shimai, Otake, Park, Peterson, & Seligman, 2006).

Research has identified certain strengths as predictive of the dimensions of adult and adolescent SWB (Brdar & Kashdan, 2010; Gillham et al., 2011; Park et al., 2004). However, few studies investigated the relationship between SWB and CSs in children, and only very limited research has provided a global perspective. One proposed reason for this lack of research is that there is no consensus as to the best-validated measures of CSs and happiness for young children because self-report measures designed for adults and adolescents may not be valid for children (Park & Peterson, 2006b). Therefore, the assessment of CSs and SWB in children often relies on observations made by teachers and parents (Park & Peterson, 2006a). For example, Park and Peterson (2006a) asked parents and guardians to describe the most prominent CSs of their children. They then assessed the resulting 680 descriptions of children aged 3 to 9 years for levels of happiness and categorized them into the 24 CSs catalogued in Peterson and Seligman's (2004) CSV. The patterns that emerged were similar to those that emerged from studies of adult and adolescent CSs; strengths of the heart, including hope, love and zest, significantly correlated with happiness in children (Park & Peterson, 2006a). However, only the levels of gratitude of older children, aged 7 to 9 years, were significantly associated with their life satisfaction—an association also found in adults. Furthermore, CSs that are more cognitively complex, such as open-mindedness, leadership and honesty, were reported less frequently in children than in studies with adults. Perhaps age affects the influence of children's CSs on their happiness. Therefore, being attentive to developmental changes in CSs may be important when investigating strengths-based SWB interventions in children.

In addition to developmental changes, children's CSs may vary across cultures. Ghosh and Deb (2016) emphasize the importance of differences in the CSs found in Indian and Western research. For example, one study including an Indian sample reported higher levels of religiosity than a Western sample (Singh & Choubisa, 2009). Knowledge of these differences is critical when identifying which CSs would be most beneficial to target in interventions intended to promote children's SWB across different nations.

Hope

Hope is one of the most frequently researched CSs in relation to children's happiness, in part because hope seems to promote life satisfaction (Bailey, Eng, Frisch, & Snyder, 2007). Hope is defined as the subjective perception of one's ability to find pathways to desired goals and to 'motivate oneself ... to use those pathways' (Snyder, 2002, p. 249). Thus, hope is comprised of both people's conceptualization of pathways to their goals, referred to as 'pathway thinking', and their motivation to use these pathways, known as 'agency thinking' (Snyder, 2002). Hope is one of the strengths that comprise the virtue of transcendence in that it connects a person with a desired future goal (Peterson & Seligman, 2004).

Given that hope encompasses a future orientation, there may be qualitative differences between how children and adults perceive it. It is, therefore, important to carefully examine children's perception and understanding of hope and determine how they relate to SWB. Snyder et al.'s (1997) thorough analysis of this topic has led to the creation of the Children's Hope Scale. This customized scale allows researchers to investigate the relationship between hope and SWB in students aged 8 to 16. For instance, studies have found significant positive correlations between children's hope and their global life satisfaction (Marques, Pais-Ribeiro, & Lopez, 2007; Merkaš & Brajša-Žganec, 2011; Valle, Huebner, & Suldo, 2006), results which were replicated in different cultures (Marques et al., 2007). For instance, Marques et al. (2007) reported a strong positive correlation between hope and life satisfaction in 367 Portuguese middle-school students. Paralleling the results with adults, studies have found a negative correlation between hope and depression in children (Snyder et al., 1997). In addition, high scores on the Children's Hope Scale were associated with higher academic achievement (Marques, Lopez, & Pais-Ribeiro, 2011). Given the benefits of hope observed across cultures, the study of SWB interventions in children that focus on hope is warranted.

Spirituality

In addition to hope, Peterson and Seligman (2004) categorized spirituality as a strength of transcendence. An inherent characteristic of both hope and spirituality is that they connect individuals with a realm beyond themselves and provide a profound sense of meaning (Peterson & Seligman, 2004). However, these constructs differ in that hope connects the individual with a desired future, whereas spirituality involves a profound connection to a belief system revolving around intangible aspects of life and the universe (Peterson & Seligman, 2004). This is not to be confused with religion, which refers to an institutional system of faith with rituals, practices and beliefs (Holder, Coleman, & Wallace, 2010; Peterson & Seligman, 2004). Many studies have not conceptually distinguished religion and spirituality, and this distinction may yield results that are more valid. Research on religion's relationship with SWB has provided less definitive findings than for hope. For example, some studies have found no significant relationship between religiosity and happiness (Francis, Ziebertz, & Lewis, 2003; Lewis, Lanigan, Joseph, & De Fockert, 1997; Lewis, Maltby, & Burkinshaw, 2000), while other studies have found significant positive associations between the two (Argyle & Hills, 2000; Francis, Robbins, & White, 2003; Lewis & Cruise, 2006). For instance, in a sample of 311 German University students, researchers failed to find a positive relationship between religion and happiness (Francis, Ziebertz, & Lewis, 2003). Moreover, studies comparing atheists to religious participants found no difference in levels of life satisfaction (Horning, Davis, Stirrat, & Cornwell, 2011) or happiness (Sillick, Stevens, & Cathcart, 2016). A major problem with these and other studies is the inconsistent use of measures of religiosity, spirituality and happiness. Moreover, Western studies often primarily focus on Christianity, thereby obscuring the diversity of religions and belief systems under a Christian conceptualization of religion.

The study of religiosity and spirituality in children poses particular challenges. There are questions surrounding young children's understanding and conceptualization of these constructs, and children are limited in their opportunities to choose their own religious practices. Parents typically '… determine the place, frequency, and duration of children's religious practices' (Holder, 2012, p. 51). Research suggests that spirituality may be a stronger predictor of happiness for children than adults, accounting for up to 26 per cent in the variance of children's happiness (Holder et al., 2010). Moreover, whereas spirituality was positively associated with children's happiness, religious practices were slightly negatively correlated. This study used self-reports and parental ratings of their children's happiness and both types of assessments gave similar results. To enable young children to self-report their happiness despite varying degrees of literacy skills, various measures were used including the faces scale, in which drawings depicted a range of faces with a continuum of sad–to–happy expressions.

Other research has demonstrated the importance of distinguishing between spirituality and religion. For instance, in a sample of 391 students in Zambia ranging in age from 7 to 12, spirituality accounted for 21 per cent of the variance in life satisfaction beyond age, gender, grade and religiosity (Holder, Coleman, Krupa, & Krupa, 2016). Although 95 per cent of the participants reported that they attended church at least once in the last month, spirituality, not religion, strongly predicted children's life satisfaction (Holder et al., 2016). Interestingly, research on spirituality and religion in adults depicts a different pattern. For example, a positive relationship between religious practices and happiness (Francis, Robbins, & White, 2003), and religious activities and life satisfaction (Chamberlain & Zika, 1988) has been reported. The importance of a clear distinction between constructs and adopting a cross-cultural perspective when studying religion and spirituality may help to explain seemingly contradictory findings. For instance, Zhang and Jin (1996) found that religious young adults (mean age=20.02) in China had more suicidal ideations, whereas religious young adults (mean age=20.94) in the United States had fewer.

These findings illustrate the need for extensive cross-cultural examinations of the relationships between religion, spirituality and SWB in children that include different spiritual and religious conceptualizations and identities. There is a need for longitudinal studies that allow researchers to trace changes that take place during childhood, which may influence the effectiveness of SWB interventions.

Appreciation of Excellence and Beauty

The CS of appreciation resembles the CSs of spirituality and hope in its transcendental nature. According to Peterson and Seligman (2004), 'a person high on this strength frequently feels awe and related emotions (including admiration, wonder and elevation) while for example, walking in the woods or in a city...' (p. 537). This strength includes an ability to perceive and take pleasure in the goodness that is inherent in the world. This description emphasizes the prominent emotional component of this strength. Peterson and Seligman identified three broad categories in which a response of awe is beneficial: (a) physical beauty, (b) virtue and (c) talent. The vastness and beauty of nature, in particular, inspires awe in many people (Kaplan & Talbot, 1983). An array of studies emphasize the benefits of contact with nature on health and SWB (Berman, Jonides, & Kaplan, 2008; Bowler, Buyung-Ali, Knight, & Pullin, 2010; Grinde & Patil, 2009). Increased time spent in nature contributes to feelings of relaxation (Korpela, Hartig, Kaiser, & Fuhrer, 2001), and improvement in children's mood (Bagot, Allen, & Toukhsati, 2015) and their ability to focus (Wells, 2000). A study of 747 children engaging with nature during a single-day trip to a park showed a significant increase in their emotional connection to nature and their commitment to environmental stewardship (Crawford, Holder, & O'Connor, 2016).

A review of research conducted from 1970 to 2015 found convergent evidence that contact with nature fostered children's physical health, cognitive functioning, self-control, psychological SWB, play and affiliation with other species and nature (Chawla & Nasar, 2015). However, despite that many studies were included in this literature review, the conclusions need to be considered with caution because many of the studies did not employ experimental designs with appropriate control groups (e.g., they were ethnographic studies or they used quasi-experimental designs). Nevertheless, studies and theories inspired by developmental researchers, including Piaget, underscore children's strong interest in, and motivation and curiosity for, exploring nature (Verbeek & de Waal, 2002). Future research to determine whether the degree to which children appreciate nature predicts higher levels of SWB is needed.

Kindness

Parents consider kindness to be one of the most important traits in their children (Diener & Lucas, 2004). Kindness is included under the category of 'Strengths of Humanity' (Peterson & Seligman, 2004,

p. 10). Kindness, 'indicating a common orientation of the self toward the other' (p. 325), has been described as altruistic love, which illustrates its relatedness to the concept of love. Kindness is an other-oriented strength that motivates us to perform actions that benefit others. Previous cross-cultural research suggests that prosocial behaviour increases happiness in individuals performing these behaviours (Dunn, Aknin, & Norton, 2008; Nelson, Layous, Cole, & Lyubomirsky, 2016; Otake, Shimai, Tanaka-Matsumi, Otsui, & Fredrickson, 2006).

Kindness requires 'the assertion of a common humanity in which others are worthy of attention and affirmation for non-utilitarian reasons ... for their own sake' (Peterson & Seligman, 2004, p. 326). This means that true kindness sparks a motivation to support people without an expectation of benefits for oneself in return (Peterson & Seligman, 2004). The frequency of giving and receiving help differed between students from Australia, Egypt, Korea, the Republic of China (Taiwan), the United States and Yugoslavia (Johnson et al., 1989). A longitudinal experiment conducted in 19 classrooms of students aged 9–11 years found that children who performed three acts of kindness each week experienced greater SWB including increases in positive affect and marginally significant increases in life satisfaction and happiness (Layous, Nelson, Oberle, Shonert-Reichl, & Lyubomirsky, 2012). A review of recent evidence-based research on kindness concluded that the initiation of kind acts is associated with increased SWB in students (Binfet, 2015). This review concluded that, rather than focusing on random acts of kindness, younger children may benefit more from conducting intentional acts of kindness in which educators and parents provide structure and deliberate support to encourage children's development of kind behaviours and social skills. These interventions would encourage children's reflection on acts of kindness and perspective-taking (Binfet, 2015). Children have different understandings and expressions of kindness and may engage in kind acts '... by offering physical help (e.g. helping up a student who has fallen), providing emotional help (e.g. comforting a lonely student), including others (e.g. inviting a student to join an established team), and sharing' (Binfet, 2015, p. 51).

There may be a relationship between children's age and their tendency to engage in acts of kindness. For instance, in a study of 3- to 16-year-olds, 7-year-old children donated fewer pennies or preferred candies when asked to do so than younger and older children (Grunberg, Maycock, & Anthony, 1985). Therefore, in addition to customizing kindness-based interventions for children to fit different cultures, researchers should consider adapting these interventions to the developmental level of the child.

CS INTERVENTIONS
What Are CS Interventions?

CS interventions are positive psychology interventions that focus on the identification, development, and use of strengths to promote flourishing or other benefits such as academic achievement (Quinlan, Swain, & Vella-Brodrick, 2011). These interventions enhance existing strengths and foster new ones (Quinlan et al., 2011). They can increase an individual's overall ability to identify and use positive CSs (Oppenheimer, Fialkov, Ecker, & Portnay, 2014). Strengths-based practices can be used with individuals or groups and are usually based on a particular classification system such as the VIA Classification of Strengths (Peterson & Seligman, 2004; Quinlan et al., 2011; Quinlan, Swain, Cameron, & Vella-Brodrick, 2014). The positive psychology literature stresses that focusing on promoting personal strengths is more beneficial than solely eliminating weaknesses (Quinlan et al., 2011).

Because various interventions are based on different classification systems and goals, some interventions are more appropriate than others in particular contexts. Thus, to fit the needs of children in different environments (e.g., school or home) CS interventions need to be carefully designed. Nevertheless, studies comparing the effectiveness of different CS interventions found that certain qualities generally produce better results regardless of the particular population targeted (Park & Peterson, 2009; Quinlan et al., 2011). For instance, longer interventions are generally more effective in achieving desired outcomes such as SWB (Park & Peterson, 2008; Quinlan et al., 2011). In this section, we analyse the empirical research conducted on interventions designed to promote children's CSs and SWB. However, before evaluating the various interventions described in the literature, we must address three questions: (a) Why are CS interventions important for children, parents and educators? (b) Who should be responsible for implementing them? (c) Which strengths should be the focus of character interventions?

Why Are CS Interventions Important?

Increasing SWB benefits children as this increase is associated with enhanced learning and creativity, and the prevention of depression (Seligman, Ernst, Gillham, Reivich, & Linkins, 2009). Because many cases of depression remain untreated, the prevention of mental illness and promotion of mental health are an essential concern (Seligman et al., 2009). Several CSs, including hope, zest and leadership, are strongly related to lower levels of depression and anxiety in children and youth (Peterson & Park, 2009). These strengths are associated with a decrease in the internalization of problems and, therefore, may act as important protective factors against mental illness (Park & Peterson, 2008). Furthermore, positive affect predicts broader attention, and is consequently conducive to creative thought (Fredrickson, 2003; Fredrickson & Branigan, 2005). Researchers and educators predict that schools that primarily focus on knowledge acquisition will not successfully adapt to the rapidly changing demands of a 21st century economy (Scoffham, 2003; Shaheen, 2010). As our societies become increasingly complex through tightening networks of communication, technology and exchange of knowledge, we will require flexible and creative modes of thought.

Studies of adults and adolescents indicate that positive psychology interventions, particularly strength-based programmes, can increase SWB (Gillham et al., 2011; Quinlan et al., 2011; Seligman, Steen, Park, & Peterson, 2005). For example, a CS intervention encouraged participants to identify and use their CSs in new ways for 6 months (Seligman et al., 2005). This intervention significantly increased the participants' SWB over the long term. These, and positive findings from similar studies with adults, encouraged the development of comparable interventions for younger people (Gillham et al., 2007; Waters, 2011). The importance of SWB interventions for promoting children's mental health is underscored by finding that they help develop resilience and decrease mental illness (Brunwasser, Gillham, & Kim, 2009; Gillham et al., 2007; Waters, 2011). Moreover, learning social and emotional skills in the early stages of development allows children to connect meaningfully with their communities (Waters, 2011).

Who Should Implement CS Interventions?

During the past century, many educational policies have overemphasized the focus that schools place on academic achievement as indicated by exam grades (Morris, 2013; Oppenheimer et al., 2014). This focus had led to schools somewhat neglecting the social, developmental and individual importance of building strong character (Morris, 2013). Importantly, educational systems that integrate 'soft' concepts of fostering CSs and other positive psychology practices led to better academic success. For instance, Finland is regularly identified as having among the highest levels of academic achievement, and has a particularly intensive focus on supporting children's emotional, social and character development (Morgan, 2014; Niemi, Toom, & Kallioniemi, 2012; Sahlberg, 2010). Prioritizing students' SWB in the classroom is beneficial because SWB is related to increased academic achievement and engagement, and improved student behaviours (Seligman et al., 2009). The positive psychology literature provides further compelling arguments for the application of more holistic education policies that focus on students' social, emotional, and mental well-being (Jenkins & Barry, 2007). For instance, there is strong scientific support for the benefits of school-based positive psychology and CSs programmes (Jenkins & Barry, 2007; Proctor, Linley, & Maltby, 2010; White & Waters, 2014).

Broader school curricula that have integrated CS interventions during the past decade show positive outcomes for children including greater student engagement (Jenkins & Barry, 2007; Quinlan et al., 2011).

Overall, schools are considered an ideal setting for programmes promoting psychological SWB (Gillham et al., 2007; Linley & Proctor, 2013). The extensive time that students spend in school can be used to effectively teach them in groups about CS use. Moreover, schools are one of the most influential social institutions with reformative impacts on individuals, families and communities (Oppenheimer et al., 2014).

Despite research identifying the benefits of positive psychology interventions in schools, internationally, few projects have been integrated into regular school routines (Sahlberg, 2010; Waters, 2011). Because schools and teachers have limited resources, novel intervention efforts are often sacrificed for traditional teaching methods that focus primarily on cognitive skills (Linkins, Niemic, Gillham, & Mayerson, 2014). The incorrect assumption that interventions focusing on emotional and social learning will not create immediate and tangible results such as improved grades often guides this approach (Sahlberg, 2010; Waters, 2011). However, a meta-analysis involving the results of 270,034 students from kindergarten to high school contradicted this assumption. It concluded that students who participated in social and emotional learning programmes scored higher on achievement tests than children who did not participate; on average students who participated scored 11 per cent higher, but only when the interventions were conducted by school personnel rather than individuals outside of the school system (Durlak, Weissberg, Dymnicki, Taylor, & Schellinger, 2011). Additionally, researchers are accumulating evidence that many other psychological dimensions, besides intellect, are equally or more predictive of academic success (Linkins et al., 2014; Lounsbury, Fisher, Levy, & Welsh, 2009). For example, CSs, including self-control, are more reliable predictors of academic achievement than IQ (Duckworth & Seligman, 2005). However, the intervention research needs to address the hesitation to integrate new interventions into school systems. To reduce this hesitation, CS initiatives need to be easy to implement, even for teachers who do not have a positive psychology background.

Though focusing on school curricula may be an effective way to introduce children to CS interventions, parents and caregivers may play a critical role in the development of their children's CSs. Parental CSs are often closely associated with those of their children (Park & Peterson, 2009). For example, parents' CSs of self-regulation and their child's global life satisfaction are strongly correlated (Park & Peterson, 2006a). A possible explanation for this correlation is that self-regulated parents provide a more stable environment for their children, which is essential for their children's SWB (Park & Peterson, 2014). In addition, research evaluating the CSs of 479 first-grade schoolchildren and their parents revealed a positive relationship between children's first-grade adjustment and parents' intellectual, interpersonal and temperance strengths (Shoshani & Aviv, 2012). The children were selected from five public elementary schools in Israel. The study described the association between children's and parents' CSs in several different ways. For instance, parents' intellectual and interpersonal strengths were predictive of their children's investment in learning. Although genetic influences on these outcomes are likely, environmental influences were also highlighted. For instance, the study showed that factors beyond inheritable intellectual ability contribute to children's achievements at school. Furthermore, the authors argue that many strengths that are important for learning, such as curiosity, naturally exist in many children. However, environmental influences can influence which CSs are enhanced or hindered (Park & Peterson, 2009). Consequently, parents play a fundamental role in creating an environment that is conducive to children's SWB and CSs development. Thus, parents should be supported in providing their children with the knowledge and encouragement necessary to practice and learn about their CSs on a daily basis.

What Strengths Should We Focus On?

Researchers have only developed a few interventions for children that focus on fostering the CSs mentioned in the previous section. One example of a CS intervention for children was a hope-based school intervention assessed with Portuguese middle school children (Marques et al., 2011). One group of students, aged 10 to 12 years, was matched with a second group of children based on similar levels of life satisfaction, academic performance, hope, mental health, self-worth and demographic factors. The students in the intervention group received five weekly 1-hour sessions that introduced them to hope theory, which holds that hope consists of goals, pathways to achieve these goals and agency thinking (Marques et al., 2011; Snyder, 2002). The students were taught how to conceptualize their goals, create pathways to reach them and acquire the attitude and energy necessary to attain them (Marques et al., 2011). At the initial assessment preceding this hope intervention, the two groups did not differ significantly on any of the measured variables. When the programme concluded, students who received the intervention showed significant increases in hope, self-worth and life satisfaction. These improvements persisted 18 months after the completion of the intervention.

Interventions that focus on fostering an appreciation for nature may be of particular value to children's development. As mentioned earlier, nature involvement not only increases commitment towards nature, it also contributes to children's health and SWB (Han, 2009; Howell & Passmore, 2013; Kellert, 2005; Wells, 2000). Park and Peterson (2008) identified the Outward Bound programme as an example of existing interventions that successfully target the CS of appreciation of beauty and excellence.

Outward Bound is a type of outdoor adventure education whose effectiveness was analysed in a meta-analysis encompassing 96 studies (Hattie, Marsh, Neill, & Richards, 1997). The meta-analysis allowed the authors to combine statistically the results of the studies, allowing for a more comprehensive evaluation of the results. Included in the analysis were 12,057 unique participants, the majority of whom were adults. Findings regarding SWB were not evaluated separately; therefore, the overall applicability of the findings should be viewed with caution. The authors found the greatest positive effects of adventure programmes to be on leadership, academic, independence, assertiveness, emotional stability, social comparison, time management and flexibility. Moreover, the improvements brought about by the interventions were mostly maintained over the long term. Not all outdoor adventure programmes were equally effective; versions of the Outward Bound courses that lasted 20+ days were most effective (Hattie et al., 1997). Because the majority of participants ranked the enjoyment of the beauty of nature very highly, the relationship with nature experienced in these programmes may be fundamental to the positive changes that were reported (Brown & Haas, 1980; Rossman & Ulehla, 1977).

These CS interventions allow researchers to establish a clearer picture of the effects of certain strengths on individuals' SWB. Nevertheless, in practical application, these interventions may not reflect children's actual CSs. Children's great diversity of CSs means that a CS intervention that focuses on a variety of strengths may be more effective and beneficial in the long term (Linkins et al., 2014). Therefore, school-based CS interventions should focus on a combination of strengths that allow children to discover and explore their own signature strengths. Next, the different types of character interventions will be compared and critically evaluated to provide a helpful overview of the research in this field.

CS Interventions

The study of CS interventions for children is still in its infancy. Different theoretical approaches concerning the application of these interventions in the classroom have been developed. Linkins et al. (2014) evaluated the concepts behind, and effectiveness of, traditional CSs initiatives in schools. They and other researchers revealed important flaws in, and misconceptions of, traditional interventions that hinder progress in the field of CS development. Many traditional CS interventions prescribe a universal set of core strengths and each student instructed to strive toward them (Linkins et al., 2014). For instance, the *Character counts!* Initiative in the United States identified six different strengths as the gold standard for all students to develop: trustworthiness, respect, responsibility, fairness, caring and citizenship (Harms & Fritz, 2001). The problem with this initiative is that it was prescriptive and imposed the value of these strengths over any other strengths (Linkins et al., 2014). The core strengths selected for CS interventions vary between countries and institutions; however, they instil particular values without providing children with the opportunity to nurture their own unique and diverse constellation of CSs (Linkins et al., 2014). This approach to CS interventions, therefore, provides a restricted definition of good character by excluding many of the strengths recognized in the 24 VIA CSs classification, and this restriction may hinder children's unique potential. Additionally, most CS-based education programmes focus on strengths from just three of the six VIA virtue categories and thus neglect a wide range of other strengths without adequate scientific justification (Linkins et al., 2014). A more expansive approach that allows children to foster their individual strengths provides a richer perspective of positive character and increases the likelihood that more children will succeed in advancing their strengths. In addition, the VIA classification provides a foundation for international CS interventions as it has cross-cultural relevancy (Linkins et al., 2014). Several of these more expansive CS interventions focus on fostering children's top strengths or encouraging the improvement of all CSs (Linkins et al., 2014). For instance, in a strength-based SWB intervention, Grade 6 students were either exposed to all 24 CSs of the VIA classification over the course of 8 weeks, or they were assigned to a control group (Rashid et al., 2013). All students completed the VIA Youth Survey which helped identify the students top five strengths. At the same time, feedback was given to parents and teachers about their children's strengths. Then these adults were asked to record any changes in the children's behaviour over the course of the intervention. In addition to being taught many ways to use their signature strengths, the intervention group learned how to employ strength-based problem-solving approaches. The children in the intervention group showed greater increases in the SWB measure than the control group. However, the two groups did not differ on measures of social skills. The intervention group's increased SWB was still apparent when assessed 6 months later. Despite these promising results, the authors argued that direct parental and teacher involvement was an important feature that was missing in this intervention. Thus, they modified this intervention to increase teachers' involvement and help them integrate the insights of the CS intervention into their curriculum (Rashid et al., 2013). The parents were also provided with after-school workshops to help them understand and support their children's strengths at home and encourage daily practice.

CS interventions can be used on their own or as an element of a larger programme or intervention. For instance, middle-school children participated in a 10-week group SWB intervention (Suldo, Savage, & Mercer, 2014). The researchers attempted to create a programme that merged several evidence-based Positive Psychology Interventions, including CSs enhancement (Suldo, Savage, & Mercer, 2014). The programme included three parts: (1) increasing hope and goal-directed thinking, (2) gratitude expressions and (3) novel uses of CSs. Compared to a control group, the intervention group showed significant increases in life satisfaction. Nevertheless, there were no significant changes in affect or psychopathology. The authors suggested that the increase in global life satisfaction, despite not concurrent increase in positive affect, was still encouraging. They contend that affect tends to be a momentary representation of a person's mood, and is thus a less stable overall indicator of SWB than life satisfaction. Interestingly, the majority of students (69%) identified the CS component as the one they would most likely continue on their own. This finding is consistent with the idea that students find CSs an inherently fascinating concept with which to engage.

Recent research has validated the benefits of giving children agency in choosing and implementing CSs interventions (Park & Peterson, 2008; Schueller, 2010). Children's agency in these interventions is linked to the effectiveness of such interventions (Schueller, 2010). For example, preference for a specific positive psychology intervention (PPI) is associated with better adherence to PPIs and greater increases in SWB following PPI completion (Schueller, 2010). Coincidentally, researchers were surprised by children's enthusiasm and interest in learning about their CSs (Park & Peterson's, 2008). To support children's agency in working with their CSs, educators, parents and researchers should use strategies that enable children's direct involvement in the intervention development (Park & Peterson, 2008). For instance, teachers can omit any speculative discussions of what constitutes good character, and instead ask students to name the traits they admire in individuals they know (Linkins et al., 2014). Researchers not only argue for the importance of schoolchildren's agency, they also claim that effective CS interventions should address the social implications of nurturing one's CSs (Quinlan et al., 2015). One classroom-based strengths intervention from New Zealand addressed the social effects of CSs education (Quinlan et al., 2015). In the study, SWB, class cohesion, engagement and relatedness were examined in 193 school students from age 9 to 12. Students were taught how to identify strengths and use them to create goal-setting strategies. Although the intervention was not accompanied by changes in life satisfaction and negative affect, several other factors, including positive affect, classroom engagement and autonomy need satisfaction, improved more in the intervention group than in the control group (Quinlan et al., 2015). Compared to the control group, the intervention class also showed enhanced group cohesion and less friction between students, therefore providing a classroom climate that was more conducive to effective learning (Quinlan et al., 2015). The enhanced classroom engagement and cohesion showed that strengths intervention may not only benefit individuals' SWB, but may also affect all students as a group.

A prominent CS intervention, the Strengths Gym, is a character-based school programme applied to young adolescent students aged 12 to 14 (Proctor et al., 2011). To test this programme's effect on students' SWB, 218 participants completed age-appropriate strengths-based activities and homework. The students also engaged in open discussions that related their newly gained knowledge and skills to their own lives. The children learned to identify their own signature strengths and were instructed on how to build their strengths, learn novel strengths and recognize strengths in others. A strong emphasis was placed on the use of CSs to build strength-based skills. Life satisfaction, affect and self-esteem were evaluated before and after the intervention took place, and all 24 VIA CSs were included in the programme booklets. Teachers employed the CSs programme during a six-month period; however, most teachers were unable to complete all of the 24 CSs lessons on time. The flexible set-up of this intervention programme allowed teachers to match the lessons to the needs of their students. Unfortunately, this flexibility may have compromised the results because students in different classes received different degrees of exposure to the intervention. Nevertheless, life satisfaction increased more for the intervention group than the control group that did not receive any interventions. These results, along with other research findings, demonstrate that positive psychology interventions, in particular those including CS lessons, increase SWB in youth and adults (Seligman et al., 2005, 2009; Sin & Lyubomirsky, 2009). More importantly, the intervention showed that a successful integration of a CSs programme into an already established curriculum was possible without the need of additional teacher training.

Summary

The findings of these and other CS interventions identify significant relationships between increased strengths use and increased SWB. When including the findings concerning the correlates of SWB, strengths such as love, zest and hope consistently emerge as the most significant CSs across all ages. However, in the context of children's character development, incorporating a full range of CSs in interventions may increase the probability of achieving long-term happiness.

Allowing children to explore and develop all CSs enables them to harness the individual benefits each of these strengths provides. For example, improvements in CSs that increase academic achievement and facilitate social relationships may build a strong foundation for happier, healthier children. Besides contributing to children's SWB, CS interventions help children develop a strong nature that allows them to emerge as moral agents. To achieve these desired outcomes, schools should track each student's CSs over time. This longitudinal research will provide a better understanding of the contributors to children's development and SWB. Studies of CS interventions also show that character education can easily be integrated into existing curricula and can be reinforced by parental engagement. Therefore, the implementation of CS interventions in schools do not need to compromise existing academic goals. Most CSs programmes offer children a variety of specific activities that allow them to use their strengths habitually, and thus increase their agency. A valuable insight derived from the CSs literature is that personalized CSs interventions that fit the need of individual children can effectively foster self-discovery, SWB and long-term adherence to the programme.

LIMITATIONS AND FUTURE RESEARCH

Research, including evaluations of intervention programmes, demonstrates that children's SWB positively influences health, academic achievement and social abilities (Huebner, 1991; Huebner, Suldo, & Gilman, 2006; Seligman et al., 2009; Suldo, Riley, & Schaffer, 2006). Recurring themes in the research literature highlight the importance of addressing limitations that hinder efforts in implementing and improving SWB and CS interventions for children (Fattore, Mason, & Watson, 2007). These limitations point to future opportunities for research including (a) developing SWB and CS measures and interventions that consider children's unique socio-economic, cognitive and cultural levels, (b) matching positive psychology interventions with each child's disposition, preferences, abilities and talents and (c) considering children's voices and autonomy in shaping research, community and educational programmes intended for them.

Consideration of Sociocultural and Economic Contexts

Systems designed to classify CSs differ in their goals, objectives, definitions and origins (Quinlan et al., 2011). Prominent examples are the StrengthsFinder (Rath, 2007), the Virtues Projects (Popov, 2000), the VIA Inventory of CSs (Peterson & Seligman, 2004) and Realise 2 (Linley, 2009). Although the effectiveness of some of the measures these systems employ has been cross-culturally validated (viz., Huebner, Laughlin, Ash, & Gilman, 1998), they were mostly developed in Western countries. Therefore, these measures may not provide important intercultural insights about children's CS. Measures originating from Western countries are not inherently flawed, but they may be limited in their ability to reflect a comprehensive view of important cultural differences or represent an unbiased conceptualization of CS. Little research has focused on examining intercultural and interpersonal influences as moderators of the effectiveness of CS interventions (Quinlan et al., 2011). Thus, there is a need to address these research gaps.

Measures that reveal predictors and correlates of children's SWB have helped to create evidence-based interventions and programmes (Huebner, 1994). Positive psychology interventions have successfully increased SWB (Sin & Lyubomirsky, 2009). For instance, instructing adolescents to count their blessings efficiently increased SWB (Froh, Sefick, & Emmons, 2008). When applying these procedures to children, researchers should note that the efficacy of any intervention can not only interact with age, but with individual differences (e.g., culture, personality and gender) as well (Gross-Manos, Shimoni, & Ben-Arieh, 2015; Uyan-Semerci & Erdoğan, 2016). Currently, there is no consensus on what measures of SWB and CS best assess these concepts. As a result, researchers use different measures which complicate comparisons across studies. By using multiple measures of SWB and CS in each study, researchers can more easily compare the findings of different studies.

Future research also needs to examine the duration of interventions and its relationship with their effectiveness and durability (Quinlan et al., 2011). Furthermore, research needs to tease apart the effects of promoting CSs in the classroom or at home from confounding variables such as increased attention, support, and social interaction between parents and teachers (Quinlan et al., 2011). The real-life application of research findings from this research would also have to be evaluated by replicating these studies in already existing schools and communities.

The 'Fit' of Positive Psychology Interventions

Studies of CS interventions generally implement a one-size-fits-all model on groups of diverse participants (Linkins et al., 2014). This approach may mask the effectiveness of interventions for specific subpopulations and decrease children's adherence to interventions that do not fit their temperament, talents and preferences. Children's continuing involvement in CS interventions is fundamental to achieving enduring increases in SWB (Park & Peterson, 2009; Quinlan et al., 2011). Therefore, it is important to enhance and maintain children's motivation for long-standing participation in interventions by making them enjoyable and engaging. Children tend to enjoy activities that support their sense of competency and learning without the pressure of meeting adult and peer expectations (Fattore et al., 2007) and children derive SWB from activities associated with their sense of self, social relationships and enjoyment of life (Ben-Arieh et al., 2001; Fattore et al., 2007). The particular type of activity was not as important to children's SWB as their ability to control its content and structure. Introducing new intervention programmes for students, in the form of games rather than tasks, may help decrease any apprehension about meeting teachers' expectations. Moreover, play has a myriad of benefits for children such as improved coping with life events, development of language skills, increased positive affect, enhanced attachment and relationships, and increased empathy, self-control and feelings of competence (Drewes & Schaefer, 2010).

Actively engaging with one's strengths each day is fundamental to achieving the long-term benefits of CS interventions. Parents play a vital role in the maintenance of their children's active engagement in CSs activities outside of school. Future research should consider the importance of systematically promoting parental involvement to increase their children's SWB through supporting their children's CSs. Furthermore, community involvement can provide additional opportunities for engaging with CS and SWB programmes. An example of such communal involvement in children's SWB is the creation of 'Walls of Well-Being' (WOWs) in public places on which children can write what happiness means to them (Holder et al., in press). To children, WOWs provide a place where they can present their thoughts and opinion. To parents and community members, the WOWs provide information about children's conceptualization of happiness so that they can better understand children's perspectives and thinking. To researchers, the walls can inform the development of interventions tailored to particular groups.

These proposed research directions will improve our understanding of the underlying mechanisms of SWB and CS interventions, and identify means through which children can become more motivated to use these interventions regularly (Quinlan et al., 2011). Especially in children, intrinsic motivation is essential for increasing interest in and adherence to activities. One study examined the effect of extrinsic rewards on preschool children's intrinsic motivation for drawing (Lepper, Greene, & Nisbett, 1973). The children showed reduced interest in drawing after receiving extrinsic rewards for drawing. These children demonstrated little interest in drawing unless they received an extrinsic reward. In contrast, children who did not receive rewards showed a consistently high level of interest in drawing. Traditional education relies heavily on extrinsic motivation. Therefore, children who are naturally curious or intrinsically interested may lose their interest in learning in classroom environments (Shoshani & Aviv, 2012). As a result, teachers may find it more difficult to engage students. In contrast, providing education and intervention programmes that fit children's preferences will likely provide intrinsic motivation.

Interventions with small effects that target only a few CSs may be more effective if they are integrated into larger SWB programmes. Creating interventions that allow children to choose which CS they want to develop and to decide which methods they prefer may increase the likelihood that the interventions will fit children's temperament and make them feel competent. For instance, in one intervention, youth wrote and then read aloud a gratitude letter to a significant person in their lives (Froh, Kashdan, Ozimkowski, & Miller, 2009). However, this activity may not be a good fit for all children; very shy children may not feel comfortable with expressing their gratitude in such a direct way, and experience increased levels of anxiety rather than positive affect (Holder, 2012).

Although many CS interventions are often intended for secondary and primary students, the underlying research that informs these interventions has been largely conducted with adult populations and university students (Mitchell, Stanimirovic, Klein, & Vella-Brodrick, 2009; Quinlan et al., 2011). This is problematic because it increases the difficulty of generalizing the research findings to children-focused interventions. Additionally, the most effective interventions start with younger children who have a greater ability to develop new CSs than adolescents or adults (Eccles & Gootman, 2002; McGabe, Bray, Kehle, Theodore, & Gelbar, 2011; Park & Peterson, 2004, 2008). Future studies should address the underrepresentation of children as research participants and provide an opportunity for children to make their voices heard as active participants.

Children's Autonomy

Current knowledge and research regarding children's psychological SWB tend to emphasize problems and deficits rather than children's potential (Pollard & Lee, 2003). For instance, there is much more research on avoiding threats to children's health and SWB than on promoting their satisfaction in life (Andrews & Ben-Arieh, 1999). Positive psychology research plays a vital role in providing a more holistic assessment of children's lives because it promotes their strengths and potentials.

A major concern with some CS research is that it has used measures of children's SWB or quality of life that tend to exclude children's direct observations and personal reports. It was common for studies to measure indirect factors such as family interactions or the parents' observations (Andrews & Ben-Arieh, 1999). Similarly, many studies do not include children's perspectives (Andrews & Ben-Arieh, 1999; Prout, 1997). Some researchers believe that children's perspectives and involvement should be a fundamental ingredient in every step of research that analyses and monitors children's SWB (Ben-Arieh & Goerge, 2001). This means including children as research participants and giving them agency to provide feedback on and influence in shaping the interventions to mitigate the effects of any adult-centric bias (Fattore et al., 2007).

Another limitation of research stems from the marginalization of children's perspectives and experiences in education. For instance, educational measures of achievement exclude children's perception regarding the quality of their education (Fattore et al., 2007). If children's voices and opinions are overlooked in research and education, the efforts of children's advocates to increase children's SWB may be hindered due to a lack of potentially valuable information (Fattore et al., 2007).

Another limitation concerns the evaluation of children's development according to standard milestones. Although developmental milestones may help identify underlying health and cognitive challenges, they do not emphasize cultural, economic and environmental influences (Lourenço & Machado, 1996). Moreover, many standardized assessments of children's development emphasize deficits and problems. They judge children based on normative standards that may not recognize the expression of individual competencies or strengths (Fattore et al., 2007). Too much emphasis is placed on predictions of how children will fare as adults, while their present experiences and contributions to the world are often overlooked. Assessing children's SWB only in terms of their future development into competent adults denies their voice, power and dignity as human beings (Qvortrup, 1991). As a distinct group, children's social and cultural realities are fundamentally different from adults. Children's understanding of SWB should reflect their present realities. Thus, children must be provided with tools that enable them to adequately express their needs and opinions (Alderson, 2000). One example is the use of graphics rather than text to illustrate concepts such as happiness (Fattore et al., 2007).

New research needs to allow for the conceptual autonomy of children in which they are recognized as knowledgeable and active agents in their own lives (Fattore et al., 2007). A study of 126 children in New South Wales represents a step forward in involving children (Fattore et al., 2007). In semi-structured interviews that included task-oriented methods, such as drawing, photography and collage, children were encouraged to illustrate their perspective of SWB. Children's conceptualization of SWB was further explored through dialogues between adults (researchers and caregivers) and the children. Children were given agency in deciding how to participate. They could choose between individual or peer-based interviews, group discussions, or the use of graphics or project-type work as a basis for discussion with the researchers. In all these dialogues and interactions, researchers minimized adult-centric bias and showed their respect for the children's autonomy and perspectives. The researchers carefully analysed children's messages regarding SWB conveyed in words and graphics. They found children's conceptualizations of SWB to be complex, ranging across themes of autonomy, safety, sense of self, material resources and shelter. Not only did children define SWB as an integration of feelings of happiness and sadness, they also stressed the importance of feeling secure and being a moral actor in social relations. Underscoring the argument for the active involvement of children in SWB interventions was the finding that children value activities in which they feel powerful and competent. The research showed that children are willing and able to participate in conversations concerning their own SWB.

A study with children in South Africa that used similar semi-structured interviews revealed prominent themes regarding children's conceptualization of happiness (Irma, 2014). These themes predominantly reflected the role of relationships with significant others, the active involvement in recreational activities and the contribution of material objects to children's happiness.

Research findings from studies, such as the two just discussed, buttress the position that future interventions need to be relevant to children. Such research is important in representing a more balanced view of children's development. Future interventions need to 'fit' children's temperament, talents, abilities and perspectives in the present to feel relevant to children. A comprehensive approach to children's SWB includes promoting their mental and physical health as well as strengthening their capacity to flourish.

CONCLUSION

The research literature summarized here shows that there are effective measures of children's CS and SWB that can be used to identify common predictors and correlates. Research with adults has demonstrated that CS interventions can increase aspects of SWB enduringly (Sheldon & Lyubomirsky, 2007). Nevertheless, the efficacy of any intervention interacts with individual differences stemming from temperament, culture, gender and age (Holder, Coleman, & Singh, 2012; Shmotkin, 1990). Moreover, it is possible that children select particular activities to increase their happiness as a function of their temperament. Future researchers, therefore, need to investigate how the fit between a PPI and the child determines the efficacy of the PPI. The self-concordance model holds that individuals' adherence to activities increases when they enjoy an activity. Thus, parents and educators, together with the child, should explore different activities and interventions aimed at increasing children's CS. Rather than unilaterally selecting an activity for the child, the child needs to be actively involved and feel autonomous in choosing a preferred activity. When children's curiosity and intrinsic motivation are triggered by a CS intervention that fits their needs and interests, educators and parents will have to exert less effort to maintain children's adherence to the intervention. Combined strategies that focus on a variety of strengths are more likely to appeal to different children. This directly relates to the idea that PPIs need to respect the unique sociocultural and economic milieu of all children, as well as strengthen children's voices in community, education and social policy. If children are taught to utilize their own potential by nurturing their strengths, they can achieve more than personal happiness. They can become agents of their own growth and thriving in society.

REFERENCES

Alderson, P. (2000). Children as researchers: The effects of participation rights on research methodology. In P. Christensen & A. James (Eds.), *Research with children: Perspectives and practices* (pp. 241–261). New York, NY: Falmer Press.

Andrews, A. B., & Ben-Arieh, A. (1999). Measuring and monitoring children's well-being across the world. *Social Work, 44,* 105–115. doi:10.1093/sw/44.2.105

Argyle, M., & Hills, P. (2000). Religious experiences and their relations with happiness and personality. *The International Journal for the Psychology of Religion, 10*(3), 157–172.

Bagot, K. L., Allen, F. C. L., & Toukhsati, S. (2015). Perceived restorativeness of children's school playground environments: Nature, playground features and play period experiences. *Journal of Environmental Psychology, 41*, 1–9. doi: 10.1016/j.jenvp.2014.11.005

Bailey, T. C., Eng, W., Frisch, M. B., & Snyder, C. (2007). Hope and optimism as related to life satisfaction. *The Journal of Positive Psychology, 2*(3), 168–175.

Ben-Arieh, A., & Goerge, R. (2001). Beyond the numbers: How do we monitor the state of our children? *Children and Youth Services Review, 23*(8), 603–631.

Ben-Arieh, A., Kaufman, N. H., Bowers Andrews, A., Goerge, R. M., Lee, J. B., & Aber, L. J. (2001). *Measuring and monitoring children's well-being* [Social Indicator Research Series, Vol. 7]. Dordrecht: Springer.

Berman, M. G., Jonides, J., & Kaplan, S. (2008). The cognitive benefits of interacting with nature. *Psychological Science, 19*(12), 1207–1212.

Binfet, J. (2015). Not-so random acts of kindness: A guide to intentional kindness in the classroom. *International Journal of Emotional Education, 7*(2), 49–62.

Bowler, D. E., Buyung-Ali, L. M., Knight, T. M., & Pullin, A. S. (2010). A systematic review of evidence for the added benefits to health of exposure to natural environments. *BMC Public Health, 10*, 456. doi:10. 1186/1471-2458-10-456

Brdar, I., & Kashdan, T. B. (2010). Character strengths and well-being in Croatia: An empirical investigation of structure and correlates. *Journal of Research in Personality, 44*, 151–154. doi:10.1016/j.jrp.2009.12.001

Brown, P. J., & Haas, G. E. (1980). Wilderness recreation experiences: The Rawah case. *Journal of Leisure Research, 12*, 229–240.

Brunwasser, S. M., Gillham, J. E., & Kim, E. S. (2009). A meta-analytic review of the Penn Resiliency Program's effect on depressive symptoms. *Journal of Consulting and Clinical Psychology, 77*, 1042–1054. doi:10.1037/a0017671

Chamberlain, K., & Zika, S. (1988). Religiosity, life meaning and wellbeing: Some relationships in a sample of women. *Journal for the Scientific Study of Religion, 27*, 411–420. doi:10.2307/1387379

Chawla, L., & Nasar, J. L. (2015). Benefits of nature contact for children. *Journal of Planning Literature, 30*, 433–452. doi:10.1177/0885412215595441

Crawford, M. R., Holder, M. D., & O'Connor, B. P. (2016). Using mobile technology to engage children with nature. *Environment and Behavior.* doi:10.1177/0013916516673870

Diener, E. (2006). Guidelines for national indicators of subjective well-being and ill-being. *Journal of Happiness Studies, 7*, 397–404. doi:10.1007/s10902-006-9000-y

Diener, M. L., & Lucas, R. E. (2004). Adults desires for children's emotions across 48 countries: Associations with individual and national characteristics. *Journal of Cross-Cultural Psychology, 35*(5), 525–547.

Drewes, A. A., & Schaefer, C. E. (2010). *School-based play therapy* (2nd ed.). Hoboken, NJ: John Wiley & Sons.

Duckworth, A. L., & Seligman, M. E. P. (2005). Self-discipline outdoes IQ in predicting academic performance of adolescents. *Psychological Science, 16*, 939–944. doi:10.1111/j.1467-9280.2005.01641.x

Dunn, E. W., Aknin, L. B., & Norton, M. I. (2008). Spending money on others promotes happiness. *Science*, *319*(5870), 1687–1688. doi:10.1126/science.1150952

Durlak, J. A., Weissberg, R. P., Dymnicki, A. B., Taylor, R. D., & Schellinger, K. B. (2011). The impact of enhancing students' social and emotional learning: A meta-analysis of school-based universal interventions. *Child Development*, *82*, 405–432. doi: 10.1111/j.1467-8624.2010.01564.x

Eccles, J., & Gootman, J. A. (2002). *Community programs to promote youth development*. Washington, DC: National Academies Press.

Engel, G. L. (1989). The need for a new medical model: A challenge for biomedicine. *Holistic Medicine*, *4*(1), 37–53.

Fattore, T., Mason, J., & Watson, E. (2007). Locating the child centrally as subject in research: Towards a child interpretation of well-being. *Child Indicators Research*, *5*, 423–435. doi:10.1007/s12187-012-9150-x

Francis, L. J., Robbins, M., & White, A. (2003). Correlation between religion and happiness: A replication. *Psychological Reports*, *92*(1), 51–52.

Francis, L. J., Ziebertz, H., & Lewis, C. A. (2003). The relationship between religion and happiness among German students. *Pastoral Psychology*, *51*(4), 273–281.

Fredrickson, B. L. (2003). The value of positive emotions. *American Scientist*, *91*(4), 330–335.

Fredrickson, B. L., & Branigan, C. (2005). Positive emotions broaden the scope of attention and thought-action repertoires. *Cognition & Emotion*, *19*(3), 313–332.

Froh, J. J., Kashdan, T. B., Ozimkowski, K. M., & Miller, N. (2009). Who benefits the most from a gratitude intervention in children and adolescents? Examining positive affect as a moderator. *The Journal of Positive Psychology*, *4*(5), 408–422.

Froh, J. J., Sefick, W. J., & Emmons, R. A. (2008). Counting blessings in early adolescents: An experimental study of gratitude and subjective well-being. *Journal of School Psychology*, *46*, 213–233. doi:10.1016/j.jsp.2007.03.005

Ghosh, A., & Deb, A. (2016). Positive psychology progress in India: Accomplishments and pathways ahead. *Psychological Studies*, *61*, 113–125. doi:10.1007/s12646-016-0367-5

Gillham, J., Adams-Deutsch, Z., Werner, J., Reivich, K., Coulter-Heindl, V., Linkins, M., & Seligman, M. E. P. (2011). Character strengths predict subjective well-being during adolescence. *The Journal of Positive Psychology*, *6*, 31–44. doi:10.1080/17439760.2010.536773

Gillham, J. E., Reivich, K. J., Freres, D. R., Chaplin, T. M., Shatté, A. J., Samuels, B., ... Seligman, M. E. P. (2007). School-based prevention of depressive symptoms: A randomized controlled study of the effectiveness and specificity of the Penn Resiliency Program. *Journal of Consulting and Clinical Psychology*, *75*(1), 9.

Grinde, B., & Patil, G. G. (2009). Biophilia: Does visual contact with nature impact on health and well-being? *International Journal of Environmental Research and Public Health*, *6*(9), 2332–2343.

Gross-Manos, D., Shimoni, E., & Ben-Arieh, A. (2015). Subjective well-being measures tested with 12-year-olds in Israel. *Child Indicators Research*, *8*, 71–92. doi:10.10.1007/s12187-014-9282-2

Grunberg, N. E., Maycock, V. A., & Anthony, B. J. (1985). Material altruism in children. *Basic and Applied Social Psychology, 6*, 1–11. doi:10.1207/s15324834basp0601_1

Han, K. T. (2009). Influence of limitedly visible leafy indoor plants on the psychology, behavior, and health of students at a junior high school in Taiwan. *Environment and Behavior, 41*(5), 658–692.

Harms, K., & Fritz, S. (2001). Internalization of character traits by those who teach character counts! *Journal of Extension, 39*(6) (Faculty Publications: Agricultural Leadership, Education & Communication Department) Retrieved from https://digitalcommons.unl.edu/cgi/viewcontent.cgi?article=1031&context=aglecfacpub

Hattie, J., Marsh, H. W., Neill, J. T., & Richards, G. E. (1997). Adventure education and outward bound: Out-of-class experiences that make a lasting difference. *Review of Educational Research, 67*, 43–87. doi:10.2307/1170619

Holder, M. D. (2012). *Happiness in children: Measurement, correlates and enhancement of positive subjective well-being*. New York, NY: Springer. doi:10.1007/978-94-007-4414-1

Holder, M. D., Coleman, B., Krupa, T., & Krupa, E. (2016). Well-being's relation to religiosity and spirituality in children and adolescents in Zambia. *Journal of Happiness Studies, 17*, 1235–1253. doi:10.1007/s10902-015-9640-x

Holder, M. D., Coleman, B., & Singh, K. (2012). Temperament and happiness in children in India. *Journal of Happiness Studies, 13*, 261–274. Retrieved from http://dx.doi.org.ezproxy.library.ubc.ca/10.1007/s10902-011-9262-x

Holder, M. D., Coleman, B., & Wallace, J. M. (2010). Spirituality, religiousness, and happiness in children aged 8–12 years. *Journal of Happiness Studies, 11*, 131–150. doi:10.1007/s10902-008-9126-1

Horning, S. M., Davis, H. P., Stirrat, M., & Cornwell, R. E. (2011). Atheistic, agnostic, and religious older adults on well-being and coping behaviors. *Journal of Aging Studies, 25*(2), 177–188.

Howell, A., & Passmore, H. (2013). Flourishing among children and adolescents: Structure and correlates of positive mental health, and interventions for its enhancement. In P. A. Linley & C. Proctor (Eds.), *Research, applications, and interventions for children and adolescents: A positive psychology perspective* (pp. 59–80). Dordrecht: Springer Netherlands.

Huebner, E. S. (1991). Correlates of life satisfaction in children. *School Psychology Quarterly, 6*, 103–111. doi:10.1037/h0088805

———. (1994). Preliminary development and validation of a multidimensional life satisfaction scale for children. *Psychological Assessment, 6*, 149–158. doi:10.1037/1040-3590.6.2.149

Huebner, E. S., Laughlin, J. E., Ash, C., & Gilman, R. (1998). Further validation of the multidimensional students' life satisfaction scale. *Journal of Psychoeducational Assessment, 16*(2), 118–134.

Huebner, E. S., Suldo, S. M., & Gilman, R. (2006). Life satisfaction. In G. G. Bear & K. M. Minke (Eds.), *Children's needs III: Development, prevention, and correction*

(3rd ed., pp. 357–368). Washington, DC: National Association of School Psychologists.

Irma, E. (2014). In pursuit of happiness: How some young South African children construct happiness. *Journal of Psychology in Africa*, *18*, 81–87. doi:10.1080/1 4330237.2008.10820174

Jenkins, R., & Barry, M. M. (2007). *Implementing mental health promotion*. London: Churchill Livingstone/Elsevier.

Johnson, R. C., Danko, G. P., Darvill, T. J., Bochner, S., Bowers, J. K., Huang, Y., ... Pennington, D. (1989). Cross-cultural assessment of altruism and its correlates. *Personality and Individual Differences*, *10*(8), 855–868.

Kaplan, S., & Talbot, J. F. (1983). Psychological benefits of a wilderness experience. In I. Altman & J. F. Wohlwill (Eds.), *Human behavior and environment: Advances in theory and research* (Vol. 6). *Behavior and the natural environment* (pp. 163–203). New York, NY: Plenum Press.

Kellert, S. R. (2005). *Building for life: Designing and understanding the human-nature connection*. Washington, DC: Island Press.

Korpela, K., Hartig, T., Kaiser, F. F., & Fuhrer, U. (2001). Restorative experience and self-regulation in favorite places. *Environment and Behavior*, *33*, 572–589. doi:10.1177/00139160121973133

Layous, K., Nelson, S. K., Oberle, E., Schonert-Reichl, K. A., & Lyubomirsky, S. (2012). Kindness counts: Prompting prosocial behavior in preadolescents boosts peer acceptance and well-being. *PloS One*, *7*(12), 1–3. doi:10.1371/journal.pone.0051380

Lee, J. N. T., Foo, K. H., Adams, A., Morgan, R., & Frewen, A. (2015). Strengths of character, orientations to happiness, life satisfaction and purpose in Singapore. *Journal of Tropical Psychology*, *5*(2), 1–21. doi:10.1017/jtp.2015.2

Lepper, M. R., Greene, D., & Nisbett, R. E. (1973). Undermining children's intrinsic interest with extrinsic reward: A test of the 'overjustification' hypothesis. *Journal of Personality and Social Psychology*, *28*, 129–137. doi:10.1037/h0035519

Lewis, C. A., & Cruise, S. M. (2006). Religion and happiness: Consensus, contradictions, comments and concerns. *Mental Health, Religion & Culture*, *9*(3), 213–225.

Lewis, C. A., Lanigan, C., Joseph, S., & De Fockert, J. (1997). Religiosity and happiness: No evidence for an association among undergraduates. *Personality and Individual Differences*, *22*(1), 119–121.

Lewis, C. A., Maltby, J., & Burkinshaw, S. (2000). Religion and happiness: Still no association. *Journal of Beliefs and Values*, *21*(2), 233–236.

Linkins, M., Niemiec, R. M., Gillham, J., & Mayerson, D. (2014). Through the lens of strength: A framework for educating the heart. *The Journal of Positive Psychology*, *10*, 64–68. doi:10.1080/17439760.2014.888581

Linley, P. A. (2009). *Realise2: Technical report*. Coventry, UK: CAPP Press.

Linley, P. A., & Proctor, C. (2013). Surveying the landscape of positive psychology for children and adolescents. In P. A. Linley & C. Proctor (Eds.), *Research, applications, and interventions for children and adolescents: A positive psychology perspective* (pp. 1–12). Dordrecht: Springer.

Lounsbury, J. W., Fisher, L. A., Levy, J. J., & Welsh, D. P. (2009). An investigation of character strengths in relation to the academic success of college students. *Individual Differences Research, 7*(1), 52–69.

Lourenço, O., & Machado, A. (1996). In defense of Piaget's theory: A reply to 10 common criticisms. *Psychological Review, 103*, 143–164. doi:10.1037/0033-295X.103.1.143

Marques, S. C., Lopez, S. J., & Pais-Ribeiro, J. L. (2011). 'Building hope for the future': A program to foster strengths in middle-school students. *Journal of Happiness Studies, 12*(1), 139–152.

Marques, S. C., Pais-Ribeiro, J. L., & Lopez, S. J. (2007). Validation of a Portuguese version of the students' life satisfaction scale. *Applied Research in Quality of Life, 2*(2), 83–94. doi:10.1007/s11482-007-9031-5

———. (2011). The role of positive psychology constructs in predicting mental health and academic achievement in children and adolescents: A two-year longitudinal study. *Journal of Happiness Studies, 12*(6), 1049–1062.

Martínez-Martí, M. L., & Ruch, W. (2014). Character strengths and well-being across the life span: Data from a representative sample of German-speaking adults living in Switzerland. *Frontiers in Psychology, 5*, 1253. doi:10.3389/fpsyg.2014.01253

McCabe, K., Bray, M. A., Kehle, T. J., Theodore, L. A., & Gelbar, N. W. (2011). Promoting happiness and life satisfaction in school children. *Canadian Journal of School Psychology, 26*, 177–192. doi:10.1177/0829573511419089

Merkaš, M., & Brajša-Žganec, A. (2011). Children with different levels of hope: Are there differences in their self-esteem, life satisfaction, social support, and family cohesion? *Child Indicators Research, 4*(3), 499–514.

Mitchell, J., Stanimirovic, R., Klein, B., & Vella-Brodrick, D. (2009). A randomised controlled trial of a self-guided internet intervention promoting well-being. *Computers in Human Behavior, 25*, 749–760.

Morgan, H. (2014). Review of research: The education system in Finland: A success story other countries can emulate. *Childhood Education, 90*, 453–457. doi:10.1080/00094056.2014.983013

Morris, I. (2013). A place for well-being in the classroom? *Research, Applications, and Interventions for Children and Adolescents*, 185–198. doi:10.1007/978-94-007-6398-2_11

Nelson, S. K., Layous, K., Cole, S. W., & Lyubomirsky, S. (2016). Do unto others or treat yourself? The effects of prosocial and self-focused behavior on psychological flourishing. *Emotion, 16*, 850–861.

Niemi, H., Toom, A., & Kallioniemi, A. (2012). *Miracle of education the principles and practices of teaching and learning in Finnish schools*. Rotterdam: Sense Publishers. doi:10.1007/978-94-6091-811-7

Oppenheimer, M. F., Fialkov, C., Ecker, B., & Portnoy, S. (2014). Teaching to strengths: Character education for urban middle school students. *Journal of Character Education, 10*(2), 91–105.

Otake, K., Shimai, S., Tanaka-Matsumi, J., Otsui, K., & Fredrickson, B. L. (2006). Happy people become happier through kindness: A counting kindnesses intervention. *Journal of Happiness Studies, 7*(3), 361–375.

Park, N., & Peterson, C. (2004). The cultivation of character strengths. In M. Ferrari & G. Potworowski (Eds.), *Teaching for wisdom* (pp. 59–77). Netherlands: Springer.

———. (2006a). Character strengths and happiness among young children: Content analysis of parental descriptions. *Journal of Happiness Studies, 7*, 323–341.

———. (2006b). Moral competence and character strengths among adolescents: The development and validation of the values in action inventory of strengths for youth. *Journal of Adolescence, 29*, 891–909. doi:10.1016/j.adolescence.2006.04.011

———. (2008). Positive psychology and character strengths: Application to strengths-based school counseling. *Professional School Counseling, 12*(2), 85–92. doi:10.5330/PSC.n.2010-12.85

———. (2009). Character strengths: Research and practice. *Journal of College and Character, 10*(4), 1–10. doi:10.2202/1940-1639.1042

———. (2014). Strengths of character in school. In M. J., R. Gilman & E. S. Huebner (Eds.), *Handbook of positive psychology in schools* (pp. 65–77). New York, NY: Routledge.

Park, N., Peterson, C., & Seligman, M. E. P. (2004). Strengths of character and well-being. *Journal of Social and Clinical Psychology, 23*, 603–619. doi:10.1521/jscp.23.5.603.50748

Peterson, C., & Seligman, M. E. P. (2004). *Character strengths and virtues: A handbook and classification.* New York; Washington, DC: American Psychological Association.

Peterson, C., Ruch, W., Beermann, U., Park, N., & Seligman, M. E. P. (2007). Strengths of character, orientations to happiness, and life satisfaction. *The Journal of Positive Psychology, 2*, 149–156. doi:10.1080/17439760701228938

Pollard, E. L., & Lee, D. P. (2003). Child well-being: A systematic review of the literature. *Social Indicators Research, 1*, 59–78. doi:10.1023/A:102128415801

Popov, L. K. (2000). *The virtues project: Simple ways to create a culture of character: Educator's guide.* Los Angeles, CA: Jalmar Press.

Proctor, C., Linley, P. A., & Maltby, J. (2010). Very happy youths: Benefits of very high life satisfaction among adolescents. *Social Indicators Research, 98*(3), 519–532.

Proctor, C., Tsukayama, E., Wood, A., M., Maltby, J., Fox Eades, J., & Linley, P. A. (2011). Strengths gym: The impact of a character strengths-based intervention on the life satisfaction and well-being of adolescents. *Journal of Positive Psychology, 6*, 377–388.

Prout, A. (1997). Objective vs. subjective indicators or both? Whose perspective counts? In A. Ben Arieh & H. Wintersberger (Eds.), *Monitoring and measuring* the state of children: Beyond survival Eurosocial Report No. 62 (pp. 89–100). Vienna: European Centre for Social Welfare Policy and Research.

Quinlan, D. M., Swain, N., Cameron, C., & Vella-Brodrick, D. A. (2014). How 'other people matter' in a classroom-based strengths intervention: Exploring interpersonal strategies and classroom outcomes. *Journal of Positive Psychology*, 10, 77–89. doi:10.1080/17439760.2014.920407

Quinlan, D., Swain, N., & Vella-Brodrick, D. A. (2011). Character strengths interventions: Building on what we know for improved outcomes. *Journal of Happiness Studies*, 13, 1145–1163. doi:10.1007/s10902-011-9311-5

Qvortrup, J. (1991). *Childhood as a social phenomenon: An introduction to a series of national reports* (2nd ed., Eurosocial Reports, Vol. 36). Vienna: European Centre for Social Welfare Policy and Research.

Rashid, T., Afroze, A., Lennox, C., Quinlan, D., Ryan, M. N., Mayerson, D., & Kazemi, F. (2013). Assessment of character strengths in children and adolescents. In C. Proctor & P. A. Linley (Eds.), *Research, applications, and interventions for children and adolescents: A positive psychology perspective* (1st ed., p. 81). Dordrecht: Springer Netherlands.

Rath, T. (2007). *StrengthsFinder 2.0*. New York, NY: Gallup Press.

Rossman, B., & Ulehla, J. (1977). Psychological reward values associated with wilderness use: A functional reinforcement approach. *Environment and Behavior*, 9(1), 41–66.

Ryan, R. M., & Deci, E. L. (2001). On happiness and human potentials: A review of research on hedonic and eudaimonic well-being. *Annual Review of Psychology*, 52, 141–166. doi:10.1146/annurev.psych.52.1.141

Sahlberg, P. (2010). Educational Change in Finland. In A. Hargreaves, A. Lieberman, M. Fullan, & D. Hopkins (Eds.), *Second international handbook of educational change* (pp. 323–348). Netherlands: Springer.

Schueller, S. M. (2010). Preferences for positive psychology exercises. *Journal of Positive Psychology*, 5(3), 192–203.

Seligman, M. E. P., Ernst, R. M., Gillham, J., Reivich, K., & Linkins, M. (2009). Positive education: Positive psychology and classroom interventions. *Oxford Review of Education*, 35(3), 293–311.

Seligman, M. E. P., Steen, T. A., Park, N., & Peterson, C. (2005). Positive psychology progress: Empirical validation of interventions. *American Psychologist*, 60(5), 410–421.

Shaheen, R. (2010). Creativity and education. *Creative Education*, 1, 166–169. doi:10.4236/ce.2010.13026.

Sheldon, K. M., & Lyubomirsky, S. (2007). Is it possible to become happier? (And if so, how?). *Social and Personality Psychology Compass*, 1, 129–145.

Shimai, S., Otake, K., Park, N., Peterson, C., & Seligman, M. E. P. (2006). Convergence of character strengths in American and Japanese young adults. *Journal of Happiness Studies*, 7(3), 311–322. doi:10.1007/s10902-005-3647-7

Shmotkin, D. (1990). Subjective well-being as a function of age and gender: A multivariate look for differentiated trends. *Social Indicators Research*, 23(3), 201–230.

Shoshani, A., & Ilanit Aviv, I. (2012). The pillars of strength for first-grade adjustment: Parental and children's character strengths and the transition to elementary school. *Journal of Positive Psychology, 7*(4), 315–326.

Sillick, W. J., Stevens, B. A., & Cathcart, S. (2016). Religiosity and happiness: A comparison of the happiness levels between the religious and the nonreligious. *The Journal of Happiness and Well-Being, 4*(1), 115–127.

Sin, N. L., & Lyubomirsky, S. (2009). Enhancing well-being and alleviating depressive symptoms with positive psychology interventions: A practice-friendly meta-analysis. *Journal of Clinical Psychology, 65*(5), 467–487.

Singh, K., & Choubisa, R. (2009). Psychometric properties of Hindi translated version of values in action inventory of strengths (VIA-IS). *Journal of Indian Health Psychology, 4*(1), 65–76.

Snyder, C. R. (2002). Hope theory: Rainbows in the mind. *Psychological Inquiry, 13*(4), 249–275.

Snyder, C. R., Hoza, B., Pelham, W. E., Rapoff, M., Ware, L., Danovsky, M., & Stahl, K. J. (1997). The development and validation of the children's hope scale. *Journal of Pediatric Psychology, 22*(3), 399–421.

Suldo, S. M., Riley, K. N., & Shaffer, E. J. (2006). Academic correlates of children and adolescents' life satisfaction. *School Psychology International, 27*, 567–582. doi:10.1177/0143034306073411

Suldo, S. M., Savage, J. A., & Mercer, S. H. (2014). Increasing middle school students' life satisfaction: Efficacy of a positive psychology group intervention. *Journal of Happiness Studies, 15*, 19–42. doi:10.1007/s10902-013-9414-2

Suls, J., & Rothman, A. (2004). Evolution of the biopsychosocial model: Prospects and challenges for health psychology. *Health Psychology, 23*, 119.

Uyan-Semerci, P., & Erdoğan, E. (2016). Child well-being indicators through the eyes of children in turkey: A happy child would be one who. *Child Indicators Research, 10*, 267–295. doi:10.1007/s12187-016-9377-z

Valle, M. F., Huebner, E. S., & Suldo, S. M. (2006). An analysis of hope as a psychological strength. *Journal of School Psychology, 44*, 393–406. Retrieved from http://dx.doi.org.ezproxy.library.ubc.ca/10.1016/j.jsp.2006.03.005

Verbeek, P., & de Waal, F. B. M. (2002). The primate relationship with nature: Biophilia as a general pattern. In P. H. Kahn & S. R. Kellert (Eds.), *Children and nature: Psychological, sociocultural, and evolutionary investigations* (pp. 1–24). Cambridge, MA: MIT Press.

Waters, L. (2011). A review of school-based positive psychology interventions. *The Australian Educational and Developmental Psychologist, 28*, 75–90. doi:10.1375/aedp.28.2.75.

Wells, N. M. (2000). At home with nature: Effects of 'greenness' on children's cognitive functioning. *Environment and Behavior, 32*(6), 775–795.

White, M. A., & Waters, L. E. (2014). A case study of 'The Good School:' Examples of the use of Peterson's strengths-based approach with students. *The Journal of Positive Psychology, 10*, 69–76. doi:10.1080/17439760.2014.920408

Zhang, J., & Jin, S. (1996). Determinants of suicide ideation: A comparison of Chinese and American college students. *Adolescence, 31*(122), 451–468.

Chapter 4

Considering Character Strength Development as an Approach to Addressing Disengagement in Secondary Schools

Nick Holton

INTRODUCTION

Recent research in the field of education, psychology and well-being has revealed two causes for alarm: declining levels of student engagement and declining levels of well-being (Ainley, 2006; Ainley & Ainley, 2011; Hidi & Harackiewicz, 2000; Hidi & Renninger, 2010; Marks, 2000; Skinner & Belmont, 1993; Switzky & Schultz, 1998). Among other issues, these declines are accompanied by upticks in student dropout rates, stress, anxiety and symptoms of depression (Broderick & Metz, 2009 as cited in Madden, Green, & Grant, 2011). Further, these rates of well-being are transferring over to adult workplaces.

In an effort to address these rising concerns researchers have begun to focus on various conceptualizations of optimal experiences, within the broader field of positive psychology. Positive psychology (Seligman, 1998) is the study of optimal human functioning; the elements of life experience that allow human beings to flourish and become the very best version of their true and authentic selves. The study of optimal experiences that move individuals towards their best self has elicited multiple important conceptualizations.

Among these conceptualizations, the identification and use of character strengths and the subjective experience of eudaimonia have recently become prominent. Character strengths have been defined as 'dispositions to act, desire, and feel that involves the exercise of judgement and leads to a recognizable human excellence or instances of human flourishing' (Yearley, 1990, p. 13, as cited in Park, Peterson, & Seligman, 2004). They are 'behaviors and virtuous activities' (Park et al., 2004) or ways of thinking and experiencing that individuals enjoy and that allows them to pursue outcomes that are of value (Quinlan, Swain, & Vella-Brodrick, 2012). Eudaimonia is a conceptualization of well-being and optimal experience based upon the ability of individuals to self-actualize and develop their perceived strengths and virtues (Ryan & Deci, 2001; Ryff, 1989; Ryff & Singer, 2006; Waterman, 2007). It is interesting to note that each of these concepts places a particular importance on the development of virtues or, in other words, perceived strengths. Each construct also has strong empirical ties to the experience of different forms of engagement (Biswas-Diener, Kashdan, & Minhas, 2011; Gander, Proyer, Ruch, & Wyss, 2012; Gillham, 2011; Holton, 2016; Madden, Green, & Grant, 2011; Peterson & Park, 2006; Proyer, Silder, Weber, & Ruch, 2012) as well as well-being (Govindji & Linley, 2007; Linley, Nielsen, Gillett, & Biswas-Disner, 2010; Quinlan et al., 2011; Shoshani & Slone, 2013).

In considering what may account for variation in these optimal experiences we may look back to both theoretical (Maslow, 1943) and empirical (Alderfer, 1969) arguments on the inherent need for personal growth. That is, seeking opportunities for developing oneself. Like self-actualization, growth needs are satisfied when individuals are able to fully engage in a manner that requires the use of current capacities and allows for further development (Alderfer, 1969). Theoretical work by Holton (2014) suggests this need to be a part of a process of self-organization, a part of an autopoietic self that is constantly organizing, growing and providing itself with feedback on that process. If these connections to inherent biological and psychological needs are deemed logical, we would expect to see organisms such as human beings fully engage in experiences that allow them to both use and develop perceived components of their authentic selves. It is also logical to expect that well-being may be the result of such experiences given their inherent satisfaction of needs which are critical to the self. Subsequently, we would expect to see relationships between empirical constructs that represent or act as components of personal growth, development and well-being, respectively.

Herein lie some interesting questions surrounding the potential of character strengths to contribute to optimal experiences and subsequent engagement. Eudaimonia and character strengths share a common conceptual bond in that each construct has perceived virtues, skills or talents as a part of their inherent make-up. As this chapter has already pointed out, when these components of our personalities are used and developed, the result is often increased engagement and well-being. The next logical step then is to consider how these various phenomena might interact with one another. Doing so may facilitate a better understanding of how we might design interventions in education and the workplace that create greater engagement and subsequent well-being.

EMPIRICAL WORK WITH CHARACTER STRENGTHS

Although a relatively young field of research, studies focusing on the impact of identifying and using character strengths can provide us with some useful insights into potential answers to our guiding question. A review of the research elicits a focus on three replicable areas of results and subsequent conclusions about empirical relationships with character strengths. They are life-satisfaction, well-being and engagement. To best understand the relationship between using and developing strengths and the subsequent enhancement of engagement, we need to review the research done in two separate yet similar fields, education and the workplace.

Character Strengths, Life Satisfaction and Well-being

Early on in the study of character strengths and their association with positive psychology experiences researchers began to see positive relationships with life satisfaction. Work by Park et al. (2004) noted the specific VIA character strengths of zest, hope, gratitude, love and curiosity. These positive associations are not limited to particular cultures either, as noted in a wealth of research (as cited in Gander et al., 2012).

Work by Seligman, Steen, Park and Peterson (2005) found that simply identifying one's strengths can lead to greater happiness and fewer symptoms of depression. However, it is important to note that individuals must understand that these strengths can change and be developed. Failure to do so may result in underperformance as a result of reliance upon those strengths as stable entities. Work conducted by Govindji and Linley (2007) found significant associations between strengths use and well-being as well. A more recent meta-analysis of these effects conducted by Quinlan, Swain and Vella-Brodrick (2012) argues increases in well-being in both adults and high school students. Likewise, positive associations were found between character strengths and subjective well-being in middle-school students as well (Shoshani & Slone, 2012).

Character Strengths and Engagement

When we investigate the impact of strength building on education, we find consistent and significant relationships with increased engagement. Early on, in the study of these relationships, Clifton and Harter (2003) noted substantial effect sizes (between 0.2 and 0.4) on GPA and declines in absenteeism when strengths developments were used. More recently, findings indicate strengths-based interventions to be related to increased motivation, engagement and effort (Louis, 2009 as cited in Biswas-Diener et al., 2011; Linley & Harrington, 2006). A follow-up study to Seligman et al. (2009) found increases in both engagement and achievement after using strengths such as gratitude and savouring (Gillham, 2011, as cited in Quinlan et al., 2012).

In the area of work, multiple studies have found significant relationships between the development of strengths and workplace engagement and satisfaction with work. Harter, Schmidt and Hayes (2002) found that employees who regularly use perceived talents tend to also be more engaged. Similar results were found after strength-based interventions in a study done across nine hospitals, as well as with a large car manufacturer (Clifton & Harter, 2003). Park, Peterson and

Seligman (2004) demonstrated associations between strengths such as zest and job satisfaction. A meta-analysis of Gallup studies across 65 companies showed an increase of employee engagement when compared to control groups. The intervention in these cases was two full years of strength-based interventions.

This engagement presumably has had greater impact on workplace satisfaction as well. Results from Stefanyszyn (2007) noted a decline in worker turnover when using perceived strengths more regularly. The same pioneering study from Park, Peterson and Seligman (2004) also found associations between character strengths such as gratitude, zest, curiosity, hope and love, and work satisfaction. Like in education research, we have also seen absenteeism from work drop when certain character strengths are in place (Wrzesniewski, McCauley, Rozin, & Schwartz, 1997, as cited in Park, Peterson, & Seligman, 2004). Gander et al. (2012) also cited a raft of research noting the positive associations between job satisfaction and character strengths such as resilience, hope and optimism.

Authentic Growth

In reviewing the wealth of research surrounding character strengths and their associations with life satisfaction, well-being and engagement, we find a few key themes. First, the findings are diverse. While many of these studies have found significant effects on well-being when character strengths are developed, others have failed to come to similar conclusions (Quinlan et al., 2012). In part, this may be due to different methods and approaches to the study of character strengths. For instance, multiple empirical sets of strengths are argued to exist. Peterson and Seligman have long advocated for the Values in Action Inventory of Strengths (VIA-IS), but this is only one example of how we might identify and measure strengths and talents. Second, the studies conducted across education and professional places of work have found increased engagement, perhaps even more consistently than enhanced well-being or life satisfaction.

However, both the resultant engagement and well-being in these studies has often been mediated by important factors relating to the authentic self and the psychological needs mentioned earlier in this chapter. For instance, the work conducted by Govindji and Linley (2007) noted that characteristics of using strengths (authenticity, yearning and intrinsic motivation to name a few) have been linked to views of human nature as 'directional tendencies' (p. 144). The authors also note goal research (Sheldon & Elliot, 1999; Sheldon & Houser-Marko, 2001) that indicates pursuing more self-concordant goals makes an individual more likely to achieve said goals and subsequently to become happier. Linley and Harrington (2006, as cited in Govindji & Linley, 2007) have also argued that strengths are linked to 'organismic valuing' (p. 144) and often come from internal desires. Linley et al. (2010) suggest that the resulting well-being achieved through these processes may even be moderated by the inherent self-concordance of the activities, goals or interventions. Progress towards these self-concordant goals was found to be associated with psychological need satisfaction, similar to the suggested growth needs posited by Maslow (1943) and Alderfer (1969).

These insights provide important theoretical posits when we return to and reconsider some of the aforementioned studies in which developing character strengths did not result in increased well-being. Take for example the findings from Seligman, Ernest, Gillham, Reivich and Linkins (2009) and Gillham (2011). These studies focused on the impact of specific character strengths on well-being, depression and anxiety and did so at two-year (Seligman et al., 2009) and three-year (Gillham) follow-ups. This chapter and this author's theoretical work (Holton, 2014) have already suggested that the *self* is likely an ongoing and ever-changing process of self-organization and identity creation. When we combine this theoretical assumption with the research on the necessity of self-concordance and authenticity for enhancing well-being, we see two important issues.

First is the nature of subjective well-being and how it may be enhanced. Research has shown that up to 40 per cent of happiness, in many cases measured as subjective well-being, can be impacted by positive activities (Sheldon & Lyubomirsky, 2004, 2006, 2007, as cited in Lyubomirsky, Dickerhoof, Boehm, & Sheldon, 2011) such as the aforementioned pursuit of goals. However, maintaining changes in well-being over time is particularly difficult due to hedonic adaptation (Frederick & Lowenstein, 1999). Nonetheless, studies have found that subjective well-being can be increased over significant periods of time. When considering character strength development and engagement, however, a critical component needs to be considered. Well-being in this sense is inherently subjective, meaning it needs to be authentic to the specific individual experiencing it. This may be why Lyubomirsky et al. (2011) found sustainable increases in happiness are only likely when optimal conditions are present, such as motivation, efficacy and effort. What this means then is that character strength development and subsequent well-being change may depend on subjective, authentic self-assessments of the particular strengths being developed as strengths of intrinsic value.

Second, even if the character strengths being used and developed in Seligman et al. (2009) were not of intrinsic value and authentic to the participants, the two- and three-year follow-up nature of the studies causes further problems for the self's subjective evaluation of well-being. Over 2–3 years an individual is likely to change and continue to construct their evolving identity. Thus, their perceived virtues and strengths are likely to change as a part of this process. Consequently, studies examining character strengths need to consider the subjective assessment by participants of what their own strengths are and keep the evolving nature of these assessments in mind if they choose to engage in longitudinal follow-up measurements of well-being.

Growth and Eudaimonic Well-being

Thus far this chapter has established three important relationships to character strength development. A wealth of research has indicated character strength identification and development often leads to enhanced well-being. This development also often leads to greater engagement. Each of these results is likely due to the sensation of authentic, self-concordant personal growth and the psychological need satisfaction accompanying that growth. These findings have not been consistently found across all character strength studies and interventions. This is likely due to the different outcome measures being used across these various studies and the inherent subjectivity involved with ensuring character strength development is authentic to the self.

Let us return then to the part eudaimonia may play in these dynamic relationships. Recall that eudaimonia is experienced when individuals feel they are actualizing their perceived virtues, talents or strengths. Given the nature of this conceptualization, it is not difficult to see the person-level subjective element included in this form of optimal experience and well-being. Nor is it a stretch to see the connection to the satisfaction of psychological needs as a consequence of personal growth via the cultivation of strengths. Further, previous empirical work suggests inherent characteristics of eudaimonia that create a synergistic conceptual fit with the research on character strengths reviewed in this chapter.

Eudaimonia as it is conceptualized and agreed upon across multiple scholars and studies holds three more consistent characteristics. First, and perhaps most important for the argument this chapter presents, is that scholars have long associated the experience of eudaimonia with *personal growth* (Huta, 2013; Ryff, 1989; Waterman, 2007; Waterman et al., 2010). Second, to experience eudaimonia one must align their actions with their true self (Huta, 2013). In that way, eudaimonia carries elements of *meaning* and *purpose*. Finally, contextual factors impact our experience of eudaimonia, including our relationships, environmental surroundings and other elements that may or may not be in line with our true self (Ryff, 1989). Each of these characteristics shares clear overlap with the associations found in the entirety of character strength research. However, the question still remains whether eudaimonia shares significant relationships with our third outcome of value—engagement.

Previous research (Holton, 2016) investigated the relationship between eudaimonia and *academic engagement* (Marks, 2000). Marks' conceptualization of engagement focuses on academic forms of attention. His work suggests academic disengagement is a result of a lack of relevant connections to the experiencer's world; in other words, a lack of congruence. The necessity of subjective congruence has been cited in other engagement research as well. Green and Miller (as cited in Appleton, Christensen, & Furlong, 2008) note significant associations between personal goal orientation and cognitive engagement. Likewise, similar associations have been found in eudaimonia research. Waterman's (1990) eudaimonistic identity theory notes predictor variables for eudaimonia such as congruence, needs fulfilment and intense involvement. Perhaps the gold standard for engagement researcher comes from Csikszentmihalyi (1975), considered to be the father of *flow*. His research (1975) on the teleonomic theory of the self suggests teleonomic flow to be indicated, in part, by 'intense involvement in activities and positive psychological functioning' (Holton, 2016, p. 14).

The further investigation of this relationship between eudaimonia and engagement revealed interesting associations. The primary study conducted in 2015 as well as the replicated study done in 2016 revealed significant correlations (>0.4, $p < 0.001$) between eudaimonia and engagement. These studies also revealed significant effects (>0.2) for eudaimonia on engagement and vice versa. Hierarchal regression analyses were also conducted to control for potentially confounding variables. The analyses also revealed significant contributions by eudaimonia to engagement (R-squared change = 0.27) and by engagement to eudaimonia (R-squared change = 0.26). Thus revealing what may be a mutual relationship between experiences of eudaimonic well-being and engagement.

SUMMARY

This chapter has suggested that the development of character strengths through interventions is a worthwhile pursuit. Previous research has indicated such interventions can lead to sustainable increases in well-being, life satisfaction and engagement. However, these findings are not consistent and studies have further suggested that the experience of well-being and engagement may be mediated by elements of authenticity to the self and the subsequent satisfaction of psychological needs. Thus leaving us with the question of how to more effectively design these interventions to harness the power of this psychological need satisfaction and congruent goal pursuits.

In looking at well-being and engagement as enhanced by character strength development, it has been argued that a subjective element of strength identification and growth may play a role in subsequent positive outcomes such as well-being and engagement. Theoretical arguments about the inherent autopoietic nature of the self and empirical research on eudaimonia have suggested eudaimonia may be a more accurate way to assess personal growth that is authentically valued as well as the well-being experienced from said growth. Recent research (Holton, 2016) provided evidence of significant relationships between eudaimonia and engagement, thus providing reasonable evidence for this argument. While this research was done in an exploratory study without experimental control groups, it nonetheless elicits interesting findings that need to be pursued and investigated further.

In the meantime, when designing character strength interventions and other personal growth initiatives for young people two considerations should be kept in mind. Character strengths and personal growth in general is, by its very nature, inherently subjective. Thus, an approach dictating to participants which strengths they will need to identify, use and develop may not be the most appropriate given the potential danger for incongruence with their true self and personal goal orientations. Further, in assessing the outcomes of these character strength interventions, a reconsideration of how well-being and engagement are being measured may be necessary. In this vein, eudaimonia, given its inherent nature, is a more subjective assessment of personal growth, and characteristics of meaning, purpose and sense of self may be a more appropriate measuring stick.

REFERENCES

Ainley, M. (2006). Connecting with learning: Motivation, affect and cognition in interest processes. *Educational Psychology Review, 18*(4), 391–405.

Ainley, M., & Ainley, J. (2011). Student engagement with science in early adolescence: The contribution of enjoyment to students' continuing interest in learning about science. *Contemporary Educational Psychology, 36*(1), 4–12.

Alderfer, C. (1969). An empirical test of a new theory of human needs. *Organizational Behavior and Human Performance, 4*(2), 142–175.

Appleton, J., Christenson, S., & Furlong, M. (2008). Student engagement with school: Critical conceptual and methodological issues of the construct. *Psychology in the Schools, 45*(5), 369–386.

Biswas-Diener, R., Kashdan, T., & Minhas, G. (2011). A dynamic approach to psychological strength development and intervention. *The Journal of Positive Psychology, 6*(2), 106–118.

Broderick, P. C., & Metz, S. (2009). Learning to BREATHE: A pilot trial of a mindfulness curriculum for adolescents. *Advances in School Mental Health Promotion, 2*(1), 35–46.

Clifton, D. O., & Harter, J. K. (2003). Investing in strengths. In A. K. S. Cameron, B. J. E. Dutton, & C. R. E. Quinn (Eds.), *Positive organizational scholarship: Foundations of a new discipline* (pp. 111–121). San Francisco, CA: Berrett-Koehler Publishers, Inc.

Csikszentmihalyi, M. (1975). Play and intrinsic rewards. *Journal of Humanistic Psychology*, 15(3), 41–63.

Frederick, S., & Loewenstein, G. (1999). Hedonic adaptation. In D. Kahneman, E. Diener, & N. Schwarz (Eds.), *Well-being: The foundations of hedonic psychology* (pp. 302–329). New York, NY: Russell Sage Foundation.

Gander, F., Proyer, R. T., Ruch, W., & Wyss, T. (2012). The good character at work: An initial study on the contribution of character strengths in identifying healthy and unhealthy work-related behavior and experience patterns. *International Archive of Occupational Environmental Health*, 85(8), 895–904.

Gillham, J. (2011). *Teaching positive psychology to adolescents: 3-year follow-up*. Paper presented as part of the symposium Positive Psychology in Schools, at the 2nd World Congress on Positive Psychology, Philadelphia, 23–26 July 2011.

Govindji, R., & Linley, A. (2007). Strengths use, self-concordance and well-being: Implications for strengths coaching and coaching psychologists. *International Coaching Psychology Review*, 1(23), 143–153.

Harter, J. K., Schmidt, F. L., & Hayes, T. L. (2002). Business-unit-level relationship between employee satisfaction, employee engagement, and business outcomes: A meta-analysis. *Journal of Applied Psychology*, 87(2), 268–279.

Hidi, S., & Harackiewicz, J. M. (2000). Motivating the academically unmotivated: A critical issue for the 21st century. *Review of Educational Research*, 70(2), 151–179.

Hidi, S., & Renninger, K. (2010). The four-phase model of interest development. *Educational Psychologist*, 41(2), 111–127.

Holton, N. (2014). Is flow enough? A review of Flow theory and its adequacy for explaining happiness and optimal experience [Unpublished practicum paper]. East Lansing, MI: Michigan State University.

Holton, N. (2016). Eudaimonia and engagement in the classroom: Using experience sampling in an exploratory study of well-being in high school students [Unpublished dissertation]. East Lansing, MI: Michigan State University.

Huta, V. (2013). Pursuing Eudaimonia versus Hedonia: Distinctions, similarities, and relationships. In A. S. Waterman (Ed.), *The best within us* (pp. 139–159). Washington, DC: American Psychological Association.

Linley, A., Nielsen, K. M., Gillett, R., & Biswas-Diener, R. (2010). Using signature strengths in pursuit of goals: Effects on goal progress, need satisfaction, and well-being and implications for coaching psychologists. *International Coaching Psychology Review*, 5(1), 6–15.

Linley, P. A., & Harrington, S. (2006). Strengths coaching: A potential-guided approach to coaching psychology. *International Coaching Psychology Review*, 1(1), 37–46.

Louis, M. C. (2009). *A summary and critique of existing strengths-based educational research utilizing the Clifton StrengthsFinder* [Internal paper]. Omaha, NE: The Gallup Organization.

Lyubomirsky, S., Dickerhoof, R., Boehm, J. K., & Sheldon, K. M. (2011). Becoming happier takes both will and a proper way: An experimental longitudinal intervention to boost well-being. *Emotion*, 11(2), 391–402.

Madden, W., Green, S., & Grant, A. (2011). A pilot study evaluating strengths-based coaching for primary school students: Enhancing engagement and hope. *International Coaching Psychology Review*, *6*(1), 71–83.

Marks, H. (2000). Student engagement in instructional activity: Patterns in elementary, middle and high school years. *American Educational Research Journal*, *37*(1), 153–184.

Maslow, A. H. (1943). A theory of human motivation. *Psychological Review*, *50*(4), 370.

Park, N., Peterson, C., & Seligman, M. (2004). Strengths of character and well-being. *Journal of Social and Clinical Psychology*, *23*(5), 603–619.

Peterson, C., & Park, N. (2006). Character strengths in organizations. *Journal of Organizational Behavior*, *27*(8), 1149–1154.

Proyer, R. T., Sidler, N., Weber, M., & Ruch, W. (2012). A multi-method approach to studying the relationship between character strengths and vocational interests in adolescents. *International Journal of Educational Vocational Guidance*, *12*(2), 141–157.

Quinlan, D., Swain, N. R., & Vella-Brodrick, D. A. (2012). Character strengths interventions: Building on what we know for improved outcomes. *Journal of Happiness Studies*, *13*(6), 1145–1163.

Ryan, R. M., & Deci, E. L. (2001). On happiness and human potentials: A review of research on hedonic and eudaimonic well-being. *Annual Review of Psychology*, *52*(1), 141–166.

Ryff, C. (1989). Happiness is everything, or is it? Exploration on the meaning of psychological well-being. *Journal of Personality and Social Psychology*, *57*(6), 1069–1081.

Ryff, C., & Singer, B. (2006). Know thyself and become what you are: A eudaimonic approach to psychological well-being. *Journal of Happiness Studies*, *9*(1), 13–39.

Seligman, M. E. (1998). What is the good life. *APA Monitor*, *29*(10), 2.

Seligman, M. E. P., Ernest, R. M., Gillham, J., Reivich, K., & Linkins, M. (2009). Positive education: Positive psychology and classroom interventions. *Oxford Review of Education*, *35*(3), 293–311.

Seligman, M., Steen, T., Park, N., & Peterson, C. (2005). Positive psychology progress: Empirical validation of interventions. *American Psychologist*, *60*(5), 410–421.

Sheldon, K., & Elliot, A. (1999). Goal striving, need satisfaction, and longitudinal well-being: The self-concordance model. *Journal of Personality and Social Psychology*, *76*(3), 482–497.

Sheldon, K. M., & Houser-Marko, L. (2001). Self-concordance, goal attainment, and the pursuit of happiness: Can there be an upward spiral? *Journal of Personality and Social Psychology*, *80*(1), 152.

Shoshani, A., & Slone, M. (2013). Middle school transition from strengths perspective: Young adolescents' character strengths, subjective well-being and school adjustment. *Journal of Happiness Studies*, *14*(4), 1163–1181.

Skinner, E., & Belmont, M. (1993). Motivation in the classroom: Reciprocal effects of teacher behavior and student engagement across the school year. *Journal of Educational Psychology, 85*(4), 571–558.

Stefanyszyn, K. (2007). Norwich union changes focus from competencies to strengths. *Strategic Human Resources Review, 7*(1), 10–11.

Switzky, H., & Schultz, G. (1988). Intrinsic motivation and learning performance: Implications for individual educational mild handicaps. *Remedial and Special Education, 9*(7), 7–14.

Vella-Brodrick, D. A., Park, N., & Peterson, C. (2009). Three ways to be happy: Pleasure, engagement and meaning; findings from Australian and US samples. *Social Indicators Research, 90*(2), 165–179.

Waterman, A. (1990). The relevance of Aristotle's conception of Eudaimonia for the psychological study of happiness. *Theoretical & Philosophical Psychology, 10*(1), 39–44.

Waterman, A. (2007). On the importance of distinguishing hedonia and eudaimonia when contemplating the hedonic treadmill. *The American Psychologist, 62*(6), 612–613.

Waterman, A., Schwartz, S. J., Zamboanga, B. L., Ravert, R. D., Williams, M. K., Bede, A. V.,... Brent, M. (2010). The questionnaire for eudaimonic well-being: Psychometric properties, demographic comparisons, and evidence of validity. *The Journal of Positive Psychology, 5*(1), 41–61.

Chapter 5

The Measurement of Character Strengths and Virtues

Zohra Ihsan and Adrian Furnham

INTRODUCTION

The first books on the psychology of happiness started appearing in the 1980s (Argyle, 2001; Eysenck, 1990). Then there appeared a few specialist academic journals but it was not until the turn of the millennium that the positive psychology movement was galvanized into action by significant grant money as well as research focus of many famous psychologists. Positive psychology today encompasses considerably more than the study of happiness. There are now various journals in this area such as the *Journal of Positive Psychology* and the *Journal of Happiness Studies*.

Psychologists working on happiness are interested in its causes and consequences. Many are very concerned with how to increase the happiness of people in general based on their research.

In this chapter, we will focus on measurement in positive psychology—that is, what tests have been devised to measure happiness as well as character strengths and virtues. There are many tests used in health psychology research on mental and physical well-being some of which have existed for a very long time and well investigated (Cheng & Furnham, 2001; Furnham & Cheng, 2000).

Most measurements of happiness are by standardized questionnaires or interview schedules. On the other hand, it can be done by informed observers—those people who know the individual well and see them regularly. There is also experience sampling when people have to report how happy they are many times a day, week or month when a beeper goes off and these ratings are aggregated. Another approach is to investigate a person's memory for happy and unhappy experiences in their recalled past. More recently, researchers have looked to physical measures such as brain scanning and saliva cortisol measures to obtain robust non-self-report measures of happiness.

This chapter is specifically concerned with the measure of strengths and virtues. Indeed one of the major turning points in the field of positive psychology was the development of a classification of character strengths and virtues. This early classification work allowed researchers to organize what was known about these constructs in an empirical, rigorously scientific manner. Science begins with taxonomic work. We saw, indeed still see this, with the 100 years of debate in personality theory where there is now reasonable consensus around the Five Factor Model. Once this has been established, it become possible to try to understand processes and mechanisms and, in due course, what personality predicts.

The original conceptualization of strengths went like this: Character strengths can be characterized as the 'psychological processes or mechanisms that define virtues' (Park & Peterson, 2006a, p. 893) and as satisfying most of the following 10 criteria:

1. Fulfilling.
2. They are intrinsically valuable, in an ethical sense (gifts, skills, aptitudes and expertise can be squandered, but character strengths and virtues cannot).
3. Moreover, they are non-rivalrous.
4. Next, they are not the opposite of a desirable trait (a counterexample is steadfast and flexible, which are opposites but are both commonly seen as desirable).
5. They are also trait-like (habitual patterns that are relatively stable over time).
6. Not a combination of the other character strengths in the CSV.

7. Personified (at least in the popular imagination) by people made famous through story, song, etc.
8. Observable in child prodigies (though this criterion is not applicable to all character strengths).
9. Absent in some individuals.
10. Nurtured by societal norms and institutions.

According to Peterson and Seligman (2004), two pioneers in the subject, there are 24 character strengths that are clustered into six 'core' virtues developed on a theoretical basis.

It is suggested that different strengths are employed to exhibit a particular virtue, although generally only one or two strengths would be exhibited from a particular virtue group. These virtues include:

1. Wisdom and knowledge (including the strengths of creativity, curiosity, open-mindedness, love of learning and perspective)
2. Courage (including bravery, persistence, honesty and zest)
3. Humanity (including love, kindness and social intelligence)
4. Justice (including teamwork, fairness and leadership)
5. Temperance (including forgiveness, modesty, prudence and self-regulation)
6. Transcendence (including appreciation of beauty and excellence, gratitude, hope, humour and spirituality).

Together, it is argued that the strengths and virtues are the foundation of psychological health, which in modern-day contexts is significantly reduced. People experience greater levels of stress and pressure that uses up their resources to cope (Hallberg, Johansson, & Schaufeli, 2007). Numerous studies have shown that the strengths of character are positively related to subjective and psychological well-being (e.g., Proyer, Buschor, & Ruch, 2013; Ruch et al., 2010). Research on the development of strengths in individuals has also showcased a decrease in depressive symptoms (Gander, Proyer, Ruch, & Wyss, 2013).

Furthermore, strengths such as gratitude, hope, zest, curiosity and, most importantly, love have been demonstrated to be related to life satisfaction (Park, Peterson, & Seligman, 2004). For example, Luthans

Table 5.1 Twenty-four Personal Strengths That Can Be Clustered into Six Core Virtues

Personal Strengths

1. **Curiosity:** interest in, intrigued by many things
2. **Love of learning:** knowing more, reading, understanding
3. **Good judgement:** critical thinking, rationality, open-mindedness
4. **Ingenuity:** originality, practical intelligence, street smart
5. **Social intelligence:** emotional/personal intelligence, good with feelings
6. **Wisdom:** seeing the big picture, having perspective
7. **Bravery:** courage, valour, fearlessness
8. **Persistence:** perseverance, diligence, industriousness
9. **Integrity:** honesty, genuineness, truthful
10. **Kindness:** generosity, empathic, helpful
11. **Loving:** able to love and be loved, deep sustained feelings
12. **Citizenship:** team worker, loyalty, duty to others
13. **Fairness:** moral valuing, equality and equity
14. **Leadership:** able to motivate groups, inclusive, focused
15. **Self-control:** able to regulate emotions, non-impulsive
16. **Prudence:** cautious, far-sighted, deliberative, discreet
17. **Humility:** modesty, unpretentious, humble
18. **Appreciative of beauty:** seeking excellence, experience of awe/wonder
19. **Gratitude:** thankful, grateful
20. **Optimism:** hopefulness, future-mindedness, positive
21. **Spirituality:** faith, philosophy, sense of purpose/calling
22. **Forgiveness:** mercy, benevolent, kind
23. **Playfulness:** humour, funny, childlike
24. **Enthusiasm:** passion, zest, infectious, engaged

Source: Peterson and Seligman (2004).

and Jensen (2002) highlighted the importance of hope in maintaining worker's motivation in an environment increasingly threatened by mergers, bankruptcies, new technologies and an uncertain global economy. Hope is a strength that allows people to overcome uncertainty. These findings have important implications for people involved in the promotion of positive development among society.

In light of such evidence, a measurement of the strengths of character and core virtues was needed. So Peterson and Seligman (2004) took up the task of assessing the positive traits that facilitate human flourishing and answering the fundamental question of how can one define the concept of a human 'strength'. Subsequently, the Values in Action Inventory of Strengths (VIA-IS) (Peterson & Seligman, 2004) was first established. Since then, various versions of this measurement have been developed, alongside other separate measurements.

THE VALUES IN ACTION INVENTORY OF STRENGTHS (VIA-IS)

The VIA-IS is a well-known questionnaire developed by Peterson and Seligman (2004) in the form of a self-report questionnaire with 240 items, which measures the 24 character strengths. This questionnaire uses a 5-point Likert scale ranging from 1 (very much unlike me) to 5 (very much like me). The 24 strengths are scored on a potential range of 10 through 50, with higher scores indicating a greater validation of a specific strength. Subscale scores are averaged across items, yielding 24 scores for each participant (i.e., one's ratings of each of the 24 strengths). The measurement was made available online and has resultantly become widespread, with over a million people completing it as a result of greater accessibility (Linley et al., 2007). The web-based version of the measurement also allows for immediate feedback about the respondent's signature strengths—the strengths that a person employs most frequently based on self-report.

The VIA-IS has been used for a variety of research purposes. For example, Park, Peterson and Seligman (2006) investigated the relative prevalence of character strengths by comparing the VIA-IS scores in 54 countries and the 50 of the United States. The researchers found that the rank order of the strengths was similar in all the countries studied. Kindness, fairness, honesty, gratitude and open-mindedness were the most commonly endorsed strengths in human beings, whereas self-regulation, prudence and modesty were the lowest ranked strengths.

Although the VIA-IS was originally developed in the United States and embody Western concepts, numerous studies have demonstrated that the character strengths have cross-generational and cross-cultural utility. Biswas-Dieners (2006) cross-cultural study of 123 members of the Kenyan Maasai, 71 seal hunters in Northern Greenland and 519 students from the University of Illinois found that there was a high rate of agreement about the existence, desirability and development of these strengths. Nevertheless, despite the apparent cultural universality of the character strengths measure, this is not replicated amongst different genders.

Significant gender differences in the prevalence of strengths of character have also been demonstrated. Linley et al. (2007) reported data on the character strengths of a UK sample of over 17,000 respondents and showed that women typically scored higher than men on almost all strengths, with the exception of creativity. The results are in agreement with those of Park et al. (2004) as well as Furnham and Lester (2012) who reported that females scored higher than males on humanity strengths such as love and kindness. These findings are found to be similar across cultures. Littman-Ovadia and Lavy (2012) conveyed higher scores from Israeli women than men on love, appreciation of beauty and excellence, and gratitude, whereas men scored higher on creativity.

Studies have also been conducted to show the correlates between various character strengths and life events. In Peterson and Seligman's (2004) three large sample studies, they found moderate correlates of strengths of character such as kindness with enjoyment of jobs where mentorship is available. Another example involves those high in curiosity tend to prefer sexually experienced romantic partners. Major life events can also affect the development of character strengths. For instance, in the aftermath of the terrorist attacks on 11 September 2001, VIA scale scores significantly increased for intimacy, kindness, gratitude, citizenship/teamwork, hope and spirituality (Peterson & Seligman, 2003), thus suggesting that individuals who have successfully recovered from serious physical or psychological difficulties or have not can score differently on the VIA-IS than they previously did.

Four measures are currently in different stages of development: The VIA-IS, the Values in Action Rising to the Occasion Inventory

(VIA-RTO), the Values in Action Inventory of Strengths for Youth (VIA-Youth) and the Values in Action Structured Interview. The VIA-Youth is a 198-item self-report questionnaire that uses a 5-point Likert scale. It has 24 subscales (strengths) and provides an indication of character traits constituting the VIA classification. As the VIA-IS is only applicable to individuals above the age of 18, the VIA-Youth was established for respondents of 10 to 17 years of age (Park & Peterson, 2006a). A summary of the main versions of the VIA is listed in Table 5.2.

Factor Structure of the VIA

A central issue is whether the factor structure describing the six virtues can be recovered from the 24 ratings. It should be pointed out that factor analysis of the full 240 item measure have often not supported the six-fold classification. Thus Peterson et al. (2008) factor analysed the responses of 1,739 people and found five factors labelled interpersonal, fortitude, cognitive, transcendence and temperance. They also factor analysed the factor scores and found two factors labelled interpersonal and cognitive.

Occasionally, studies have attempted to examine the factor structure of the VIA (Singh & Choubisa, 2010) to assess whether the respective strength loads on the virtue it was allocated to. Only moderate empirical support has been provided for the conceptual structure of Peterson and Seligman's (2004) original model which identified six virtues. Yet most researchers and practitioners have accepted the distinctiveness of the 6 virtues and 24 strengths at face value without empirical evaluation (Brdar & Kashdan, 2009).

In fact, the character strengths do not empirically map as theoretically claimed. Instead, five factors (restraint, intellect, interpersonal skills, emotion and theology) have emerged (Peterson & Seligman, 2004) instead of six. Nevertheless, further research has demonstrated different number of factors ranging between three to five factors (McGrath, 2014) and the content of the labels given to the factors also varied. This may be a reflection of the cultural differences (the studies were conducted in different countries) or methodological differences. This included which methods were used to determine the number of factors to retain as well as the factor analytic method.

Table 5.2 *Brief Descriptions of the Different Versions of the VIA-IS*

Versions of the VIA	What It Is
The VIA-Youth Classification	An alternative measure of the VIA was developed for youths aged 10–17 (Park & Peterson, 2006a). Similar to the original, it is a self-report questionnaire consisting of 198 items and 24 subscales that uses a 5-point Likert scale.
The VIA-120	A 120-item short version of the VIA-IS—the 5 items with the largest corrected item-total correlations from the original 10 items per subscale were chosen to be included. Different from the other versions as this is suggested to act as a replacement for the standard 240-item questionnaire.
Self-rated Character Strengths	A short 24-item measure of strengths was developed by Furnham and Lester (2012) to provide a short measure. It involves individuals rating each item on a normal bell-curve distribution with a mean of 100 and a standard deviation of 15 points.
The Abbreviated Character Strengths Test (ACST)	The ACST uses single items to capture each of the 24 character strengths of the VIA–IS using an 11-point Likert scale ranging from 0 (never/rarely) to 10 (always), with higher scores reflecting higher levels of character strength.
Character Strengths Rating Form (CSRF)	The German version of the VIA consisting of 24 items with a 9-point Likert scale that measures the 24 VIA character strengths; each of the items of the CSRF describes one of the 24 strengths. Suggested to be a valid measure showing high convergence with the VIA-IS.

In an important recent paper, researchers Ruch and Proyer (2015) highlighted that Peterson and Seligman (2004) did not specify how their model should be tested, and never claimed that the classification of character strengths under the six core virtues would empirically emerge from the former, but was rather simply a classification scheme. Therefore, they suggest that factor analysis is perhaps not the best way to test the classification and provide an alternative method. They examined how good an example each of the 24 strengths is for the six virtues by utilising expert judgements in order to develop a standardized understanding of what the virtues are.

Seventy experts from various backgrounds including psychology, philosophy and theology as well as forty-one regular people rated how protypical the strengths are for each of the six virtues. Results showed that the experts overall assigned the strengths to the virtues in the same way that Peterson and Seligman (2004) did, with only one strength (humour) being not considered protypical. Thus, providing support for the internal structure of the VIA classification. Another important conclusion from their study is that factor analyses of the classification will inevitably fail. Their findings showcased that several strengths relate to more than one virtue suggesting that factor analysis is not ideally suited to test the relation between strengths and virtues.

Is the VIA-IS a Valid Measure?

This measurement has been subjected to scrutiny regarding whether it is a reliable and valid test of character strengths. Peterson and Park (2009) suggested that all scales are reliable and valid with α coefficients >0.70, that test–retest correlations were also >0.70 (across a period of 4 months) and that scores meaningfully varied (although they were skewed to the right). Moreover, the predictive validity of the measurement is promising. Gayton and Kohoe (2015) highlighted that self-reported character strengths do have predictive utility in the Australian Special Forces selection process, specifically because it is a negative predictor of success. Findings showed that the absence of three self-reported character strengths of integrity, team worker and persistence in the top four ranks was a clear predictor that an applicant would almost certainly fail.

Many studies have tried to examine the factor structure of the VIA (Singh & Choubisa, 2010). Only moderate empirical support has been provided for the conceptual structure of Peterson and Seligman's original model (2004) which identified six virtues. Yet, most researchers and practitioners have accepted the distinctiveness of the six virtues and 24 strengths at face-value without empirical evaluation (Brdar & Kashdan, 2009).

Macdonald, Bore and Munro (2008) related the 24 strengths to the Big Five personality traits and social desirability. They set out to test a theoretically derived model relating the six 'higher order' virtues to the Big Five traits: Temperance would correlate with Conscientiousness; Wisdom and Knowledge with Openness; Humanity and Justice with Agreeableness; Courage with emotional stability; but they predicted no correlate of the virtue Transcendence. They factor analysed the 24 scales and found four factors which they labelled positivity, intellect, conscientiousness and niceness, and which did not confirm the Peterson and Seligman (2004) hypothetical structure. Again, by looking at Big Five personality trait correlates of the new scale, evidence of concurrent validity may be established.

One study has looked at the stability of character strengths over time (Martinez-Marti & Ruch, 2014). They examined the relationship between character strengths and subjective well-being (e.g., life satisfaction, positive affect and negative affect) across the life span in a representative sample of German-speaking adults living in Switzerland.

Using the German version of a VIA brief test (CSRF) (Ruch, Martínez-Martí, Proyer, & Harzer, 2014), they found that in younger aged group, honesty and subjective well-being were correlated closely; in middle aged group, hope, zest and humour were more essential for subjective well-being; yet in the older aged group, gratitude and love of learning became more important as they are freed from professional responsibility. Subsequently this highlights that some character strengths were more important for subjective well-being in different life stages.

Proyer, Gander, Wellenzohn and Ruch (2015) have further demonstrated that specific strengths are more important than others, particularly when targeted during strength-based interventions. This received initial support from a study where interventions targeting those five strengths that are highly correlated with life satisfaction led to an increase in life satisfaction, while this effect did not occur for a group that trained in five low-correlated strengths (Proyer et al., 2013). The study involved comparing interventions based on using 'signature strengths' (individual's five highest ranked strengths) and an intervention using 'lower strengths' (individual's five lowest ranked strengths). They showed that subjective well-being increased in both conditions over six months; however, it is more beneficial for individuals reporting higher levels of strengths to work on their lower strengths and vice versa.

Additional research has been conducted that identifies limitations beyond validity. One study using a large data set indicated that none of the 24 character strengths were unidimensional (Ng, Cao, Marsh, Tay, & Seligman, 2016). Additionally, the sheer size of the instrument (240 items) which imposes severe time constraints and attention demands on many respondents, particularly limiting its use in real world settings. Thus, it can be problematic because data collection efforts are often limited by time constraints and test takers' attention and motivation levels. As such, the VIA-IS measure, while ground breaking and vital for positive psychology research, may not be adequate for measuring strengths and virtues. Subsequently, various other shorter measures were generated which are summarized in Table 5.3.

VIRTUES, CHARACTER STRENGTHS AND THE BIG FIVE

The Big Five personality traits stem from the five-factor model that suggests that there are five dimensions (extraversion, agreeableness, conscientiousness, neuroticism and openness) that serve as the building blocks to personality (McCrae & Costa, 1995). There is a significant amount of research studying the Big Five in relation to academic achievement, cultural differences, personality disorders and work success, just to name a few.

An interesting development in the topic of strengths and virtues is its correlation to the Big Five traits and whether there is an overlap between these constructs. Table 5.4 illustrates Peterson and Seligman's (2004) observations of the approximate corresponding character strengths to the big five traits.

Littman-Ovadia and Lavy (2012) provide one of the few studies that provide an empirical report of associations between the Big Five personality traits and specific strengths. Character strengths contributing to the wisdom and knowledge virtue (creativity, curiosity) have been suggested to highly correlate with the trait of openness to experience, whereas character strengths contributing to the courage virtue (persistence, vitality) have been proposed to be related with conscientiousness (Peterson & Seligman, 2004). The humanity virtue has been correlated with the agreeableness and extraversion traits; the justice virtue has also been weakly correlated to these traits as well. Temperance virtue scores

Table 5.3 Brief Descriptions of the Different Existing Measures of Character Strengths

Measurements of Virtues/ Strengths	What It Is
Strengthscope	Drawing from a set of 24 strengths, the assessment highlights the top 7 significant strengths as well as 'bubbling under' strengths.
Strengths Finder 2.0	The StrengthsFinder instrument was created to measure 34 strengths of employees in organizations across talent themes to reveal a brief set of strengths (top 5) that are applicable in a work context.
R2 Strengths Profiler	Measures 60 strengths. Identifies strengths as the energising nature of strengths is key to understanding what makes them intrinsically motivating and sustaining as some behaviours may yield high performance yet may in fact be draining.
Adapted Inventory of Virtues and Strengths	A measure of rehabilitation of clients' virtues and character traits. This instrument measures an individual's virtues in a clinical context, as reflected in one's character strengths. The items include a total of 64 adjective pairs that describe the meaning of a certain character strength.
Multi-component Gratitude Measure	Measures the specific virtue of gratitude by assessing individuals' concept of gratitude, e.g., (a) feelings of gratitude, (b) attitudes of appropriateness (of gratitude), (c) behavioural shortcomings, (d) rituals/noticing benefits, (e) expressions of gratitude and (f) attitudes to gratitude.

to relate most strongly to conscientiousness and agreeableness scores. And transcendence virtue scores relate most strongly to agreeableness, extraversion and openness scores, albeit this virtue is the most unclear out of the six.

Previous studies have provided empirical support for these proposals such as the one conducted by Macdonald, Bore and Munro (2008) as well as Steger, Hicks, Kashdan, Krueger and Bouchard (2007) who have

Table 5.4 *The Corresponding Character Strengths to the Big Five Traits*

Big Five Trait	Correlated Virtues	Correlated Character Strengths
Neuroticism	None	None
Extroversion	Justice	Citizenship, fairness, leadership
	Humanity	Kindness, gratitude
Openness to Experience	Wisdom and knowledge	Curiosity, creativity
Agreeableness	Humanity	Kindness, gratitude
Conscientiousness	Courage	Perseverance, vitality

found moderate to strong relationships between character strengths and personality measures. More recent research has reported similar results where strengths of character correlated highly with personality dimensions (Noftle, Schnitker, & Robins, 2011).

These findings would normally suggest low differential validity of the VIA as high correlations between several strengths and the personality traits suggest that the VIA-IS actually measures the Big Five personality traits. Due to this issue being raised from such research, it is important to empirically study whether character is distinctive from personality and to demonstrate that character is not redundant with current taxonomies of personality. Ng, Tay and Kuykndall (2017) attempted to resolve this in their development of a character scale—the Comprehensive Inventory of Virtuous Instantiations of Character. They reported that character cores and personality domains mostly share the same latent structure, but are still more or less distinguishable depending on the level of analysis and which dimensions are being examined.

With regard to predictive validity, Noftle et al. (2011) questioned the utility of character strengths in incrementally predicting salient outcomes (e.g., well-being) beyond personality traits after their results indicated inconsistent support. These oversights need redressing to establish any measure of character and the virtues that describe it as construct valid.

Table 5.5 Correlations of the VIA-IS's Scales with SWB (Subjective Well-being, N = 184), SWLS (Satisfaction with Life Scale, N = 635), PANAS (Positive = PA and Negative Affect = NA, N = 184), and Big Five Dimensions (N = Neuroticism, E = Extroversion, O = Openness, C = Conscientiousness, A = Agreeableness, N = 184)

Strengths	SWB	SWLS	PA	NA	N	E	O	C	A
Creativity	0.37***	0.21***	0.41***	−0.05	−0.11	0.31***	0.67***	0.23***	0.09
Curiosity	0.53***	0.37***	0.52***	−0.30***	−0.34***	0.39***	0.59***	0.19**	0.26***
Perspective	0.48***	0.33***	0.47***	−0.19**	−0.31***	0.31***	0.41***	0.34***	0.23***
Open-mindedness	0.41***	0.23***	0.44***	−0.11	−0.17*	0.11	0.38***	0.44***	0.17*
Love of Learning	0.46***	0.22***	0.52***	−0.14	−0.11	0.22**	0.57***	0.29***	0.21**
Persistence	0.39***	0.24***	0.41***	−0.09	−0.12	0.09	0.19**	0.66***	0.18*
Bravery	0.33***	0.23***	0.36***	−0.06	−0.15*	0.36***	0.40***	0.24***	0.07
Honesty	0.31***	0.19***	0.35***	−0.12	−0.13	0.09	0.15*	0.43***	0.15*
Zest	0.57***	0.39***	0.57***	−0.27***	−0.30***	0.49***	0.48***	0.28**	0.20**
Social Intelligence	0.33***	0.26***	0.35***	−0.15*	−0.24***	0.44***	0.43***	0.22**	0.17*
Kindness	0.32***	0.22***	0.32***	−0.15*	−0.22**	0.18*	0.26***	0.23***	0.49***
Love	0.43***	0.34***	0.34***	−0.26***	−0.26***	0.34***	0.14	0.22**	0.28***
Leadership	0.33***	0.25***	0.33***	−0.13	−0.23**	0.21**	0.25***	0.33***	0.45***

(Continued)

Table 5.5 *(Continued)*

Strengths	SWB	SWLS	PA	NA	N	E	O	C	A
Fairness	0.29***	0.17***	0.30***	−0.08	−0.14*	−0.01	0.17*	0.27***	0.51***
Teamwork	0.38***	0.24***	0.35***	−0.22**	−0.25***	0.11	0.13	0.31***	0.52***
Forgiveness	0.25**	0.25***	0.17*	−0.10	−0.17*	−0.03	0.04	0.17*	0.60***
Self-regulation	0.47***	0.24***	0.42***	−0.25***	−0.19*	0.09	0.13	0.50***	0.18*
Prudence	0.29***	0.26***	0.26***	−0.07	0.07	−0.21**	0.06	0.38***	0.27***
Modesty	0.24**	0.12**	0.18*	−0.05	−0.04	−0.32***	0.03	0.20**	0.44***
Spirituality	0.22**	0.27***	0.13	−0.08	−0.04	−0.09	0.16*	0.18**	0.29***
Appreciation of Beauty	0.26***	0.18***	0.31***	−0.02	−0.03	0.25***	0.62***	0.12	0.20**
Hope	0.55***	0.43***	0.49***	−0.34***	−0.39***	0.16*	0.20**	0.35***	0.29***
Gratitude	0.46***	0.40***	0.40***	−0.22**	−0.24***	0.17*	0.25***	0.31***	0.38***
Humour	0.36***	0.19***	0.38***	−0.15*	−0.22**	0.38***	0.33***	0.06	0.14

Source: Littman-Ovadia and Lavy (2012).

Notes: *$p<0.05$, **$p<0.01$, ***$p<0.001$.

OVERUSED STRENGTHS

Pendleton and Furnham (2012) had a similar approach based on two dimensions: competence and personality. There are four components:

1. A *natural strength* where a person has a competency which is helped by their personal makeup. The central idea is WORK WITH this ability to rejoice in this strength.
2. A *potential strength* where people do not have a competency but their personality, ability and values would help them acquire and express it. They are encouraged to WORK ON it, so to develop it further.
3. A *fragile strength* where a person has a salient competency but their personality hinders the expression of it. The suggestion is the WORK ON it to develop it further.
4. A *resistant limitation* where a person does not have a competency nor the personality profile to support it. It is suggested that they try to WORK AROUND the issue.

The overuse of strengths has been identified as a major cause of leadership failure and derailment. It has been noted that overexploiting a strength can result in harmful effects on both individuals and organizations.

It is recommended that people should use what comes naturally to them; that is realise and exploit what they are good at, but not overuse them. There are many researchers who challenge the strength-based approach suggesting that overusing strengths leads poor and lopsided leadership (Kaiser & Overfield, 2011; Kaplan & Kaiser, 2009).

The reason is twofold. First, many people are unaware of their strength because they are not open to affirmation of their positive qualities or they have been taught to focus more on criticism. They also might, quite simply, lack self-awareness which is not a rare phenomenon. Personality test, performance management or coach feedback is often necessary in order for one to reveal strengths.

Second, strengths become weaknesses where they are overused. It is wrong to assume a linear positive relationship between strengths and overall outcomes such as job satisfaction, performance, productivity and general happiness. The data suggest that the function is better represented by an inverted U, which is the idea of optimal rather than maximal.

All work behaviours can be rated on a variety of linear scales such as 'too little', 'right amount' and 'too much'. In many cases, people rated as displaying 'too much' of one specific leadership style suggests it has become weakness. Strengths become weaknesses because they prohibit people from engaging in contrasting but complementary behaviours.

Thus, paradoxically, finding and exploiting a strength can be a weakness. Being very agreeable and empathic can result in a leader not confronting poor performance. Equally being very optimistic can make a leader insufficiently vigilant about potential problems ahead.

Thus a leader can display excellent technical skills but poor interpersonal skills: High IQ but low EQ. It is important to confront the question: 'What should I stop doing, what should I continue doing and what should I start doing?' This can clearly indicate what people overdo, what they ignore. Another way to prevent strengths becoming weaknesses is by comparing self-evaluation with peers.

The now established paradox of overused strengths occurs where extremes of anything, even desirable traits and skills, are considered undesirable. Extremes of anything are to be avoided.

CONCLUSION

For a field to move forward in psychology, it has always been important to carefully define and then operationalize the variables under consideration. Defining and categorizing strengths and virtues has been a major, and as yet unfinished, undertaking in positive psychology. Just as personality psychology struggled for years with contrasting models, theories and measures, so there is some evidence of this in positive psychology.

To some extent, it is surprising how few competing measures of the strengths and virtues exist as there has been an active interest in the area for 15 to 20 years. One reason for this is that positive psychologists have seemed less interested in experimental research compared to personality theorists. It is expected that over the years new and psychometrically valid measures will be developed to support research in positive psychology.

REFERENCES

Argyle, M. (2001). *The psychology of happiness*. London: Routledge.
Brdar, I., & Kashdan, T. B. (2010). Character strengths and well-being in Croatia: An empirical investigation of structure and correlates. *Journal of Research in Personality, 44*, 151–154.
Biswas-Diener, R. (2006). From the equator to the north polo: A study of character strengths. *Journal of Happiness Studies, 7*(3), 293–310.
Bowling, A. (2005). *Measuring health*. Maidenhead: Open University Press.
Bradburn, N. (1969). *The structure of psychological well-being*. Chicago, IL: Aldine.
Burns, R. (1979). *Self-concept*. London: Longman.
Cantril, H. (1967). *The pattern of human concerns*. New Brunswick: Rutgers University Press.
Cheng, H., & Furnham, A. (2001). Attributional style and personality as predictors of happiness and mental health. *Journal of Happiness Studies, 2*(3), 307–327.
Costa, P. T., Jr., & McCrae, R. R. (1995). Domains and facets: Hierarchical personality assessment using the Revised NEO Personality Inventory. *Journal of Personality Assessment, 64*, 21–50.
Diener, E. (2000). Subjective well-being. *American Psychologist, 55*(1), 34–41.
———. (2009). Frequently asked questions about subjective well-being. (Happiness and Life Satisfaction). Retrieved from https://internal.psychology.illinois.edu/~ediener/faq.html#SWB
Eysenck, M. (1990). *Happiness: Facts and myths*. Hove: LEA.
Furnham, A. (2000). Parents' estimates of their own and their children's multiple intelligence. *British Journal of Developmental Psychology, 18*(4), 583–594.
———. (2001). Self-estimates of intelligence: Culture and gender differences in self and other estimates of general and multiple intelligences. *Personality and Individual Difference, 31*(8), 1381–1405.
———. (2004). Are lay people lumpers or splitters? *Learning and Individual Differences, 14*(3), 153–168.
———. (2005). Gender and personality differences in self and other ratings of business intelligence. *British Journal of Management, 16*(2), 91–103.
———. (2009). Sex differences in mate selection preferences. *Personality and Individual*.
Furnham, A., & Cheng, H. (2000). Perceived parental behaviour, self-esteem and happiness. *Social Psychiatry and Psychiatric Epidemiology, 35*(10), 463–470.
Furnham, A., & Lester, D. (2012). The development of a short measure of character strength. *European Journal of Psychological Assessment, 28*, 95–101.
Furnham, A., & McManus, I. C. (2004). Student attitudes to university education. *Higher Education Review, 36*(2), 29–38.
Furnham, A., Hosoe, T., & Tang, T. (2002). Male hubris and female humility: A cross-cultural study of ratings of self, parental and sibling multiple intelligence in America, Britain and Japan. *Intelligence, 30*(1), 101–115.

Gander, F., Proyer, R. T., Ruch, W., & Wyss, T. (2012). The good character at work: An initial study on the contribution of character strengths in identifying healthy and unhealthy work-related behavior and experience patterns. *International Archives of Occupational and Environmental Health, 85*, 895–904.

Gayton, S.D., & Kehoe, E.J. (2015). Character strengths and hardiness of Australian Army Special Forces Applicants. *Military Medicine, 180*(8), 857–862.

Hallberg, U. E., Johansson, G., & Schaufeli, W. B. (2007). Type A behavior and work situation: Associations with burnout and work engagement. *Scandinavian Journal of Psychology, 48*, 135–142.

Holder, M., & Coleman, B. (2007). The contribution of social relationships to children's happiness. *Journal of Happiness Studies, 9*, 279–302.

Hogan, H. (1978). IQ self-estimates of males and females. *Journal of Social Psychology, 106*(1), 137–138.

Judge, T. (2009). Core self-evaluations and work success. *Current Directions in Psychological Science, 18*(1), 58–62.

Judge, T., Erez, A., Bono, J., & Thorensen, C. (2003). The core self-evaluation scale. *Personnel Psychology, 56*(2), 303–331.

Kaiser, R. B., & Overfield, D. V. (2010). Assessing flexible leadership as a mastery of opposites. *Consulting Psychology Journal: Practice and Research, 62*(2), 105–118.

Kaplan, R. E., & Kaiser, R. B. (2009). Stop overdoing your strengths. *Harvard Business Review, 87*, 100–103.

Linley, A. (2008). *Average to A+*. Coventry: CAPP Press.

Linley, P., Maltby, J., Wood, A., Joseph, S., Harrington, S., Peterson, C., Park, N., & Seligman, M. (2007). Character strengths in the United Kingdom: The VIA Inventory of Strengths. *Personality and Individual Differences, 43*(2), 341–351.

Littman-Ovadia, H., & Lavy, S. (2012). Character strengths in Israel: Hebrew adaptation of the VIA Inventory of Strengths. *European Journal of Psychological Assessment, 28*, 41–50.

Luthans, F., & Jensen, S. M. (2002). Hope A new positive strength for human resource development. *Human Resource Development Review, 1*, 304–322.

Macdonald, C., Bore, M., & Munro, D. (2008). Values in action scale and the Big 5. *Journal of Research in Personality, 42*(4), 787–799.

Martinez-Martí, M. L., & Ruch, W. (2014). Character strengths and well-being across the life span: Data from a representative sample of German-speaking adults living in Switzerland. *Frontiers in Psychology, 5*, 1253. doi:10.3389/fpsyg.2014.01253

McGrath, R. (2014). Scale- and item-level factor analyses of the VIA inventory of strengths. *Assessment, 21*, 4–14.

McManus, I. C., & Furnham, A. (2006). Aesthetic activities and aesthetic attitudes: Influences of education, background and personality on interest and involvement in the arts. *British Journal of Psychology, 97*(4), 555–587.

McManus, I. C., Smithers, E., Partridge, P., Keeling, A., & Fleming, P. (2003). A levels and intelligence as predictors of medical careers in UK doctors: 20 year prospective study. *British Medical Journal, 327*(7407), 139–142.

Myers, D. (1992). *The pursuit of happiness.* New York, NY: Avon.
Nevid, J., Rathus, S., & Greene, B. (1997). *Abnormal psychology in a changing world.* Upper Saddle River, NJ: Prentice Hall.
Ng, V., Cao, M., Marsh, H. W., Tay, L., & Seligman, M. P. (2016, October 13). The factor structure of the Values in Action Inventory of Strengths (VIA-IS): An item-level exploratory structural equation modeling (ESEM) bifactor analysis. *Psychological Assessment.* Advance online publication.
Ng, V., Tay, L., & Kuykendall, L. (2017). The development and validation of a measure of character: The CIVIC, *Journal of Positive Psychology.* Advanced online publication. doi: 10.1080/17439760.2017.1291850
Noftle, E. E., Schnitker, S. A., & Robins, R. W. (2011). Character and personality: Connections between positive psychology and personality psychology. In K. M. Sheldon, T. B. Kashdan, & M. F. Steger (Eds.), *Designing positive psychology* (pp. 207–227). New York, NY: Oxford University Press.
Park, N., & Peterson, C. (2006a) Moral competence and character strengths among adolescents. *Journal of Adolescence, 29*(6), 891–909.
———. (2006b). Methodological issues in positive psychology and the assessment of character strengths. In A. Ong & M. van Dulmen (Eds.), *Handbook of methods in positive psychology* (pp. 292–305). New York, NY: Oxford University Press.
Park, N., & Peterson, C. (2009). Strengths of character in schools. In R. Gilman, E. S. Huebner, & M. J. Furlong (Eds.), *Handbook of positive psychology in schools* (pp. 65–76). New York, NY: Routledge.
Park, N., Peterson, C., & Seligman, M. (2004). Strengths of character and well-being. *Journal of Social and Clinical Psychology, 23*(5), 603–619.
Park, N., Peterson, C., & Seligman, M. (2006). Character strengths in fifty-four nations and fifty. *Personality and Individual Differences, 43*(2), 341–351.
Pendleton, D., & Furnham, A. (2012). *Leadership: All you need to know.* London: Palgrave Macmillan.
Peterson, C., & Seligman, M. (2004). *Character strengths and virtues: A handbook of classification.* Washington, DC: APA Press.
Peterson, C., Park, N., & Seligman, M. (2006). Greater strengths of character and recovery from illness. *Journal of Positive Psychology, 1*(1), 17–26.
Peterson, C., Park, N., Pole, N., D'Andrea, W., & Seligman, M. (2008). Strengths of character and posttraumatic growth. *Journal of Traumatic Stress, 21*(2), 214–217.
Positive Psychology Centre: Frequently Asked Questions. Retrieved from www.ppc.sas.upenn.edu/faqs.htm
Proyer, R. T., Gander, F., Wellenzohn, S., & Ruch, W. (2015). Strengths-based positive psychology interventions: A randomized placebo-controlled online trial on long-term effects for a signature strengths—vs. a lesser strengths—intervention. *Frontiers in Psychology, 6*, 456. doi:10.3389/fpsyg.2015.00456
Proyer, R. T., Ruch, W., & Buschor, C. (2013). Testing strengths-based interventions: A preliminary study on the effectiveness of a program targeting curiosity,

gratitude, hope, humor, and zest for enhancing life satisfaction. *Journal of Happiness Studies, 14*(1), 275–292.

Rosenberg, M. (1965). *Society and the adolescent self-image*. Princeton, NJ: Princeton University Press.

Ruch, W., Martínez Martí, M. L., Proyer, R. T., & Harzer, C. (2014). The Character Strengths Rating Form (CSRF): Development and initial assessment of a 24-item rating scale to assess character strengths. *Personality and Individual Differences, 68*, 53–58.

Ruch, W., & Proyer, R. T. (2015). Mapping strengths into virtues: The relation of the 24 VIA-strengths to six ubiquitous virtues. *Frontiers in Psychology, 6*(April), 1–12.

Ruch, W., Proyer, R. T., Harzer, C., Park, N., Peterson, C., & Seligman, M. E. P. (2010). Values in Action Inventory of Strengths (VIA-IS): Adaptation and validation of the German version and the development of a peer-rating form. *Journal of Individual Differences, 31*(3), 138–149.

Seligman, M. (2002). *Authentic happiness*. New York, NY: Free Press.

Seligman, M., & Rosenhan, D. (2001). *Abnormal psychologist*. New York, NY: W. W. Norton.

Shimai, S., Otake, K., Park, N., Peterson, C., & Seligman, M. (2006). Convergence of character strengths in American and Japanese young adults. *Journal of Happiness Studies, 7*, 311–322.

Singh, K., & Choubisa, R. (2010). Empirical validation of values in action-inventory of strengths (VIA-IS) in Indian context. *National Academy of Psychology India Psychological Studies, 55*(2), 151–158.

Steger, M. F., Hicks, B., Kashdan, T. B., Krueger, R. F., & Bouchard, T. J., Jr. (2007). Genetic and environmental influences on the positive traits of the values in action classification, and biometric covariance with normal personality. *Journal of Research in Personality, 41*, 524–539.

Swami, V., & Furnham, A. (2008). *The psychology of physical attractiveness*. Hove: Psychologist Press.

Tsaousis, I., Nikolaou, I., Serdaris, N., & Judge, T. (2007). Do the core self-evaluations moderate the relationship between subjective well-being and physical and psychological health. *Personality and Individual Differences, 42*(8), 1441–1452.

Chapter 6

People's Theatre on Character Strengths Development with Youth

Lui Ka Ki David

INTRODUCTION

Positive psychology approaches suggest that our major mission is no longer to intervene in problems but to develop strengths and potentials so as to obtain mental and physical well-being of people (Hutchinson, Stuart, & Pretorius, 2010). The discussion of implementation on positive psychology had been explored in different human service settings which included schooling (Clonan, Chafouleas, McDougal, & Riley-Tilman, 2004), coaching (Biswas-Diener & Dean, 2010) or even very specific professional education such as law (Peterson & Peterson, 2009). It is concluded and believed that recognition and enhancement of personal strength is a very important task on not only our livelihood, but also our development on knowledge, value and capability to work and live in the society with pressure and challenges. A person with all-round development of character strength should be open to both cognitive and emotional development, and focus on both self and others (Peterson, 2006).

When it comes to strength development of young people, the positive youth development approach had been introduced to focus on bonding, competence and person's quality of young people (Catalano, Berglund, Ryan, Lonczak, & Hawkins, 2002). The relationship of young people with others and the communities had also become an important factor to construct the context for them to obtain positive development (Pittman, 1991).

In a practical sense, different media including arts had been applied to foster positive psychological development in different communities including youth since arts provide a process for people to express themselves, causing positive impact on people's willingness to increase self-awareness and build relationship with others (Gussak & Rosal, 2016).

In the previous paragraphs, information is gathered to conclude that character strength development in positive psychology is not just a psychological issue, but also a social one, and arts certainly play a role in it. In this chapter, the author will demonstrate the impact of theatre work, grounded by the 'Theatre of the Oppressed' and the critical social perspective, on character strength development on young people. An example of a local theatre group FM Theatre Power will be introduced, especially the development of the group, and the way it applies theatre with young people in Hong Kong to develop their strength.

CONCEPTS ON THEATRE FOR CHARACTER STRENGTH DEVELOPMENT

Seligman and Csikszentmihalyi (2014) agree that art has a contribution on positive psychological development of communities. In youth service sectors such as social work (Dutton, 2001) and education (Jackson, 2002), different theatre forms had been applied to work with the young people. Dutton (2001) also states that theatre work with young people encourages them to develop skills, communications and beliefs to make contributions and positive changes on their communities. In this process, the self-worthiness and strength of the youth will be established. Before the people, especially the young people, believe that they are capable to makes changes in the society, they must have the opportunity to review and find out the issues and problems in the social system, which require a critical perspective on the society. In the coming paragraphs, the integration of critical perspective and positive psychology will be discussed, and the development of theatre models with critical perspective will be introduced.

A Critical Social Perspective on Positive Psychology

Critical social theory provides a perspective suggesting that the society is an oppressive system (Mullaly, 2010) and that the structure of power inequalities is established to grant privilege to some groups (Glasberg & Shannon, 2011). For the oppressed groups, they will not have the awareness of the systematic oppression—they will rather accept or even fulfil the negative label on them by believing in their weaknesses and the stereotypes imposed on them (Cudd, 2006), and also stop believing that they have the right and capability to participate in social changes, thereby ultimately being dehumanized (Freire, 1993).

The consciousness towards reality of dehumanized and oppressed people will be alienated, affecting the development of their character strength. In the industrialized society, people usually have two different tendencies to construct their attitude to live—they may either be obeying law and order without questions and awareness about their own right and duty, or intentionally ignore or even show contempt for social reality. It is difficulty for the people to understand and live with the reality, believing in their own existence as a factor to make changes (Freire, 1973).

Psychological resilience is also difficult to be established and nurtured in the social oppression. Resilience as a concept has strong connection with character strength (Hutchinson et al., 2010) and refers to our willingness and readiness to face challenges (Tusaie & Dyer, 2004). If a person is obeying or ignoring the social reality, he/she is probably unwilling to play an active role in the society, and will naturally be refusing or escaping when faced with challenges.

To conclude, the critical perspective pointed out that a person who believed in his/her own weaknesses is under oppression and lacks resilience, and also considered difficult to discover and develop his/her personal strength to survive and develop his/her community and the society. Capacity building as a preparation to face oppression in the society is also considered an important mission of positive psychology development (Bohart & Greening, 2001). In this sense, the promotion and development of positive psychology in youth community is a very important aspect of anti-oppression practice.

Development of Theatre Model Against Oppression

During 1950–1970s, Paulo Freire developed his theory Pedagogy of the Oppressed (Freire, 1993), which started the worldwide movement to promote 'critical pedagogy' which applies critical theory to education to achieve conscientization through an interactive and empowering process to develop a bidirectional student–teacher relationship (Kincheloe & Steinberg, 2008). Pedagogy of the Oppressed encourages the students to raise questions on knowledge, social reality or even the educational system to nurture their 'critical consciousness' (Freire, 1973). The ideal outcome of Pedagogy of the Oppressed is our awareness and sensitivity on oppression in social context and our willingness to make changes against it. In this perspective, education is not only applicable to the traditional school and the teacher–student relationship, but also provides a general view of the society.

Inspired by Pedagogy of the Oppressed, the Theatre of the Oppressed was developed by Boal (1985) to turn the movement of critical theory to a new dimension. Having conceptualized Theatre of the Oppressed as a professional theatre and its artists being trained under traditional theatre aesthetics, Boal reflected on the nature of traditional arts and arrived at the conclusion that the one-way relationship between performers and audience actually becomes a source of oppression in the society, while the people are forced to accept the values hidden in the plays, and theatre becomes part of the political agenda for governors to incept pro-social values. Staying in the role of 'spectator', people will lack competence to develop consciousness of their situation and strength to face or change it. Theatre of the Oppressed, as a theory developed on such understanding about oppression in the society, stresses on the reflection process of people on the systematic oppression, and the contextual and self-inflicted limitation set up by the people in their mind and body (Boal, 1985). As a theatre model with participatory nature, people will also experience the process to face social conflicts during theatrical conflicts in the process to create, perform and interact. The goal of Theatre of the Oppressed is to conduct a 'rehearsal of life and revolution' (Boal, 1985), ultimately leading to direct actions and social change initiated by the people themselves.

Conclusion

Theatre of the Oppressed, under the integrated sense of positive psychology and critical social perspective, enhances one's psychological well-being and social competence at the same time, which integrate the process of character strengths development, social consciousness development and professional theatre practice.

OVERVIEW OF THEATRE IDEOLOGY AND APPROACHES

People's Theatre

In the past century, a large number of theatre groups are developed in different countries with attention on applying theatre in communities or neighbourhoods to foster dialogue among people from different cultural backgrounds (Van Erven, 2005). These theatre groups are known as the worldwide force of Community Theatre, Applied Theatre or People's Theatre. With different forms to create and perform in accordance with disparate and unique cultures and social structures, a very wide spectrum of aesthetics and ideas are developed with similar missions, encouraging the people to go beyond the position as audience in arts.

In such a worldwide scale of theatre development and movement, use of public spaces (such a street, squares, settlements and plazas), conservation of traditional folk culture and events (such as folk songs and dance, puppets shows and festivals) and exploration on social issues (on both livelihood and political systems) are some very important common features (Mok & Lam, 1994). Some of the theatre groups even played very important role in the countries' history in different ways such as organizing and participating in anti-dictatorship campaigns, establishing an educational and community-based cultural and arts platform to start up many different projects with different communities (Balanon, 2012).

Methodologies from Theatre of the Oppressed

Boal (2001) designed different theatre forms to facilitate the process of conscientization and strength development. Games are designed for people to experience different theatre-related elements such as sensations, energy flow, conflict and dynamics; image theatre to construct basic theatrical scenarios with physical approaches; forum theatre to facilitate dialogue between performers and audience by a participatory process so as to discuss on social issues and related solutions. Besides with these most well-known forms used in interactive performance and workshops, newspaper theatre is conducted to study specific social issues; also, theatre exercises such as Cops in the Head and Rainbow of Desire are developed to review participants' inner limitations and oppressions (Boal, 1985).

Strength Development from Body to Mind

A very common oppression prevalent in the society is the alienation of body by the industrialized system of society (Boal, 1985). When people need to work and study in certain mode, their body needs to stay in constant positive posture, which stops people from exploring their weaknesses and strengths in a physical sense. Theatre sees our body as a very important instrument to perform (Stanislavsky & Hapgood, 2003); exercises are invented and explored to arouse our physical and cognitive sensitivity. The process of body and mind exploration can be considered as a preparation to be an actor and citizen at the same time.

Theatre as Storytelling and Social Interaction

Theatre creation and performance is a process for performers to tell stories (Johnstone, 2014), and story can be based on personal experience in different social contexts. If a group of people with similar or different experiences in the society can be gathered and made to listen to stories from each other, their personal actions will be turned into a community-based social activity. In such a process, self-expression and mutual empathy are both encouraged, and the stories will be reviewed in theatre to explore life and social issues behind. Boal (1985) also provide approaches such as Photoromance, Newspaper Theatre and Forum Theatre to create room for further discussions based on stories told, to enhance participations of both storytellers and listeners.

Improvisation as Challenges

Except a storytelling process, Johnstone (2014) also demonstrates theatre as a process to improvise. Telling stories is the first step to construct theatre, and the next step is to further react and push forward stories. Improvisation lets the performer continue the theatrical conflict and dynamic by performing with no script; in the process, people need to be ready to create and perform under unknown progress of the play—every new line spoken can trigger new changes and possibilities. Readiness and willingness to face challenges is necessary during improvisation, which is also an important psychological strength a person can develop in theatre.

Professional Development in Theatre

Theatre is a profession which entails a process of coaching and preparation for the people to undergo and master, actually skills and mindset will be trained during the experience (Stanislavsky & Hapgood, 2003). The discussions on theatre and its features in previous paragraphs showed that not only for actors, theatre can be more than a leisure interest to the people in any community. Theatre, in a board sense, is a combination of different professions including skill-based professions such as sound, lighting and performance; creativity-based profession such as playwright, directing and acting; value-based profession such as community development and education, and even administration. Different strengths are inquired during theatre work, which makes theatre itself a medium for positive development.

Theatre and Flow Experience

Csikszentmihalyi (1997) suggested that a flow experience happens when we are well engaged in a here-and-now experience with enjoyment. A flow experience can happen in a host of situations, including work, entertainment or performance. People who are able and ready to keep themselves present and be focused on their experience, and to stay away from distractions are more likely to achieve and enjoy a flow. Theatre, as a process to build attachment among self, characters, space and performance, provides many contributing factors for people to start flow experiences. Also, improvisation in theatre has high requirement for the actors to stay in here and now since they are asked to react to immediate happening with other actors on stage, or even the audience. Concentration is a very important factor, and it probably leads to flow experience for both the actors and audiences.

Conclusion

In theatre, we review lives, listen to and learn from others' lives so as to recreate life stories for future changes; we become expressive in both body and mind, so we communicate with our teammates and the community we are interacting with; we develop professional and constructive attitude to create plays which show our attention on civilization, environment and society, so as to position ourselves as global citizens and local neighbours at the same time. We conduct theatre for the people, with the people and by the people, and we recognize ourselves as part of the people and communities. Theatre, under the People's Theatre ideology, can be seen as a way to develop and apply social sciences, which support the development of people and community on physical, cognitive, emotional, interpersonal and spiritual aspects. It is a process of empowerment and conscientization when the people can become the subject to study and take actions spontaneously (Freire, 1973).

APPLICATION OF THEATRE ON CHARACTER STRENGTH DEVELOPMENT

Twenty-four measurable character strengths, categorized into six virtues, namely, wisdom, courage, humanity, justice, temperance and transcendence, had been listed by Peterson and Seligman (2004) as directions for positive psychology practitioners to work on. The application of these strengths in our work, life and professional development is the key to life with happiness and well-being (Seligman, 2011).

Wisdom Development in Theatre Creation

Wisdom refers to creativity, competence to have insight and judgement, and the attitude to learn and maintain one's curiosity about the world (Peterson & Seligman, 2004). Theatre provides a creative process for people to build connection among self, environment, the society and the world. When we are devising a play, or thinking of the way to perform, we need to transform our internal thoughts, feelings and experience to prepare for a purposeful and insightful expression; we will need to make judgements on the way we create a play. This process will become a sustainable one to keep our mind fresh since every creation is distinctive from the others, which also becomes a contributing factor to keep ourselves curious and willing to keep learning in the world.

Courage Development in Theatre Production

Courage, as a character strength virtue, consists of passion, frankness, diligence and audacity (Peterson & Seligman, 2004), which can be considered closely related to productivity. In theatre production, people need to develop positive manner and attitude to work, and be ready to work hard not only to their fulfil duty but also responsibility. Integrity and commitment are also very important qualities for a productive theatre worker, no matter whether he/she is working on a creative, technical or administrative position.

Humanity Development in Theatre Interaction

Love, kindness and social intelligence are very important personal qualities to build up our humanity (Peterson & Seligman, 2004). Theatre approaches need to encourage people to conduct interactive theatre performance and projects in neighbourhoods or communities; theatre participants will be trained to pay close attention to the living conditions and issues of different communities including those in need or disadvantages. Sensitivity to the issue of social oppression will need to be nurtured. Correspondingly, empathy for the suffering of people needs to be aroused.

Justice Development in Theatre Movement

Justice can be defined as leadership, team spirit and the sense and pursuit of fairness (Peterson & Seligman, 2004). In the process to promote and organize community-based movement (not necessarily a protest, also possible to be the establishment of civil societies) by theatre in approaches from People's Theatre, every theatre and all civil participants will have opportunities to review their role in the organizations and communities. Everyone, although having different positions and competences, can make contributions to the team in their own ways spontaneously, with a collective consciousness.

Temperance Development in Theatre Profession

People who are capable to self-regulate with prudence and to forgive with humility are strong in temperance (Peterson & Seligman, 2004). As a combination of performance, production and creation which can be applied in social movement in community-based interaction, theatre is actually a profession which requires efforts to master. To fulfil different objectives in the professional development in theatre, self-request and commitment are indispensable, blaming will not be a practice to be encouraged in the process of professional development.

Transcendence Development in Theatre Aesthetics

Appreciation of beauty, life, future, humour, self and others are integrated to become the final virtue—transcendence (Peterson & Seligman, 2004). Transcendence is, to a higher extent, the pursuit of spirituality in different dimensions. Theatre as an art form originated from ancient Greek arts including tragedy, comedy and Sartrean drama which explore philosophical, social and political concerns, and myth. The broad range of theme and performance forms is an encouragement for people to develop sense and taste to enjoy and savour arts and life. In a long term, a community with habits to appreciate theatre plays not merely from commercial channels will also become mature and active audience with transcendence.

Conclusion

Development of the virtues in character strengths are actually interrelated like the different dimensions of theatre work. The discussion in the previous paragraphs comprises a logical demonstration to show relationships between different strengths and theatre elements. In a practical context to implement theatre with positive psychological practices, a thorough understanding of theatre ideology and aesthetics (like Theatre of the Oppressed) is necessary; experiments and observations are also essential.

FM THEATRE POWER: A HONG KONG THEATRE GROUP WITH STRONG YOUTH PARTICIPATION

In Hong Kong, a theatre group named FM Theatre Power, founded in year 2000, had been seen as a phenomenon, triggering a lot of discussion on youth community and arts (Shiu & Wong, 2012). FM Theatre Power was founded and developed by a group of young artists in their 20s with multi-arts directions that included 'street and public space theatre', 'community based theatre', 'interactive theatre', People's Theatre, 'traditional theatre production' and 'international theatre exchange'. Until year 2017, considering the inclusion of new young members regularly, major groups of members happen to be still in their 20s or early 30s. In the group, participations of systematically trained theatre workers, experience-based practitioners and amateurs are all very common. With continuing participation of young force, FM Theatre Power maintains its image as a young theatre group with relatively long developmental life span to review on. In the following paragraphs, some features of the group will be explored, and evaluation of the impact on character strength development will be discussed.

The Integration of People's Theatre and Traditional Theatre

The founder of FM Theatre Power, Banky Yeung, studied both People's Theatre approaches and traditional theatre aesthetics as a graduate of the Hong Kong Academy of Performing Art, the major theatre worker training institute in Hong Kong. The training led Yeung to have an exposure to both directions in theatre work, and make FM Theatre Power an inclusive group with members from different disciplines including theatre workers and artists, social workers, therapists, teachers and students. As a result, FM Theatre Power integrated ideology from different perspectives, which let most of the members of the team to be capable to exchange knowledge and skills to implement different practices inclusive of, but not limited to, therapeutic work, interactive performance, improvising, workshop facilitation and performance. They also integrate different approaches to develop their own unique theatre forms, such as Playforward Theatre—an integration of Playback theatre (a classical humanistic theatre approach) and Theatre of the Oppressed (application of critical perspective in theatre)—and different skills of performance and creation. Development of FM Theatre Power equips its members with strengths to perform and create by trial and error, resulting in very unique achievements.

Youth-based Collective Creativity

Theatre creations and productions of FM Theatre Power can be considered as 'youth-oriented' theatre in terms of aesthetics and creativity. In every play performed by FM Theatre Power, devising theatre is applied, which every actor is sharing the responsibility to create and contribute for the scenes to be performed (Oddey, 2013), the play writer and director, share the position to facilitate instead of to control the creative process. As a result, a number of plays conducted by FM Theatre Power are constructed from a youth perspective with different developmental issues, big group chorus with touches to show personal strength and characteristics of every single actor becomes a common scenery in FM Theatre Power's plays.

Multi-participation of Young People in Theatre

Not only acting, young participants and members of FM Theatre Power are also in charge of every single position in theatre. From stage management, technical design to administration and logistic, every member of FM Theatre Power is able to experience the whole operation in theatre. Young members are always welcomed to join in production and technical meetings, and to co-work with operators of technical system in the very front line. The full participation and involvement of young people in theatre actually builds a linkage between them and the product they are constructing (that is, the play) which significantly raises their motivation and commitment to prevent alienation (Kanungo, 1979). Moral competence with all-round development of skills, knowledge and motivation will be developed (Park & Peterson, 2006).

Work in Community and School Settings

FM Theatre Power apples its theatre methodology in different spaces including street, public spaces, schools and community service centres. Except a challenging process to adapt different environment, the work manner of the group also provided the young members chances to interact with totally different audiences and communities. For instance, rich experience to perform Playback theatre enhances their understanding towards issues in different communities and cultural contexts of FM Theatre Power members (Asian People's Theatre Festival Society, 2001), also making them a group of active listeners with empathy, making them capable to care about others. They are also trained to react and accept offers raised by different audiences, establishing a multi-level professional identity.

International Exploration

In year 2017, FM Theatre Power participated in the International Community Arts Festival (ICAF) Rotterdam, a festival gathering community of arts developers, organizers, pioneers and workers (Van Erven, 2016). The team was invited to perform one main stage show, one interactive performance workshop and to show a short film. The team attended the festival including its founding members and recently joined members, applying their competence and professional sense in theatre and community work. The successful exchange and performance conducted by a theatre group developed in Hong Kong proved the success of FM Theatre Power to apply their local experience on international level.

Conclusion

A true conscientization and empowering process happens when we can hand over the power to the service users, and let them become part of the committee. When young people step forward from the position of learning and being served, they develop their skills with professional value and attitude, social and emotional perspective on self, others and environment. They pass through a process of anti-oppression by developing character strengths with creativity, kindness to others, maturity to work, courage to acquire new knowledge and accept challenges, and commitment to make positive changes in the society.

OPPORTUNITIES AND CHALLENGES ON POSITIVE PSYCHOLOGICAL THEATRE PRACTICE

Theatre can be considered a form of community, so the humanistic work established in theatre can turn a group of people, although not trained in some performing art academy, into a community (Halperin, 2002) by way of a strength development process to face challenges in daily life. The integration of human service and arts has always been an issue to discuss. Positive psychology practitioners can certainly be a group of stakeholders to explore the development of a positive psychological theatre practice, by fostering cross-profession collaboration in two dimensions, namely, (a) to start up projects involving practitioners from different professions and (b) to create new or support the development of an integrated professional discipline.

Theatre in Community Organization and Advocacy to Enhance Resilience

It is common to see theatrical elements in social actions organized by civil societies such as the use of slogans, special props or costumes for the protesters to highlight the issues, or even dramatic dialogues to be performed. When it is believed that the process of community organization is to collect and organize opinions in order to present in unforgettable ways, theatre actually plays a strong role in community organization and advocacy. Theatre of the Oppressed itself is the theatre approach for the people to review issues related to their livelihood and to enhance awareness on social oppressions (Boal, 1985). In the resilience-building process of communities, application of theatre approaches will be a significant supportive factor in social and psychological competence development.

Community-oriented Theatre Centre

There are limitations for community centre to organize theatre projects and programmes, as the major mission and competence for community service is not to organize arts-related projects. However, galleries and theatre generally are not set up to fulfil social and humanistic goals. A community-oriented theatre centre should be welcomed to organize arts projects for the people, with the people and by the people. Although it is not very common to see such setting, some successful cases do exist, including Sarwanam Theatre in Nepal (Davis, 2009), Philippine Educational Theatre Association in Manila (Balanon, 2012) and Islemunda in Rotterdam (Van Erven, 2016). These theatres spaces are constructed with high production standard which allow the communities to experience a complete theatrical experience, also letting the owner of the theatre to generate income by working on commercial projects, making use of the hardware and software in the theatre spaces, to sustain their community-based development.

To Develop a Community-based Arts Training System

Mok and Ng (2014) introduced the rise of the model of community cultural development—a combination of approaches which suggest that everyone can be an artist to participate in community arts projects. A lot of artists, educators and organizers start to show interest in learning community cultural and arts approaches so that they can implement these approaches in different occasions. However, in current education systems, arts and community work are generally still treated as different disciplines. A new systematic development of integrated ideologies and approaches has become a gap in education nowadays. Curriculum and pedagogy need to be discussed and developed under cooperation among artists, performers, producers, social workers, educators, neighbours and any possible stakeholders.

A Challenge: Theatre as Just a 'Tool'?

In a number of situations, arts inclusive of theatre is described as a tool (Doss, 1999; Johnson, 2008) when people believe they are 'making use of the innovative means and method under their professional framework and idea'. We certainly might have different interpretation to the word 'tool' and not all people using this word pay no attention to ideology behind arts, especially community arts that includes People's Theatre, but for every individual who is willing to apply arts and theatre in human service, it is important to alert that theatre is not just a combination of a set of skills to be applied. To elaborate the previous discussion on cross-profession collaboration, equipping theatrical mindsets is an important mission for human service practitioners, service providers and organizers, researchers and educators who are willing to implement theatre approaches.

Also, when theatre is just considered as a 'tool', it will be difficult for the workers to obtain sufficient resources which include capital, venue and manpower to sustain theatre development with the communities.

Conclusion

For arts and human service practitioners, working together is the beginning of integration. However, if people from different disciplines are just gathered by projects and occasions, it is not guaranteed that they will have consensus and mutual understanding on the way to work and use resources. Conflict is predictable and is also an unavoidable process on the route to develop the real integrated approach with an integrated system of training, practising and evaluating.

CONCLUSION

When a lot of youth service practitioners believe that their mission is to conduct developmental services for young people, the most common programme they can organize is voluntary work (Centre for Youth Research and Practice, Hong Kong Baptist University, 2010). A wide vision on youth positive psychology is suggested to be adapted. When a group of people are able to create arts work together to share their stories and attention on communities and society, the community cultural development process is established (Mok & Ng, 2014) to be an empowering element to strengthen the people in community as individuals and groups to live with resilience in the changing environment and with mutual support for each other.

Long-term exploration and continuing studies are required for human service practitioners to integrate their knowledge and skills with theatre approaches under a critical social perspective, but the development of community-based theatre is undoubtedly effective on character strength development of young people. It is a direction of development in our disciplines which is worthy to be looked forward to. It has come to the age for young people to strengthen themselves by working with others; theatre is certainly a suitable space to contain this process.

REFERENCES

Asian People's Theatre Festival Society. (2001). *Fluid sculpture: Playback theatre in Hong Kong*. Hong Kong: Asian People's Theatre Festival Society.

Balanon, F. G. (2012). *Rate P3G Pamilya, Paaralan, at Pamayanan: A PETA cultural campaign*. Quezon City: Philippine Educational Theater Association.

Biswas-Diener, R., & Dean, B. (2010). *Positive psychology coaching: Putting the science of happiness to work for your clients*. Hoboken, NJ: John Wiley & Sons.

Boal, A. (1985). *Theatre of the oppressed*. New York, NY: Theatre Communications Group.

———. (2001). *Games for actors and non-actors*. New York, NY: Routledge.

Bohart, A. C., & Greening, T. (2001). Humanistic psychology and positive psychology. *American Psychologist, 56*(1), 81–82.

Catalano, R. F., Berglund, M. L., Ryan, J., Lonczak, H. S., & Hawkins, J. D. (2002). Positive youth development in the United States: Research findings on evaluations of positive youth development programs. *Prevention & Treatment, 5*, Article 15.

Centre for Youth Research and Practice, Hong Kong Baptist University. (2010). *Review on the service of integrated child and youth service centres*. Retrieved from http://www.cheungkwokche.hk/sites/default/files/20101120_ICYSC_ReportSummar.pdf

Clonan, S. M., Chafouleas, S. M., McDougal, J. L., & Riley-Tillman, T. C. (2004). Positive psychology goes to school: Are we there yet? *Psychology in the Schools, 41*(1), 101–110.

Csikszentmihalyi, M. (1997). Finding flow. Retrieved from http://wiki.idux.com/uploads/Main/FindingFlow.pdf

Cudd, A. E. (2006). *Analyzing oppression*. New York, NY: Oxford University Press.

Davis, C. C. (2009). Decade of dreams: Democracy and the birth of Nepal's engaged stage, 1980–1990. *Asian Theatre Journal, 26*(1), 94–110.

Doss, E. (1999). 'Revolutionary art is a tool for liberation': Emory Douglas and protest aesthetics at *the black panther*. *New Political Science, 21*(2), 245–259.

Dutton, S. E. (2001). Urban youth development—Broadway style: Using theatre and group work as vehicles for positive youth development. *Social Work with Groups, 23*(4), 39–58.

Freire, P. (1973). *Education for critical consciousness*. New York, NY: Continuum.

———. (1993). *Pedagogy of the oppressed*. New York, NY: Continuum.

Glasberg, D. S., & Shannon, D. (2011). *Political sociology: Oppression, resistance, and the state*. Los Angeles, CA: Pine Forge.

Gussak, D., & Rosal, M. L. (2016). *The Wiley handbook of art therapy*. Chichester: John Wiley & Sons.

Halperin, D. (2002). The play's the thing: How social group work and theatre transformed a group into a community. *Social Work with Groups, 24*(2), 27–46.

Hutchinson, A. M. K., Stuart, A. D., & Pretorius, H. G. (2010). Biological contributions to well-being: The relationships amongst temperament, character strengths and resilience. *SA Journal of Industrial Psychology, 36*(2), 1–10. Retrieved from http://www.scielo.org.za/scielo.php?script=sci_arttext&pid=S2071-07632010000200009&lng=en&tlng=es

Jackson, A. (Ed.). (2002). *Learning through theatre: New perspectives on theatre in education*. London: Routledge.

Johnson, L. M. (2008). A place for art in prison: Art as a tool for rehabilitation and management. *Southwest Journal of Criminal Justice, 5*(2), 100–120.

Johnstone, K. (2014). *Impro for storytellers*. New York, NY: Routledge.

Kanungo, R. N. (1979). The concepts of alienation and involvement revisited. *Psychological Bulletin, 86*(1), 119–138.

Kincheloe, J. L., & Steinberg, S. R. (2008). *Changing multiculturalism*. Berkshire: Open University Press.

Mok, C. Y., & Ng, E. (2014). The birth and development of a cultural advocacy group in Hong Kong: Centre for community cultural development. In C. Leung & S. H. Lo (Eds.), *Creativity and culture in Greater China: The role of government, individuals, and groups* (pp. 230–240). Los Angeles, CA: Bridge21 Publications.

Mok, C. Y., & Lam, P. Y. (1994). *People's theatre and grassroot democracy*. Taipei: Tang Shan.

Mullaly, B. (2010). *Challenging oppression and confronting privilege: A critical social work approach* (2nd ed.). Canada: Oxford University Press.

Oddey, A. (2013). *Devising theatre: A practical and theoretical handbook*. London: Routledge.

Park, N., & Peterson, C. (2006). Moral competence and character strengths among adolescents: The development and validation of the Values in Action Inventory of Strengths for Youth. *Journal of Adolescence, 29*(6), 891–909.

Peterson, C., (2006). *A primer in positive psychology*. New York, NY: Oxford University Press.

Peterson, C., & Seligman, M. E. P. (2004). *Character strengths and virtues: A handbook and classification*. New York, NY: Oxford University Press, & Washington, DC: American Psychological Association.

Peterson, T. D., & Peterson, E. W. (2009). Stemming the tide of law student depression: What law schools need to learn from the science of positive psychology. *Yale Journal Health Policy, Law & Ethics, 9*(2), 357.

Pittman, K. J. (1991). Promoting youth development: Strengthening the role of youth-serving and community organizations. *School K-12*, Paper 42. Retrieved from http://digitalcommons.unomaha.edu/slcek12/42

Seligman, M. E. P. (2011). *Flourish: A visionary new understanding of happiness and well-being*. New York, NY: Free Press.

Shiu, J., & Wong, Y. (2012). *Emotionalists: A case of FM Theatre Power*. Hong Kong: Red Publish.

Seligman, M. E. P., & Csikszentmihalyi, M. (2014). Positive psychology: An introduction. In M. Csikszentmihalyi (Ed.), *Flow and the foundations of positive psychology: The collected works of Mihaly Csikszentmihalyi* (pp. 279–298). Netherlands: Springer.

Stanislavsky, K., & Hapgood, E. R. (2003). *An actor prepares*. New York, NY: Routledge/Theater Arts Books.

Tusaie, K., & Dyer, J. (2004). Resilience: A historical review of the construct. *Holistic Nursing Practice, 18*(1), 3–8.

Van Erven, E. (2005). *Community theatre: Global perspectives*. London: Routledge.

———. (2016). Towards a new cutting edge: Where Avantgarde meets community art. *TDR/The Drama Review, 60*(4), 92–107.

Wang, S. (2010). *The civilization of Greece*. Taipei: Jia he wen hua xing xiao chu ban.

Chapter 7

Resiliency, Positive Coping and Posttraumatic Growth in Survivors of Child Abuse and Neglect

Jennifer M. Foster

INTRODUCTION

In the wake of child abuse and neglect (CAN), some child victims and adult survivors demonstrate positive coping, strength and resilience (Anderson & Hiersteiner, 2008; Jenmorri, 2006; Leckman & Mayes, 2007; Sandoval, Scott, & Padilla, 2009; Tedeschi & Calhoun, 2004; Wright, Crawford, & Sebastian, 2007). Research indicates that following victimization, about half of children experience severe distress (e.g., post-traumatic stress disorder); yet, approximately one-third show no signs of poor functioning or mental health problems immediately following CAN (Adler-Nevo & Manassis, 2005). In fact, some child victims seem to flourish (Leckman & Mayes, 2007). Children's narrative accounts of their abuse and recovery indicate an overwhelming sense of optimism, hope and readiness to move forward towards a positive future following adversity (Foster, 2017b; Foster & Hagedorn,

2014b). Similarly, the empirical literature on adult survivors supports the potential for positive adjustment (Wright et al., 2007).

The purpose of this chapter is to explore the lived experiences of resilient survivors of trauma who have experienced posttraumatic growth and positive coping. The chapter will provide a description of victims of CAN, explore character strengths of survivors, discuss specific applications for counselling, review strengths, weaknesses, opportunities and challenges, and provide a clinical case study. The chapter will conclude with a discussion of future directions, with an emphasis on prevention of CAN (Carson, Foster, & Tripathi, 2014; Kumar, Bhagyalakshmi, & Foster, 2018). This chapter illuminates the recovery process for children and adults who have experienced CAN and demonstrates that healing is possible (Carson, Foster, & Chowdhury, 2015).

DEMOGRAPHICS OF VICTIMS OF ABUSE AND NEGLECT

The abuse and neglect of children, often referred to as child maltreatment, is a pervasive global problem that can result in immediate negative effects on children, followed by problems throughout the lifespan if the trauma is unresolved (Briere, 2002; Wolf, Reinhard, Cozolino, Caldwell, & Asamen, 2009). There is no one face of a victim. Children of any age, race, socio-economic status or religion can be affected.

Child maltreatment is often organized into four broad categories, namely, (a) physical abuse, (b) sexual abuse, (c) emotional abuse and (d) neglect, and younger children are the most vulnerable (Green, 2008). Witnessing violence between parents/caregivers, substance abuse or crime in the home, parental discord, mental illness and community violence have also been recognized as adverse childhood experiences that affect neurodevelopment. The large-scale Adverse Childhood Experiences (ACE) study documented that these types of personal or familial experiences significantly influence one's health and well-being in the long term (Felitti et al., 1998). In an effort to cope, many victims engage in negative coping mechanisms, such as substance abuse, disordered eating and risky sexual behaviour. Further, as adults, they are more likely to suffer social problems, disabilities, financial hardship and serious health conditions such as heart disease, cancer, obesity and premature morbidity.

The ACE study also documented that these types of experiences are common (Felitti et al., 1998). In a sample of over 17,000 participants, 28 per cent reported physical abuse and 21 per cent reported sexual abuse. Additionally, substance abuse, mental illness and parental divorce/separation in one's childhood home were also common. Further, 40 per cent of the sample reported experiencing two or more types of adverse events, and 12.5 per cent experienced four or more. New research is now examining the effects of experiencing multiple forms of abuse during childhood, which has been termed 'polyvictimization'.

The reported incidents of abuse by participants in the ACE studies do not account for individuals who did not disclose their CAN on the surveys. Sexual abuse, for example, is frequently undisclosed, with some experts estimating that the majority of victims never tell anyone (London, Bruck, Ceci, & Shuman, 2005). Moreover, males disclose less frequently than females and many wait until adulthood to disclose, if they tell at all (Gagnier & Collin-Vézina, 2016).

Each type of CAN has the potential to hinder children's growth and development (Cicchetti & Toth, 2006; Goodman, Quas, & Ogle, 2010) and place children at risk for a host of mental health disorders. Examples of negative mental health outcomes include 'anxiety, depression, anger, cognitive distortions, posttraumatic stress, dissociation, identity disturbance, affect dysregulation, interpersonal problems, substance abuse, self-mutilation, bulimia, unsafe or dysfunctional sexual behavior, somatization, aggression, suicidality, and personality disorder' (Briere & Lanktree, 2008, p. 8). Furthermore, children who have experienced CAN frequently show signs of social, cognitive, academic, physical, spiritual and emotional difficulties (Goldfinch, 2009; Tomlinson, 2008; Young & Widom, 2014).

Yet while many children show warning signs of CAN, others are not as easy to identify. Some may be excellent students in school, accomplished musicians and high-performing athletes. Although there are established warning signs of CAN, not every child shows clear signs and symptoms. Further, while some victims fare poorly following CAN, others show posttraumatic growth and resilience. The following section highlights factors that contribute to strength and resiliency in the face of adverse childhood experiences.

CHARACTER STRENGTH DEVELOPMENT OF SURVIVORS OF ABUSE AND NEGLECT

The research literature has documented that following CAN some child victims and adult survivors demonstrate positive coping, strength and resilience (Anderson & Hiersteiner, 2008; Jenmorri, 2006; Leckman & Mayes, 2007; Sandoval et al., 2009; Tedeschi & Calhoun, 2004; Wright et al., 2007). Resilience has been defined as the ability to adapt positively to crises, disasters and traumas (Glenn, 2014). The journey through and beyond CAN is arduous, and 'for survivors of childhood trauma, resilience appears in the fragile spaces between healing and devastation' (Glenn, 2014, p. 37).

Researchers and clinicians have questioned what causes some children to experience posttraumatic growth, healing and resiliency whereas others experience severe distress. For children, belief and support of non-offending parents/caregivers following a disclosure and during counselling is crucial. Moreover, caregiver mental health and familial characteristics correlates with resilience in young children. For adults, learning new coping strategies, connecting with other survivors, drawing strength from friends and family, and exploring one's personal beliefs enhance resiliency. Each of these catalysts for resilience is explored in the following.

When children are believed about their traumatic experiences following disclosure, they are more likely to move towards resolution of their trauma. Many adverse childhood experiences are committed by known adults and older children that the child victims were taught to love, trust and obey. Children are rarely abused by a stranger (Finkelhor et al., 2008). This makes disclosure of the abuse extremely difficult. Many children fear disclosing abuse because they worry that they will not be believed, fear for their personal safety or the safety of their loved ones, feel embarrassed or guilty, or love their perpetrator (Foster & Hagedorn, 2014a, b). Children take a significant risk by disclosing abuse, including the risk that they will be further silenced and the abuse will continue or become worse.

Unfortunately, some adults respond to children's disclosures of CAN by communicating disbelief, continuing a relationship with the perpetrator, accusing the child for the abuse, or indicating that the abuse should be kept a family secret. This disbelief and failure to protect the child victim causes substantial harm. Yet, when adults respond with belief, protection and support, they can foster hope and cultivate healing (Foster, 2014).

Children need adults' support during a disclosure, and they need continued support during the counselling process. Counsellors working with child victims can improve treatment outcomes through including non-offending, supportive parents or caregivers (Cohen & Mannarino, 2000; Feather & Ronan, 2009; Silverman et al., 2008). It is critical for child victims to have at least one safe adult who will support them as they process their trauma. Children are often not able to begin their journey towards healing until they are believed and supported.

Parents of child victims frequently necessitate support as well. Recent research has indicated that parental characteristics influence young children's resiliency. One study examined parental characteristics of young resilient children who experienced CAN. Nearly half (48%) of the maltreated children in the sample were resilient (Dubowitz et al., 2016). Children who were resilient were more likely to come from smaller households and have parents who were not depressed and held employment. The researchers asserted that addressing caregiver's mental health may further promote resilience in young children, and paediatricians are ideal professionals to screen parents and refer to counselling services. Access to counselling and parental follow-through may be enhanced through the employment of mental health professionals within paediatric settings so that physicians can provide a warm handoff. Parents need to process their own reactions to their children's trauma, learn how to support their children and in some cases process their own personal experiences of CAN (Foster, 2014).

Adults who have a history of CAN also have the potential for positive adjustment (Wright et al., 2007). Learning new coping strategies, engaging in counselling, connecting with other survivors and exploring the meaning of their experiences can foster resilience.

Numerous adults who seek counselling have carried the burden of their abuse in silence and alone. Many of these adults survived through coping in the best way that they could, often seeking solace through substances, food or risky sexual behaviours. Although these coping mechanisms provided a temporary salve for their wounds, they were ineffective at erasing memories. They are also connected to a myriad of negative outcomes, including addiction, obesity, sexually transmitted diseases and other social and legal consequences. Counselling provides a safe place to explore the pain of the past and learn new ways of coping. Adult survivors must take the risk of putting aside their old ways of coping with their pain and try new strategies. Instilling hope is crucial, and counsellors ask adults to take a chance to hope again and believe that things can be better.

Further, adults who have experienced CAN experience increased resilience and healing when they learn that they are not alone. Counselling helps expose them to others who have walked similar roads. Counsellors accomplish this through sharing stories through bibliotherapy as well as in the context of group counselling for trauma survivors. The powerful realization that one is not alone and that the abuses experienced were not the fault of the child is transformative for many adults. Additionally, many adults find that they can draw strength from supportive friends and family members on their healing journey. As they begin to share their story, they often meet other survivors among their family and friends and draw strength from their collective experiences.

Along with drawing strength from the support of others, a survivor's personal beliefs may help them identify meaning in their experiences (Glenn, 2014). For many adults this includes religious and/or spiritual beliefs, which may bring solace and hope. Survivors also necessitate an opportunity to explore the impact of their trauma on their beliefs. They need an opportunity to ask difficult questions such as, 'Is God still good and in control? Where was God when my abuse happened?' Forgiveness may also be explored during this time. Although many adults choose to forgive, this is a personal choice and does not require reconciliation and a restored relationship with the abuser if that person is still living.

There are many paths that lead to resilience for those who have experienced CAN. Adverse experiences can be a catalyst for personal growth and finding meaning in life (Wright et al., 2007). Counsellors play an important role in this process by recognizing personal resources and strengths. The following section discusses applications for counselling trauma survivors.

APPLICATIONS

Research indicates that adults who received counselling for CAN experienced improved coping skills, increased ability to relate to others, enhanced inner strength and heightened gratitude (Tedeschi & Calhoun, 2004). Moreover, adults who shared their experiences with others were believed and validated, identified meaning and attained support, and demonstrated posttraumatic growth (Anderson & Hiersteiner, 2008).

Although there are many approaches to treatment for CAN, trauma-focused cognitive behavioural therapy (TF-CBT) is the only approach that is significantly more effective than a placebo and other forms of treatment (Silverman et al., 2008). Randomized controlled studies indicate that TF-CBT results in a reduction of trauma-related symptoms for victims of sexual abuse, and is more effective than other types of counselling immediately following treatment and at one year after the intervention (Cohen, Mannarino, & Knudsen, 2005). TF-CBT with a survivor of abuse is explored in the case study section of this chapter.

In order for evidence-based approaches such as TF-CBT to be effective, counsellors need specific trauma training. Unfortunately, many counsellors-in-training lack critical knowledge and feel unprepared to provide services to victims. One study surveyed counsellors-in-training ($N = 304$) and found 69 per cent of students reported low levels of competence and feelings of preparedness for working with child sexual abuse victims, which is of one of the most common types of trauma (Foster, 2017a). Training is especially important as lack of preparation may result in negative outcomes for counsellors (e.g., burnout, compassion fatigue, vicarious trauma, feeling incompetent and unethical behaviour) and clients (e.g., improper referral, inadequate treatment and further silencing) (Adams & Riggs, 2008; Cavanagh, Read, & New, 2004; Pearlman & Saakvitne, 1995; Read, Hammersley, & Rudegeair, 2007).

Therefore, counselling preparation programmes must help students increase their knowledge about trauma and counselling skills for working with survivors. Developing students' knowledge can be accomplished through classroom instruction, web-based training, integration in multiple courses, trauma-specific courses and supervised field experiences. In the area of sexual abuse, the following must be taught for minimum competency: (a) reporting procedures and laws,

(b) assessment of abuse, (c) symptoms, (d) offenders, (e) nature of child sexual abuse relationships, (f) disclosure, (g) blaming the victim/non-offending mother, (h) empirically based treatments for child sexual abuse, (i) values and beliefs and (j) self-care/vicarious traumatization (Kenny & Abreu, 2015). This approach could be expanded so students are proficient in all types of CAN.

In addition to a lack of trained counsellors, in many parts of the world there is insufficient access to mental health services. In areas where professional counselling is unavailable, lay counsellors can serve a vital role with children and adults who have experienced traumas. Lay counsellors are especially vital in developing countries in which there are few trained clinicians and access to mental health services is scant or non-existent. A lay counsellor model was implemented in South and Southeast Asia. Ministry leaders in religious organizations were taught basic counselling skills and how to respond to victims of trauma using a train-the-trainer approach (Carson, Lawson, Casado-Kehoe, & Wilcox, 2011). Such a model could be expanded and adapted so that it is culturally sensitive and addresses critical trauma needs in the area in which it is implemented (e.g., genocide and human trafficking).

This section demonstrates that counselling is effective for individuals who have experienced CAN and evidence-based approaches have been established. Trained clinicians and lay counsellors are needed to meet the needs of trauma survivors. The following section discusses some of the particular challenges and opportunities associated with trauma work.

STRENGTHS, WEAKNESSES, OPPORTUNITIES AND CHALLENGES

When working with survivors of CAN, there are weaknesses and challenges as well as strengths and opportunities. This section will detail each of these with an emphasis on how to increase the likelihood of successful treatment in which counsellors join their clients as they journey from victims to survivors.

A strength-based approach is often neglected in trauma work; yet, every client who has survived CAN has strengths that can help facilitate the healing process. These may be individual character qualities (e.g., tenacity, courage, perseverance, interpersonal skills, creativity and resourcefulness) or external (e.g., stable employment, financial security and supportive loved ones). Counsellors must identify their clients' strengths and help clients acknowledge and utilize their strengths in the healing process. If counsellors assess their clients' situations as hopeless, they will cause further harm.

Counsellors can also harm clients if they are unable to be fully present and listen empathetically to clients' painful experiences. It can be extremely challenging to hear the atrocities and evils that clients experienced, often at the hands of people who should have loved and protected them (e.g., parents/caregivers). When counsellors become overwhelmed by these stories, they are at risk for secondary traumatic stress and compassion fatigue (Jenmorri, 2006). Counsellors who work with survivors necessitate proper training, supervision and self-care (Foster, 2014). Counsellors are human and are affected by clients' horrific experiences, thus they need support as they face the unimaginable realities of victims.

When counsellors can identify clients' strengths and empathetically hear clients' stories, there are opportunities for healing. Counsellors can provide psychoeducation about trauma, teach coping strategies and provide a safe space to explore one's personal narrative, which are elements of TF-CBT (Cohen, Mannarino, & Deblinger, 2006). Counsellors must also be prepared to discuss children's past, current and future fears. Children have an intense need to feel safe and protected, and many children report feeling unsafe following abuse (Foster, 2017b; Foster & Hagedorn, 2014a). Restoring a sense of safety and protecting children from further abuse is critical.

Furthermore, for counselling to be successful, counsellors must be aware of common challenges during the counselling process. Two frequent obstacles are increased symptomology as trauma is explored and premature dropout (Chasson, Vincent, & Harris, 2008). Dropout risk is related to the severity of the child victim's symptoms at the start of treatment and familial dynamics, which include low socio-economic status, single parent household, and minority status. Moreover, parental stress and depression, uncertainty regarding the efficacy of counselling, and a poor therapeutic relationship increase dropout risk (Nock, Phil, & Kazdin, 2001). Parents frequently terminate treatment prematurely if they observe increased symptoms in their child (Chasson et al., 2008). To address these risks, it is vital that counsellors frequently assess children's symptoms and communicate openly with parents. Psychoeducation for parents can help them understand the treatment process and normalize the common occurrence that symptoms often become worse temporarily before they improve.

In sum, working with trauma survivors presents a myriad of opportunities and challenges. The following section provides a case study from the author's clinical work. A pseudonym was utilized and details were changed to protect the identity of the client. The case illustrates the healing journey of one trauma survivor.

A Survivor Case Study

Leanne was a 40-year-old married mother who entered the counselling office complaining of depression. She described feeling tired, unmotivated and having difficulty thinking clearly. She stated that she had felt this way most of her life, although there were periods of time that seemed better than others.

When asked what encouraged her to seek help now, she said she wanted to start feeling better for her daughter, who was five. Her eyes filled with tears as she explained that she felt like the days were slipping away from her. She felt too tired to play with her daughter or care for her in the way she would like by keeping her home clean and preparing healthy meals. The client was overweight, and she said the paediatrician had indicated her daughter was also overweight. Leanne shared that her husband worked 50 to 60 hours a week while she stayed at home. With her daughter now in school, she had considered returning to work as a secretary, but she stated she did not know where to start with looking for a job.

Leanne was asked to complete a basic intake form asking a number of questions about past experiences and present concerns. When I reviewed her paperwork, I noted that she had checked 'yes' to sexual abuse. I asked if she could tell me more about her abuse experience. She responded with saying that she was unsure as I was the first person she had told. I let her know we would take it slow and that at any point we could take a break if she needed. She was able to provide some basic information. She shared that she was 13 when the abuse started, and the perpetrator was 19 years old. He was the older sibling of her childhood friend. The abuse occurred over the course of a year nearly every week. She stated that her parents did not know then and still do not know. She had also never shared it with her husband.

As a counsellor, I thought that her unprocessed sexual abuse was likely connected to her persistent feelings of depression, lack of self-esteem and poor self-image. I also wondered if she used food to cope with negative emotions. My client had several important strengths that I noted as well, including perseverance, a solid support system and financial stability. My counselling approach included TF-CBT along with several other experiential interventions. TF-CBT has eight components (spelling the acronym PRACTICE) that are delivered in order, as they build on each other: (a) psychoeducation and parenting skills, (b) relaxation skills, (c) affective regulation skills, (d) cognitive coping skills, (e) trauma narrative and cognitive processing, (f) in vivo mastery of trauma reminders, (g) conjoint child–parent sessions and (h) enhancing safety and future developmental trajectory (Cohen et al., 2006). I modified these to fit the needs of my client.

My first priority in counselling was to establish a strong therapeutic relationship with Leanne that demonstrated empathy, positive regard and congruence. During the beginning stages of counselling, I also worked to provide psychoeducation about sexual abuse, such as how common it is and how victims often feel they are to blame. Leanne said that learning the myths and facts about sexual abuse helped her realize that she is not alone and begin to see the offender as at fault for the abuse.

Following psychoeducation, we worked to build coping skills and relaxation strategies. I taught Leanne deep breathing, progressive muscle relaxation and guided imagery. During these exercises, she worked on visualizing her safe place. Leanne reported that she had started utilizing these coping skills at home when she felt triggered by a traumatic memory and that they were working to help her feel grounded. During sessions, we worked on affective regulation as well as cognitive coping. Leanne was able to examine the connection between her thoughts, feelings and behaviours. She kept a journal during the week and would bring in examples to share.

After several months, Leanne's depression started to improve. One day Leanne came in to her session and said, 'I'm ready. I'm ready to go there'. She said she had been thinking about telling her whole story, but she kept waiting because she was afraid that it would make everything worse again. I shared with her that when we explore trauma, symptoms can get worse, but that it is temporary. I used the metaphor of cleaning out an infected wound. I explained that it is painful to open it up and clean it, but then when it is done, it can heal properly. I asked if she would be willing to try writing out her story by hand during sessions, organized into chapters, which is referred to as a trauma narrative. She agreed and outlined her book with the following chapters: My Life Before the Abuse, The First Time the Abuse Happened, My Worst Memories, Wanting to Tell, How the Sexual Abuse Affected My Life, and My Hope and Dreams for the Future.

Leanne detailed a carefree childhood. Her family had a nice home that was in a good neighbourhood. She felt loved by her parents and aimed to please them through performing well in school and sports. She was an only child, which meant she felt at ease with adults, but she sometimes was a bit lonely. She enjoyed having many friends at school and often spent time at their houses.

During the 8th grade when Leanne was 13, her mother took a promotion, which meant longer hours. Her mother arranged for Leanne to go to her friend Sarah's house after school until she could pick her up around dinnertime. Sarah had an older brother named Jake who was 19. He was very interested in Leanne, and in the beginning, she always looked forward to spending time with him. He made her feel like she was interesting, smart and beautiful. Sarah teased her that she liked Jake, and Leanne said she remembered thinking she did.

The first time the abuse happened was when her friend Sarah had to leave earlier than expected to go to a theatre audition. Sarah suggested that Leanne could just stay home and wait for her mom instead of coming with her since her brother was home. Leanne agreed and felt excited to spend some extra time with Jake.

Leanne recalled that as soon as Sarah left with her mom for the audition, Jake invited her up to his room. Although she felt a bit nervous, as this was her first time alone with him, she followed him up the stairs. She wrote in her narrative that she knew something was wrong when he locked the door behind her. She wanted to leave, but she did not want to seem rude. He asked to lay on the bed, and she did. He then pulled a knife out of a drawer and said, 'If you scream, I will cut your throat. If you tell anyone about this, I will kill you and your family'. Leanne was unable to speak but nodded her head. She recalled the pain of the assault. When it was done, he left the room to shower while she tried to put her clothes back on and went downstairs to wait for her mom to pick her up. When he came back down the stairs, he acted as if nothing had happened and asked if she wanted something to eat.

Leanne said that the attacks continued for the next year anytime Jake could be alone with her. He even assaulted her while his mom and sister were home, saying that he was going to help Leanne with her homework in his room. Although she begged her mom to not have to go to Sarah's house anymore, her mom insisted that she had to continue to go because she did not want her staying home alone until she was older. The abuse ended when Leanne's mom let her stay home on her own the following year. She thought frequently of telling, but she was worried she would be blamed. In her mind, she should have never stayed in his room that first time. She should have screamed or tried to get out or called the police. She believed Jake was capable of killing her and her family. She decided that it was not worth jeopardizing their safety. She saw Jake a handful of times in the community and at events like graduation. He always acted like the perfect gentleman, and no one ever suspected that he had assaulted her. Sometimes it did not even seem real to her.

Leanne then wrote a chapter about how the abuse had affected her life. Although she tried to forget that horrific year, the past continued to haunt her. When she had a serious boyfriend and had consensual intercourse, memories of the abuse came flooding back. Although she and her husband had intercourse, she stated she never really enjoyed it and would feel numb. Now, as a mom, she felt an intense need to protect her daughter from harm. When her daughter started kindergarten this year, Leanne felt her daughter's safety was slipping from her hands, and she worried constantly that her daughter would be abused.

Leanne's final chapter shared her hopes and dreams for her future. She dreamed of feeling more connected with her husband, having the energy to do fun activities together as a family, and not worrying constantly about her daughter. She hoped to feel strong enough to share her story with other victims so they would know that they are not alone.

Together we processed the narrative and explored her thoughts, feelings and beliefs about her sexual abuse. She confronted cognitive distortions, such as the reason that I was a target was because there was something wrong with me. We discussed her fears that her daughter would also be abused, and we explored prevention strategies for helping keep her safe. We also discussed her sharing the narrative with her husband. Over time, Leanne grieved her losses associated with the trauma including a loss of innocence and the belief that people are good. She also explored questions like where was God when this was happening.

Leanne indicated that she was ready to bring her husband into counselling. He listened empathetically to her narrative and cried with her. The couple came for several more sessions together to talk about the way the abuse had affected their marriage. Not long after, Leanne was ready to graduate from counselling. She had rediscovered her strengths and had a positive outlook for her future. Light had returned to her eyes and her laugh was infectious. Leanne is a survivor.

FUTURE DIRECTIONS

Prevention of CAN is of paramount importance (Carson et al., 2014; Kumar et al., 2018). Prevention must be viewed as the responsibility of parents and caregivers as well as community members. Children are defenceless against perpetrators, and adults need to take responsibility for protecting them (Wurtele, 2009). This section will detail prevention strategies that can be implemented in schools and communities.

Sexual abuse is one type of CAN that has been targeted through prevention efforts. Currently, most sexual abuse prevention programmes delivered in schools are designed for young children, and parent education is often a small part of the curriculum (e.g., take home assignments) or is completely absent. Parents/caregivers necessitate information about perpetrators and need training on ways to protect their children. Programmes can be improved through incorporating parent-only sessions that teach parents potential trauma symptoms, how to respond empathetically to disclosure of abuse and how to talk with their children about healthy sexuality and body safety.

In addition to parents and caregivers, all community members (e.g., educators, childcare workers, healthcare workers, religious leaders, law enforcement, lawyers and professional helpers) who work with children and families need abuse and neglect prevention training. Trainings can help individuals examine their beliefs about CAN and mobilize them to take action steps to prevent CAN in their homes, schools, religious institutions and communities.

Teachers may be a key group to collaborate with in prevention efforts as well as resilience-building strategies (Koch, 2015). Teachers are mandated reporters of CAN and need to know the warning signs of abuse. In every classroom, there are likely children who have experienced abuse, including some who have never disclosed. Teachers may be the one caring adult in a child's life, and resiliency research indicates that having a healthy adult who is invested in the child's life enhances resilience (Masten & Coatsworth, 1998). Teachers have a potential to influence children as they spend a significant amount of time with their students. Teachers can promote resilience through 'positive expectations, ongoing opportunities for participation, and care and support' (Koch, 2015, p. 33). Thus, teachers need tools and resources to create trauma-informed classrooms that promote resilience.

Prevention is the only way to stop CAN. This will require a shift from blaming victims to holding perpetrators accountable. Additional research is needed to establish effective prevention programmes and strategies. Furthermore, public awareness and action are required to create systemic change.

CONCLUSION

Individuals across the globe experience adverse childhood experiences prior to the age of 18 at staggering rates. The experience of CAN affects children of all socio-economic levels, races and religions, and often causes 'wounds [that] penetrate deeply to the core of their spirit' (Crenshaw & Hardy, 2007, p. 162). When trauma is unprocessed, victims stay victims and they cannot become survivors.

This chapter underscores the important message that healing is possible for victims of abuse and neglect (Carson et al., 2015). Some children do not experience maladaptive symptomology following CAN, which is often a result of their resilience (Yancy, Hansen, & Naufel, 2011). Resiliency is enhanced for adults and children through (a) social support, (b) religious or spiritual beliefs, (c) positive outlook, (d) counselling services and (e) supportive non-offending parents/caregivers for child victims (Foster, 2014; Foster & Hagedorn, 2014a, b; Tarakeshwar, Hansen, Kochman, Fox, & Sikkema, 2006).

The effectiveness of counselling with individuals with trauma histories has been well documented. Counsellors can help clients identify their sources of strength, such individual character qualities, supportive friends and loved ones to lean on during the healing process, beliefs in something larger than themselves (God or higher power) and an optimistic outlook. Finally, the opportunity to share one's story and explore its meaning is a critical component of the healing process. Counsellors have the incredible responsibility of creating a safe place to explore trauma through the therapeutic relationship. By instilling hope and communicating empathy, counsellors help clients share their stories, some for the first time. It is a sacred privilege to journey alongside clients during the transformation from hopeless to hope filled, terrified to secure, imprisoned by the past to freed, and victim to survivor.

REFERENCES

Adams, S. A., & Riggs, S. A. (2008). An exploratory study of vicarious trauma among therapist trainees. *Training and Education in Professional Psychology, 2*(1), 26–34.

Adler-Nevo, G., & Manassis, K. (2005). Psychosocial treatment of pediatric Posttraumatic Stress Disorder: The neglected field of single-incident trauma. *Depression and Anxiety, 22*(4), 177–189. doi:10.1002/da.20123

Anderson, K. M., & Hiersteiner, C. (2008). Recovering from childhood sexual abuse: Is a 'storybook ending' possible? *American Journal of Family Therapy, 36*(5), 413–424. doi:10.1080/01926180701804592

Briere, J. (2002). Treating adult survivors of severe childhood abuse and neglect: Further development of an integrative model. In J. E. B. Myers, L. Berliner, J. Briere, C. T. Hendrix, T. Reid, & C. Jenny (Eds.), *The APSAC handbook on child maltreatment* (2nd ed.) (pp. 175–203). Newbury Park, CA: SAGE Publications.

Briere, J., & Lanktree, C. (2008). Integrative treatment of complex trauma for adolescents (ITCT-A): A guide for the treatment of multiply-traumatized youth. Retrieved from http://johnbriere.com/articles.htm

Carson, D. K., Foster, J. M., & Chowdhury, A. (2015). *Child sexual abuse in India: Understanding and impacting individuals, families, and socio-cultural systems.* Saarbrücken, Germany: Lambert.

Carson, D. K., Foster, J. M., & Tripathi, N. (2014). Child sexual abuse in India: Current issues and research. *Psychological Studies, 58*(3), 318–325.

Carson, D. K., Lawson, D. A., Casado-Kehoe, M., & Wilcox, D. A. (2011). *International lay counselor training: A short term training-the-trainers program for Christian leaders and workers in developing countries.* Parker, CO: Outskirts Press.

Cavanagh, M., Read, J., & New, B. (2004). Sexual abuse inquiry and response: A New Zealand training programme. *New Zealand Journal of Psychology, 33*(3), 137–144.

Chasson, G. S., Vincent, J. P., & Harris, G. E. (2008). The use of symptom severity measured just before termination to predict child treatment dropout. *Journal of Clinical Psychology, 64*(7), 891–904. doi:10.1002/jclp.20494

Cicchetti, D., & Toth, S. L. (2006). Building bridges and crossing them: Translational research in developmental psychopathology. *Developmental Psychopathology, 18*, 619–622. Retrieved from http://ezproxy.lib.ucf.edu/login?URL=http://search.ebscohost.com/login. aspx?direct=true&db=psyh&AN=2006-10905-001&site=ehost-live

Cohen, J. A., & Mannarino, A. P. (2000). Predictors of treatment outcome in sexually abused children. *Child Abuse and Neglect, 24*, 983–994. doi:10.1016/S0145-2134(00)00153-8

Cohen, J. A., Mannarino, A. P., & Deblinger, E. (2006). *Treating trauma and traumatic grief in children and adolescents*. New York, NY: The Guilford Press.

Cohen, J. A., Mannarino, A. P., & Knudsen, K. (2005). Treating sexually abused children: 1-year follow-up of a randomized controlled trial. *Child Abuse and Neglect, 29*(2), 135–145. doi:10.1016/j.chiabu.2004.12.005

Crenshaw, D. A., & Hardy, K. V. (2007). The crucial role of empathy in breaking the silence of traumatized children in play therapy. *International Journal of Play Therapy, 16*(2), 160–175.

Dubowitz, H., Thompson, R., Proctor, L., Metzger, R., Black, M. M., English, D.,... Magder, L. (2016). Adversity, maltreatment, and resilience in young children. *Academic Pediatrics, 16*(3), 233–239.

Feather, J. S., & Ronan, K. R. (2009). Trauma-focused CBT with maltreated children: A clinic-based evaluation of a new treatment manual. *Australian Psychologist, 44*, 174–194. doi:10.1080/00050060903147083

Felitti, V. J., Anda, R. F., Nordenberg, D., Williamson, D. F., Spitz, A. M., Edwards, V.,... Marks, J. S. (1998). Relationship of childhood abuse and household dysfunction to many of the leading causes of death in adults: The adverse childhood experiences (ACE) study. *American Journal of Preventive Medicine, 14*(4), 245–258.

Finkelhor, D., Hammer, H., & Sedlak, A. J. (2008). *Sexually assaulted children: National estimates and characteristics*. Bureau of Justice Statistics, U.S. Department of Justice. Retrieved from http://www.ncjrs.gov/pdffiles1/ojjdp/214383.pdf

Foster, J. M. (2014). Supporting child victims of sexual abuse: Implementation of a trauma narrative family intervention. *The Family Journal, 22*(3), 332–338.

———. (2017a). A survey of students' knowledge about child sexual abuse and perceived readiness to provide counseling services. *The Journal of Counselor Preparation and Supervision, 9*(1). doi:10.7729/91.1165

———. (2017b). The fears and futures of boy victims of sexual abuse: A narrative analysis. *Journal of Child Sexual Abuse, 26*(6), 710–730. doi:10.1080/10538712.2017.1360426

Foster, J. M., & Hagedorn, W. B. (2014a). A qualitative exploration of fear and safety with child victims of sexual abuse. *Journal of Mental Health Counseling*, 36(3), 243–262. doi:10.17744/mehc.36.3.0160307501879217

———. (2014b). Through the eyes of the wounded: A narrative analysis of children's sexual abuse experiences and recovery process. *Journal of Child Sexual Abuse*, 23, 538–577. doi:10.1080/10538712.2014.918072

Gagnier, C., & Collin-Vézina, D. (2016). The disclosure experiences of male child sexual abuse survivors. *Journal of Child Sexual Abuse*, 25(2), 221–241. doi:10.1080/10538712.2016.1124308

Glenn, C. T. B. (2014). A bridge over troubled waters: Spirituality and resilience with emerging adult childhood trauma survivors. *Journal of Spirituality in Mental Health*, 16(1), 37–50. doi:10.1080/19349637.2014.864543

Goldfinch, M. (2009). 'Putting humpty together again': Working with parents to help children who have experienced early trauma. *Australian & New Zealand Journal of Family Therapy*, 30(4), 284–299. doi:10.1375/anft.30.4.284

Goodman, G. S., Quas, J. A., & Ogle, C. M. (2010). Child maltreatment and memory. *Annual Review of Psychology*, 61(1), 325–351. doi:10.1146/annurev.psych.093008.100403

Green, E. J. (2008). Reenvisioning Jungian analytical play therapy with child sexual assault survivors. *International Journal of Play Therapy*, 17(2), 102–121. doi:10.1037/a0012770

Jenmorri, K. (2006). Of rainbows and tears: Exploring hope and despair in trauma therapy. *Child & Youth Care Forum*, 35(1), 41–55. doi:10.1007/s10566-005-9002-7

Kenny, M. C., & Abreu, R. L. (2015). Training mental health professionals in child sexual abuse: Curricular guidelines. *Journal of Child Sexual Abuse*, 24(5), 572–591.

Koch, S. L. (2015). *Child abuse and neglect in elementary school children and how teachers can help foster resilience* (Doctoral Dissertation). Retrieved from Proquest. (UMI No. 3689456).

Kumar, A. P., Bhagyalakshmi, K. C., & Foster, J. M. (2018). Child sexual abuse: Evaluating the school based prevention programs in India. In R. T. Gopalan (Ed.), *Handbook of research on social, psychological, and forensic perspectives on sexual abuse*. Hershey, PA: IGI Global.

Leckman, J. F., & Mayes, L. C. (2007). Nurturing resilient children. *Journal of Child Psychology and Psychiatry*, 48, 221–223. doi:10.1111/j.1469-7610.2007.01743.x

London, K., Bruck, M., Ceci, S. J., & Shuman, D. W. (2005). Disclosure of child sexual abuse: What does the research tell us about the ways that children tell? *Psychology, Public Policy, and Law*, 11(1), 194–226. doi:10.1037/1076-8971.11.1.194

Masten, A. S., & Coatsworth, J. D. (1998). The development of competence in favorable and unfavorable environments. *American Psychologist*, 53(2), 205–220.

Nock, M. K., Phil, M., & Kazdin, A. E. (2001). Parent expectancies of child therapy: Assessment and relation to participation in treatment. *Journal of Child and Family Studies*, 10(2), 155–180.

Pearlman, L. A., & Saakvitne, K. W. (1995). *Trauma and the therapist: Countertransference and vicarious traumatization in psychotherapy with incest survivors.* New York, NY: Norton & Co.

Read, J., Hammersley, P., & Rudegeair, T. (2007). Why, when, and how to ask about childhood abuse. *Advances in Psychiatric Treatment, 13*, 101–110. doi:10.1192/apt.bp.106.002840

Sandoval, J., Scott, A. N., & Padilla, I. (2009). Crisis counseling: An overview. *Psychology in the Schools, 46*(3), 246–256. doi:10.1002/pits.20370

Silverman, W. K., Ortiz, C. D., Viswesvaran, C., Burns, B. J., Kolko, D. J., ... Amaya-Jackson, L. (2008). Evidence-based psychosocial treatments for children and adolescents exposed to traumatic events. *Journal of Clinical Child and Adolescent Psychology, 37*, 156–183. doi:10.1080/15374410701818293

Tarakeshwar, N., Hansen, N. B., Kochman, A., Fox, A., & Sikkema, K. J. (2006). Resiliency among individuals with childhood sexual abuse and HIV: Perspectives on addressing sexual trauma. *Journal of Traumatic Stress, 19*(4), 449–460. doi:10.1002/jts.20132

Tedeschi, R. G., & Calhoun, L. G. (2004). Posttraumatic growth: Conceptual foundations and empirical evidence. *Psychological Inquiry, 15*, 1–18. doi:10.1207/s1532796Child 12li1501_01

Tomlinson, P. (2008). Assessing the needs of traumatized children to improve outcomes. *Journal of Social Work Practice, 22*(3), 359–374. doi:10.1080/02650530802396684

Wolf, G. K., Reinhard, M., Cozolino, L. J., Caldwell, A., & Asamen, J. K. (2009). Neuropsychiatric symptoms of complex posttraumatic stress disorder: A preliminary Minnesota Multiphasic Personality Inventory scale to identify adult survivors of childhood abuse. *Psychological Trauma: Theory, Research, Practice, and Policy, 1*(1), 49–64. doi:10.1037/a0015162

Wright, M. O., Crawford, E., & Sebastian, K. (2007). Positive resolution of childhood sexual abuse experiences: The role of coping, benefit-finding and meaning-making. *Journal of Family Violence, 22*(7), 597–608. doi:10.1007/s10896-007-9111-1

Wurtele, S. K. (2009). Preventing sexual abuse of children in the twenty-first century: Preparing for challenges and opportunities. *Journal of Child Sexual Abuse, 18*(1), 1–18. doi:10.1080/10538710802584650

Yancy, C. T., Hansen, D. J., & Naufel, K. Z. (2011). Heterogeneity of individuals with a history of child sexual abuse: An examination of children presenting to treatment. *Journal of Child Sexual Abuse, 20*, 111–127. doi:10.1080/10538712.2011.554341

Young, J. C., & Widom, C. S. (2014). Long-term effects of child abuse and neglect on emotion processing in adulthood. *Child Abuse & Neglect, 38*(8), 1369–1381. doi:10.1016/j.chiabu.2014.03.008

Chapter 8

If the Character Is Lost....! Strength and Value-based Solutions to Maintain the Character of the Victimized

Santhosh Kareepadath Rajan and
Ruopfuvinuo Pienyu

Abusive experiences can have a direct influence on the character of the children. After abusive experiences, there is a higher chance that the children ponder over their 'character weaknesses'. This can lead to various disorders which may emerge out due to the deficiencies in virtues. Scanning through different studies, about 20 to 35 per cent of the victimized have later become victimizer or perpetrator (Glasser et al., 2001). What happens to the rest of 65–80 per cent of the victimized? Little information is available in the literature regarding this. It can be assumed that this significant segment did not become perpetrators. A factor that made them stand away from the tendency to perpetrate could be their character. In one occasion or other, they might have got the opportunity to identify their character strengths, a capacity for feeling, thinking and behaving in a way that allows optimal function in the pursuit of valued outcomes (Snyder & Lopez, 2007). Strength- and value-based solutions have to be instilled since childhood to help the individuals to overcome the tendency of perpetration. The concept of value strengths (Peterson, 2006; Peterson & Seligman, 2004) introduced by positive psychology pioneers could be a back up to such an approach. The present chapter will discuss various elements that could contribute to the strengths and values of the victimized children.

Character strengths are the essential part of an individual's personality that enables to bring out the best and is something that is ethically valued (Park & Peterson, 2009). Having a good character does not portray that a person is without any flaws or deficit, but rather has well-established positive traits (Park & Peterson, 2009). It implies that the person tries to maximize the positive traits to the most and endeavours to minimize the attention on the flaws and deficit. The character of a person is plural (Peterson & Seligman, 2004). An individual is not characterized by a single characteristic but includes a family of positive strengths. Each individual's character is customized and has a family of unique strengths. These strengths are expressed according to the setting of the condition. For instance, leadership and teamwork strengths may come handy in work, but not in writing an exam.

Despite its importance, this topic has been one of the least researched areas in the 20th century (Park & Peterson, 2009). The study on character strengths was put to light with the introduction of positive psychology, which characterized it as a key to maintain a good psychological life (Selingman & Csikszentmihalyi, 2000). Positive experiences of a person such as pleasure, flow and mindfulness is empowered by character strengths (Peterson, Ruch, Beermann, Park, & Selingman, 2007). They are the universal traits that are morally esteemed by the person who follows it. They are developed by the individual's willingness, action, thinking and feeling. Positive psychology considers character strengths as the basic building blocks of human flourishing and human goodness (Peterson & Seligman, 2004). Understanding one's ability and strengths will result in having a realistic goal. It will also prevent adversities of life (Weissberg & Greenberg, 1998). Character strengths act as a cushion for the individual against undesirable negative emotions. For instance, good characters such as self-control, hope and social intelligence safeguard the person from stress and trauma (Park & Peterson, 2009). They help the people to succeed and achieve their desired outcomes (Peterson & Park, 2004).

Twin studies have revealed that character strengths can be both a result of nature and nurture (Steger, Hicks, Kashdan, Krueger, & Bouchard, 2007). The good character even if innate has to be moulded by the environment to maximize the use of it. It can also be learned and can become a healthy habit with proper practice. Most of the character strengths are interrelated to each other and function based on the context they are put in. When a student tops the class, he/she will feel a combination of both happiness and satisfaction. Therefore, the context and the situation also play a vital role in determining the character of a person. Knowledge about strengths among the victimized, for instance, gambles with the chance of stigmatization in a collectivistic social setting. Victimized children in the collectivistic societies undergo this challenge, and hence realization of the strengths seems to be a puzzle at least for a small segment of this population.

A BRIEF OVERVIEW OF CHILD VICTIMIZATION IN THE CURRENT SCENARIO

A child exposed to victimization will have the detrimental effect and have prolonged psychological and physical consequences (Santhosh, 2016). Child victimization or child abuse is a global phenomenon which is characterized by a state of physical, emotional and sexual maltreatment dispensed to a child below the age of 18 years (Jaishankar & Ronel, 2011). It includes hitting, smacking, kicking, caning, negligence, maltreatment, scolding, verbal abuse, psychological tensions, sexual abuse and so on. Case registration of child victimization in India has tremendously increased over the years. A study done by Straus (2010) showed India among the nations with high use of corporal punishment with 54.4 per cent children experienced corporal punishment by their families. The Indian NGO Save the Children reported (2016) that cases registered against child victimization increased from 8,904 in 2014 to 14,913 in the year 2015. Among that 81 per cent cases of the crimes were kidnapping and sexual offences. There were even instances that the child was tortured even by the mother. A nine-year-old boy was found to be assaulted by his mother. He was beaten, tortured, locked up and was not given food for several days

(Rajendran, 2016). Recently, in September 2017, a four-year-old kid was sexually assaulted by a security guard (*Deccan Chronicle*, 2017).

Home to 19 per cent of the world's children population, India is the most spoken country in the world when it comes to issues relating to children. India is the second largest country in the world, where 37 per cent of the population consists of children (Centre for Child Rights, 2017). Therefore, protection of the child is very essential. A healthy childhood will determine the country's future. However, when it comes to children, India has been in the news for all bad reasons in the past. Practices such as discrimination against the girl child, child marriage, child labour, child beggars and malnutrition were some of the significant topics India that made headlines around the world. These negatively impacted the kids and increased the vulnerability of neglect and victimization.

They also have the risk of engaging in criminal behaviour later in their life. Children may find it difficult to regulate their emotions after going through severe punishments. These emotions then will result in negative and aggressive feelings. Children who were corporally punished were aggressive and pessimistic (Kawabata, Alink, Tseng, Ijzendoom, & Crick, 2011; Ulman & Straus, 2003). These kinds of aggression in the victims can later take the role of the victimizer. Children who are neglected during their childhood can later engage delinquent and criminal behaviours (Mason, Hitch, Kosterman, McCarty, Herrenkohl, & Hawkins, 2010). Studies show the relationship between child victimisation and antisocial behaviour in children (Hecker, Hermenau, Isele, & Elbert, 2014; Nakpodia, 2012). Similarly, the literature review on different studies by Glasser et al. (2001) reveals that about 20–35 per cent of the victimized later became victimizer or perpetrator.

CHARACTER WEAKNESSES AMONG THE VICTIMIZED

Experiencing victimization can have a direct influence on the character of the child. Their interpretation of the victimization can lead to the development of negative attributions. These can further lead to the formation of a detrimental character later in their life. Smith, Schneider, Smith, and Ananiadou (2004) reported some negative developmental consequences for children who had experienced corporal punishment, including disruptive and antisocial behaviour. After abusive experiences, there is a higher chance that the children will be more pondering over their 'character weaknesses' (Santhosh, 2016). Here the individual will find it difficult to appraise the good characteristics and will also be overpowered by negative thoughts. This can lead to various disorders that may emerge due to the deficiencies in virtues.

According to Santhosh (2016), the four major disorders commonly seen in perpetrators are disorders of love, disorders of justice, disorders of temperance and disorders of transcendence (cf. Peterson, 2006). Disorder of love and intimacy is characterized by distorted thoughts and feelings (Peterson, 2006). Perpetrators suffer from emotional promiscuity due to their lack of intimacy and weak social intelligence. Lack of justice refers to the feeling of lack of fairness as perceived by the perpetrator. This is an effect of prejudice and partisanship, and they lack the ability to sense and understand the feelings and rights of others (Out of the FOG, 2015). Disorder of prudence is the inability to be farsighted and the propensity to act recklessly. They are mostly arrogant and lack the ability to forgive others. The absence of the ability of the individual to appreciate gratitude, humour, beauty or excellence, hope and spirituality is called the disorder of transcendence.

CHARACTER STRENGTHS AMONG THE VICTIMIZED

In the review by Glasser et al. (2001), 20–30 per cent of the victims later turn out to be victimizers or perpetrator. From these statistics, we can infer that more than half percentage of these victims are did not become perpetrators. Synder and Lopez (2007) said that some people are capable of identifying their character strengths. Such understandings and self-realization will help them distaste the idea of becoming a perpetrator. The concept of value strengths talks about the ability to thrive in the midst of stressful situation (Peterson, 2006; Peterson & Seligman, 2004). Instead of focusing on the deficits, we can give importance of what is prolific in a person.

With the growing rate of child victimization in India, there is a necessity of bringing out interventions which will help in building the character of the child and reducing the probability of the child to indulge in anti-social behaviour. Character strengths are deep-rooted into the basic idea of positive psychology, which talks about focusing on the positives and nurturing it. Subsequently, two main classifications which talk about strengths are the 34 Clifton Strength Finder themes and the VIA Classification. The 34 Clifton StrengthsFinder themes are developed by Dr Clifton and, measures 34 different kinds of strengths. Clifton's primary motive to develop this measure was based on simple questions 'what will happen if we study what is right with people?' The measure tries to analyse which of the strengths are more prominent for the person who is taking the test. Some of the examples of the StrengthFinder are achiever, adaptability, consistency, connectedness, positivity, responsibility, strategy and so on.

Dr Mayerson founded the Value in Action (VIA) Institute in accord with Dr Seligman. It envisions practising good character in the lives of people. Years of research in understanding the best in humans have help in the development of the VIA Classification. It aims at developing these characters for the best for oneself and others. The VIA has six broad classifications namely courage, transcendence, humanity, temperance, wisdom and justice. The Clifton StrengthsFinder is identified within us and is innate, whereas the VIA Classification is identified as important for the person and is learned throughout the years. But both of these advocate the importance of understanding the strength of the person and nourishing it to its optimum.

Certain studies show that interventions to overcome the tendency to be a perpetrator can be conducted successfully. One of the best examples is the study by Olds et al. (1997). They examined the long-term effects of a programme of prenatal and early childhood home visitation by nurses on women's life course and child victimization. The study used randomized trial design in a sample of 400 consecutive pregnant women with no previous live births enrolled and in which 324 participated in a follow-up study when their children were 15 years old. Prenatal and early childhood home visitation by nurses reduced later child victimization and neglect on the part of the mother. Co-ordinated Action Against Domestic Abuse's (CAADA) Insights National Dataset 2012–2013 for adult victims of abuse show that 69 per cent of domestic abuse ceased at the point of case closure after support from an independent domestic violence advisor (IDVA) (CAADA, 2014).

There is a need to detect the problem and put efforts on strengthening upright characters in the victims so that the change of victims becoming victimizers will decrease. To warrant that the victim's character strengths have developed fully, their problems have to be analysed thoroughly and required support should be provided to them. Unrealistic beliefs and irrational thoughts can lead to the development of the 'disorder of love' among the victims. Such problems may be addressed by giving appropriate solution focused psychotherapies that enhance the rational and distinctive thoughts (Santhosh, 2016). This kind of measures can bring about change in the thoughts of the victims, which if not addressed can lead to dangerous consequences. Also, victims may have an opposition to the principles of equality and respect which most of the people follow (Zurbriggen, 2013). Therefore, the intervention shall emphasize on upgrading the importance of justice and fairness. This can be achieved when the person tries to uplift the strength of justice, where the individual is trained by the notion of treating the people with justice and fairness.

The inability to be prudent denotes the disorder of temperament as it has been mentioned in VIA Classification. Interventions may concentrate to enhance the capabilities of forgiveness or mercy, humility or modesty, prudence and self-regulation in the individual. For victims with a disorder of transcendence, interventions need not be designed to reduce the pessimism in them. The objectives of the intervention have to be to enhance the capacity to appreciate beauty or excellence, to be thankful, to be hopeful, to be humorous and to be spiritual.

REFERENCES

CAADA. (2014). *In plain sight: Effective help for children exposed to domestic abuse*. Bristol: CAADA.

Centre for Child Rights. (2017). *Budget for children 2016–2017: Not even halfway through its demographic dividend*. New Delhi: HAQ Centre for Child Rights.

Deccan Chronicles. (2017, September 2017). *Bengaluru: 4-year-old girl sexually assaulted by security guard*. Retrieved 23 September 2017, from Deccan Chronicles: https://www.deccanchronicle.com/nation/crime/130917/bengaluru-4-year-old-girl-sexually-assaulted-by-security-guard.htmlGlasser, M., Kolvin, I., Campbell, D., Glasser, A., Leitch, I., & Farelly, D. (2001). Cycle of child sexual abuse: Links between being a victim and becoming a perpetrator. *The British Journal of Psychiatry, 179*(6), 482–494.

Hecker, T., Hermenau, K., Isele, D., & Elbert, T. (2014). Corporal punishment and children's externalizing problem: A cross-sectional study of Tanzanian primary school aged children. *Child Abuse & Neglect, 38*(5), 884–892.

Jaishankar, K., & Ronel, N. (2011). *First International Conference of the South Asian Society of Criminology and Victimology (SASCV), 15–17 January 2011.* Jaipur, India: SASCV.

Kawabata, Y., Alink, L. R., Tseng, W., Ijzendoom, M. H., & Crick, N. R. (2011). Maternal and paternal parenting styles associated with relational aggression in children and adolescents: A conceptual analysis and meta-analytic review. *Developmental Review, 31*(4), 240–278.

Mason, W. A., Hitch, J. E., Kosterman, R., McCarty, C. A., Herrenkohl, T. I., & Hawkins, D. J. (2010). Growth in adolescent delinquency and alcohol use in relation to young adult crime, alcohol use disorders, and risky sex: A comparison of youth from low-versus middleincome backgrounds. *Journal of Child Psychology and Psychiatry, 51*(12), 1377–1385.

Nakpodia, E. D. (2012). Principals' attitude towards corporal punishment in Nigeria secondary schools. *Global Journal of Human Social Sciences, 12*(11), 13–17.

Olds, D. L., Eckenrode, J., Henderson, C. R., Kitzman, H., Powers, J., Cole, R.,...Luckey, D. (1997). Long-term effects of home visitation on maternal life course and child abuse and neglect: Fifteen-year follow-up of a randomized trial. *JAMA, 278*(8), 637–643.

Out of the FOG. (2015). *Objectification.* Retrieved 20 November 2017, from Out of the Fog: outofthefog.net/CommonBehaviors/objectification.htm

Park, N., & Peterson, C. (2009). Character strengths: Research and practice. *Journal of College and Character, 10*(4), 1–10.

Peterson, C. (2006). The values in action (VIA) classification of strengths. In M. Csikszentmihalyi & I. S. Csikszentmihalyi (Eds.), *A life worth living: Contributions to positive psychology* (pp. 29–48). New York, NY: Oxford University Press.

Peterson, C., & Park, N. (2004). Classification and measurement of character strengths: Implications for practice. In P. A. Linley & S. Joseph (Eds.), *Positive psychology in practice* (pp. 433–446). Hoboken, NJ: John Wiley & Sons.

Peterson, C., & Seligman, M. E. (2004). *Character strengths and virtues: A handbook and classification.* New York, NY: Oxford University Press.

Peterson, C., Ruch, W., Beermann, U., Park, N., & Selingman, M. (2007). Strengths of character, orientations to happiness and life satisfaction. *The Journal of Positive Psychology, 2*(3), 149–156.

Rajendran, S. (2016). *Kerala boy brutalized by mother: Corporal punishment by parents is common in India.* Kerala: The News Minute.

Santhosh, K. R. (2016). A review on the perpetrators of the child abuse. *Review of Social Sciences, 1*(3), 45–52.

Save the Children. (2016, September 8). *Recent statistics of child abuse.* Retrieved 22 January 2018, from Save the child: https://www.savethechildren.in/resource-centre/articles/recent-statistics-of-child-abuse

Selingman, M. E., & Csikszentmihalyi, M. (Eds.). (2000). Happiness, excellence, and optimal human functioning [Special issue]. *American Psychologist, 55*(1), 5–183.

Smith, J. D., Schneider, B. H., Smith, P. K., & Ananiadou, K. (2004). The effectiveness of whole-school antibullying programs: A synthesis of evaluation research. *School Psychology Review, 33*(4), 548–561.

Snyder, C. R., & Lopez, S. J. (2007). *Positive psychology: The scientific and practical explorations of human strengths.* New Delhi: SAGE.

Steger, M. F., Hicks, B. M., Kashdan, T. B., Krueger, R. F., & Bouchard, T. J. (2007). Genetic and environmental influences on the positive traits of the values in action classification, and biometric covariance with normal personality. *Journal of Research in Personality, 41*(3), 524–539.

Straus, M. A. (2010). Prevalence, societal cause, and trends in corporal punishment by parents in world perspective. *Law and Contemporary Problems, 73*(2), 1–30.

Ulman, A., & Straus, M. A. (2003). Violence by children against mothers in relation to violence between parents and corporal punishment by parents. *Journal of Comparative Family Studies, 34*(1), 41–60.

Weissberg, R. P., & Greenberg, M. T. (1998). School and community competence-enhancement and prevention programs. In W. Damon, I. E. Sigel, & K. A. Renninger (Eds.), *Handbook of child psychology: Child psychology in practice* (pp. 877–954). Hoboken, NJ, US: John Wiley & Sons.

Zurbriggen, E. L. (2013). Objectification, self-objectification, and societal change. *Journal of Social and Political Psychology, 1*(1), 188–215.

Chapter 9

Children's Developing Emotional Competence in a Global Context

Vaishali V. Raval and Jennifer H. Green

Emotional or affective competence is a significant developmental task in childhood that is heavily influenced by both biological (e.g., temperament) and social (family, school, community) and cultural context (e.g., Eisenberg & Morris, 2002; Morris, Silk, Steinberg, Myers, & Robinson, 2007; Saarni, 1999). Emotional competence refers to awareness of one's own and others' emotions, the ability to cope with distressing emotions and express emotions in culturally appropriate ways and understanding the role of emotion communication in interpersonal relationships (Saarni, 1999). Emotional competence is a key attribute of social competence, and social competencies are among the 40 developmental assets identified by Benson (1990), which refer to skills, experiences, resources, relationships and environments, and that help young people become successful members of the society. The development of emotional competence is related to positive adaptation across a variety of contexts including home, school, work, family and social relationships (e.g., Durlak, Domitrovich, Weissberg, & Gullotta, 2015; Eisenberg et al., 1995; Eisenberg, Spinrad, & Morris, 2002; Saarni, 1999). In contrast, deficiencies in emotional competence are linked to negative outcomes such as poor interpersonal relationships and internalizing and externalizing problems (e.g., Cicchetti, Ackerman, & Izard, 1995; Frick & Morris, 2004; Kranzler et al., 2016).

Consider the following scenario: Seven-year-old Rohan is completing his assigned work in his classroom at school. Another child, who is sitting behind, kicks him. Rohan ignores this and continues his work. The other child whispers, throws a piece of paper at him and pulls his arm. Rohan may be feeling angry and frustrated because he is not able to concentrate on his work. He continues to looks down at his notebook as though he is still doing his assigned work. Is Rohan aware of how he is feeling? Will he tell others how he is feeling, and would that be considered acceptable? Is his approach to coping (e.g., continuing to do his work) adaptive? The answer depends on the classroom context, school and family norms, and the larger culture in which he lives.

Another child, eight-year-old Emily likes to play basketball on a team in her community. Emily has average skill in basketball. However, she becomes increasingly frustrated and upset when the other team scores basket after basket and her team is losing the game. When a player on the opposing team jumps up and blocks her shot (a legal play), Emily pushes the opposing player onto the ground and starts screaming that the other player is a cheater. She continues to yell at the referee and the players on the other team. When she is asked to leave the game, Emily purposefully knocks over a table of snacks and drinks on her way out of the gym. Why does Emily struggle with emotion and behaviour regulation? Can she learn a different way to cope with strong emotions? The answer to why Emily struggles is a complex one. Biological, social, family and cultural factors all influence emotional competence, and how children regulate strong emotions. We hope that Emily can learn new, more adaptive ways to regulate her emotions and behaviour. Understanding her family, social and cultural context will give us clues about how to most effectively support Emily in building her emotional competence and self-regulation skills.

MODELS OF EMOTIONAL COMPETENCE

A number of models for emotional competence and related constructs have been suggested in Western developmental and clinical child psychology literature. Saarni (1999) details eight skills of emotional competence including (a) awareness of one's own emotions, (b) the ability to discern and understand others' emotions, (c) the ability to use vocabulary of emotion and expression, (d) the capacity for empathic involvement, (e) the ability to differentiate internal subjective experience from external emotional expression, (f) the capacity for adaptive coping with adverse emotions and distressing circumstances, (g) awareness of emotional communication within relationships and (h) the capacity for emotional self-efficacy.

A related construct, emotional intelligence (Goleman, 1995; Mayer & Salovey, 1997), has been popular in self-help literature, which includes components such as perceiving and appraising others and one's own emotions, accessing and generating emotions, recognizing and analysing emotions in others, and regulating emotions. Another group of scholars (Halberstadt, Denham, & Dunsomore, 2001) refer to affective social competence, which is comprised of three components: sending affective messages, receiving affective messages and experiencing affect. Within each of these components, skills of emotional awareness, identification, working within a social context, as well as emotion management and regulation are considered essential. Along the same lines, a model of social–emotional learning (SEL) has emerged (Weissberg, Durlak, Domitorvich, & Gullotta, 2015). The Collaborative for Academic, Social and Emotional Learning (CASEL) has identified five competencies that promote social and emotional learning for children, namely, (a) self-awareness, (b) self-management, (c) social awareness, (d) relationship skills and (e) responsible decision-making. While the CASEL model is focused on the facilitation of social and emotional learning in the school setting, the identified competencies converge nicely with Saarni's (1999) model. Furthermore, while Saarni's (1999) model highlights emotional competence, Saarni also emphasizes the importance of the social context, noting the reciprocal influence of social and emotional experiences.

Across these models, emotional competence requires that an individual has self-awareness and can identify his or her own emotions. The CASEL model adds that understanding how thoughts, feelings and actions are connected promotes self-awareness. Saarni (1999) specifies that the ability to verbalize and use a vocabulary of emotions is also important. Identifying emotions involves recognizing physiological signs of an emotion (e.g., rapid heartbeat and breathing), connecting the emotion to the current situation and labelling the emotion with words. Simply expressing 'I am feeling mad' or 'I am so sad right now' are examples of emotion identification and verbal expression that may be common in Western, European and American cultures. While self-awareness is linked to positive adaptation, low emotional awareness has recently been linked to symptoms of anxiety and depression in youth (Kranzler et al., 2016).

The CASEL competence of social awareness seems to encompass Saarni's skills of discerning and understanding others' emotions and empathy. Both models point to the ability of the individual to take the perspective of others. To have emotional competence, one must be able to recognize others' emotions and feel empathy and compassion for another person's experience.

The capacity for adaptive coping with adverse emotions and distressing circumstances (Saarni, 1999) and self-management (Weissberg et al., 2015) suggest that regulating emotions and behaviour, controlling impulses and managing stress are all aspects of emotional competence. A person with emotional competence can cope adaptively with strong feelings of anger, sadness and fear as well as regulate more positive emotions such as happiness and excitement. These skills converge with the well-known concept of emotion regulation. Eisenberg and Spinrad (2004) define emotion-related self-regulation as

> the process of initiating, avoiding, inhibiting, maintain, or modulating the occurrence, form, intensity or duration of internal feeling states, emotion-related physiological, attentional processes, motivational states and/or the behavioral concomitants of emotion in the service of accomplishing affect related biological or social adaptation or achieving individual goals. (p. 338)

Emotion regulation involves both conscious and unconscious processes that help individuals to respond adaptively to their emotions. Modulating and responding in socially acceptable and developmental-appropriate ways to emotions such as happiness, sadness, anger and fear is necessary to experience success across a variety of important contexts and relationships (e.g., family, school, work and community). Thus, the ability to regulate one's emotions has important implications for adaptive functioning and healthy development (e.g., Durlak et al., 2015; Eisenberg et al., 2002; Saarni, 1999). Furthermore, deficits in emotion regulation have been linked to internalizing and externalizing disorders and maladaptive outcomes (e.g., Cicchetti et al., 1995; Frick & Morris, 2004; Kranzler et al., 2016).

Saarni and the CASEL model identify the significance of attending to relationships in attaining emotional competence. Relationship skills include the behaviours necessary to develop and maintain positive relationships within a child's particular cultural and social context. Specific behaviours include communication and listening skills, cooperation and conflict resolution skills (Weissberg et al., 2015). Of note, social awareness, perspective-taking, empathy and the ability to regulate and manage emotions are all integrally related to relationships skills. According to Saarni (1999), awareness of emotional communication within relationships suggests recognition that emotions may be communicated differently in the context of different types of relationships. For example, a child may feel safer communicating his/her frustration or disappointment in the context of a parent–child relationship than in the context of a teacher–student relationship. Thus, the ability to differentially regulate and express emotions across different contexts and relationships is an important part of emotional competence.

Saarni's eighth skill—the capacity for emotional self-efficacy—highlights an individual's acceptance and validation of one's own feelings. Emotional self-efficacy does not imply that one experiences only positive emotions, but instead suggests that a person is confident in his or her ability to regulate a range of emotions and learn from emotional experiences (Saarni, 1999). A person with emotional self-efficacy trusts his or her emotional experience and may use it to guide future behaviour and choices in an adaptive way.

Finally, the CASEL model of social–emotional learning includes emphasis on responsible decision-making. Responsible decision-making involves use of the aforementioned skills and competencies to make prosocial choices that result in positive outcomes for the person and others. In addition to being aware of others and their feelings, responsible decision-making requires the individual to consider safety, behavioural norms and the consequences of different courses of actions. Responsible decision-making then may be an important and positive product of the other skills and domains (e.g., self-awareness, self-management, social awareness and relationships skills).

As noted throughout this discussion, the skills and domains of emotional (and social-emotional) competence are highly interrelated and dependent upon one another. Awareness of one's own emotions certainly precedes the ability to regulate and manage strong emotions. Social awareness of other's emotions, perspective-taking and empathy are all related to relationship skills. The ability to self-manage and regulate or cope with adverse emotions at all is necessary to differentially express emotion across different relationships. Emotion self-efficacy requires an awareness of all these processes and competencies.

It is important to point out that all of these skills and competencies develop within a developmental framework. Ideally, children learn and eventually master these important skills of emotional competence slowly and over time from infancy through adolescence.

UNDERSTANDING EMOTIONAL COMPETENCE IN A CULTURAL CONTEXT

Much like any other domain of child's development, emotional competence develops through intersecting influences of children's biologically based predisposition (e.g., temperament) and the social environment in which they live (Bronfenbrenner, 1979). The social environment includes multiple ecological systems such as the child's family, school, neighbourhood and community, and the larger culture in which the child resides. Culturally shared worldviews influence the ways in which competence is defined.

In some cultural groups, people define their sense of self primarily in relation to others in their life (Markus & Kitayama, 1991). One's familial and social roles (such as, being a father, being a daughter, being a teacher and being a citizen of a country) are primary in one's self-conceptualization, and cognitions that focus on expectations of others, one's duties and shared cultural norms guide one's behaviour in emotion-eliciting situations. Emotions may be experienced and expressed with the goal of maintaining one's relationships with others (Kitayama, Mesquita, & Karasawa, 2006). Such interdependent (Markus & Kitayama, 1991), sociocentric (Shweder & Bourne, 1984) or familial (Roland, 1988) self is considered to be most salient for individuals in Asia, Africa, the Middle East and South America.

In other cultural groups, people define their sense of self primarily in terms of their inner attributes (i.e., personality traits, feelings and thoughts), and other people are important because they provide validation of these inner attributes. For these individuals, their emotion-related decisions may be guided by their needs, desires, inner thoughts and feelings, and communication of emotions may signify their individuality (Kitayama et al., 2006). Such an independent (Markus & Kitayama, 1991) or egocentric (Shweder & Bourne, 1984) self-construal is considered to be more salient in middle-class Caucasian families in North America and Western Europe. Some psychologists (viz., Kağıtçıbaşı, 1996) have argued that urban, educated, middle-class families around the world are becoming more homogeneous due to their easy access to global media and technology, and that individuals in these families are likely to develop a more hybrid sense of self that includes an emphasis on both autonomy and relatedness. Moreover, other factors such as one's gender (Cross & Madson, 1997), family and local community, and socio-economic class (Kusserow, 2004) may also contribute to one's conceptualization of oneself along the dimensions of independence and interdependence.

The way in which one conceptualizes oneself has implications for a wide range of psychological processes including emotions. Cultural models of independence and interdependence may guide scripts about emotions, beliefs about the role of emotions in our lives, views regarding certain emotions as helpful versus harmful, as well as cultural norms about whether and how to express emotions and to whom (Kitayama et al., 2006). For example, Miyamoto and Ma (2011) suggest that in many Western cultures, one of the major scripts related to emotions is to maximize happiness, while in many Asian cultures, emotion scripts suggest a balance between positive and negative emotions. Given these differing cultural scripts, it is not surprising that individuals in Asia report feeling positive emotions less frequently than do Americans (Miyamoto & Ryff, 2011). In another study, college students in Japan reported experiencing emotions that promote social relationships (i.e., friendly feelings and guilt) more frequently and emotions that disengage or disrupt oneself from others (e.g., anger and pride) less frequently than students in the United States. This research suggests that the frequency with which people feel different emotions may vary across cultures.

Cultural differences have also been found in whether and how one expresses their emotion. In a study of school-age children, those in India were less likely to report expressing their feelings of anger and sadness than children in the United States (Wilson, Raval, Salvina, Raval, & Panchal, 2012). When they chose to express these emotions, children in India were less likely to use direct verbal expressions (e.g., saying 'I am angry') than children in the United States. The children were also able to provide fairly sophisticated rationale for these emotion-related decisions. For example, when asked about their reasons for controlling or expressing their emotions, consistent with the cultural task of interdependence, Indian children reported a desire to maintain social norms as a reason to control anger and sadness more frequently than US children. In contrast, consistent with the cultural task of independence, US children reported a desire to communicate felt emotion as a reason to express their feelings more than Indian children (Wilson et al., 2012).

Individualistic and Relational Emotional Competence

To make sense of these cultural differences in emotion-related processes, Fredlmeier, Corapci and Cole (2011) distinguish between individualist emotional competence (for individuals with independent self-construal) and relational emotional competence (for individuals with interdependent self-construal). Although the authors do not outline specific components of these two forms of emotional competence, it is possible to discuss major components of emotional competence across models we outlined earlier (e.g., Halberstadt et al., 2001; Saarni, 1999) and how they might differ for individualistic versus relational forms of emotional competence. Specifically, awareness and identification of emotion is considered to be a critical component of emotional competence (Halberstadt et al., 2001; Saarni, 1999; Weissberg et al., 2015), which relies heavily on perceiving and appraising one's social situation (including other people one is interacting with), as well as making sense of physiological changes in one's body and one's accompanying thoughts. Some research suggests cultural differences in introceptive awareness, which is the awareness of one's bodily sensations, and differences in the conditions under which processing of bodily signals is enhanced (Maister & Tsakiris, 2014). Research also supports cultural differences in how people interpret the emotion-eliciting situation. For example, in one study where participants were asked to think about times when they succeeded, Americans were more likely to attribute it to themselves and reported feeling proud, whereas the Japanese attributed the success to luck (Imada & Ellsworth, 2011). It is likely that for individuals for whom interdependence is salient, the appraisal focuses on other people's expectations, their responses and the dynamics of the interpersonal relationship, whereas for individuals for whom independence is salient the appraisal focuses on one's own physiological reactions and cognitive processes.

Saarni (1999) specifically refers to using emotion vocabulary as an important skill for emotional competence. Studies have shown that the use of emotion words is much more common in North America than in many Asian cultures. For example, in a study where mothers and children were asked to discuss past events, Chinese immigrant children used fewer emotion words than White American children (Fivush & Wang, 2005). A series of comparative studies showed that both school-age children (Wilson et al., 2012, discussed earlier) and emerging adults (Crowe, Raval, Trivedi, Daga, & Raval, 2012) in India were less likely to directly state their feelings as a way to express them than their counterparts in the United States.

Models of emotional competence proposed in Western psychological literature (Halberstadt et al., 2001; Saarni, 1999; Weissberg et al., 2015) also refer to skills for emotion management or regulation focusing on adaptive coping. Scholars typically discuss three possible ways of responding to one's emotions. Under-regulation refers to an individual's inability to adequately control the outward expression of emotions leading to culturally inappropriate forms of expressions (e.g., hitting others or screaming when angry, crying inconsolably when sad). Over-regulation refers to exercising too much control that may lead to suppression or inhibition of emotion. Finally, adaptive regulation may include being able to control and calmly deal with the situation (Zeman, Shipman, & Suveg, 2002) or reappraisal of the situation (Gross & John, 2003). Studies have shown that under-regulation of negative emotions such as anger or sadness seems to have negative consequences across cultures. For example, children's appropriate regulation of emotion is associated with adaptive outcomes such as good peer relations, social competence or fewer behaviour problems in the United States (Eisenberg et al., 2001) and India (Raval et al., 2013). In contrast, children's under-regulation of anger and sadness has been related to child internalizing and externalizing problems across cultures including in China (Raval, Li, Deo, & Hu, 2017), India (Raval, Raval, & Deo, 2014; Raval et al., 2017) and the United States (Zeman et al., 2002). Over-regulation of emotion, specifically suppression, has been associated with poor interpersonal (Gross & John, 2003) and psychological functioning (e.g., depressed mood) among adults in the United States (Soto, Perez, Kim, Lee, & Minnick, 2011). However, these negative effects of suppression on interpersonal functioning are moderated by culture such that for Asian American women who endorsed Asian cultural values, there were fewer negative interpersonal consequences than for White American women (Butler, Lee, & Gross, 2007), and for Chinese students in Hong Kong, emotional suppression was unrelated to their psychological functioning (Soto et al., 2011).

PARENTAL CONTRIBUTIONS TO THE DEVELOPMENT OF CHILDREN'S EMOTIONAL COMPETENCE ACROSS CULTURES

Parents are a critical aspect of children's immediate ecological system, along with other adult caregivers (such as, grandparents, uncles and aunts) in the family. A large body of psychological literature focuses on the ways in which parents socialize their children with respect to emotions. This includes both direct and indirect methods of emotion socialization (Saarni, 1985). The direct methods include parents' responses to children's emotions (e.g., what parents do or say when their child expresses an emotion) and parents' discussion of emotion (e.g., while reading a storybook, discussing how characters in the story feel, or while discussing an event from the child's life). The indirect methods of socialization include parental modelling (e.g., what parents do when they experience an emotion), where children learn by observing their parents. An emerging body of research shows that there are differences in these methods of socialization employed by parents across cultures.

With respect to the first method of emotion socialization, several research studies have examined cross-cultural differences in parents' responses to children's emotions. For example, in a study that compared parents' responses to children's emotions between two communities in Nepali villages (Cole, Tamang, & Shreshta, 2006), researchers found that caregivers in Buddhist Tamang families tended to respond to children's shame by ignoring but also teaching and nurturing while caregivers in Hindu Brahmin families predominantly responded by ignoring. In contrast for children's anger, Brahmin caregivers responded with reasoning while Buddhist caregivers were more likely to reprimand. The researchers explained how these different ways of responding fit with the differences in broader religious philosophy (Buddhist and Hindu) and social organization in the two communities. In another study, where researchers compared mothers' responses to children's emotions across two communities in India (old city and suburban) as well as middle-class mothers in United States, mothers in India were more likely to 'make their children understand' than American mothers (Raval et al., 2003). American mothers were more likely to problem solve with their children than Indian mothers. In particular, Indian mothers would help their child understand family roles, norms about emotional expression, nuances of emotion-eliciting situation in order for them to better adjust to the situation, whereas American mothers focused more on helping the children to change the situation in some form. Interestingly, both forms of parents' responses—those that focus on making the children understanding and those that help them problem solve—are related to effective emotion regulation and adaptive functioning in their respective cultural contexts (Criss, Morris, Ponce-Garcia, Cui, & Silk, 2016; Raval et al., 2014). However, parents' responses that involve scolding or punishing the child when the child expresses an emotion are related to under-regulation of emotion and maladaptive child outcomes across cultures (e.g., see Eisenberg, Fabes, & Murphy, 1996, for the United States, and Raval et al., 2014, for India).

With respect to the second method of emotion socialization—discussion of emotion—researchers have coded pre-recorded conversations between mothers and children about events from their lives or as they read a storybook together. In such conversations, it has been found that Chinese immigrant mothers referred to mental states less (Doan & Wang, 2010), used emotion words less (Fivush & Wang, 2005) and provided fewer emotion explanations and elaborations (Wang, 2001) than White American mothers. Unfortunately, researchers have not yet investigated whether the frequency of use of emotion words or references to mental states are related to children's emotional competence.

With respect to the third method of emotion socialization, parents' modelling, researchers have examined parents' reports of the extent to which they express positive and negative emotions within the family context. Overall, parents across cultures do not differ in the extent to which they express negative emotions within the family context (Raval & Walker, 2018). Further, when parents report higher likelihood of expressing negative emotions, their children are more likely to have maladaptive problems (such as, more behaviour problems and lower social competence), and this has been the case, across cultures. However, findings regarding parents' expression of positive emotion portrayed a different story. Overall, mothers in China (Camras et al., 2008) and Indian immigrant mothers in USA (McCord & Raval, 2016) were less likely to report expressing positive emotions to family members than White American mothers. Interestingly, the extent to which mothers expressed positive emotions did not seem to matter for child outcomes in an Asian sample (Eisenberg et al., 2001).

In addition to these specific methods of socialization, emotional competence develops in the context of a warm and nurturing parent–child relationship (Morris et al., 2007). Although parents across cultures may differ in how they express warmth and affection to their children, when children experience empathy from their caregivers, they are more likely to display empathy themselves (Taylor et al., 2013).

PROMOTING CHILDREN'S EMOTIONAL COMPETENCE: RECOMMENDATIONS FOR PARENTS AND EDUCATORS

Overall, the information we have summarized in this chapter suggests that various aspects related to emotional competence may differ across families, communities and cultures. With such variation, it may be difficult to outline general recommendations about how parents and educators can help children in developing skills for emotional competence that are consistent with the broader cultural norms. While we have robust frameworks and models that detail specific skills comprising emotion competence (e.g., emotion awareness, empathy, regulation and problem-solving), it is important to consider cultural and individual family factors to ensure that we are building skills in ways that are consistent with family and cultural goals.

Awareness and identification of one's emotions is an important aspect of emotional competence. To enhance the awareness of the child's own emotions, caregivers and teachers can practice modelling awareness and expression of one's own emotions. Adults may also help children to attend to and identify their bodily signals (e.g., heart rate and breathing), as well as identify their thoughts. Depending on the broader cultural norms, in some situations, directly stating how one feels (e.g., 'I am angry' or 'I am sad') may be an appropriate way of expressing one's feeling. In other situations, subtle or implicit expressions (e.g., communicating anger through the tone of voice, describing the emotion-eliciting situation and letting the other person infer what one is feeling) may be the most appropriate course of action. What is appropriate may depend on the child's age, who is present, public versus private setting and norms about how emotions are expressed in a particular culture or setting. Parents and teachers can discuss with the child whether it is appropriate to express how they feel in the given situation and, if so, what would be an appropriate way of expressing emotion. In summary, helping children to become aware of how they are feeling may be relevant across family and cultural contexts, as well as helping them to express their emotion in culturally appropriate ways (i.e., direct verbal, non-verbal).

There may also be cultural differences in how individuals make sense or understand a situation that causes strong emotions. For example, people from more individualistic cultures may focus on the individual's internal states such as feelings of sadness, frustration or excitement experienced as a result of a particular situation. People from more collectivistic cultures may acknowledge these internal states and focus more on the situation's impact on one's relationships with others or impact on a group. Parents and teachers can also help children make sense of the situation that caused the emotion in a way that is consistent with their family and cultural norms.

Emotional competence in relationship to others can be facilitated by parents and teachers who model awareness of others' emotions and empathetic responses to children. Likewise, engaging children in prosocial behaviour (e.g., volunteering time and donating money/goods) that demonstrates compassion for others will support the development of emotional competence in relationships. Jennings and Greenberg (2009) describe the 'prosocial classroom' where 'emotionally competent teachers set the tone of the classroom' by modelling respectful and empathic behaviours (p. 492).

Parents and teachers are salient models for emotion regulation and problem-solving. Children learn to cope with strong emotions by watching the people around them. Children observe what their mother, father, other adults in the family and teachers do when they get angry or upset. These are important learning opportunities for children where they learn cultural norms about how to behave when one is feeling a certain emotion. As such, adults can teach skills for emotional competence by demonstrating adaptive coping in their own lives. Caregivers and teachers can model strategies such as taking deep breaths, moving away from the situation to calm down or to reappraise the situation when feeling distressed. In addition to modelling, adults can explicitly teach children to take deep breaths, walk away from a situation or find something else to do to distract themselves from a distressing event. It is useful for adults and children to practise these strategies in neutral and non-distressing emotional times and plan together for situations in which these strategies may be useful.

In terms of the regulation of strong emotions and behaviour, parents and teachers may also take a more active role in helping children to regulate their emotions, particularly if they observe that the child is not being able to control the outward expression as evident in behaviours such as aggression, screaming, or crying inconsolably. Specifically, parents and teachers can help children to calm down by gently talking to them, by physically comforting them (e.g., a gentle pat on the shoulder), helping them to think about the situation in a different way, or helping them to focus on something else. Depending on the cultural norms and the situation, parents may provide explanations (e.g., about social roles, about the situation and others' behaviour, and about the nature of the emotion) or they may help children in resolving the situation. Consideration of the child's age is really critical here so much so such that with preschool-age children, the parents and teachers may use strategies such as physical comforting or distraction whereas with older children, helping them to problem solve or providing them with an expiation may be possible. Research across cultures shows that at times when children are experiencing intense emotions, if parents themselves become distressed or angry and engage in punitive behaviours (e.g., scolding the child, telling the child they will be punished or will not get a desired item), this does not help children in calming down and in the long run parents' punitive responses may lead to child behaviour problems. Relatedly, when parents and teachers themselves experience emotions such as anger and sadness, it is important that they model for children how to calmly respond. Research across cultures shows that when parents express intense negative emotions in the family context, their children are less likely to learn how to regulate their emotions, and in turn, may be more likely to experience behaviour problems.

Let us return to the examples of Emily and Rohan that we discussed at the beginning of this chapter. Both Emily and Rohan would benefit from adult support in becoming aware of their emotional experiences. Rohan would benefit from identifying his feelings and thinking through possible ways of coping, which may include taking deep breaths to continue to stay calm, seeking adult help by approaching a teacher and describing the situation, and if no adult is immediately available, focusing on something else. It may be that Rohan continues to look down as though he is still doing the assigned work because he is not sure how to best express his feelings or to approach the child who is engaging in disruptive behaviours. The adult may coach Rohan regarding how he can express his frustration in a culturally appropriate way within the classroom setting (e.g., through subtle facial or verbal expression), as well as how he can approach the other child (e.g., calmly ask the other child to stop).

Emily would benefit from instruction in identifying how her behaviour (e.g., pushing and yelling) makes others feel. She could be taught to recognize early signs of frustration and identify culturally appropriate ways to express her frustration (e.g., by stating that she is angry) and cope with her feelings. The verbal expression of emotion might prompt adults (e.g., coach and parents) to support Emily in coping with her difficult feelings. This support will be important for Emily to be able to enact adaptive emotion regulation skills. Upon realizing that Emily is distressed, a coach could calmly and physically guide her out of the situation and prompt her to use an adaptive coping strategy (e.g., taking deep breaths). Emily will benefit from specific instructions and opportunities to practise new emotion regulation skills when she is calm. Once Emily has learned how to calm down and regulate her emotions, she can learn about problem-solving and making adaptive choices. The pros and cons of behaviours such as pushing and yelling may be considered alongside of the consequences for remaining calm, following the rules of the game and working hard at basketball. Emily can practise considering the consequences of her actions through role-play and discussion. Direct instruction in problem-solving will help Emily identify and ultimately enact behavioural choices that result in positive consequences for her and for others around her.

In summary, skills in calming down and making prosocial behavioural choices can be modelled and explicitly taught and reinforced by parents, adult family members, teachers, counsellors or other school professionals in a home or school setting and can be practised at home. In thinking through the most appropriate strategies for emotion regulation, consideration of the child's age, family or school context and the broader cultural norms are critical.

REFERENCES

Bronfenbrenner, U. (1979). *The ecology of human development.* Boston, MA: Harvard University Press.

Benson, P. L. (1990). *The troubled journey: A portrait of 6th–12th grade youth.* Minneapolis, MN: Search Institute.

Butler, E. A., Lee, T. L., & Gross, J. J. (2007). Emotion regulation and culture: Are the social consequences of emotion suppression culture-specific? *Emotion, 7*(1), 30–48.

Camras, L., Kolmodin, K., & Chen, Y. (2008). Mothers' self-reported emotional expression in Mainland Chinese, Chinese American and European American families. *International Journal of Behavioral Development, 32*(5), 459–463.

Cicchetti, D., Ackerman, B. P., & Izard, C. E. (1995). Emotions and emotion regulation in developmental psychopathology. *Development and Psychopathology, 7*(1), 1–10.

Cole, P. M., Tamang, B. L., & Shrestha, S., (2006). Cultural variations in the socialization of young children's anger and shame. *Child Development, 77*(5), 1237–1251.

Cross, S. E., & Madson, L. (1997). Models of the self: Self-construals and gender. *Psychological Bulletin, 122*(1), 5–37.

Criss, M. M., Morris, A. S., Ponce-Garcia, E., Cui, L., & Silk, J. S. (2016). Pathways to adaptive emotion regulation among adolescents from low income families. *Family Relations, 65*(3), 517–529.

Crowe, M. L., Raval, V. V., Trivedi, S. S., Daga, S. S., & Raval, P. H. (2012). Processes of emotion communication and control: A comparison of India and United States [Special issue: 'Culture as process: Dynamics of cultural stability and change']. *Social Psychology, 43*(4), 205–214.

Doan, S. N., & Wang, Q. (2010). Maternal discussions of mental states and behaviors: Relations to emotion situation knowledge in European American and immigrant Chinese children. *Child Development, 81*(5), 1490–1503.

Durlak, J. A., Domitrovich, D. E., Weissberg, R. P., & Gullotta, T. P. (Eds.). (2015). *Handbook of social and emotional learning research and practice*. New York, NY: The Guilford Press.

Eisenberg, N., Fabes, R. A., & Murphy, B. C. (1996). Parents' reactions to children's negative emotions: Relations to children's social competence and comforting behavior. *Child Development, 67*(5), 2227–2247.

Eisenberg, N., Fabes, R. A., Murphy, B., Maszk, P., Smith, M., & Karbon, M. (1995). The role of emotionality and regulation in children's social functioning: A longitudinal study. *Child Development, 66*(5), 1360–1384.

Eisenberg, N., Gershoff, E. T., Fabes, R. A., Shepard, S. A., Cumberland, A. J., Losoya, S. H., & Murphy, B. C. (2001). Mother's emotional expressivity and children's behavior problems and social competence: Mediation through children's regulation. *Developmental Psychology, 37*(4), 475–490.

Eisenberg, N., Liew, J., & Pidada, S. U. (2001). The relations of parental emotional expressivity with quality of Indonesian children's social functioning. *Emotion, 1*(2), 116.

Eisenberg, N., & Morris, A. S. (2002). Children's emotion-related regulation. In R. V. Kail (Ed.), *Advances in child development & behavior* (Vol. 30, pp. 190–229). San Diego, CA: Academic Press.

Eisenberg, N., & Spinrad, T. L. (2004). Emotion-related regulation: Sharpening the definition. *Child Development, 75*(2), 334–339.

Eisenberg, N., Spinrad, T. L., & Morris, A. S. (2002). Regulation, resiliency, and quality of social functioning. *Self and Identity, 1*, 121–128.

Fivush, R., & Wang, Q. (2005). Emotion talk in mother—child conversations of the shared past: The effects of culture, gender, and event valence. *Journal of Cognition and Development, 6*(4), 489–506.

Frick, P., & Morris, A. S. (2004). Temperament and developmental pathways to severe conduct problems. *Journal of Clinical Child and Adolescent Psychology, 33*(1), 54–68.

Friedlmeier, W., Corapci, F., & Cole, P. M. (2011). Emotion socialization in cross-cultural perspective. *Social and Personality Psychology Compass, 5*(7), 410–427.

Goleman, D. (1995). *Emotional intelligence: Why it can matter more than IQ*. New York, NY: Bantam books.

Gross, J. J., & John, O. P. (2003). Individual differences in two emotion regulation processes: Implications for affect, relationships, and well-being. *Journal of Personality and Social Psychology, 85*(2), 348–362.

Halberstadt, A. G., Denham, S. A., & Dunsmore, J. C. (2001). Affective social competence. *Social Development, 10*(1), 79–119.

Imada, T., & Ellsworth, P. C. (2011). Proud Americans and lucky Japanese: Cultural differences in appraisal and corresponding emotion. *Emotion, 11*(2), 329–345.

Jennings, P. A., & Greenberg, M. T. (2009). The prosocial classroom: Teacher social and emotional competence in relation to student and classroom outcomes. *Review of Educational Research, 79*(1), 491–525.

Kağıtçıbaşı, C. (1996). The autonomous-relational self: A new synthesis. *European Psychologist, 1*(3), 180–186.

Kitayama, S., Mesquita, B., & Karasawa, M. (2006). Cultural affordances and emotional experience: Socially engaging and disengaging emotions in Japan and the United States. *Journal of Personality and Social Psychology, 91*(5), 890–903.

Kranzler, A., Young, J. F., Hankin, B. L., Abela, J. R., Elias, M. J., & Selby, E. A. (2016). Emotional awareness: A transdiagnostic predictor of depression and anxiety for children and adolescents. *Journal of Clinical Child and Adolescent Psychology, 45*(3), 262–269.

Kusserow, A. (2004). *American individualisms: Child rearing and social class in three neighborhoods.* New York, NY: Palgrave Macmillan.

Maister, L., & Tsakiris, M. (2014). My face, my heart: Cultural differences in integrated bodily self-awareness. *Cognitive Neuroscience, 5*(1), 10–16.

Markus, H. R., & Kitayama, S. (1991). Culture and the self: Implications for cognition, emotion, and motivation. *Psychological Review, 98*(2), 224–253.

Mayer, J. D., & Salovey, P. (1997). What is emotional intelligence? In P. Salovey & D. Sluyter (Eds.), *Emotional development and emotional intelligence: Educational implications* (pp. 3–31). New York: Basic Books.

McCord, B. L., & Raval, V. V. (2016). Asian Indian immigrant and White American maternal emotion socialization and child socio-emotional functioning. *Journal of Child and Family Studies, 25*(2), 464–474.

Miyamoto, Y., & Ma, X. (2011). Dampening or savoring positive emotions: A dialectical cultural script guides emotion regulation. *Emotion, 11*(6), 1346–1357.

Miyamoto, Y., & Ryff, C. D. (2011). Cultural differences in the dialectical and non-dialectical emotional styles and their implications for health. *Cognition and Emotion, 25,* 22–39.

Morris, A. S., Silk, J. S., Steinberg, L., Myers, S. S., & Robinson, L. R. (2007). The role of the family context in the development of emotion regulation. *Social Development, 16*(2), 361–388.

Raval, V. V., Li, X., Deo, N., & Hu, J. (2017). Reports of maternal socialization goals, emotion socialization behaviors, and child socio-emotional functioning in China and India [Advance online publication]. *Journal of Family Psychology.* doi:10.1037/fam0000336

Raval, V. V., Raval, P. H., & Deo, N. (2014). Mothers' socialization goals, mothers' emotion socialization behaviors, child emotion regulation, and child socio-emotional functioning in urban India. *Journal of Early Adolescence, 34*(2), 229–250.

Raval, V. V., Raval, P. H., Salvina, J., Wilson, S., & Writer, S. (2013). Mothers' socialization of children's emotion in India and United States: A cross- and within-culture comparison. *Social Development, 22*(3), 467–484.

Raval, V. V., & Walker, B. L. (2018). Unpacking 'culture': Caregiver socialization of emotion and child functioning in culturally diverse families. Manuscript under review.

Roland, A. (1988). *In search of self in India and Japan: Towards a cross-cultural psychology.* Princeton, NJ: Princeton University Press.

Saarni, C. (1985). Indirect processes in affect socialization. In L. Michael & C. Saarni (Eds.), *The socialization of emotions* (pp. 187–209). New York, NY: Plenum Press.

———. (1999). *The development of emotional competence.* New York NY: Guilford Press.

Shweder, R. A., & Bourne, E. J. (1984). Does the concept of the person vary cross culturally? In R. A. Shweder & R. A. Levine (Eds.), *Cultural theory* (pp. 158–199). Cambridge, MA: Cambridge University Press.

Soto, J. A., Perez, J., A., Kim, Y., Lee, E. A., & Minnick, M. R. (2011). Is expressive suppression always associated with poorer psychological functioning? A cross-cultural comparison between European Americans and Hong Kong Chinese. *Emotion, 11*(6), 1450–1455.

Taylor, Z. E., Eisenberg, N., Spinrad, T. L., Eggum, N. D., & Sulik, M. J. (2013). The relations of ego-resiliency and emotion socialization to the development of empathy and prosocial behavior across early childhood. *Emotion, 13*(5), 822–831.

Thompson, R. A., & Meyer, S. (2007). Socialization of emotion regulation in the family. In J. J. Gross (Ed.), *Handbook of emotion regulation* (pp. 249–268). New York, NY: Guilford Publications.

Wang, Q. (2001). 'Did you have fun?' American and Chinese mother–child conversations about shared emotional experiences. *Cognitive Development, 16*(2), 693–715.

Weissberg, R. P., Durlak, J. A., Domitrovich, D. E., & Gullotta, T. P. (2015). Social and emotional learning: Past, present, and future. In J. A. Durlak, D. E. Domitrovich, R. P. Weissberg, & T. P. Gullotta (Eds.), *Handbook of social and emotional learning research and practice* (pp. 3–19). New York, NY: The Guilford Press.

Wilson, S., Raval, V. V., Raval, P. H., Salvina, J., & Panchal, I. N. (2012). Emotional expression and control in school-age children in India and United States. *Merrill-Palmer Quarterly, 58*(1), 50–76.

Zeman, J., Shipman, K., & Suveg, C. (2002). Anger and sadness regulation: Predictions to internalizing and externalizing symptoms in children. *Journal of Clinical Child and Adolescent Psychology, 31*(3), 393–398.

Chapter 10

Self-compassion as a Foundation for the Development of Character Strengths in Young Adults

Salome Divya Vijaykumar, Ranjitha Kumar,
Avneet Kaur, Vibha Bhat, Ritu Verma
and Anirudh Kedia

In the face of failure and threat, what defines us as individuals is not the misfortune itself, but how we overcome threats to develop traits of love, empathy and resilience. Failure, misfortune and challenges are an unfortunate but a necessary part of our lives that provide us the base to becoming better human beings. In the recent years, the primary measure of psychological health and the predictor of resilience-related qualities has been self-esteem. Though the literature on self-esteem is vast, William James, one of the primary thinkers in psychology, proposed in 1890 that self-esteem involves evaluating personal performances in comparison to set in domains of perceived importance, and looking to others' evaluations of the self.

However, self-esteem has been consistently criticized for the incomplete role it plays in development of positive mental health over the past few years; the repercussions of having a sense of esteem, derived from social consensus, significantly outweighed the positive mental health benefits (Neff, 2003a). Furthermore, an overemphasis on self-esteem has been shown to lead to the development of an inflated sense of self and out-group prejudice. Neff in 2003 was one of the few researchers who attempted to introduce an alternate concept that dealt with attitude towards oneself. Her concept, self-compassion, is the subject of this article. She defines self-compassion as

> being touched by and open to one's own suffering, not avoiding or disconnecting from it, generating the desire to alleviate one's suffering and to heal oneself with kindness…involves offering non-judgmental understanding to one's pain, inadequacies and failures, so that one's experience is seen as part of the larger human experience. (Neff, 2003a, pp. 86–87)

Self-compassion as a construct has also been explored beyond its definitions. There are three faces to self-compassion, namely, (a) self-kindness, that is, the process of extending kindness to oneself as a replacement of harsh judgement, (b) common humanity, that is, seeing one's experiences as part of the larger human experience, and (c) mindfulness, that is, holding one's thoughts and feelings in balanced awareness rather than overidentifying with them (Neff, 2003a).

Self-compassion has also been equated with 'mental space' through which one offers kindness to oneself. By not overidentifying with one's emotional experience through the face of mindfulness, individuals allow themselves to define their experience as incidents not isolated, but a part of the broader experience of existence (Neff, 2003a). However, it is important to note that self-compassion is a construct that has many similar and overlapping variables; self-compassion is a concept distinct from self-pity, self-concept and self-esteem.

SELF-COMPASSION: A DEMOGRAPHIC UNDERSTANDING

Self-compassion is a highly multidimensional construct. It has been posited that the adolescence represents the period of lowest self-compassion in comparison to all the other developmental stages (Neff, 2003a). With an increase in cognitive capabilities of self-reflection, metacognition and perspective-taking, combined with environmental factors such as peer pressure and hostility from social groups, can lead to the outcomes of unfavourable self-evaluations and increased self-absorptions—two factors that contribute negatively to the development of self-compassion.

Neff (2003b) found that women had significantly less self-compassion than men; the subscales which contributed to these scores included a higher score of self-judgement, isolation when confronted with painful situations and overidentification of negative emotions. Common parlance would dictate women to be higher in levels of self-compassion, but due to the variables of self-criticism and evaluation, women significantly are less self-compassionate. However, it is interesting to note that Buddhist men and women did not possess a significant difference in self-compassion when administered with the same scale (Neff, 2003b). The study went on to suggest that perhaps the practice of Buddhist meditation is a possible means of achieving mental health and wellness.

Though self-compassion is a concept derived from Eastern cultures especially that of Buddhism, people from Asian countries have lesser levels of self-compassion (Neff, 2003b). Although individuals from collectivistic cultures have more interdependent sense of self, due to which they are likely to possess more self-compassion, this was not the case. The variables of self-criticism and negative self-evaluation significantly influence level of self-compassion, resulting in lower self-compassion among Asians from Eastern cultures.

From the review of self-compassion as a positive construct, there are certain observable qualities of self-compassion that can be made: (a) although it facilitates growth at a personal level, its effects manifest at a macro level, (b) when internalized, it can be a powerful source for change, (c) the benefits of self-compassion as a self-related construct has benefits that outweigh problems of excess and (d) it leads to a stable sense of self-worth. Research also shows positive associations between self-compassion, self-esteem and self-concept with constructs of character-strengths such as optimism, wisdom and curiosity (Neff, Kirkpatrick, & Rude, 2007). This chapter attempts to review the relationship and effects of self-related constructs, and compare the effects of shortages with those of excesses. Self-compassion is seen as a positive self-related construct that can buffer against such excesses, for example, an inflated self-esteem, which could be detrimental to the development of certain character strengths. Self-compassion has also been proven to alleviate levels of anxiety and depression and reduce paranoid beliefs (Abercrombie, Zamora, & Korn, 2007; Mills, Gilbert, Bellew, McEwan, & Gale, 2007). There is evidence to show how self-compassion can also work preventively in mental health: it acts as a buffer against pathology, prevents burnout and helps during periods of transition (Terry, Leary, & Mehta, 2012). It has been effective across various populations such as adolescents, counsellors, clergy, cancer patients and war veterans (Barnard & Curry 2012; Beaumont, Durkin, Martin, & Carson, 2016; Dahm et al., 2015).

Self-compassion helps an individual treat oneself with kindness and hold all aspects of oneself in mindful awareness, thereby facilitating self-acceptance. Self-acceptance plays a crucial role in meeting the developmental needs of intimacy and love during young adulthood.

It is during this stage where crystallization of various aspects of identity, including character strengths, takes place. Self-compassion by nature is an internalizing process with its effects manifesting in the social environment. This study proposes a model basing self-compassion as a foundation for the development of character strengths in young adults. A mindfulness-based self-compassion intervention has been developed for young adults between ages 18 and 21 to establish the model.

SELF-COMPASSION IN RELATION TO SELF-ESTEEM AND SELF-CONCEPT

Self-compassion helps one to face and recognize pain and not avoid it. Self-compassion is often confused with two similar terms—self-esteem and self-concept. However, they are not the same and must be differentiated while defining self-compassion. As mentioned earlier, self-esteem is the degree to which the self is judged to be competent in life domains which are deemed important (James, 1890). One important thing to note while discussing self-esteem is that it also entails the perceived evaluations of self on the part of the others apart from one's own assessment of oneself (Cooley, 1964, as cited in Neff & Vonk, 2009). Therefore, although self-esteem and self-compassion may seem similar in that they are both related to the experience of positive emotions towards the self, self-esteem seems to be based solely on positive self-evaluations (Harter, 1999, as cited in Neff & Vonk, 2009). Self-compassion, contrastingly, does not relate to evaluations or cognitive representations about the self but refers to an acceptance of all aspects of one's experience. Moreover, self-esteem is related to agency and competition whereas self-compassion is related more to caring and communion (Helgeson & Fritz, 1999). This distinction is reflected in the social mentality theory: Self-compassion leads to the inhibition of the threat system, activated in times of insecurity and defensiveness and promotes the functioning of the self-soothing system which is associated with feelings of secure attachment (Gilbert, 1989, as cited in Neff & Vonk, 2009).

High level of self-esteem has its drawbacks. The attainment of high self-esteem has been related to narcissistic personality traits and self-rumination (Neff & Vonk, 2009). Individuals with an inflated self-esteem tend to make exaggerated assessments of their capabilities, leading to commitments that fall outside their actual capabilities, causing failure (Baumeister, 1993). This failure may lead to self-criticism, causing anxiety.

Contrastingly, self-compassion predicted more stable feelings of self-worth and was less dependent on specific consequences as compared to self-esteem (Neff & Vonk, 2009). A higher level of self-compassion also leads to a more mindful perception of one's inadequacies. This marks a shift from extensive processing of thoughts related to the self, to experiencing the present (Gilbert, 1989). Self-compassionate individuals also form a more accurate self-concept than individuals with high self-esteem; as individuals with high self-esteem are dismissive of negative feedback from others and take less responsibility for damaging actions (Sedikedes, 1993). Self-compassionate individuals, on the other hand, are more accepting of their inadequacies and form a self-concept that is based in reality (Neff & Vonk, 2009).

Self-compassion is often used interchangeably with the term 'self-pity'. However, they are not the same thing. Self-pity can be defined as the sympathetic heartfelt sorrow for oneself prompted by one's own physical or mental suffering, distress or unhappiness (Stober, 2003). Self-pity as a construct makes the individual feel highly disconnected from others; individuals experiencing this emotional state tend to overidentify with their own suffering. They are engrossed in their own emotional reaction to the extent that it becomes difficult for them to remove themselves from the situation and look at it more objectively (Bennett-Goleman, 2001, as cited in Neff, 2003b). It entails a certain degree of self-absorption and does not involve being self-centred (Neff,

2003b). Since self-compassion requires metacognitive processing that makes allowance to relate one's experiences to that of others, it breaks the cycle of overidentification and decreases the egocentric feelings. This helps one have a larger perspective on their suffering which in turn offers greater clarity on the same (Neff, 2003b).

CRYSTALLIZATION OF PERSONALITY

Researchers hold different opinions as to when personality of an individual crystallizes, while most identify adolescence or young adulthood as the milestones for crystallization of personality (Costa & McCrae, 1988; McCrae & Costa, 1982; Stein, Newcomb, & Bentler, 1986), some also suggest that personality stability should not be studied independent of stability in the external social environment (Ardelt, 2000). Personality, along with self-concept, is highly stable from years 25 to 90, attaining stability at 30 (Costa & McCrae, 1988); measures of self-concept for 30-year-olds are a good predictor for personality at the age of 80 (McCrae & Costa, 1982). During the transition from adolescence to adulthood, there is an increase in maturity, along with maturity-stability effects (individuals with mature personalities during adolescence show lesser changes in personality during adulthood) (Donnellan, Conger, & Burzette, 2007; Roberts, Caspi, & Moffitt, 2001). Furthermore, personality is the most stable during the transition towards young adulthood (Stein, Newcomb, & Bentler, 1986). Personality stability is usually related to genetic factors while changes in personality traits are attributed to the environmental changes (McGue, Bacon, & Lykken, 1993).

Personality maturation is moderated by formation of the first partner relationship, occurring in young adulthood. It is during this age that people are entering the workforce and also form committed partner relationships (Neyer & Lehnart, 2007; Srivastava, John, Gosling, & Potter, 2003). Furthermore, changes in social relationships contribute to a stability rather than change in personality (Neyer & Voigt, 2004), and regulatory relationship changes stabilize the personality of an individual (Lang, Reschke, & Neyer, 2006). Similarly, personality development is influenced by peer and family relationships (Neyer & Lehnart, 2007).

The rationale of choosing the age group of 18–21 was that this is the age at which young adults experience the conflict between intimacy vs.

isolation (Erikson & Erikson, 1998). Furthermore, it is during this age that individuals begin to form intimate connections, the consequences of which could enhance or hinder the attainment of the virtue, that is, love, which, as explained later on, leads internally to the development of self-compassion.

Intimacy vs. Isolation and Self-compassion

Social Connectedness

Social connectedness can help one overcome the feelings of isolation and loneliness through participation in activities, such as voluntary work, playing sports, shopping and culture-related activities, which involve interaction with other people (Toepoel, 2013). Self-compassion is related to sense of connectedness (Neff, 2003b); individuals reported feeling more socially connected on inculcating self-compassion (Neff, Kirkpatrick, & Rude, 2007). Social connectedness, in turn, along with a lower usage of first person plural pronouns (e.g., we, our) has been linked with lesser scores on depression scales (Neff, Rude, & Kirkpatrick, 2007). Moreover, individuals who used first person plural pronouns while talking about their weaknesses showed more self-compassion (Neff, Kirkpatrick, & Rude, 2007). Loving-kindness meditation, a form of meditation specific to inculcating self-compassion, increases social connectedness as well as positive feelings even towards people one does not know (Hutcherson, Seppala, & Gross, 2008).

Self-compassion and Romantic Relationships

Romantic relationships are one of the main hubs of intimate connections, an important form of intimacy explored by Erikson in the psychosocial stage of 'intimacy vs. isolation' (Beyers & Seiffge-Krenke, 2010; Erikson & Erikson, 1998). Self-compassion helps in the maintenance of relationships when the individuals have the motivation to make up for their mistakes (Baker & McNulty, 2011). This motivation is dependent upon the gender and personality factors, such that men who scored high on conscientiousness measures showed higher motivation to correct their interpersonal mistakes and vice versa; for women, self-compassion always produced positive results for their relationships as well as motivation to correct interpersonal mistakes, regardless of their scores on conscientiousness (Baker & McNulty, 2011). High self-compassion is linked to compromise in relationships, authenticity, relational well-being and low preference of one's own needs over the other's (Yarnell & Neff, 2013). Furthermore, self-compassion in individuals is associated with positive relationship behaviour (Neff & Beretvas, 2012).

High self-compassion is related to forgiveness, compassion for humanity, greater empathy and so on among adults and practising mediators (Neff & Pommier, 2013). These are important qualities that help in development of secure relationships. Forgiveness in romantic relationships is an important factor during an incident of infidelity (Gunderson & Ferrari, 2008). Empathy affects relationship satisfaction (Davis & Oathout, 1987), and perception of partner empathy is related positively to relationship satisfaction (Long, Angera, Carter, Nakamoto, & Kalso, 1999).

Attachment and Self-compassion

Attachment styles themselves can be seen as different forms or degrees of intimacy, or as precursors to future romantic relationships. Attachment styles are linked to adult romantic relationships; and in fact, attachment style in childhood can act as a predictor for future adult relationships (Feeney & Noller, 1990). Attachment in infancy as well as adulthood is an important factor that determines the extent to which one fulfils the need to develop romantic love and relationships (Snyder & Lopez, 2007). Self-compassion mediates the relationship between attachment orientation (i.e., secure, anxious, disorganized or avoidant) and mental health; attachment anxiety and attachment avoidance are significantly negatively associated with self-compassion (Raque-Bogdan, Ericson, Jackson, Martin, & Bryan, 2011). Furthermore, self-compassion mediates the relationship between attachment anxiety and subjective well-being (Wei, Liao, & Tsun-Yao Ku, 2011).

Development of Self-compassion

Self-compassion must be promoted for benefits without the side effects of self-esteem (Neff, 2009). Self-compassion protects one against social comparison, closed-mindedness, stable self-worth and so on (Neff & Vonk, 2009). Furthermore, parental (especially maternal) support, secure attachment, as well as pleasant functioning of the family—all predict higher self-compassion among teenagers (Neff & McGehee, 2009). Fear of compassion towards oneself is related to fear of compassion from others; and that one of the factors that both self-compassion and compassion for others are associated with is insecure attachment (Gilbert, McEwan, & Matos, 2011). Cognitive factors as well as family are important predictors of individual differences in self-compassion among adolescents and young adults (Neff & McGehee, 2009). Childhood abuse and neglect is related to low self-compassion (Tanakaa, Wekerle, Schmuck, Paglia-Boak, & Team, 2011). Certain interventions have been proposed in order to enhance the development of self-compassion, which will be discussed further.

DEVELOPMENT OF CHARACTER STRENGTHS

According to the VIA classification, character is inherently assumed to be plural (Park & Peterson, 2009). Strengths, which are specific and distinguishable psychological mechanisms defining virtues, exist in degrees. The commonly held view is that character strengths are trait-like, or aspects of personality that are considered to be morally valuable. Character strengths are markers and causes of healthy lifelong development; they prevent undesirable life outcomes and buffer against stress and trauma. Young people thrive with the help of character strengths, exercising of which is associated with desirable outcomes such as leadership, school success, kindness, altruism, tolerance and ability to delay gratification. The following character strengths are consistently associated with life satisfaction: gratitude, zest, hope, curiosity and, most importantly, love. Since life satisfaction is an important predictor of well-being, it is evident that individuals must cultivate certain strengths for a psychologically good life. As society focuses on good character in young people, it is necessary that assessments of character strengths take place in an academic setting. Strengths such as love and gratitude are more closely associated with well-being than those such as creativity, appreciation of beauty and excellence, and critical thinking. Education in a formal academic setting focuses on the latter.

Thus, it is interesting to incorporate these findings into programmes that target the youth (Park & Peterson, 2006a, b, 2009; Park, Peterson, & Seligman, 2004).

Character strengths among adults and among youth are relatively stable across time. Their development across an individual's life span shows a predictable direction. Development of character strengths is influenced by a number of factors, one of which is cognitive maturation. Character strengths that are least common among children and adolescents are those that require cognitive maturation, such as forgiveness, open-mindedness, appreciation of beauty and excellence, and modesty (Park & Peterson, 2006a, b; Park, Peterson, & Seligman, 2006). An assortment of variables influences the development of character strengths and good character; these include genetic inheritance, family, community and peers. Twin studies showed that each of the character strengths were moderately heritable and so were individual differences (Steger, Hicks, Kashdan, Krueger, & Bouchard, 2007). Family environment was also found to have an influence on certain strengths (Park & Peterson, 2009).

Adolescence is a stage of character development and in early young adulthood, signs of crystallization of strengths are seen. A range of moral skills are developed, assessed and refined which allows for effective social engagement among adolescents (Hart & Carlo, 2005). The movement into formal operational stage of thinking allows the individual to interpret the social environment in novel ways (Piaget, 1952, as cited in Park & Peterson, 2009). These reflect in terms of advances in perspective-taking skills (Kohlberg, 1981), prosocial behaviours, development of altruistic tendencies (Eisenberg, Zhou, & Koller, 2001) and moral judgement oriented towards the other. Adolescence marks the beginning of an increase in the number of character strengths as the individual develops (Shoshani & Slone, 2013).

A look at brain development studies provides some answers but also raises many questions especially in terms of it practical implications and public policy. The neuronal connectivity present in the frontal lobes, which are responsible for functions such as working memory, planning, impulse control and judgement, is likely to be fully developed by early to mid-20s (Johnson, Blum, & Giedd, 2009; Sowell, Thompson,

Holmes, Jemigan, & Toga, 1999). The brain's functional organization largely consists of local interactions in children while it shifts to a more 'distributed architecture' in young adults. The weakening of connections contributed more to prediction of maturity than strengthening of connections. This is under the condition that functional connections in the brain are divided as the following: (a) strengths which were positively correlated (strengthening) with chronological age and (b) those that were negatively correlated (weakening) with chronological age. Among many identified networks, the cingulo-opercular network was found to be significant in predicting functional maturity. The anterior prefrontal cortex was also relatively significant in predicting brain maturity (Dosenbach et al., 2010).

SELF-COMPASSION AND CHARACTER STRENGTHS/VIRTUES

Peter and Seligman in the year 2005 analysed different philosophical schools and religious traditions in order to understand and classify the positive traits. With the help of the philosophies of the West, South Asia and China emerged with the understanding of moral behaviour and good life. This led to the understanding of six virtues as mentioned earlier. The convergence of the different traditions led to the development of the six virtues. Peterson and Seligman then went on to understand character strengths with the help of which core virtues could be expressed (Dahlsgaard, Peterson, & Seligman, 2005).

Self-compassionate individuals tend to show certain character strengths such as self-kindness, empathy and common humanity; other findings support these primary faces of self-compassion (Gilbert, Clarke, Hempel, Miles, & Irons, 2004; Neff, 2003b).

As discussed earlier, there exists a positive correlation between self-compassion and empathy, compassion for humanity and forgiveness. High self-compassion is associated with higher altruism, perspective-taking, tolerance and less personal distress. The association, however, differed among the participant group and the genders (Deniz, Kesici, & Sümer, 2008; Neff, 2012). Development of negative emotions leads to an inability to understand self as well as others, leading to lesser levels of tolerance and compassion (Deniz, Kesici, & Sümer, 2008).

SELF-COMPASSION AS A FOUNDATION FOR THE DEVELOPMENT OF CHARACTER STRENGTHS: A MODEL

Literature tells us the variety of roles self-compassion plays in the growth of an individual; it aids in developing self-kindness, it enables the development of empathy, and it enriches positive self-evaluation. However, most importantly, self-compassion acts as a base or a foundation on which one develops important character strengths that are translated into behaviour one has towards oneself and others.

The following is a proposed model that attempts to highlight the role that self-compassion plays in the development of character strengths.

The development of self-compassion in an individual, especially during late adolescence and young adulthood (the developmental period that is considered to be a point of lowest self-compassion), has multiple positive effects; self-acceptance being the enabler to the next step of development. The 'mental space' that an individual gives to oneself in order to not only adopt flexibility in terms of accepting mistakes, but also reducing overidentification with negative emotions is a catalyser in the resolution of the psychosocial conflict, intimacy versus isolation, as given by Erikson (1959). The resolution of this conflict not only takes one to the next psychosocial stage, but also bestows one with the virtues of love and intimacy. Love and intimacy are the central and perhaps the most important components of self-compassion, that is, an internal manifestation of self-compassion itself. Development of certain character strengths fortifies and reinforces others; the development of love and intimacy provides an individual fodder for the nourishment of related character strengths. These strengths are manifested in the social environment through social behaviour, that is, the external manifestation of self-compassion. Figure 10.1 illustrates the proposed model.

DEVELOPING LOVE BY INCULCATING CHARACTER STRENGTHS THROUGH SELF-COMPASSION AND MINDFULNESS: AN INTERVENTION

The intervention is designed for young adults, between the age of 18 and 21, and the purpose of this intervention is to guide the resolution of the conflict of intimacy vs. isolation as explained by

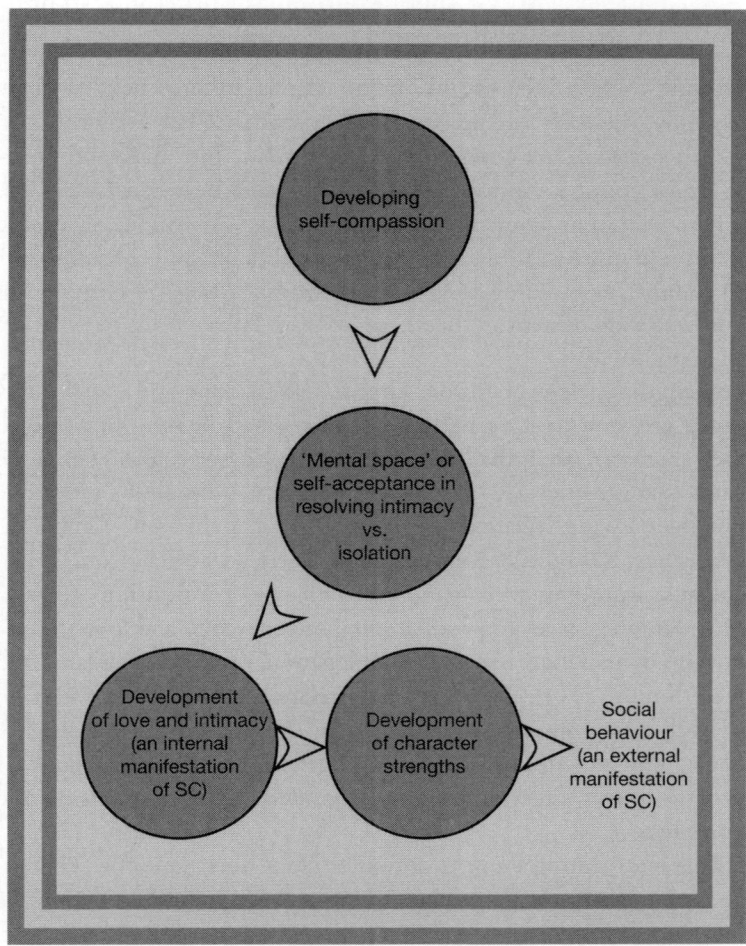

Figure 10.1 *Self-compassion as a Foundation for the Development of Character Strengths*

Erikson (1959). This intervention aims at improving the young adults' capacity to overcome the conflict, and achieve the virtue of love, by inculcating and strengthening their character strengths of gratitude, forgiveness, kindness, zest, hope and social intelligence. Love is a trait that shows how one values others and close relations in their lives. Love can be shown in the form of sharing and caring and that being reciprocated among individuals with close relations (Niemiec, 2017b). On the other hand, self-love is a way to appreciate one's self, which grows out of actions done to help us grow physically, mentally and spiritually (Khoshaba, 2012). According to Erikson's psychosocial stages of development, the successful completion of young adulthood, which is the stage between 18 and 40, leads to the attainment of the virtue of love. At this stage, young adults build more relationships, are involved in making commitments and indulge in building long-lasting bonds. Successful completion leads to the attainment of the virtue of love; failure leads to isolation (McLeod, 2017).

Strengths such as gratitude, kindness, zest, hope and social intelligence are seen to have highest correlates with love as opposed to other character strengths (Niemiec, 2017b). Love is also seen to be related to forgiveness (Al-Mabuk, Enright, & Cardis, 2006). Gratitude influences loving 'relationship maintenance' behaviour (Kubacka, Finkenauer, Rusbult, & Keijsers, 2011, as cited in Nicholson, 2011). Gratitude improves well-being and enhances relationships (Erwin, 2017). Kindness leads to positive spiral of generosity and love in relationships by making partners feel understood, cared for, validated and loved (Smith, 2014). Zest is strongly related to love, life satisfaction and well-being among students and in the workplace (Chompoo, 2016). The development and strengthening of these character strengths in this intervention will be guided by self-compassion and mindfulness.

This intervention consists of four sessions over a month. There is one session per week. For each of these sessions, a mindfulness exercise is conducted first, after which there is a discussion of the homework, accompanied by new exercises and, finally, there is an announcement of the homework for the next session. Except for the first session, this pattern is followed for all sessions. Each session has a theme, which reflects the main focus and aim of the session. The sessions are aimed at guiding the individuals through their mindful journey towards attaining love by using their character strengths; finally leading to them fully accepting and loving themselves.

Session 1
Theme: Breaking the Ice   **Time: 3 hours**

The session begins with a mindfulness self-compassion meditation, called affectionate breathing (Germer & Neff, 2013), in order to give them an idea about self-compassion mindfulness meditation. After this, participants are asked to talk about their experience while doing the meditation.

First, an ice breaker activity is conducted, wherein people get to know each other. Individuals will be paired, and some amount of time will be given to them to get to know their partner. After some time, they are asked to introduce to everyone, what they know about their partner.

Further, they are given an introduction to the concepts of self-compassion and mindfulness, the relationship between the two, as well as an introduction to character strengths in general. The aims and purpose of the intervention, along with its benefits, will be briefed to the individuals.

Finally, homework is assigned to the individuals, which involves them practising 'affectionate breathing' and 'compassionate body scan' meditation (Germer & Neff, 2013) every day, for the coming week. They are also asked to keep a self-compassion journal (Germer & Neff, 2013), and read up about their top 5 character strengths.

Session 2
Theme: Incorporating Character Strengths   **Time: 3 hours**

Now that the participants know their character strengths, they practise 'mindfulness meditation targeting a character strength' (Niemiec, 2017a), focusing especially on one of their top 5 character strengths. After the meditation, the participants talk to each other about why they picked that character strength, along with a story from their life where they used that strength.

From the second session onwards, there is a 'sharing session', where the participants talk about their experiences of practising their homework throughout the previous week, and this happens for half an hour.

Further, the individuals are told about the importance of positive self-talk in developing self-compassion, and 'taking care of the caregiver' technique (Germer & Neff, 2013) is taught to them.

As an activity to incorporate the character strength of hope, the participants are asked to formulate a future map for themselves, incorporating where and what they want to be in the next 10 years. For the strength of gratitude, participants are tasked with writing a Gratitude Letter, thanking anyone or anything as they see fit (Ackerman & Oppland, 2017). The Counting Kindness activity is initiated. This activity involves listing acts of kindness by others as well as self (Otake, Shimai, Tanaka-Matsumi, Otsui, & Fredrickson, 2006). The Compass Points game is conducted for social intelligence (Allen, 2015). Identification of grudges, the emotions they produce and how these affect one's behaviour is done by participants (Rashid & Anjum, 2005). The participants also write a self-compassionate letter addressed to themselves.

Finally, the homework is given to them, which involves them practising 'self-compassion break' as well as 'noting your emotions', which are mindfulness meditation techniques (Germer & Neff, 2013), every day, for the coming week. The participants are also asked to do one thing that they love on any one day in the coming week, for an hour, and they must continue to maintain their self-compassion journal. They are also asked to practise 'in the moment loving acts' (Niemiec, 2017b). They will be asked to maintain a Gratitude Jar; they will write down three things that they are grateful for everyday and put it in the jar. The Counting Kindness activity will continue for the rest of the week. The participants are also encouraged to engage in any physical activity of their choosing to boost zest. Participants write five personal feelings daily for four weeks and monitor patterns (Rashid & Anjum, 2005). Participants make a list of individuals against whom they hold a grudge, then either meet them personally to discuss it or visualize whether bygones can be bygones (Rashid & Anjum, 2005).

Session 3

Theme: Overcoming the Barriers **Time: 3 hours**

The third session begins with Strong Mindfulness (Niemiec, 2017a), a technique that helps one overcome the barriers one might face while engaging in mindful meditation through their character strengths.

The participants then share their experience for half an hour of doing the homework that was assigned to them in the previous session.

Further, 'the criticizer, the criticized, and the compassionate observer' technique (Germer & Neff, 2013) is taught to the individuals, and all of them are advised to come forth and try the technique. The technique of Self-Compassion Pause (Germer & Neff, 2013), which helps one deal with instances that entail negative thoughts about self, is taught to the participants, and they are given a Self-Compassion Pause worksheet as a hand-out.

As an activity to incorporate the character strength of hope, the participants are instructed to take five minutes to think of some optimistic ideas for themselves or for their future, and write them down on a paper. A meditation session on gratitude is conducted where participants are encouraged to contemplate on gratitude and it significance as seen in their lives. Self-kindness exercise is done by participants as they write down ways in which they can and will try to be kind to themselves. For the strength zest, individuals are asked to list down activities they enjoy engaging in and that provide them with a sense of purpose. The opposition listening task is done (Treder-Wolff, 2014). Participants are asked to remember times when they offended someone and were forgiven (Rashid & Anjum, 2005).

Finally, the session ends with homework, which includes continued writing of the self-compassion journal and practising the 'Soften, Soothe, Allow' meditation (Germer & Neff, 2013) every day for the coming week. Furthermore, the participants are instructed to read up about any personality who overcame adversities and to use that as an inspiration. Participants are encouraged to go on brief Gratitude Walks where they appreciate their surroundings (Ackerman & Oppland, 2017). They are encouraged to indulge in one act of kindness per day. It is suggested that they enjoy a leisure hour everyday so as to energize themselves (Hood, 2014). Acts of love include sitting together with loved ones and discuss how the day went for them and yourself. Perceiving and acknowledge three sincere gestures of a friend is another task (Rashid & Anjum, 2005).

Session 4
Theme: Spreading the Love   **Time: 3 hours**

The last session starts with a meditation called 'Lovingkindness for Someone You Care About', followed by 'Lovingkindness for Ourselves'; these techniques are originally from Making Friends with Yourself (MFY), a self-compassion intervention for teens and young adults (Bluth, Gaylord, Campo, Mullarkey, & Hobbsc, 2016).

The participants then share about their previous week's homework, and about how they have felt writing the self-compassion journal for this entire month. The participants are asked to think about one of the things they dislike about themselves. Then, they are asked to write a letter about the same to their own self, but as someone else who loves and cares for them. This could be an actual or an imaginary person. This is the technique of 'exploring self-compassion through writing' (Germer & Neff, 2013).

As an activity to incorporate the character strength of hope, the participants are asked to think of some of the recent negative things that happened to them, and list out one positive thing about each of these negative events. In order to inculcate zest and kindness, the participants are asked to go around and socialize with each other while saying something kind about them. After this, participants are asked about the number of times they said 'thanks' and whether they meant it (Rashid & Anjum, 2005). Practice to use the Using Emotional Freedom Technique is done (Santilli, 2015).

The mp3 files for all meditations and more are provided to the individuals, using which they can continue working on their self-compassion levels, as well as on their character strengths. To continue incorporating optimism, the participants are suggested to rehearse a challenge they anticipate is yet to come, so they are better equipped to deal with it. Participants are encouraged to continue the exercises that enhance their character strengths in novel and different ways.

IMPLICATIONS

The theory, model and intervention in this chapter provide young adults with an opportunity to explore a deep and meaningful way to connect with oneself and others. There is an overall emphasis on capitalizing on strengths for personal growth and using a multi-modal approach in connecting (through writing, guided practice, communicating and so on). The intervention integrates emotional, evaluative as well as interactive components. The direction of change and development is from the inside towards the outside. This direction is advantageous because change that is intrinsically driven is sustainable. The proposed model can serve as a basis for developing interventions for other populations. Further research can be carried out to empirically test the model and the effects of the intervention.

CONCLUSION

This chapter focused on the role of self-compassion in the development of character strengths among young adults. A new perspective, namely, meeting the developmental tasks of the stage to catalyse the development of character strengths, emerged as part of the model. The model and intervention proposed in this chapter can be seen as a way to promote sustainable psychosocial development in young adults.

REFERENCES

Abercrombie, P. D., Zamora, A., & Korn, A. P. (2007). Providing a mindfulness-based stress reduction program for low-income multiethnic women with abnormal pap smears. *Holistic Nursing Practice 21*(1), 26–34.

Ackerman, C., & Oppland, M. (2017, April 28). 31 gratitude exercises that will boost your happiness (+PDF). Retrieved from https://positivepsychologyprogram.com/gratitude-exercises/

Allen, G. (2015). A simple exercise to strengthen emotional intelligence in teams. Retrieved from https://www.kqed.org/mindshift/40880/a-simple-exercise-to-strengthen-emotional-intelligence-in-teams

Al-Mabuk, R. H., Enright, R. D., & Cardis, P. A. (2006). Forgiveness education with parentally love-deprived late adolescents. *Journal of Moral Education, 24*(4), 427–444.

Ardelt, M. (2000). Still stable after all these years? Personality stability theory revisited. *Social Psychology Quarterly, 63*(4), 392–405.

Baker, L., & McNulty, J. K. (2011). Self-compassion and relationship maintenance: The moderating roles of conscientiousness and gender. *Journal of Personality and Social Psychology, 100*(5), 853–873.

Barnard, L. K., & Curry, J. F. (2012). The relationship of clergy burnout to self-compassion and other personality dimensions. *Pastoral Psychology, 61*(2), 149–163.

Baumeister, R. F. (1993). When ego threats lead to self-regulation failure: Negative consequences of high self-esteem. *Journal of Personality and Social Psychology, 64*(1), 141–156.

Beaumont, E., Durkin, M., Martin, C. J. H., & Carson, J. (2016). Measuring relationships between self-compassion, compassion fatigue, burnout and wellbeing in student counsellors and student cognitive behavioural psychotherapists: A quantitative survey. *Counselling and Psychotherapy Research, 16*(1), 15–23.

Bennett-Goleman, T. (2001). *Emotional alchemy: How the mind can heal the heart.* New York, NY: Three Rivers Press.

Beyers, W., & Seiffge-Krenke, I. (2010). Does identity precede intimacy? Testing Erikson's theory on romantic development in emerging adults of the 21st century. *Journal of Adolescent Research, 25*(3), 387–415.

Bluth, K., Gaylord, S. A., Campo, R. A., Mullarkey, M. C., & Hobbsc, L. (2016). Making friends with yourself: A mixed methods pilot study of a mindful self-compassion program for adolescents. *Mindfulness, 7*(2), 479–492.

Campbell, W. K., & Baumister, R. F. (2001). Is loving the self necessary for loving another? An examination of identity and intimacy. In Garth G. O. F. & Margaret S. C. (Eds.), *Blackwell handbook of social psychology, Vol. 2: Interpersonal processes* (pp. 437–456). London: Blackwell.

Chompoo. (2016, March 25). Zest: The character strength for satisfaction in work and life. Retrieved from https://positivepsychologyprogram.com/zest/

Cooley, C. H. (1964). *Human nature and the social order.* New York, NY: Schocken Books.

Coopersmith, S. (1967). *The antecedents of self-esteem.* New York, NY: Freeman.

Costa, J. P., & McCrae, R. R. (1988). Personality in Adulthood: A six-year longitudinal study of self-reports and spouse ratings on the NEO Personality Inventory. *Journal of Personality and Social Psychology, 54*(5), 853–863.

Crocker, J., & Park, L. E. (2004). The costly pursuit of self-esteem. *Psychological Bulletin, 130*(3), 392–414.

Dahlsgaard, K., Peterson, C., & Seligman, M. E. (2005). Shared virtue: The convergence of valued human strengths across culture and history. *Review of General Psychology, 9*(3), 203.

Dahm, K. A., Meyer, E. C., Neff, K. D., Kimbrel, N. A., Gulliver, S. B., & Morissette, S. B. (2015). Mindfulness, self-compassion, posttraumatic stress disorder symptoms, and functional disability in U.S. Iraq and Afghanistan war veterans. *Journal of Traumatic Stress, 28*(5), 460–464.

Davis, M. H., & Oathout, H. A. (1987). Maintenance of satisfaction in romantic relationships: Empathy and relational competence. *Journal of Personality and Social Psychology, 53*(2), 397–410.

Deniz, M., Kesici, Ş., & Sümer, A. S. (2008). The validity and reliability of the Turkish version of the Self-Compassion Scale. *Social Behavior and Personality: An International Journal, 36*(9), 1151–1160.

Donnellan, M. B., Conger, R. D., & Burzette, R. G. (2007). Personality development from late adolescence to young adulthood: Differential stability, normative maturity, and evidence for the maturity–stability hypothesis. *Journal of Personality, 75*(2), 237–264.

Dosenbach, N. U., Nardos, B., Cohen, A. L., Fair, D. A., Power, J. D., Church, J. A., . . . Schlaggar, B. L. (2010). Prediction of individual brain maturity using fMRI. *Science, 329*(5997), 1358–1361. doi:10.1126/science.1194144

Eisenberg, N., Zhou, Q., & Koller, S. (2001). Brazilian adolescents' prosocial moral judgment and behavior: Relations to sympathy, perspective taking, gender-role orientation, and demographic characteristics. *Child Development, 72*(2), 518–534.

Elkind, D. (1967). Egocentrism in adolescence. *Child Development, 38*, 1025–1034. doi:10.2307/1127100.

Erikson, E. H. (1959). Identity and the life cycle: Selected papers. *Psychological Issues, 1*(1), 1–171.

Erikson, E. H., & Erikson, J. M. (1998). *The life cycle completed* (Extended version). New York, NY: W. W. Norton.

Erwin, M. (2017, February). The power of gratitude. Retrieved from https://journal.thriveglobal.com/the-power-of-gratitude-64ac2a4dbcde

Feeney, J. A., & Noller, P. (1990). Attachment style as a predictor of adult romantic relationships. *American Psychological Association, 58*(2), 281–291.

Gardner, D. G., & Pierce, J. L. (1998). Self-esteem and self-efficacy within the organizational context: An empirical examination. *Group & Organization Management, 23*(1), 48–70.

Germer, C., & Neff, K. (2013). Self-compassion in clinical practice. *Journal of Clinical Psychology, 69*(8), 856–867.

Gilbert, P. (1989). *Human nature and suffering.* Hove: Lawrence Erlbaum.

Gilbert, P., Clarke, M., Hempel, S., Miles, J. N., & Irons, C. (2004). Criticizing and reassuring oneself: An exploration of forms, styles and reasons in female students. *British Journal of Clinical Psychology, 43*(1), 31–50.

Gilbert, P., McEwan, K., & Matos, M. (2011). Fears of compassion: Development of three self-report measures. *Psychology and Psychotherapy: Theory, Research and Practice, 84*(3), 239–255.

Gunderson, P. R., & Ferrari, J. R. (2008). Forgiveness of sexual cheating in romantic relationships: Effects of discovery method, frequency of offense, and presence of apology. *North American Journal of Psychology, 10*(1), 1–14.

Hart, D., & Carlo, G. (2005). Moral development in adolescence. *Journal of Research on Adolescence, 15*(3), 223–233. doi:10.1111/j.1532-7795.2005.00094.x

Harter, S. (1999). *The construction of the self: A developmental perspective.* New York, NY: Guilford Press.

Helgeson, V. S., & Fritz, H. L. (1999). Unmitigated agency and unmitigated communion: Distinctions from agency and communion. *Journal of Research in Personality, 33*(2), 131–158.

Hood, D. (2014, October 25). Improving well-being: Developing zest for life. Retrieved https://writingcreativenonfiction.wordpress.com/2014/10/25/improving-well-being-developing-zest-for-life/

Hutcherson, C. A., Seppala, E. M., & Gross, J. J. (2008). Loving-kindness meditation increases social connectedness. *Emotion*, *8*(5), 720–724.

Hwang, S., G. Kim, G., Yang, J.-W., & Yang, E. (2016). The moderating effects of age on the relationships of self-compassion, self-esteem, and mental health. *Japanese Psychological Research*, *58*(2), 194–205.

James, W. (1890). *The principles of psychology*. New York, NY: Dover Publications.

Johnson, S. B., Blum, R. W., & Giedd, J. N. (2009). Adolescent maturity and the brain: The promise and pitfalls of neuroscience research in adolescent health policy. *Journal of Adolescent Health*, *45*(3), 216–221. doi:10.1016/j.jadohealth.2009.05.016

Jopling, D. A. (2000). *Self-knowledge and the self*. New York, NY: Routledge.

Jost, J. T., Glaser, J., Kruglanski, A. W., & Sulloway, F. J. (2003). Political conservatism as motivated social cognition. *Psychological Bulletin*, *129*(3), 339–375.

Khoshaba, D. (2012). A seven-step prescription for self-love. Retrieved from https://www.psychologytoday.com/us/blog/get-hardy/201203/seven-step-prescription-self-love

Kohlberg, L. (1981). *The philosophy of moral development: Moral stages and the idea of justice*. San Francisco, CA: Harper & Row.

Kubacka, K. E., Finkenauer, C., Rusbult, C. E., & Keijsers, L. (2011). Maintaining close relationships: Gratitude as a motivator and a detector of maintenance behavior. *Personality and Social Psychology Bulletin*, *37*(10), 1362–1375.

Lang, F. R., Reschke, F. S., & Neyer, F. J. (2006). Social relationships, transitions, and personality development across the life span. In D. K. Mroczek & T. D. Little (Eds.), *Handbook of personality development* (pp. 455–466). Mahwah, NJ: Lawrence Erlbaum.

Long, E. C., Angera, J. J., Carter, S. J., Nakamoto, M., & Kalso, M. (1999). Understanding the one you love: A longitudinal assessment of an empathy training program for couples in romantic relationships. *Family Relations*, *48*(3), 235–242.

McCrae, R. R., & Costa, J. P. (1982). Self-concept and the stability of personality: Cross-sectional comparisons of self-reports and ratings. *Journal of Personality and Social Psychology*, *43*(6), 1282–1292.

McGue, M., Bacon, S., & Lykken, D. T. (1993). Personality stability and change in early adulthood: A behavioral genetic analysis. *Developmental Psychology*, *29*(1), 96–109.

McLeod, S. (2017). Erik Erikson. Retrieved from https://www.simplypsychology.org/Erik-Erikson.html

Mills, A., Gilbert, P., Bellew, R., McEwan, K., & Gale, C. (2007). Paranoid beliefs and self-criticism in students. *Clinical Psychology and Psychotherapy*, *14*(5), 358–364.

Neff, K. (2003a). Self-compassion: An alternative conceptualization of a healthy attitude toward oneself. *Self and Identity*, *2*(2), 85–101.

———. (2003b). The development and validation of a scale to measure self-compassion. *Self and Identity*, *2*(3), 223–250.

Neff, K. D. (2009). The role of self-compassion in development: A healthier way to relate to oneself. *Human Development, 52*(4), 211–214.
———. (2012). The science of self-compassion. In C. Germer & R. Siegel (Eds.), *Compassion and wisdom in psychotherapy* (pp. 79–92). New York: Guilford Press.
Neff, K. D., & Beretvas, S. N. (2012). The role of self-compassion in romantic relationships. *Self and Identity, 12*(1), 78–98.
Neff, K. D., & McGehee, P. (2009). Self-compassion and psychological resilience among adolescents and young adults. *Self and Identity, 9*(3), 225–240.
Neff, K. D., & Pommier, E. (2013). The relationship between self-compassion and other-focused concern among college undergraduates, community adults, and practicing meditators. *Self and Identity*, 160–176. doi:10.1080/15298868.2011.649546
Neff, K. D., & Vonk, R. (2009). Self-compassion versus global self-esteem: Two different ways of relating to oneself. *Journal of Personality, 77*(1), 23–50.
Neff, K., Kirkpatrick, K., & Rude, S. (2007). Self-compassion and adaptive psychological functioning. *Journal of Research in Personality, 41*(1), 139–154.
Neff, K., Rude, S., & Kirkpatrick, K. (2007). An examination of self-compassion in relation to positive psychological functioning and personality traits. *Journal of Research in Personality, 41*(4), 908–916.
Niemiec, R. M. (2017a). Mindfulness. In R. M. Niemiec (Ed.), *Character strengths interventions: A field guide for practitioners* (pp. CSI65–70). Toronto, Canada: Hogrefe Publishing.
———. (2017b). Virtue: Humanity. In R. M. Niemiec (Ed.), *Character strengths interventions: A field guide for practitioners*. Toronto, Canada: Hogrefe Publishing.
Neyer, F. J., & Lehnart, J. (2007). Relationships matter in personality development: Evidence from an 8-year longitudinal study across young adulthood. *Journal of Personality, 75*, 535–568.
Neyer, F. J., & Voigt, D. (2004). Personality and social network effects on romantic relationships: A dyadic approach. *European Journal of Personality, 18*(4), 279–299.
Nicholson, J. (2011, September 28). How gratitude influences loving behavior. Retrieved from https://www.psychologytoday.com/blog/the-attraction-doctor/201109/how-gratitude-influences-loving-behavior
Otake, K., Shimai, S., Tanaka-Matsumi, J., Otsui, K., & Fredrickson, B. L. (2006). Happy people become happier through kindness: A counting kindnesses intervention. *Journal of Happiness Studies, 7*(3), 361–375. doi:10.1007/s10902-005-3650-z
Park, N., & Peterson, C. (2006a). Character strengths and happiness among young children: Content analysis of parental descriptions. *Journal of Happiness Studies, 7*(3), 323–341.
———. (2006b). Moral competence and character strengths among adolescents: The development and validation of the Values in Action Inventory of Strengths for Youth. *Journal of Adolescence, 29*(6), 891–909.

Park, N., & Peterson, C. (2009). Character strengths: Research and practice. *Journal of College and Character, 10*(4). doi:10.2202/1940-1639.1042

Park, N., Peterson, C., & Seligman, M. E. (2004). Strengths of character and wellbeing. *Journal of Social and Clinical Psychology, 23*(5), 603–619.

———. (2006). Character strengths in fifty-four nations and the fifty US states. *The Journal of Positive Psychology, 1*(3), 118–129.

Peterson, C., & Seligman, M. E. (2004). *Character strengths and virtues: A handbook and classification.* New York, NY: Oxford University Press, and Washington, DC: American Psychological Association.

Piaget, J. (1952). *The origins of intelligence in children.* New York, NY: International University Press.

Raque-Bogdan, T. L., Ericson, S. K., Jackson, J., Martin, H. M., & Bryan, N. A. (2011). Attachment and mental and physical health: Self-compassion and mattering as mediators. *Journal of Counseling Psychology, 58*(2), 272–278.

Rashid, T., & Anjum, A. (2005). 340 ways to use VIA character strengths. Retrieved from http://www.actionforhappiness.org/media/52486/340_ways_to_use_character_strengths.pdf

Roberts, B. W., Caspi, A., & Moffitt, T. E. (2001). The kids are alright: Growth and stability in personality development from adolescence to adulthood. *Journal of Personality and Social Psychology, 81*(4), 670–683.

Santilli, E. (2015). 8 ways to increase your self-love. Retrieved from https://www.huffingtonpost.com/elyse-gorman/8-ways-to-increase-your-self-love_b_6883702.html

Sedikedes, C. (1993). Assessment, enhancement, and verification determinants of the self-evaluation process. *Journal of Personality and Social Psychology, 65*(2), 317–338.

Shoshani, A., & Slone, M. (2013). Middle school transition from the strengths perspective: Young adolescents' character strengths, subjective well-being, and school adjustment. *Journal of Happiness Studies, 14*(4), 1163–1181. doi:10.1007/s10902-012-9374-y

Smith, E. E. (2014, June 12). Masters of love. Retrieved from https://www.theatlantic.com/health/archive/2014/06/happily-ever-after/372573/

Snyder, C. R., & Lopez, S. J. (2007). *Positive psychology: The scientific and practical explorations of human strengths.* Thousand Oaks, CA: SAGE.

Sowell, E. R., Thompson, P. M., Holmes, C. J., Jernigan, T. L., & Toga, A. W. (1999). In vivo evidence for post-adolescent brain maturation in frontal and striatal regions. *Nature Neuroscience, 2*(10), 859–861. doi:10.1038/13154

Srivastava, S., John, O. P., Gosling, S. D., & Potter, J. (2003). Development of personality in early and middle adulthood: Set like plaster or persistent change? *Journal of Personality and Social Psychology, 85*(5), 1041–1053.

Steger, M. F., Hicks, B. M., Kashdan, T. B., Krueger, R. F., & Bouchard, T. J. (2007). Genetic and environmental influences on the positive traits of the values in action classification, and biometric covariance with normal personality. *Journal of Research in Personality, 41*(3), 524–539. doi:10.1016/j.jrp.2006.06.002

Stein, J. A., Newcomb, M. D., & Bentler, P. (1986). Stability and change in personality: A longitudinal study from early adolescence to young adulthood. *Journal of Research in Personality, 20*(3), 276–291.

Stober, J. (2003). Self-pity: Exploring the links to personality, control beliefs, and anger. *Journal of Personality, 71*(2), 183–220.

Tanakaa, M., Wekerle, C., Schmuck, M. L., Paglia-Boak, A., & Team, T. M. (2011). The linkages among childhood maltreatment, adolescent mental health, and self-compassion in child welfare adolescents. *Child Abuse & Neglect, 35*(10), 887–898.

Terry, M. L., Leary, M. R., & Mehta, S. (2012). Self-compassion as a buffer against homesickness, depression, and dissatisfaction in the transition to college. *Self and Identity, 12*(3), 1–13.

Toepoel, V. (2013). Ageing, leisure and social connectedness: How could leisure help reduce social isolation of older people? *Social Indicators Research, 113*(1), 355–372.

Treder-Wolff, J. (2014). Improvisation games & exercises for developing emotional intelligence. Retrieved from http://www.livesinprogress.net/2014/01/improvisation-games-exercises-for.html

Wei, M., Liao, K. Y.-H., & Tsun-Yao Ku, P. A. (2011). Attachment, self-compassion, empathy, and subjective well-being among college students and community adults. *Journal of Personality, 79*(1), 191–222.

Wispe, L. (1991). *The psychology of sympathy.* New York, NY: Plenum Press.

Yarnell, L. M., & Neff, K. D. (2013). Self-compassion, interpersonal conflict resolutions, and well-being. *Self and Identity, 12*(2), 146–159.

Chapter 11

Nurturing Character Strength in Children
Agents of Socialization to Promote Well-being

Bhagyalakshmi K. C. and Raseela K. N.

INTRODUCTION

Nurturing is the most challenging part of childrearing. The psychological well-being is largely dependent on the inputs of emotional and moral feeds of childhood. Inculcation and promotion of positive traits at the young age is crucial for well-being. One of the central concerns discussed in this chapter is about increasing positive experiences and strengthening the virtue of character strength (CS) through agents of socialization. The evolutionary theory often speculates that individual differences in traits are grounded in biology (Park, Peterson, & Seligman, 2004). CS being one of the most important correlates of well-being (Upadhyay & Arya, 2015) becomes a key ingredient of life satisfaction in later life (Park & Peterson, 2006). Well-being encompasses the hedonic and eudaimonic components. The hedonic components include high positive and low negative emotions which are more related to subjective and personal well-being. On the other hand, eudaimonic well-being is characterized by real strength of character which embodies meaning and purpose in life. The interplay of the two sustains psychological engagement of humans which promotes well-being (Gallagher, 2009).

Nurturing CS in children is a priority concern in childrearing and socialization practices. The capacity to reflect on one's strengths promotes well-being. It is the influence of socializing agents that helps children build on their natural strengths to a most fulfilling one (Linley & Harrington, 2006). The study of early manifestation of CS in children becomes most important in this context so that adequate strategies can be adopted to understand and measure them and develop best interventions at an early age (Park & Peterson, 2006). Development of CS does not restrict to prevention of psychopathology and problems but also promotes flourishing and thriving (Upadhyay & Arya, 2015). The strengths also vary in meanings and manifestations across different cultures in terms of salience and applications in different developmental stages. The cultural values and norms also influence the expressions of strengths in different contexts (Tripathi, Banu, & Mehrotra, 2015).

SOCIALIZATION CONCEPTS AND VIEWS

According to *Oxford Dictionary of Psychology* (Colman, 2009) socialization is the process beginning in infancy, whereby one acquires the attitudes, values, beliefs, habits, behaviour patterns and accumulated knowledge of one's society, through childrearing, education and modification of one's behaviour to conform with the demands of the society or group to which one belongs.

Socialization is the process by which acceptable cultural beliefs and behaviours are shaped. Agents of socialization include parents/family, teachers/school and peer groups. Modern day socialization also includes the influence of media. Sociologists categorize the process into six kinds:

1. Primary socialization: learning of attitudes and values appropriate to a given culture
2. Secondary socialization: learning appropriate behaviour as a member of a small group mostly found during adolescence and young adulthood

3. Developmental socialization: learning of social skills in the context of a social institution
4. Anticipatory socialization: learning to socialize for future relationship, occupation and position
5. Resocialization: learning to discard old patterns of behaviour for important transitions in life and accepting new ones
6. Reverse socialization: learning of desired behaviour from younger people also called enculturation of old and new generations (Ozmete, 2011)

Socialization makes humans the functional members of society. Though like primates most of the human behaviours are biologically set, social experiences help us to learn and survive in society.

A domain approach to socialization put forth by Grusec and Davidov (2010) in their theoretical perspectives of socialization gives a broad understanding of the concept. They categorize five domains to explain socialization mechanism: protection, reciprocity, control, guided learning and group participation. Each domain requires different mechanisms and is found to have different outcomes for children.

1. *Protection:* The main feature of this domain is proximity to caregiver and the children develop a sense of trust and security. It is also claimed that a sensitive caregiving in this area makes them more competent and also have emotional control as adults.

2. *Reciprocity:* Includes exchange of favours as well as unconditional mutuality. This gives a sense of equal status to partners. This is more pronounced to be active when children are engaged in play. The caregiver's responsibility here involves accommodating reasonable requests for compliance to reciprocate favours. In essence, reciprocity promotes receptive compliance.

3. *Control:* This domain is very important to make children understand concepts of sanctions and costs of deviance. The cultural beliefs take form and also involve conflicts with control agents. The effect of control is beneficial if it is capable of producing desired effect. The individual differences provide scope for specific interactions depending

on the social contexts. The central aspect of this domain is exerting appropriate amount of authority. And care should be taken to not overly threaten the child's sense of autonomy. It is in this domain that our children develop moral and principled behaviours. Thus the internalization of correct moral standards should take place in this process of socialization.

4. *Guided learning:* Socialization in this stage requires interactions from all agents. The cognitive, physical and emotional development becomes more concrete and highly complex. The role of agents involves provision of structure, strategies and feedback to develop skills and learn independently. The child develops into a mature cognitive and socio-emotional being.

5. *Group participation:* Emphasizes the participation of children in cultural practices. The innate tendency of humans to be part of social groups facilitates more socialization with agents. The preference for group activities becomes more common and children are exposed to a range of options with in-group expectations and norms. The exposure provides ample opportunities to reflect and seek support from agents. The parents or other agents can mould behaviour by structuring the environment for more desired options and avoid undesirable exposures. It is crucial here for children to identify with positive models. These get more strongly internalized and promote positive growth.

According to the present authors, there are numerous interplays between the domains and the socializing agents should be sensitive in combining features when children are expected to model upon. Anything unhealthy and disorganization recognized should be addressed more positively to bring out the best in children.

Socialization carried out by parents and organizations is a two-way process—one that they act upon the child and the other they act on behalf of the larger society. Each of them also has different levels of impact (Handel, 2006). The process does not end in childhood but continues for life. The internalization of social character from a mere reflexive being when born, the process of socialization is a remarkable and exhaustive journey from a biological being to a social one.

The impact of environment on brain–biological systems is explored for decades now. The bidirectional process of individuation and social self is enumerated in detail in *Childhood Socialisation* (Damon, 2006; Handel, 2006). Here the development of individual personality and social development is termed as a paradoxical affair. Personality is more bound to identify individual distinctiveness from others. Whereas social development is a resultant of establishing connections with others, the kind of incentives received during socialization determines the kind of integration with social values and norms. These incentives begin with biological need fulfilment like physical care to more complex fulfilment of emotional needs. The processor individuation helps identify with idiosyncratic characteristics and balancing them in ideal relationships. Individuation is a step by step process of differentiation and later moves to realize its independent self. During the differentiating function a coherent identity develops. This state of affairs is crucial because conflicts herein lead to confusion and despair. In short socialization and individuation are distinct process but each can significantly impact one another positively or negatively. Hence it is in this process that a regulative mechanism needs to be worked out to promote prosocial attitude in children which can lay foundations for positive adult behaviours.

After the process of differentiation and individuation it is the initiation of social interaction. It is these interactions that help children mature both physically and mentally. Socialization should provide all possible experiences of social world. Providing opportunities to learn and mature is the key in increasing brain plasticity. A clear understanding of prescribed and penalized behaviour also gets in to shape. Along with this develops the self. In the course of acquiring language and vocabulary the child also learns set of rules and can understand symbols as well. The acquisition of these language skills accelerates the development of self, that is, to view oneself as distinct from people and objects around. The booming and buzzing confusion in interactions created through a range of physical and mental sensations gradually gains definition and self emerges. The emergence of self helps children to regulate their own conduct and develop the capacity for self-direction. Henceforth the interaction with significant adults is of utmost importance. The 'looking glass self' concept of Charles Horton Cooley (1922) explains the child becomes capable of reflecting on how his actions affect significant others when the self is fully developed. Similarly, the 'I' and 'Me' concepts given by George Herbert Mead (1934) emphasizing that communicating the 'good' and 'bad' behaviour by socializing agents become increasingly patterned and organized and leads to the formation of 'Me'—the self-object of others. Over time the sum of others' attitudes becomes subjective and personal and gets oriented to physical self. In short he claims individuals have individuality as well as social characteristics.

SOCIALIZATION AND BIOLOGICAL SYSTEMS

A classic paper on evolution of human character by E. D. Cope (1883) proposes the profound influences of biological system. The author explains the primary components of mind includes the emotions; to include the likes and dislikes which also forms the bases for passion, intellect; to include the authority to organize experiences in the order desired, which will be based on the likes, dislikes and pure necessities, the will; the ultimate power which direct and restrains experiences. With these components working the active physical senses (touch, vision, taste, smell, audition and movement sensation) the organism builds consciousness. This doctrine is more or less found in primitive beings but through evolution higher mental activities takes place with the development of memories for experiences. The quality and quantity of experiences in combination of all the aforementioned emotions, intellect and the will characterize individual behaviour and belief. The more the area of the brain involved in intense activity at a given time the more the energy produced and vice versa. Accordingly the pathology of the mind arises from the disruptions in the quality and quantity and activities in the brain tissues. Impressibility and sensitiveness of stimulation help the mind acquire positive or negative qualities. In this context, the sense of justice or moral development is a function of emotion of benevolence and intellectual capacity of discrimination. These guides the noble human attribute of sympathy, and thus noble capacities should be nurtured to harvest a positive mind. These exercises of stimulation and interaction are provided and protected by the society and socializing agents. And thus have a critical role in nurturing positive traits and promotion of well-being.

Mulford (1921) discusses the development of infant brain beginning at the fourth month of prenatal stage and continuing up to eight years of postnatal growth. The differentiating feature of the anthropoid brain is the extending growth of the frontal regions. He further states that only the foundations of human brain laid at prenatal stage and the social stimulation and interaction complete the fully developed brain which is termed the 'man brain'. The developing brain is expressed as a 'child mind' with 'child brain'. The child brain has to build upon the experiences and establish higher-level functions. Through different stages the new emerging brain fights against old, purely reflexive functions and progresses towards more conscious and self-directed function. The automatic responses to the environment of the child brain slowly develop the growth of different centres of the brain in sequence. It is during this developmental phase that the interaction with the environment becomes crucial. The mother is the first point after birth for receiving an array of responses and over time widen with other family members. As a child grows, the social experiences shape the attitude, thoughts and emotions that condition to respond in a pattern which can be termed as 'behaviour' in general. Parental impact of emotional socialization lays foundation for emotional competence (Denham, 1997) that builds character. The skills of socialization are acquired through these interactions underlying which are the biological bases (Grusec & Davidov, 2010).

Rösler and Röder (2014) explain the importance of neurobiology in the socialization process. The following summarizes their views:

1. The structure and functions of nervous system always work based on interaction of heredity disposition and influences from the environment. The nervous system does not automatically develop if there are no environmental stimulations. The early growing-up years have important implications in this regard.

2. The key structures in the brain attain full capacity only when associated behavioural patterns develop and sustain. Lack of this would lead to deficits and if these are not targeted in early stages and intervened in, they remain a problem area for entire life. The early education on building positive character becomes a disable strategy here.
3. The attainment of linguistic competence is predetermined and this is very important to carry forward the development process. Specific techniques to identify the linguistic competency must be applied at a very early age.
4. The environmentally dependent learning and outcome process collectively contribute to formation of general intelligence. A challenging and supportive environment helps children attain a high-level cognitive function.
5. The skills of self-regulation, that is, to make inhibitory choices and delay gratification also rely on social factors.
6. The understanding of the bases of the neuroplasticity helps make sensitive and critical periods of socialization more rewarding.
7. Prenatal factors also have a long-lasting impact on socialization.
8. Early investigations and interventions will be more effective if both physiological and social factors are considered. The views of the authors are illustrated in Figure 11.1.

Positive psychology being the scientific exploration of well-being, morally valued positive trait development in the early years of life gains enormous significance. Research evidences show a significant relationship between strengths and life satisfaction (Park & Peterson, 2006; Park et al., 2004; Peterson & Seligman, 2004). The CS is more trait-like and as discussed earlier biological factors also play a vital role in educating and socializing children for positive traits. Cultivating CS facilitates positive attitude as adults and provides with better coping abilities. This in turn promotes health and well-being. There would definitely be a beneficial impact on children if strategically the social and physiological determinants are assigned equal place. Ambitious, actively coping and socially supportive individuals can be produced only with

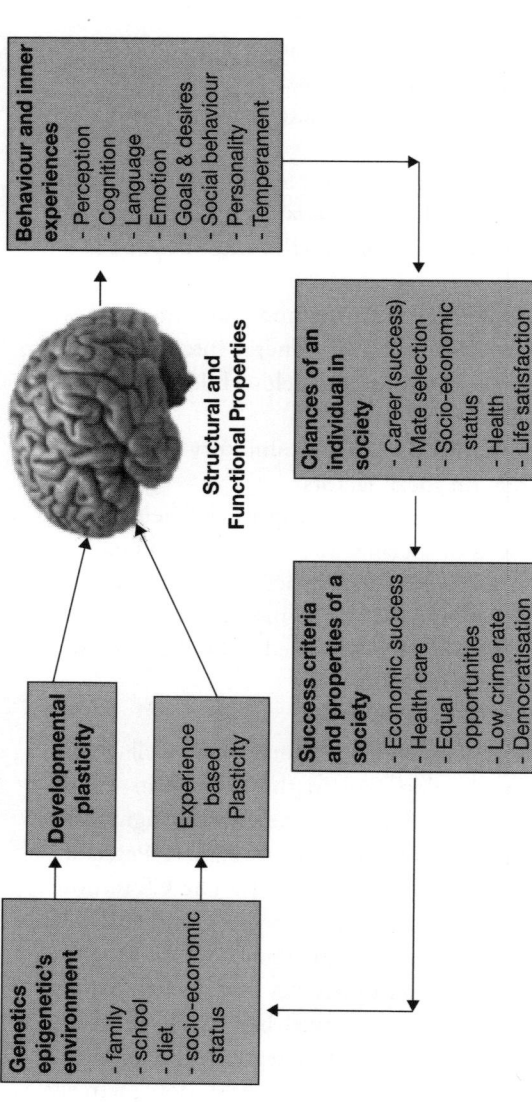

Figure 11.1 Socialization: *Influencing Factors and Consequences*

Structural and functional properties of the brain determine an individual's behaviour and inner experience (top right). This is expressed in perception, language, cognition, emotions, goals and desires, social behaviour and temperament. The properties of the brain–mind system develop on the basis of two mechanisms: functional and structural changes in the brain (plasticity), a process occurring as a result of maturation and experience. These two forms of plasticity are dependent on gene C, epigene C as well as environmental factors. The lower set of connections in the diagram indicates how an individual's behaviour determines his/her chances in society (bottom right) and how, at the same time, this and the interactions between individuals influence the characteristics of an individual in society (bottom left). In turn, these societal and cultural characteristics then influence the maturational and experience-based plasticity (top left).

Source: Rösler and Röder (2014).

positive and scientific engagement in the early socialization process. The maladaptive patterns detected in childhood also can be corrected to a large extent by suitable alterations in the social interactions termed as strength-based interventions. Intellectual and interpersonal traits can be strengthened by conscious and active socialization.

ROLE OF SOCIALIZING AGENTS IN NURTURING CS

In a busy world where people look for flaws in others rather than appreciate their strengths, it is necessary to make a change in attitude among the ones who are growing up through showing them the right way to look up on strengths. Parents are hastily making moves to rectify their children's shortcomings and seldom do they spend time in identifying their child's strengths, to be specific, 'character strengths'. Unless and until actions to develop and enhance these strengths are taken, these are of no use.

A place where a child spends his plenty of time is school which is for sure the best place to inculcate CSs in a child. Schools play an important role in the overall development of a child. The teachers, the curriculum and the system followed are important in an individual's life. Best schools are the ones which take effort in finding out a person's potentials and nurture it.

Peer groups are also important when CSs are considered. They contributes equally in enhancing the abilities and potentials of a child. In the following section, briefings regarding all these three aspects are given.

Role of Parents in Developing Character Strengths

Several researches have been conducted in the past regarding the contribution of 'nature' and 'nurture' in an individual. In a study conducted by Peterson and Seligman (2004), the CSs except spirituality have no evidence of being inherited. CSs are only moderately heritable and the rest are inculcated throughout the development process (Steger,

Hicks, Kashdan, Krueger, & Bouchard, 2007). All these researches suggest a possibility that during the developmental span, one can take actions to cultivate CSs in their children and hence it is important to devise strategies of parenting which have a major role in moulding the future generation.

Darling and Steinberg (1993) defined parenting practices as specific behaviours that parents use to socialize children. There are two dimensions in parenting which are 'parental responsiveness' and 'parental demandingness'. Parental responsiveness refers mainly to parental warmth and supportiveness. In this, parents 'foster individuality, self-regulation, and self-assertion by being attuned, supportive and acquiescent to children's special needs and demands'. Parental demandingness in a sense refers to behavioural control wherein the parents 'claim the children to become integrated to their family whole by their maturity demands, supervision, disciplinary efforts and willingness to confront the child who disobeys' (Baumrind, 1991).

In neuroscience, parenting is actually a process of regulating our internal 'states of mind', a *state regulation system* that is under development in early childhood (Porges, 2011). It relies upon our social engagement system which refers to a brain–body state which enables us to be close to others without being defensive.

Baumrind (1991) identified three types of parenting styles—authoritarian, permissive and authoritative. The authoritative parenting refers to a rigid pattern wherein parental demandingness is more whereas permissive parents are low on demandingness and are either highly responsive or irresponsive, ignorant and indifferent at times and are extremely flexible. In between these two extremes lies the authoritative style where the parents are demanding as well as responsive but not overindulgent. They understand their children better. They set realistic limits and this style therefore induces positive discipline among children. Scarr (1992) states that for children to develop their innate potentials, parents need to provide a basically warm, supportive and nurturant environment for their children. Although the positive outcomes are discussed in many researches, some researches focus on the negative approaches adopted by the parents and their effects. For example, a mother who rejects her children makes them become aggressive (Mackinnon, Starnes, Volling, & Johnson, 1997). All these shed light on the point that positive parenting strategies are required to enhance the CSs of children.

There are some key rules to effective parenting—set reasonable yet high standards (teach them to expect much from themselves), stay alert for good behaviour and rewarding it, explain the reasons when one asks a child to do something (encourages self-control in a child), encourage children to take the perspective of others (encourages moral development and empathy), enforce rules consistently (Weiten & Lloyd, 2007) and such others.

One of the best examples of parenting approach to be adopted to inculcate CSs in children is the 'strength-based parenting' approach introduced by Lea Waters (2017). In this, she introduced the powerful tool fundamental to parenting—the Strength Switch—which emphasizes on focusing on a child's strengths rather than weaknesses. The basic aim in this approach is to identify the CSs of children and build up their strengths and positive qualities. The parents are made to find out if the parenting style they adopt is deficit based or strength based. Even parents who use an authoritative stance do block their child's strength development through being deficit based. The teenagers whose parents used a strength-based parenting approach were reported to have higher levels of life satisfaction, higher extents of positive emotions, a better understanding of their strengths, and hence they better utilized their strengths, coped with stress in proactive ways and reported low levels of daily stress (Waters, 2017).

Understanding strengths of a child is an important process. Strength can be either skills, abilities, characteristics, traits or talents. Strength has three key elements—performance, energy and high use. Performance refers to 'being good at something', energy refers to 'feeling good doing it' and high use refers to 'choosing to do it'. Other additional clues in identifying a child's strength are:

1. Presence of yearning or drive in a child to use a particular skill or practice
2. Observing the natural behaviour of a child wherein the parent has to observe how he or she acts and speaks
3. Noting whether a child loses track of time when engaged in a particular activity, that is, *flow experiences*

The development of strengths requires both ability and effort. A paradox is that if a child has knowledge about his strength, it will help him overcome his limits. Strength-based parenting helps in increasing competence, self-assurance and happiness. Early childhood is the best time to build a child's strengths (Waters, 2017).

There are three different phases in life corresponding to which strengths unfold. In the first phase, namely, the Romantic Phase, the child plays, explores and has fun with his potential strengths. Here, the parents can help their children to develop their passions through giving low-pressure opportunities to engage them and to reinforce their strengths. As children explore newer experiences, the grey matter in their brain grows substantially which is named as 'overproduction phase' by the neuroscientists. Therefore, it is important to encourage play, autonomy and passion in children at this phase. The second phase is the Precision Phase, which comprises the middle years between early to mid-adolescence, where a child has better clarity regarding his potential and systematically enhances one's strengths. As a parent, one should make sure that the child is provided opportunities such as classes, clubs, camps, volunteer work, equipment, coaches and tutors which help them 'strengthen their strengths'. Both the parent and child have to take effort in this phase. There is a major change in the brain at this phase, that is, the brain has a massive growth spurt different from that of childhood. The overproduction phase is corrected in order to meet the demands of upcoming adulthood through neural pruning. The more used neural networks are maintained while the ones that are less frequently used lose the battle. As a result of this process, the child gets more efficient at things he or she practises more frequently. At this phase, it is also important to protect the teenager from physical, social, psychological and emotional anger. A parent has to generate trust in his/her child and help them use their strengths to overcome the peer pressure to involve in risky behaviours. The next phase is the Integration Phase, which refers to the late adolescence where they learn to use their strengths situation specifically. Here the strengths are mastered better by the teenager and they becomes a part of his identity (Waters, 2017).

In strength-based parenting, basically, four foundational psychological processes are used to support strengths development—mindset management, role modelling, scaffolding and proximal development practices. Mindset management refers to encouraging a 'growth mindset' (a belief that personal qualities can be modified) by discarding a fixed mindset which views qualities as static and unchangeable. To do this, a parent too should have a growth mindset. Role modelling in a way tells parents to display behaviours which help the child to develop his strengths. If a particular strength is absent in a parent, he/she can expose the child to strength helpers such as teachers, tutors and accomplished people who possess the same strength. Strength-based scaffolding is the process where the parents make sure that children have the resources and support necessary for building their strengths. Proximal development practices involve helping the child to reach a higher level of understanding than one could have achieved alone by giving an opportunity to practise a task by increasing the challenges. The assistance given is at minimal level so that the child learns to master it himself (Waters, 2017).

Intersubjectivity, which refers to reciprocal relationship between a parent and child, has a lot to do in a child's development. Openness, receptiveness and sharing one's experience comprise it. Such reciprocal moments allow the parent and child to deeply engage with one another. It influences the child's development in a positive manner as well as induces a positive effect on the parent. It also helps the child to get over from states of extreme emotions, distractible thoughts, impulsive behaviours and in building resilience and emotional competence. Playfulness, one of the key components of parenting process, is helpful in generating hope. It includes fully engaged interactions involving facial expressions, eye contact, voice prosody and rhythm, gestures, postures and touch. Both the parent as well as the child enters into a state of pleasure, deep joy and fascination with one another and with the shared activity. Acceptance by parents is another key component which help the kids to feel free to express their inner feelings and desires, thoughts, perceptions, intentions and memories. It increases the child's interest in engaging in the social world (Hughes & Baylin, 2012).

Positive parenting is another approach which helps the parents to raise empowered, confident and strong children with a firm sense of well-being and the ability to maintain contentment throughout life. It emphasizes on a warm relationship where good behaviours are praised, clear rules are set and children are listened to, and positive disciplining strategies are used instead of punishments (Batra, 2013). One of the factors mentioned here, praise, by adjusting the communication build a child's CS. In toddlers through adults, praise is related to task achievement, enjoyment and motivation which correspond to performance, energy and use, respectively. 'Strength-based praise' works better because it acknowledges action as well as strengths (Waters, 2017).

In addition to identifying one's own strength, a child can also develop his strengths through understanding others' strengths and finding new role models. It can be done through showing good movies and making children read books which reflect strengths (Mitchell, 2017).

Family relationships predict the strengths in a child. A parent–child relationship which involves care, challenges growth, provides support, shares power and expands possibilities was found to have a significant effect on the development of CSs. The quality of parent–child relationship is powerful in predicting whether children are developing critical CSs they need to be their best in school and in life (www.parentfurther.com, 2015).

All the aforementioned approaches, if put into practice, would definitely help a child to develop his CSs and enhance his well-being and happiness.

Role of Schools in Developing Character Strengths in Children

The application of positive psychology in classrooms has gained popularity recently as the synergy between learning and positive emotions show that skills to acquire happiness should be taught in schools. An effective preventive strategy which can be used in schools is that of enhancing the strengths and virtues of students. Seligman and Peterson (2004) suggested the use of positive psychology principles in services like school consultation. Amplifying an individual's strengths works wonders than repairing their weaknesses.

The field of 'positive education' emerged due to the aforementioned need. Seligman, Ernst, Gillham, Reivicha and Linkins (2009) stated that teaching well-being in schools can help in reducing depression rates, increase life satisfaction and improve learning. Individuals have a set of signature strengths and engaging in these virtues results in a good life. Positive education programmes target a broad array of strengths.

Positive education focuses mainly on clear-eyed optimism, deep wells of emotional energy and motivation, springy resilience, sturdy hope, strong relationships, clearly understood values, refined purpose, challenging and motivating goals. There are various obstacles which make the application of positive education a tedious process—lack of a unifying framework to bring together the evidence-informed practices together, difficulties in training personnel in positive psychology and the absence of targeted evaluation and research programmes (Kumar, 2011).

Promoting safe and supporting school environments through constructing a respectful school culture, ensuring safety and security, building positive relations among educators and students and understanding level of social and behavioural expectation is an important aspect. Communication, problem-solving and coping skills can be taught to students and prosocial activities can be encouraged which may help in increasing resilience and hope in students. Learning opportunities which require the application of student's strengths such as mini courses or enrichment clusters, independent studies, multilevel instructions-based curriculum strategies and mentoring will be helpful in strengthening the students. To an extent, strengths such as courage can be inculcated in schools through communicating to students in time of failure that it is a chance to extend themselves. Students should not feel left alone with failure. In case he or she takes an effort to succeed, it has to be praised. These qualities should be encouraged and recognition should be given. Teachers should also be hopeful and optimistic as it is also a key aspect of education.

In fact, teachers play an important role in identifying a student's signature strengths. The assessment should also include the observation of their behaviour during the lunch and recess hour, where they get an opportunity for social interaction. Lessons can be planned such that each student is able to apply their signature strengths multiple times in a day. Many students let their past determine their future. This in turn causes sorrow. In such a student, change can be brought about through improving their forgiveness and gratitude. Teachers can apply strategies like making students write down five things that they were grateful for the day and five things that they could improve upon at the end of every school day (Kumar, 2011).

There have been certain programmes which were implemented to enhance CSs in schools. Some such programmes are 'Project Wisdom' and 'Wise Skills' which promote many of the CSs. It was found by Leslie Matula in 1992 (as cited in Knowles & Smith, 2006). It is a widely used character education programme in the United States. It uses proverbs and maxims to teach CSs to children. On every school day, a short message referred to as 'words of wisdom' are read over the school's public address (PA) system or in-house TV to reach everyone in the school. It also provides the educators online access to weekly messages and lesson plans. Mini posters and parental resources are also made available. The schools encourage the students to apply these words in their real-life settings. Project Wisdom is functional in over 17,000 schools across the United States and around 4 million students are reached by this programme. The evaluation of this programme showed that it positively affected the school climate, increased students' self-awareness, social awareness and self-management. It also encouraged student conversations about character and improved teacher morale (Manke, 2004). Wise Skills programme is based on monthly character themes provided to school, family and community. Teachers are provided with classroom packages including character cards and posters and a curriculum notebook. Families are assigned family activities and communities are provided ways to connect with classrooms.

Sternberg (2001) developed a curriculum referred to as *balanced curriculum* to teach the strength 'wisdom' to students by incorporating critical and wise thinking to eighth grade history. Activities that foster critical, creative and practical thinking, dialogical thinking, dialectical thinking, critical discussion, role modelling and reflection of values using maxims were included in the curriculum. Another attempt following this was the English Teacher Wisdom Project (Ferrarie et al., 2011). It was a secondary school English classroom based project wherein literature was used to inculcate wisdom in schools. Here, a contextualized analysis of characters and actions in literature is done. But this required an active effort from the part of the teachers (cf. Ferrari & Guthrie, 2014).

Overall, it is obvious that using a strength-based approach in educational institutions will be better than taking a problem-focused approach.

The Influence of Peers on Character Strength

The term 'peer' actually refers to a companion of approximately the same age and developmental level (Bukatko & Daehler, 2012). Peers can also play an important role in inculcating strength among children in the course of their development.

Most infants and toddlers are found to meet their peers on a regular basis, and many have long lasting friendships that start from birth (Hay, Castle, Davies, Demetriou, & Stimson, 1999). When a child relates more to his peers, that is, when he is more similar to a peer, it increases interaction, and ultimately helps in developing social skills.

Toddlers who engaged in complex play were found to be high in competence in dealing with other children in their preschool years as well as middle childhood (Ladd & Troop-Gordon, 2003). There are evidences that having early friendships helps in preventing psychological disorders in future (Criss, Pettit, Bates, Dodge, & Lapp, 2002).

The way through which peers influence a child's behaviour is through modelling and reinforcement. These may be positive as well as negative. Therefore, making sure that the child shares a part in a good group is important so as to empower his strengths. Else, it would lead to a deteriorative effect. Peers also give direct feedback about how one is performing in all domains. This in turn helps in increasing his self-esteem (Bukatko & Daehler, 2012). Friends can also increase the tendency to perform prosocial behaviour. When friends are prosocial, adolescents express more altruistic behaviour (Barry & Wentzel, 2006). All these aspects inculcate strengths in a child if he has a good peer circle.

Even if a brief idea has been given in the preceding paragraphs regarding the influence of parenting, education and peers on the development of CSs, there is a broad array of information regarding these. Numerous studies have been done till date on all these aspects which have helped in spreading awareness about the importance of CSs and virtues and of inculcating them in a child. This glimpse will help in giving importance to these aspects and help in the flourishing of the child as CSs influence well-being.

Role of Culture in Character Strength

The terms 'character' and 'conduct' are often used interchangeably. Every society and culture has accepted codes of conduct. Conduct in this regard can be understood as a mode in which a response is made for a given circumstance (Alexander, 1893). We often categorize individuals based on their dominant traits and fix the term 'character' to exemplify a courageous character, soft character and so on. The religion, ethnicity, culture and belief system play a dominant role in strengthening character. The manners in which positive traits are acquired and transferred are unique to each culture. Sets of cultural practices are unique to each culture. Such practices are embedded in social contexts and are deeply associated with our emotions (Denham, Bassett, & Miller, 2017). The American culture is more emotionally expressive in nature while the African Americans take emotions more placidly (Parker et al., 2012). There is a dearth of research in this area wherein the universal traits of CS virtues take different shapes and are formed through culturally-based socialization.

The universal aspects of human development—relationship formation, knowledge acquisition and balance between autonomy and relatedness—were studied by Greenfield et al. (2003). The study was carried on adolescent groups. The development of cultural pathways is drawn upon three major theories: (a) the eco-cultural theory—to include the responses conditioned to the materialistic aspects of environment, (b) value theory—to include conditioning towards the ideal and meaningful human values and (c) sociohistorical theory—to include the interactional process influenced by cultural learning in the historical context. The value approach is central to the development of CS in children. This lays the foundation for universal positive traits by way of deep-rooted cultural pathways. The cross-cultural research focuses on the independent value-based approach and interdependent pathways. Further, the development of 'altruism' and 'egoism' are outcomes of different socialization and environmental contexts. The independent and interdependent interactions are very important for development.

The former expects individuation and independence, and the latter group membership and interdependence. The dominance of sociocentric or collectivistic attitude is necessary for social harmony and peace. In a related study conducted by Hutcheon (2000), the impact of culture and socialization through interdependence was explored. The present authors deliberate on purposeful guidance and nurturance for developing desirable habits and behaviour. The role of culture in this context must be to inspire, inform and uplift virtues. According to the authors, the cultural relativism only promotes subjectivism and perspectivism, thus denying the characteristic feature of universality of human values and virtues. Further, there are some which are better than the others, and one should strive to achieve the higher. Accordingly, multiculturalism in this context only breeds division and isolation, and undresses the harmony and unity of cultures. The authors propose interculturalism for breaking barriers between groups and promote development of original cultures, thereby bringing enriched cultures into existence. The crisis of values of the modern society is said to be due to a host of modern cultures such as those of poverty, affluence, culture of violence, misunderstood sexuality, self-indulgence, alienation and very critical the culture of fantasy. The culture of fantasy is said to be the state of absence of rational thinking and is embodiment of the irrational (e.g., mindless entertainment, celebrity culture and gambling). Another standpoint is that cultural frameworks determine the conception of self and social relation based on the alternatives of (a) duty based and (b) morality based (Turiel, 2008). In this context, children are viewed as developing moral systems; hence participation and communication about cultural practices is of significance.

Deep-rooted cultures do have a significant impact on the way we think, feel and act. Though socialization has a predominant influence on the virtues that we develop, influence of culture should be more understood in terms of universalities. For example, love of a mother towards her child is a universal phenomenon. Similarly, the cultivation of positive human values at a young age is possible with deliberate and conscious training and education of children. The culture of human values then can be realized as a ubiquitous phenomenon. The involvement of all agents of socialization in this regard needs much effort and commitment. It is the adult social agents and organizations who can imbibe qualities of sympathy, hope and sincerity in our growing up children. The crisis values of this generation can be resolved only when socializing agents take responsibility and commit themselves to positive childrearing practices.

Recommendations

The aim of the present chapter is to explore the role of socializing agents in building CS as a virtue for promotion of well-being. The phenomenon of socialization begins at early age and developing a human being in this phase is a lot more malleable and must be carefully utilized for positive growth. In light of the preceding discussion and reviews, an attempt is made here to provide recommendations for nurturing CS in children for well-being.

1. Morality cannot be psychologicized or biologicized (Turiel, 2008). The influence of both depends on many extraneous factors. The inclination towards the sensible and the right should begin at an early age. The agents of socialization interact upon the predisposed biological being, and strong psychological mechanisms have to be incorporated while teaching the young. Promotion of reciprocal interactions and moral concepts is the responsibility of immediate relatives of the child. According to Nussbaum (1999), despite their social context human beings are capable of and have the power of moral choice and can live in accordance with it. The traditional psychology which has constantly focused on manipulating and controlling behaviour needs a paradigm shift giving due accord to positive promotion of well-being, choice of a better and planned life. With the universality of moral beliefs, the methods to harness the positive traits must be explored, and the best approaches to make children more human should be adopted.
2. The phenomena of cultural differences can be contrasted with the efforts of positive psychologists to unify different domains of culture under one roof. The commonalities can be given effective treatments to develop the culture of positive traits and virtues. Parental values and practices must serve as a model to imitate, and in the due course development becomes an integral part of self.

3. An individual's goals and expectations about future can be tuned with the character virtue by representing the life with hopeful future expectations (Callina et al., 2017). The individuals would then be able to function effectively, and the prospect of a better life for future motivates them to adopt fair means to reach goals.
4. Intentional culture creation (Sokatch, 2017) in schools can promote long-lasting proactive behaviour in children. School environment and teachers have an important role to play in creating a classroom environment with informed practices, for teachers and other school members constitute an important step towards building CS. The nurturing of CS through high-quality skill development programmes for long-term positive outcomes should be worked out for each school setting. For this, specifically developed programmes should no doubt be implemented with commitment and rigour.
5. It is very important to mentally represent adult concepts (of morality) in a unitary fashion (Maas, 2008). Such representations or prototypes are very important at different points in development. The child in the context of various experiences shall then have a frame of references to make a choice and adopt positive approach to life. The crisis of modernity can be said to be the absence of such framework for young children who end up in juvenile homes and conflict with the legal systems.
6. Dishonesty and lying most commonly found in children should be replaced by moral character and ethical behaviour. Clark and Soutter (2016) argue that a multidimensional and broad approach is indispensable for the development of CS. The interactions of the intellectual character and the moral character of the young along with social experiences reframe the purpose of education and commitment to civic actions. A cooperative effort from the family, parents, older adults, school, teachers and community is needed, and all formal and informal agencies have to put in efforts to make a morally sound society. Moral characters often oppose and discourage deviance and promote integrity.
7. Bolstering human capacities by virtues of character strengthens children against delinquency, trauma and depression. Enhancing creativity, tolerance and non-judgemental attitude also promotes leadership (Thun, 2009). CS-based leadership outcomes are more in conjunction with the qualities of a transformational leader.

8. Stress and coping are also the hallmarks of the developing child. The cognition of the stressor and display of an appropriate positive coping strategy is an important exercise. The understanding and restructuring of problems in a positive manner is highly cognitive in nature (Gustems-Carnicer & Calderón, 2016). The development of virtues and character empowers individuals to constructively deal with demanding situations and express a positive outlook towards life in general. Such attitudes promote resilience, compliance and tolerance for others. Proactive coping strategies help children to integrate themselves easily in social contexts since they are equipped with multiple resources to cope with stress. In cases of depression, positive affective strengths such as gratitude, love, hope and bravery promote easy and early recovery and better coping (Zhou, Siu, & Liu, 2013).

9. Often faulty parental socialization (of negative emotions) are related to child psychopathology (O'Neal & Magai, 2005). Further, rewarding socialization of comfort, empathy and support benefits children in the long run. The punitive style of discouragement, disapproval and neglect (ignoring the emotional needs of the child) promote disregard and deviance from the moral standards. Over time negative emotions magnify in cognitive domain, and negative and deviant behaviour patterns develop. Hence parental socialization should combine positive affect strategies to prevent deviance and dysregulation. Thus emotional management of children and psychopathology are linked to childhood experiences of socialization, and positive parenting approaches can prevent derangement in cognition and personality.

Conclusion

The building block of every human development is inclusive of physiological mechanisms as well as psychosocial interactions. The children of today are blessed with massive exposure of technology and hi-tech trends. The same however has left very little scope for a morally rooted and culturally sensitive way of life. The competitive world and race for success often have people to overlook traditional human values and concern for fellow beings. The most democratic and secular nations today are all in search of peace and harmony. Vengeance, violence and war are becoming the first options for dealing with chaos and scarcity. The crisis of human values can only be resolved with adept and conscious socialization of children from a very young age. Parenting and childrearing practices today are also bound to be influenced by social change and metamorphosis of modern values. The highly materialistic world has to now yearn for human love and care, and the well-being of people is at stake. The positive traits and virtues are hence to be consciously made mandatory in parenting and socialization processes. Different phases of development have specific significance in inculcating positive and empathetic attitude in children. The efforts of schools and the teaching environment have to tap and nurture the best traits in the child and provide a conducive and encouraging environment to sustain the attitude of hope and trust throughout life. Such an encouraging environment would provide constant motivation to thrive on positive values and virtues, and promote well-being of not only self but also the fellow beings. CS in this chapter is dealt within the context of socialization and interactions of parents, school and peer group, in promoting well-being as both supplementary and complementary functions. The role of culture, especially the universality of culture in the context of CS, is of great significance in adopting universal approaches to promote value-based well-being.

REFERENCES

Alexander, S. (1893). Character and conduct. *International Journal of Ethics*, *3*(4), 466–489.

Barry, C. M., & Wentzel, K. R. (2006). Friend influence on prosocial behavior: The role of motivational factors and friendship characteristics. *Developmental Psychology*, *42*(1), 153–163.

Batra, P. (2013). Positive parenting: Meaning and methods. *Indian Journal of Positive Psychology*, *4*(4), 528–533.

Baumrind, D. (1991). Parenting styles and adolescent development. In J. Brooks-Gunn, R. M. Lerner, & A. C. Petersen (Eds.), *The encyclopedia on adolescence* (pp. 746–758). New York, NY: Garland Publishing.

Bukatko, D., & Daehler, M. W. (2012). *Child development: A thematic approach* (6th ed.). Belmont, CA: Wadsworth.

Callina, K. S., Johnson, S. K., Tirrell, J. M., Batanova, M., Weiner, M. B., & Lerner, R. M. (2017). Modeling pathways of character development across the first three decades of life: An application of integrative data analysis techniques to understanding the development of hopeful future expectations. *Journal of Youth and Adolescence, 46*(6), 1216–1237. doi:10.1007/s10964-017-0660-1

Clark, S., & Soutter, M. (2016). A broad character education approach for addressing America's cheating culture. *Journal of Research in Character Education, 12*(2), 29–42.

Colman, A. M. (2009). *Oxford dictionary of psychology*. Newark: Oxford University Press.

Cooley, C. H. (1922). The social self: The meaning of 'I'. Chapter 5 in *Human nature and social disorder* (pp. 168–210). New York, NY: Charles Scribner's Sons. Retrieved from https://campus.fsu.edu/bbcswebdav/institution/academic/ social_sciences/sociology/Reading%20Lists/Social%20Psych%20 Prelim %20Readings/I.%20Classics/1968%20Cooley%20-%20The%20 Social%20Self.pdf

Cope, E. D. (1883). The evolutionary significance of human character. *The American Naturalist, 17*(9), 907–919.

Criss, M. M., Pettit, G. S., Bates, J. E., Dodge, K. A., & Lapp, A. L. (2002). Family adversity, positive peer relationships, and children's externalising behavior: A longitudinal perspective on risk and resilience. *Child Development, 73*(4), 1220–1237.

Damon, W. (2006). Socialisation and individuation. In G. Handel (Ed.), *Childhood Socialisation* (2nd ed). (New Brunswick transaction publishers. 2006). Retrieved from: http://www.world cat.org/title/childhood-socialization/oclc/971493678

Darling, N., & Steinberg, L. (1993). Parenting style as context: An integrative model. *Psychological Bulletin, 113*(3), 487–496.

Denham, S. A. (1997). 'When I have a Bad Dream, Mommy Holds Me': Preschoolers' conceptions of emotions, parental socialisation, and emotional competence. *International Journal of Behavioral Development, 20*(2), 301–319.

Denham, S. A., Bassett, H. H., & Miller, S. L. (2017). Early childhood teachers' socialization of emotion: Contextual and individual contributors. *Child & Youth Care Forum, 46*(6), 805–824. doi:10.1007/s10566-017-9409-y

Ferrari, M., & Guthrie, C. E. (2014). Positive education and teaching for wisdom. In A. C. Parks & S. M. Schueller (Eds.), *The Wiley-Blackwell handbook of positive psychological interventions*. Malaysia: Vivar Printing.

Ferrari, M., Peskin, J., Allen, G., Petro, a., Waugh, C., & Martin-Smith, A. (2011). Teaching for wisdom in Highschool English Class. Poster presented at the *Canadian Psychology Association*. Toronto, ON.

Gallagher, M. W. (2009). Wellbeing. In S. J. Lopez (Ed.), *The encyclopaedia of positive psychology* (Vol. 1, pp. 1030–1034). Chichester, UK: Wiley-Blackwell. Retrieved from http://simbi.kemenag.go.id/pustaka/images/materibuku/the-encyclopedia-of-positive-psychology.pdf

Greenfield, P. M., Keller, H., Fuligni, A., & Maynard, A. (2003). Cultural pathways through universal development. *Annual Review of Psychology, 54*, 461–490.

Grusec, J. E., & Davidov, M. (2010). Integrating different perspectives on socialization theory and research: A domain-specific approach. *Child Development*, *81*(3), 687–709.

Parent Further. (n.d). Great relationships don't just happen. Retrieved from https://www.parentfurther.com

Gustems-Carnicer, J., & Calderón, C. (2016). Virtues and character strengths related to approach coping strategies of college students. *Social Psychology of Education: An International Journal*, *19*(1), 77–95. doi:http://dx.doi.org/10.1007/s11218-015-9305-y

Handel, G. (Ed.). (2006). *Childhood socialization* (2nd ed.). New Brunswick: Transaction Publishers. 2006. Retrieved from https://books.google.co.in/books?id=3R65_edfKlcC&printsec=frontcover#v=onepage&q&f=false

Hay, D. F., Castle, J., Davies, L., Demetriou, H., & Stimson, C. A. (1999). Prosocial action in very early childhood. *Journal of Child Psychology and Psychiatry*, *40*(6), 906–916.

Hughes, D. A., & Baylin, J. (2012). *Brain-based parenting: The neuroscience of caregiving for healthy attachment*. New York, NY: W.W. Norton.

Hutcheon, P. D., & Hoecker-Drysdale, S. (2000). Building character & culture. *EAF Journal*, *15*(1), 45.

Knowles, E., & Smith, M. (2006). *Character builders: Books and activities for character education*. Westport, Conn.: Libraries Unlimited.

Kumar, P. (2011). *Positive psychology: Approach to education*. Canada: Apple Academic Press.

Ladd, G. W., & Troop-Gordon, W. (2003). The role of chronic peer difficulties in the development of children's psychological adjustment problems. *Child Development*, *74*(5), 1344–1367.

Linley, P. A., & Harrington, S. (2006). Playing to your strengths. *Psychologist*, *19*(2), 86–89.

Mackinnon, L. C., Starnes, R., Volling, B., & Johnson, S. (1997). Perception of parenting as predictors of boys sibling and peer relations. *Developmental Psychology*, *33*(6), 1024–1031.

Maas, F. K. (2008). Children's understanding of promising, lying, and false belief. *Journal of General Psychology*, *135*(3), 301–322.

Manke, B. (20014). 2004 program evaluation executive summary. Retrieved from: https://www.projectwisdom.com/ERS/Resource_Public.asp?key=ExecSummary_04

Mead, G. H. (1934). Social attitudes and physical world. *Mind, self and society*. Chicago, IL: University of Chicago Press.

Mitchell, M. P. (2017). Positive youth development with parents, schools and communities. Retrieved from https://www.rootsofaction.com/developing-character-strengths-a-vital-goal-of-education part-2.html

Mulford, H. (1921). The child mind. *The American Journal of Psychology*, *32*(2), 179–195. doi:10.2307/1413740

Nussbaum, M. C. (1999). *Sex and social justice.* New York, NY: Oxford University Press.
O'Neal, C. R., & Magai, C. (2005). Do parents respond in different ways when children feel different emotions? The emotional context of parenting. *Development and Psychopathology, 17*(2), 467–487.
Ozmete, E. (2011). Building social capital in micro environment: The family attachment theory and socialisation. *Nurture, 5*(1), 1–7.
Parker, A. E., Halberstadt, A. G., Dunsmore, J. C., Townley, G., Bryant, A., Jr., Beale, K. S., & Thompson, J. A. (2012). 'Emotions are a window into one's heart': A qualitative analysis of parental beliefs about children's emotions across three ethnic groups. *Monographs of the Society for Research in Child Development, 77*(3), 1–136.
Park, N., & Peterson, C. (2006). Character strengths and happiness among young children: Content analysis of parental descriptions. *Journal of Happiness Studies, 7*(3), 323–341.
Park, N., Peterson, C., & Seligman, M. E. P. (2004). Strengths of character and wellbeing. *Journal of Social and Clinical Psychology, 23*(5), 603–619.
Peterson, C., & Seligman, M. E. P. (2004). *Character strengths and virtues: A classification and handbook.* New York: Oxford University Press & Washington, DC: American Psychological Association.
Porges, S. (2011). *The polyvagal theory: Neurophysiological foundations of emotions, attachment, communication and self-regulation.* New York, NY: W. W. Norton.
Rösler, F., & Röder, B. (2014). *Socialisation in early childhood: Biological, psychological, sociological and economic perspectives.* Berlin: German National Academy of Sciences Leopoldina. Retrieved from http://www.akademienunion.de/fileadmin/redaktion/user_upload/Publikationen/Stellungnahmen/2014_Stellungnahme_Sozialisation_EN_web.pdf
Scarr, S. (1992). Developmental theories for the 1990s: Development and individual differences. *Child Development, 63*(1), 1–19.
Seligman, M. E. P., Ernst, R. M., Gillham, J., Reivich, K., & Linkins, M. (2009). Positive education: Positive psychology and classroom interventions. *Oxford Review of Education, 35*(3), 293–311.
Sokatch, A. (2017). Toward a research agenda: Building character strengths in school settings. *Journal of Youth and Adolescence, 46*(6), 1238–1239. doi: 0.1007/s10964-017-0657-9
Steger, M. F., Hicks, B., Kashdan, T. B., Krueger, R. F., & Bouchard, T. J., Jr. (2007). Genetic and environmental influences on the positive traits of the Values in Action classification, and biometric covariance with normal personality. *Journal of Research in Personality, 41*(3), 524–539.
Sternberg, R. J. (2001). Why schools should teach for wisdom: The balance theory of wisdom in educational settings. *Educational Psychologist, 36*(4), 227–245.
Thun, N. B. (2009). *Character strengths in leadership* (Order No. NR58326). Available from ABI/INFORM Global; ProQuest Central; ProQuest Dissertations & Theses Full Text. (250178736).

Tripathi, R., Banu, H., & Mehrotra, S. (2015). Self-perceived character strengths in urban Indian youth: Observations and reflections. *Journal of the Indian Academy of Applied Psychology, 41*(3), 175–186.

Turiel, E. (2008). The development of children's orientations toward moral, social, and personal orders: More than a sequence in development. *Human Development, 51*(1), 21–39.

Upadhyay, U. T., & Arya, S. (2015). A critique of research studies on application of positive psychology for augmenting children's emotional wellbeing. *Indian Journal of Positive Psychology, 6*(4), 417–421.

Waters, L. (2017). *The strength switch: How the new science of strength-based parenting can help your teen and child to flourish.* New York, NY: Avery Publishers.

Weiten, W., & Lloyd, M. A. (2007). *Psychology applied to modern life-adjustment in the 21st century* (8th ed.). Delhi: Thomson-Wadsworth Learning.

Zhou, Y., Siu, A. F., & Liu, X. (2013). What does not kill me makes me stronger: The relationship between depression history, character strengths and coping strategies. *Indian Journal of Health and Wellbeing, 4*(6), 1249–1254.

Chapter 12

Scope for Character Strength Development in Organizations

Vijayalaya Srinivas T., Vijaya R., Lijo Thomas and Hitankshi M. Trivedi

The great hope of society is in individual character.

—William Ellery Channing

Within a decade of the turn of the century, the world has seen enough of large corporations collapsing ranging from WorldCom, Enron, AIG, Lehman Brothers, Freddie Mac to Satyam. Juxtaposing the quote of William Ellery Channing (1780–1842) with the events of 21st century makes it obvious that the recognition of the role of individual character is something that is longstanding (Wright & Goodstein, 2007). The reasons for such corporate frauds including lack of leadership, integrity, zest for work and psychological well-being shall be related to the perceived decline in individual character and its formation (Peterson, Park, Hall, & Seligman, 2009). Even Henry Ford had emphasized on the benefits of having individuals with strengths of character in one's employ (Lacey, 1986, as cited in Wright & Huang, 2008). All these point to the vitality of the role played by the character of individual employees in the organizational effectiveness. As Walton (2001) argues, the idea of good *polis* (community)—not unmanageably large, united in purpose, with distributed but not necessarily democratic decision-making authority—given by Aristotle (384–322 BC) shall be related with the modern day organizations. This paves the way for the extension of application of character strengths development in the community to the organizations as well. Taking cognizance of the aforementioned, this chapter focuses on the scope for character strengths and its development in the organizational settings along with the plausible areas of applications and recommendations for future research.

BASIC CONCEPTS

Character Strengths

The Oxford Dictionary defines 'character' as the mental and moral qualities distinctive to an individual. Character strengths are personality traits which refer to internal psychological processes that define the character and the specific aspects of personality that are morally valued (Park, Peterson, & Seligman, 2004). These character strengths are different from strengths of our innate talents, abilities, skills, external resources and supports. Though these strengths are important, character strengths are the foundation upon which the edifice of these strengths shall be built. Character strengths are defined as a family of positive traits reflected in thoughts, feelings and behaviours (Park & Peterson, 2006b). Institutions, one of the criteria for character strength development, are the deliberate target of societal practices and rituals that try to cultivate the character strengths (Park, Peterson, & Seligman, 2004). Therefore, the scope for character strength development in organizations is quite apparent.

The Values in Action (VIA) Institute led by Peterson and Seligman (2004) identified 24 distinct character strengths as a result of the completion of a large-scale project. When the VIA strengths were subjected to factor analysis (Park & Peterson, 2006a), four factors emerged prominently that got replicated across studies, namely, Temperance (e.g., authenticity, prudence, self-regulation and perseverance), Intellectual (e.g., love of learning, creativity and curiosity), Transcendence (e.g., hope, religiousness, spirituality, gratitude and zest) and Interpersonal strengths (e.g., modesty, social intelligence, kindness and teamwork).

Signature Strengths

Out of all the identified 24 character strengths, it has been found that in general any individual will possess up to seven character strengths as his/her top or core character strengths. These top seven core character strengths are known as the signature strengths of an individual (Peterson & Seligman, 2004). These signature strengths will be of prime importance while designing strength-based intervention techniques for enhancing organizational effectiveness.

Associated Outcomes

Character strengths are found to be positively associated with school success, prosocial behaviour, self-esteem and perceived competence (Scales et al., 2000; Skinner & Wellborn, 1994, as cited in Park & Peterson, 2006b). Further, it is also found to be negatively associated with depression (Snyder et al., 1998), delinquency and violence (Benson et al., 1998; Cardemil et al., 2002, both as cited in Park & Peterson, 2006b). For easier understanding, broad classifications such as 'Head' strengths and 'Heart' strengths are introduced. 'Head' strengths refer to the intellectual strengths such as curiosity, creativity and love for learning, while the 'Heart' strengths refer to aspects such as zest, kindness, hope and teamwork. Park and Peterson (2010) have identified that the 'heart' strengths are more helpful than the 'head' strengths for adjustments in diverse situations.

Most of the studies on character strengths have only focused on happiness and life satisfaction of the respondents which pushed the importance of intellectual strengths to the backburner. The study of the influence of character strengths on organizational effectiveness from the perspective of the managers may bring out the importance of the 'head' strengths or the intellectual strengths of the employees. Positive psychology embodies an effort or movement from psychological problems and deficits to human strengths and virtues which make life worth living (Seligman & Csikszentmihalyi, 2000) and thus highlights that character strengths contribute to individual well-being, happiness and life satisfaction.

Universal Virtues

In their handbook on character strengths and virtues, Peterson and Seligman (2004) have identified certain six universal virtues such as

- wisdom (cognitive strengths related to acquisition and use of knowledge),
- courage (emotional strengths related to exercise of will to achieve something despite opposition),
- humanity (interpersonal strengths involving tending and befriending others),
- justice (civic strengths such as justice, leadership and teamwork),
- temperance (strengths that protect against excess) and
- transcendence (strengths that forge connections with larger universe).

These virtues are considered to be broad based having commonality across various cultures, religions and moral standings.

Focus on such universal virtues helped in the consideration of virtue ethical frameworks that shall guide the organizations through the hectic process of ethical decision-making (Crossan, Mazutis, & Seijts, 2013).

Organizational-level Virtues

In order to make it much more specific to the needs of the organizational requirements, the following five organizational-level virtues were identified (Peterson & Park, 2006),

- Purpose: a shared vision of the moral goals of the organization
- Safety: protection against threat, danger and exploitation which affect physical and psychological well-being
- Fairness: equitable rules
- Humanity: mutual care and concern
- Dignity: equal treatment irrespective of their positions

APPLICATIONS
Corporate Social Responsibility

Corporate social responsibility (CSR) is one of the cornerstones of an organization which helps in brand building, employee engagement and paying back to the society as well. Recently developing countries like India have made it mandatory under the New Companies Act, 2013. In these circumstances, exploring the scope for character strengths in CSR and understanding its role in making it effective becomes all the more pertinent. A huge responsibility of ensuring proper CSR activity in the organization rests on the type of leadership prevailing in the organization as well (Angus-Leppan, Metcalf, & Benn, 2010).

Charity sport events: Unlike organizing events such as ALS Ice Bucket Challenge and no makeup selfie challenge, the charity sports events combine the awareness campaign and fundraising activities along with a physically engaging workout. According to New Economics Foundation (NEF, 2011), charity sports events provide consistent support for five pathways to well-being such as

- being active,
- giving,
- connecting,
- learning and
- being mindful.

These pathways are found be highly related to the interpersonal strengths and intellectual strengths expected from an employee. Research has shown that leisure activity might trigger certain event-specific character strengths that shall result in well-being outcomes. The activation of character strengths shall happen at three different phases; pre-event (e.g., citizenship and generosity), during the event (e.g., perseverance and leadership) and post-event (e.g., gratitude and enthusiasm). The leader should identify the evoked strengths and organize the event matching the needs of the organization (Coghlan & Filo, 2016).

Small and medium enterprises (SMEs): Worldwide, 90 per cent of the business and 50–60 per cent of employment opportunities are provided by small and medium enterprises (SMEs) (Jenkins, 2004). The word 'corporate' in CSR has unfortunately focused only on multinational companies and left out the contributions of SMEs. However, Jenkins (2006) identified that due to their scale of operations, they establish a very strong stakeholder relationship. These relationships are invariably laced with trust, informal communication networks, teamwork and higher importance to interpersonal relationship. This naturally enables them to sacrifice their profits in the wake of achievement of greater societal goals (Vives, 2006). Scholars of the field prefer to call this as 'silent CSR' or 'sunken CSR' activities. The scope for harnessing interpersonal strengths and transcendence strengths are very much available among the SMEs.

Positive youth development: Organizations focusing on positive youth development would be an ideal way of promoting and building character strengths among employees. Strumpfer (1995) identified that the best way to build strengths for well-being is to start off at more points, namely, work, marriage, parenthood and so on. Like the faith-based institutions, conducting positive parenting workshops for the employees might very well be considered as a CSR activity.

Strength-based parenting is an approach where parents deliberately identify and cultivate positive states, processes and qualities in their children. It is about connecting your kids with their inborn strengths such as strengths of character (e.g., humour and kindness) as well as their talents such as writing or sporting ability. These strengths are the inner resources contained within our kids that help boost their life satisfaction (Waters, 2016). Parents who are already exposed to character strength development programmes in the organization will be primed towards identifying such strengths among their children. Organizing positive parenting workshops for the employees as a CSR activity shall enable them to excel in strength-based parenting.

Ethical Decision-making

One of the most crucial actions in an organization is decision-making, especially so when it involves ethical dilemmas. Though there are three different approaches to solve such kind of ethical dilemmas, most of the times the ethical decisions are based only on the following two approaches (Nyberg, 2007):

- Consequentialism approach: justifying the means or the processes through the ends or final outcomes
- Deontological approach: Kantian philosophy of justifying a noble end through noble means

More often than not, the ethical decisions are influenced by the self-interest only view of character of the decision-maker. Recently, this self-interest view has been put to scrutiny (Wright & Goodstein, 2007, as cited in Wright & Huang, 2008) and the alternative methods have been focused upon. The third and the most relevant approach is known as the 'virtue ethics approach'—a framework focusing on the excellence of personal character to define moral behaviour. This approach believes on the inherent virtues of the individual to arrive at ethical decisions. According to Peterson and Seligman (2004), character strengths are the psychological ingredients that define human virtues.

Virtue-based Orientation (VBO) model: This is the revised version of Rest's (1986) Ethical Decision-making (EDM) model after the incorporation of virtue ethics approach to it. Initially Rest's model focused on the processes such as awareness, judgement, intent and behaviour to be in a linear relationship. Introduction of the concept of self-reflection as a mediator in Rest's EDM model has eventually changed the linear relationship into a circular one.

Virtuous mean: The origin of this concept shall be traced back to *Nicomachean Ethics* of Aristotle. It does not imply the average or moderation of an individual's virtues. It just represents the display of character strength when they are at the best of human condition. Further, it is important to ensure that the development of character strengths is within the virtuous mean rather than falling prey to the vices of excess or deficiency of those strengths (Crossan, Mazutis, & Seijts, 2013). For instance, if the character strength of bravery is taken for consideration, it shall range from cowardice (deficiency) to absolute recklessness (excess).

Situational pressures: Another prominent factor influencing decision-making is the context in which those decisions are made. Determinants such as organizational policies, environmental factors, job context and interpersonal communication networks which comprise of organizational climate shall have an impact on the ethical decisions made (Fritzsche, 2000). Zimbardo (2008) through the replication studies of Milgram experiment proved the significant influence of situational pressure on human behaviour. However, he also pointed out a huge range of variance in human compliance attributable to individual differences. This individual difference is the scope for character strengths to influence the ethical decision-making in overcoming the immediate situational pressures.

Figure 12.1 shows the virtual-based orientation (VBO) model of ethical decision-making which is a refurbished Rest's (1986) four component model of EDM model incorporating the aspects such as self-reflection, virtuous mean and situational factors. It is believed that the VBO model will act as a buffer to overcome the situational pressures while making ethical decisions (Crossan, Mazutis, & Seijts, 2013).

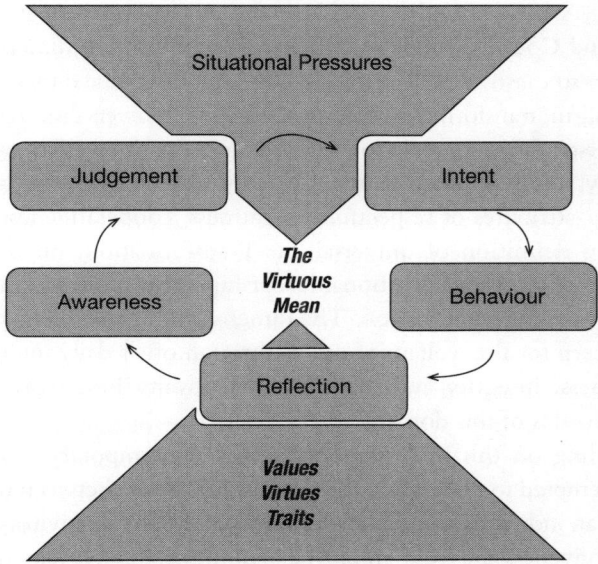

Figure 12.1 *VBO Model of Ethical Decision-making*
Source: Crossan, Mazutis and Seijts (2013).

Leadership

Given the current scenario of organizational demands, the managers are mandated to replace their act of merely getting things done with influencing the subordinates and achieving the organizational effectiveness. This is where the leadership traits and core strengths are getting emphasized upon.

In order to cater to the emerging complexities of the organizations, Avolio and colleagues (Avolio et al., 2004; Luthans & Avolio, 2003, both as cited in Jensen & Luthans, 2006) proposed a new model of leadership known as authentic leadership style. An authentic leader is one who knows what he is doing, takes ethical decisions, works with optimism, confidence and hope, and is widely known and respected for his integrity (Sarros & Cooper, 2006). This approach draws a lot from positive psychology and focuses on building strengths, adding value and sense of right to decision-making, enhancing trust and remaining positive.

Characters of an individual also form a part of his personality. It can be understood as an outward expression of personal values and integrity, which intends to achieve morally appropriate outcomes. Sarros and Cooper (2006) recognized three important dimensions of character strengths that determine a good leader. These dimensions are universalism, transformation and benevolence. Universalism represents an understanding, appreciation and tolerance for the welfare of people generally, and is a macro perspective approach to work and life. The character attributes of respectfulness, fairness, cooperativeness fit best with this definition of universalism. Transformation, on the other hand, relates to transformational leadership. This dimension includes values of courage and passion. The dimension of benevolence focuses on concern for the welfare of others through one's daily interactions. Selflessness, integrity and organizational loyalty best represent the characteristics of this domain.

Building on this understanding, many contemporary researchers have attempted to understand the relationship, if any, between the character of an individual and his leadership qualities. In an environment of love, forgiveness and trust, employee commitment and loyalty rise multifold. It instils in the employees a sense of self-discipline, self-control and self-respect accompanied by high levels of self-esteem (Caldwell & Dixon, 2010). It also encourages employees to take ownership of their work and take on extra role behaviour. This positive outlook in an organization is possible only under the guidance and supervision of an effective leader.

Luthans and Avolio (2003) have identified that the strengths of a leader and his/her well-being will have a 'contagion effect' on the well-being of the subordinates as well (as cited in Wright & Huang, 2008). The employees are expected to work within the value system and the ideals of the organization. They thus get conditioned to working with these values day in and day out, leading to the development of certain similar character strengths in them. Research studies conducted demonstrate that subordinates learn those values and ideals emphasized and focused upon by the leaders (Kraft & Austin, 2015). A transformational leader will focus on ideals such as courage, justice, honesty and accountability (Sarros & Cooper, 2006). Thus, these are focused upon and passed on to the employees, leading to their character strength development as well.

Employees who follow authentic leaders are found to be enjoying work–family enrichment rather than the usual work–family conflict (Braun & Nieberle, 2017). Implicit CSR activities are those which are promoted by leaders who follow emergent and authentic leadership styles (Angus-Leppan, Metcalf, & Benn, 2010). This can come in handy to understand and promote the 'silent CSR' happening in the SMEs which can be highly driven by the leaders of such organizations. All these clearly brings to the fore the influence of character strengths of the leader and its eventual impact on the employees and the effectiveness of the organization.

Theodora Effect

This effect is named after Byzantine Empress Theodora who supported her husband, Emperor Justinian through the Niko revolt and later became the pioneer in the fight for women's liberation and their rights. She was instrumental in bringing into effect certain women-friendly legislations in the Byzantine Empire.

Theodora effect refers to the common set of character strengths found among high-performing women executives. Those common set of character strengths are as follows: judgement, honesty, love, creativity, fairness, humour and kindness. Women executives possessing these character strengths are found to be engaged in positive deviant behaviours in an organization (Joyner, 2014).

Gerzema and D'Antonio (2013) in their famous book *The Athena Doctrine* have described how the world is expecting a relief in the form of feminine leadership. Focusing on these common feminine character strengths shall bring in the welcome respite to the existing more masculine leadership styles involving aggression, competition, control and black-and-white thinking.

Strength-based Intervention

Character strengths are not something that is inherited. They are malleable, however, at least some character strengths when changed in short term are found to have staying power. This provides the scope for interventions to build on them and have an avenue for character strength development through character education (Peterson & Seligman, 2003). As Strumpfer (2006) argues in his strengths perspective, it can be nurtured and developed through *Fortigenesis,* which comes from Latin *fortis* meaning 'strong' and Greek *genesis* meaning 'production'.

Holocaust survivors were not supermen but their stories were all examples of just how remarkable humans can be when subjected to undue stress and agony (Helmreich, 1992, as cited in Strumpfer, 2006). Post 9/11 attacks, Peterson and Seligman (2003) conducted studies and identified the role played by crises as a crucible for building character strengths. Therefore, crisis simulation trainings and case studies shall support the character strength development process.

Hodges and Asplund (2010) have identified that the application of character strengths in organizational settings leads to increase in productivity by 12.5 per cent and reduction in turnover rates by almost 50 per cent (as cited in Harzer & Ruch, 2014).

Signature strengths of the individuals are positively related to the job performance which comprises of subdimensions namely task performance, job dedication, interpersonal facilitation and organizational support at the workplace (Harzer & Ruch, 2014). Further, they designed a web-based intervention and proved that signature strengths help in improving the tendency to perceive the job as one's calling—a consuming and meaningful passion that people experience towards a domain like one's work (Harzer & Ruch, 2016).

Sadler-Smith (2012) found that virtues are developed over time through habitual practice which means that ethical decision-making shall be learnt from previous contextual references. Dimow (2004) pointed out that people who resisted authority in Milgram experiment were found to be having earlier such experiences in political and military organizations (as cited in Crossan, Mazutis, & Seijts, 2013).

These studies clearly point out that the character strengths can be developed through exposure to similar experiences either through simulation trainings or case study methods. Further, it can be developed by habituating the practices of character strengths as part of the organizational culture itself.

CASE STUDY
Maple Leaf Foods

In August 2008, Canadian Food Inspection Agency (CFIA) started receiving complaints from public about the nationwide spread of listeriosis. Even before the source was identified beyond doubt, Maple Leaf Foods establishment issued a 'voluntary' recall. The first recall issued on 17 August 2008 was limited to only 23 ready-to-eat packaged meat products. Later as the death toll rose to 22 and many more started falling sick, the recall was expanded to include all 220 products since 1 June 2008.

Media found fault with the lax Canadian government policy on food safety unlike the US government. The reason was identified as the accumulation of the bacteria *Listeria monocytogenes* in the meat-slicer machine. Though the slicer manufacturer and Maple Leaf Foods were blaming each other, the establishment had to be closed for months for extensive cleaning and replacement of certain parts. Later the president of Maple Leaf Foods, Michael McCain, acknowledged that across the brand the sales had plummeted by up to 50 per cent.

The turning point happened on 23 August 2008, when the president of Maple Leaf Foods, Michael McCain took complete responsibility for the outbreak of listeriosis and tendered a public apology through a video message. Post-apology, the press response turned the corner and gradually Maple Leaf Food establishment regained its lost position and currently remains one of the leading food safety establishments in Canada.

The federal government and the Parliament appointed Sheila Weatherill to investigate the listeriosis crisis. Despite the investigation coming up with evidences of Listeria contamination ever since 2007, Maple Leaf Foods could not be held liable as it was not mandatory for the company to report the same in those days.

The effect of the good press which reported that McCain was making the apology against the advice of his legal advisors and at a time when the Ontario's Apology Act was not even in force reduced the reduction of sales from 50 per cent to 15 per cent within just two months (Stevenson, 2008).

Analysis

In the aforementioned case study, the president McCain neither took a consequentialist ethical approach to protect the narrow interest of the shareholders and denied the responsibility for the contamination nor took a deontological ethical approach and delayed response by weighing in the rights and responsibilities of each and everyone involved. Instead he resorted to the virtue-based ethical approach driven by his character strengths and responded swiftly by assuming responsibility and apologizing to the public (Crossan, Mazutis, & Seijts, 2013).

FUTURE DIRECTIONS

Given the scope of character strengths in the organizational settings, it is equally important to highlight the challenges which shall be overcome only through more empirical research. Organizational culture is mostly transmitted to most of the employees of any organization. Employee orientation is very critical to the success of any firm (Beatty, 1988). More studies need to be carried to understand the influence of culture on character strengths. Although Kitayama et al. (2000) argued that the positive feelings associated with character strengths would mean interdependence for Japanese and independence for Americans, later studies revealed more of convergence in the character strengths of Japanese and American culture (as cited in Shimai, Otake, Park, Peterson, & Seligman, 2006). However, there is still scope to compare, like the monotheist American approach with the Buddhist and Shintoist Japanese approaches to religiosity (Shimai et al., 2006).

Considering the role of character strengths in CSR activities, more needs to be done in the form considering the relationship between event-related signature strengths and charity sports events. More direct studies have to be conducted to explore the scope of character strengths in SMEs towards promotion of CSR activities. There is an absolute lack of studies relating the organizational climate and its induced character strengths with the parenting styles of the employees of the organization. Such studies shall take the entire gamut of CSR activities of an organization to the next level.

As far as ethical decision-making is concerned, more studies have to be conducted to understand the practical realization of 'virtuous mean' that might help in designing realistic strength-based intervention programmes. This would further improve the standards of ethical decision-making, and thereby reduction of conflict and negative deviant behaviours in the organizations.

In the realm of leadership, authentic leadership style is a relatively new concept that emerged out of positive psychology influences in the aftermath of repeated corporate frauds. Though there is huge scope for the character strengths, people have already started pointing out the redundancy between the authentic and transformative style of leadership (Banks, McCauley, Gardner, & Guler, 2016). Moreover, there is lot of scope to explore the specific feminine character strengths associated with leadership qualities. Therefore, future studies should focus more on tapping the influence of character strengths on leadership taken in a wholesome and comprehensive manner.

More studies have to be carried out in ascertaining the signature strengths specific to the jobs in an organization. Focused research on signature strengths might help in enhancing the person–environment (P–E) fit in an organization, and thereby job performance and satisfaction. The importance of the intellectual or head strengths have to be tested against job performance rather than against the widely compared life satisfaction to identify and tap specific character strengths appropriate for industrial/organizational settings. Conducting longitudinal studies to understand the staying power of the strength-based intervention programmes would be highly pertinent here.

Once the scope of character strengths in the organizational settings is realized and put to practical use through evidence-based approaches, then the herculean task of unleashing the human potential in an organization would become a child's play for any human resource manager.

REFERENCES

Angus-Leppan, T., Metcalf, L., & Benn, S. (2010). Leadership styles and CSR practice: An examination of sensemaking, institutional drivers and CSR leadership. *Journal of Business Ethics, 93*(2), 189–213. Retrieved from http://www.jstor.org/stable/40605337

Banks, G. C., McCauley, K. D., Gardner, W. L., & Guler, C. E. (2016). A meta-analytic review of authentic and transformational leadership: A test for redundancy. *Leadership Quarterly, 27*(4), 634–652. doi:10.1016/j.leaqua.2016.02.006

Beatty, S. E. (1988). An exploratory study of organizational values with a focus on people orientation. *Journal of Retailing, 64*(4), 405–425.

Braun, S., & Nieberle, K. W. (2017). Authentic leadership extends beyond work: A multilevel model of work–family conflict and enrichment. *Leadership Quarterly, 28*(6), 780–797. doi:10.1016/j.leaqua.2017.04.003

Caldwell, C., & Dixon, R. D. (2010). Love, forgiveness, and trust: Critical values of the modern leader. *Journal of Business Ethics, 90*(1), 91–101. doi:10.1007/s10551-009-0184-z

Coghlan, A., & Filo, K. (2016). Bringing personal character strengths into the production of the leisure experience. *Leisure Sciences, 38*(2), 100–117. doi:10.1080/01490400.2015.1087355

Crossan, M., Mazutis, D., & Seijts, G. (2013). In search of virtue: The role of virtues, values and character strengths in ethical decision making. *Journal of Business Ethics, 113*(4), 567–581. doi:10.1007/s10551-013-1680-8

Fritzsche, D. J. (2000). Ethical climates and the ethical dimension of decision making. *Journal of Business Ethics, 24*(2), 125–140. doi:10.1023/A:1006262914562

Gerzema, J., & D'Antonio, M. (2013). *The Athena doctrine: How women (and the men who think like them) will rule the future*. San Francisco, CA: Jossey Bass.

Harzer, C., & Ruch, W. (2014). The role of character strengths for task performance, job dedication, interpersonal facilitation, and organizational support. *Human Performance, 27*(3), 183–205. doi:10.1080/08959285.2014.913592

Harzer, C., & Ruch, W. (2014). (2016). Your strengths are calling: Preliminary results of a web-based strengths intervention to increase calling. *Journal of Happiness Studies, 17*(6), 2237–2256. doi:10.1007/s10902-015-9692-y

Jenkins, H. (2004). A critique of conventional CSR theory: An SME perspective. *Journal of General Management, 29*(4), 55–75. doi:10.1177/030630700402900403

———. (2006). Small business champions for corporate social responsibility. *Journal of Business Ethics, 67*(3), 241–256. doi:10.1007/s10551-006-9182-6

Jensen, S., & Luthans, F. (2006). Relationship between entrepreneurs' psychological capital and their authentic leadership. *Journal of Managerial Issues, 18*(2), 254–273. Retrieved from http://www.jstor.org/stable/40604537

Joyner, A. M. (2014). The Theodora Effect: Character strengths and performance in executive women (Unpublished work). Retrieved from ProQuest Dissertations Publishing (3619454).

Kraft, C. R., & Austin, K. (2015). The character of achievement: An analysis of teacher's instructional practices for character education. *Journal of Character Education, 11*(2), 109–128.

New Economics Foundation (NEF). (2011). *Sustainable development and wellbeing: Relationships, challenges and policy implications*. London: Department for Environment, Food and Rural Affairs.

Nyberg, D. (2007). The morality of everyday activities: Not the right, but the good thing to do. *Journal of Business Ethics, 81*(3), 587–598. doi:10.1007/s10551-007-9530-1

Park, N., & Peterson, C. (2006a). Moral competence and character strengths among adolescents: The development and validation of the values in action inventory of strengths for youth. *Journal of Adolescence, 29*(6), 891–910. doi:10.1016/j.adolescence.2006.04.011

Park, N., & Peterson, C. (2006b). Character strengths and happiness among young children: Content analysis of parental descriptions. *Journal of Happiness Studies, 7*(3), 323–341. doi:10.1007/s10902-005-3648-6

Park, N., & Peterson, C. (2010). Does it matter where we live? The urban psychology of character strengths. *American Psychologist, 65*(6), 535–547. doi:10.1037/a0019621

Park, N., Peterson, C., & Seligman, M. (2004). Strengths of character and wellbeing. *Journal of Social and Clinical Psychology, 23*(5), 603–619. doi:10.1521/jscp.23.5.603.50748.

Peterson, C., & Park, N. (2006). Character strengths in organizations. *Journal of Organizational Behavior, 27*(8), 1149–1154. doi:10.1002/job.398

Peterson, C., & Seligman, M. (2003). Character strengths before and after September 11. *Psychological Science, 14*(4), 381–384. Retrieved from http://www.jstor.org/stable/40063813

Peterson, C., & Seligman, M. E. P. (2004). *Character strengths and virtues: A classification and handbook*. New York/Washington, DC: Oxford University Press/American Psychological Association.

Peterson, C., Park, N., Hall, N., & Seligman, M. E. P. (2009). Zest and work. *Journal of Organizational Behavior, 30*(2), 161–172. doi:10.1002/job.584

Rest, J. R. (1986). *Moral development: Advances in research and theory*. New York, NY: Praeger.

Sadler-Smith, E. (2012). Before virtue: Biology, brain, behaviour, and the 'moral sense'. *Business Ethics Quarterly, 22*(2), 351–376. doi:10.5840/beq201222223

Sarros, J., & Cooper, B. (2006). Building character: A leadership essential. *Journal of Business and Psychology, 21*(1), 1–22. Retrieved from http://www.jstor.org/stable/25473467

Seligman, M. E. P., & Csikszentmihalyi, M. (Eds.). (2000). Positive psychology [Special issue]. *American Psychologist, 55*(1).

Shimai, S., Otake, K., Park, N., Peterson, C., & Seligman, M. (2006). Convergence of character strengths in American and Japanese young adults. *Journal of Happiness Studies, 7*, 311–322. doi:10.1007/s10902-005-3647-7

Snyder, C. R., Lapointe, A. B., Crowson, J. J., Jr., & Early, S. (1998). Preferences of high- and low-hope people for self-referential feedback. *Cognition and Emotion, 12*(6), 807–823. doi:10.1080/026999398379448

Stevenson, C. P. (2008). Maple leaf case study: An example of crisis management. Retrieved from https://www.swlawyers.ca/docs/Maple-Leaf-Case-Study-Colin-Stevenson.pdf.

Strumpfer, D. (1995). The origins of health and strength: From 'salutogenesis' to 'fortigenesis'. *South African Journal of Psychology, 25*(2), 81–89. doi:10.1177/008124639502500203

———. (2006). The strengths perspective: Fortigenesis in adult life. *Social Indicators Research, 77*(1), 11–36. Retrieved from http://www.jstor.org/stable/27522571

Vives, A. (2006). Social and environmental responsibility in small and medium enterprises in Latin America. *The Journal of Corporate Citizenship, 21*, 39–50. Retrieved from http://www.jstor.org/stable/jcorpciti.21.39

Walton, C. (2001). Character and integrity in organizations: The civilization of the workplace. *Business and Professional Ethics Journal, 20* (3/4), 105–128.

Waters, L. (2016). The value of strength-based parenting. Retrieved from https://pursuit.unimelb.edu.au/articles/the-value-of-strength-based-parenting

Wright, T. A., & Goodstein, J. (2007). Character is not 'dead' in management research: A review of individual character and organizational-level virtue. *Journal of Management, 33*(6), 928–958. doi:10.1177/0149206307307644

Wright, T.A., & Huang, C.-C. (2008). Character in organizational research: Past directions and future prospects. *Journal of Organizational Behavior, 29*(7), 981–987. doi:10.1002/job.521

Zimbardo, P. G. (2008). *The Lucifer effect: Understanding how good people turn evil*. New York, NY: Random House.

Chapter 13

Heroes Begin Early
Parenting and the Development of Character Strengths

Bishakha Majumdar and Sibnath Deb

INTRODUCTION

The positive psychology movement that arose in the last decade of the 20th century has created a significant mindset change in orienting research attention from pathology to positivity (Heyne & Anderson, 2012). One of the first proponents of this field, Seligman and Csikszentmihalyi (2014), proposed that since the ultimate aim of psychological interventions is to lead individuals to optimal living, it may be advisable to identify, emulate and promote factors that enhance positive behaviour rather than to focus on reducing negative and undesirable behavioural traits. The study of character strengths, as drivers of psychological health, integrity and satisfaction, has contributed significantly to proactive measures to promote health and well-being among individuals of all ages (Anderson & Heyne, 2012; Saleebey, 2006).

Research in positive psychology has the concept of strengths for a long time (Seligman & Csikszentmihalyi, 2000). As early as 1924, Poffenberger and Carpenter proposed that certain character traits, such as care for detail or perseverance, lead to success in academic ventures at the school level (Poffenberger & Carpenter, 1924). Smith, in 1967, proposed the concept of strength of character, comprised of social maturity, resourcefulness, self-reliance and the like, which lead to school performance. Bennett (1993) provided his own categorization of desired youth outcomes such as compassion, faith, courage and perseverance.

Jach, Sun, Loton, Chin and Waters (2017) state that strengths are

> Capacities, characteristics, and processes that are energizing and authentic, and are manifested through patterns of thoughts, feelings, and behaviour. Strengths can be considered moral virtues such as honesty, talents such as creative writing ability, or Big Five personality traits such as conscientiousness. They are stable over time like a trait, but also dynamic and alterable by environmental influences and effort.

The concept of character strength was originally proposed by Peterson and Seligman (2004) in their Values in Action (VIA) model. These were conceptualized to counter the approach of psychopathology that focused on disorders, by developing what is known to be a Manual of the Sanities (Peterson & Seligman, 2004). The authors essentially viewed character as 'plural, rather than singular', meaning that it is multi-dimensional rather than an either–or affair (Park & Peterson, 2009). Strengths are morally valued, relatively stable, satisfying to self, and not counterproductive for others (Peterson & Seligman, 2004; Ruch et al., 2010). Park and Peterson (2009) clarify that, despite their relatively permanent nature, character strengths do not signify underlying traits.

CLASSIFICATION OF CHARACTER STRENGTHS

In the VIA model, Peterson and Seligman (2004) listed 24 values or strengths that people possess in various degrees, which form the basis of human positivity and effectiveness throughout the life span (Platt, Ruch, Gander, & Hofmann, 2017). Based on prior literature and writings of religious leaders and philosophers (e.g., Dahlsgaard, Peterson, & Seligman, 2005), Peterson and Seligman (2004) classified character strengths as mechanisms or processes leading to six broad virtues (Peterson, 2006):

1. *Wisdom and knowledge:* Incorporating curiosity, creativity, open-mindedness, love of learning and perspective

2. *Courage:* Incorporating bravery, persistence, honesty and zest
3. *Humanity:* Incorporating love, kindness and social intelligence
4. *Justice:* Incorporating teamwork, fairness and leadership
5. *Temperance:* Incorporating forgiveness, modesty, prudence and self-regulation
6. *Transcendence:* Incorporating appreciation of beauty and excellence, gratitude, hope, humour and religiousness

Peterson (2006) stated that character strengths may be distinguished on two dimensions:

1. Strengths that relate to the *mind or cognitive abilities* (e.g., open-mindedness and perseverance) and strengths that relate to the *heart or emotional states* (e.g., humour and love)
2. Strengths that relate to *self-enhancement, exploration or enjoyment* (e.g., creativity and hope) and strengths that relate to *others in the environment* (e.g., teamwork and forgiveness)

The strengths that are the strongest for a given individual are called the signature strengths. Signature strengths need to be identified and practised every day for fulfilment and effectiveness (Seligman, Steen, Park, & Peterson, 2005).

Based on Peterson's nomenclature (2006), Weber and Ruch (2012) presented the classification of the 24 character strengths as shown in Figure 13.1.

CHARACTER STRENGTHS AND LIFE OUTCOMES

The role of character strengths has been studied in various contexts, such as school, life adjustment and work (Gander, Proyer, Ruch, & Wyss, 2012; Harzer & Ruch, 2014, 2015). In the context of young people, Weber and Ruch (2012) demonstrated that character strengths build in an individual a desire to make efforts towards improvement or doing what is felt to be the right thing, which in turn leads to improvement in school performance. Along similar lines, Lounsbury, Fisher, Levy and Welsh (2009) showed a significant relation between character strength and grade point average (GPA), while Shoshani and

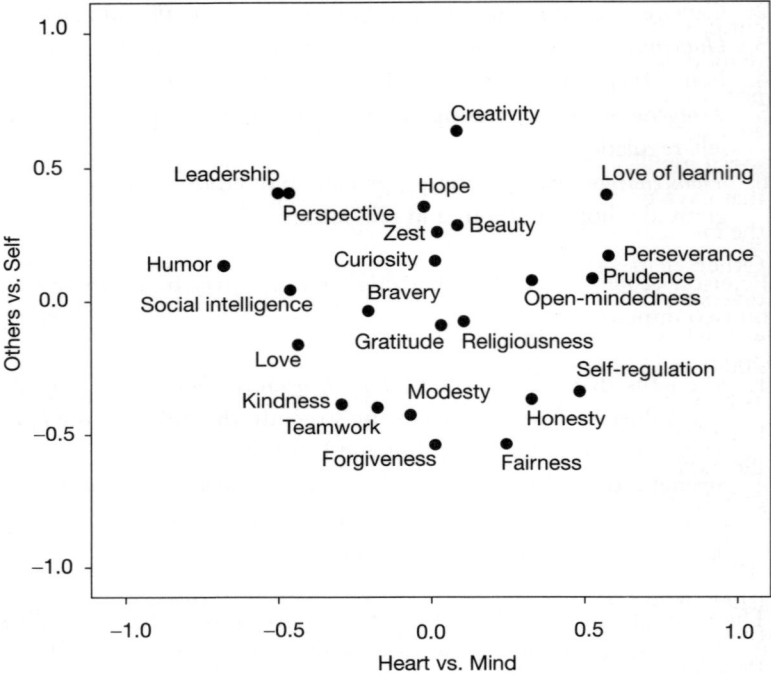

Figure 13.1 *Classification of Character Strengths on the 'Heart vs. Mind' and 'Others vs. Self' Dimensions*

Source: Adapted from Weber & Ruch (2012).

Aviv (2012) reported that character strengths have also been found to smoothen school transition.

When it comes to adults, Seligman et al. (2005) stated that strengths lead to happiness, self-efficacy and hope. Character strengths have also been positively associated with advancement towards life goals (Linley et al., 2010). Finally, Botvin, Baker, Dusenbury, Botvin and Diaz (1995) showed that character strengths reduce propensity of mental illnesses and undesirable life outcomes.

There is a difference in the relative contribution of the character strengths in determining life outcomes. For instance, Park, Peterson and Seligman (2004) demonstrated that the character strengths that are most strongly correlated with life satisfaction are hope, zest, gratitude, curiosity, love and persistence (Park & Peterson, 2006), while the traits of modesty, creativity, appreciation of beauty and love of learning were not correlated with life satisfaction. Spirituality/religiousness is associated with meaningful living (Park & Peterson, 2009). Hope, kindness, social intelligence, self-control and perspective are character strengths that have preventive roles, that is, they reduce stress and thus prevent the incidence of mental disorders (Park, 2004; Park & Peterson, 2009). Other character strengths, such as leadership, tolerance, valuing of diversity, ability to delay gratification, kindness and altruism, have been associated with positive student outcomes, such as school success (Park, 2004) and recovery from illness, as have been character strengths such as bravery and appreciation of beauty. Character strengths have also been found to grow in response to dramatic events, such as accidents, illnesses, trauma or other tragedies (Peterson, Park, Pole, D'Andrea, & Seligman, 2008).

Demographic differences have been reported in the incidence of specific character strengths. Strengths requiring cognitive maturity (such as modesty, appreciation of beauty and forgiveness) are relatively rare among young children (Park & Peterson, 2006; Park, Peterson, & Seligman, 2006). Again, women are found to score better in the humanity dimension than men, while playfulness and humour are found to be higher among younger adults than older adults (Ruch et al., 2010).

Parenting styles directed at generating positive experiences include responsiveness, warmth and freedom in life activities for children (Milevsky, Schlechter, Netter, & Keehn, 2007). On the other hand, ineffective parenting styles might lead to destruction of positive attributes in a person. Irvine, Biglan, Smolkowski and Ary (1999) listed various ineffective parenting styles such as laxness (e.g., permissive and inconsistent) and overreactivity (e.g., anger and threats) (Chand, Farruggia, Dittman, Sanders, & Ting Wai Chu, 2013).

Research has shown that interventions to promote effective parenting lead to effective parent–child relationships (Eyberg, Nelson, & Boggs, 2008). Evidence demonstrated that participation in brief seminars designed to enhance positive parenting enhances subsequent display of positive parenting behaviour among caregivers (Chand et al., 2013).

PARENTING AND CHARACTER STRENGTH

The apparent trait-like quality of character strengths has made researchers explore whether character strengths are hereditary or created by environmental conditions. In a research on twins and on parents and children, Steger, Hicks, Kashdan, Krueger and Bouchard (2007) found that there is some extent of heritability in character strengths. However, it was seen that shared family environment played a greater influence in determining the levels of strengths in children and adolescents, with parents and teachers having the greatest role in what strengths an individual will possess later in life (Dunn & Plomin, 1992), both as role models (Sprafkin, Liebert, & Poulos 1975) and as influencers.

Character strengths, although trait-like, show reasonable evidence of trainability and amenability to environmental influences (Biswas-Diener, Kashdan, & Minhas, 2011; Peterson, 2006). This has made the role of parenting and caregiving an important concern in the study of character strengths (Baumrind, 1991). Positive parenting has been associated with life satisfaction, self-esteem and well-being as an adult (DeVore & Ginsburg, 2005; Sanders, Markie-Dadds, & Turner, 2003). Further, other researches show that the mean score of character strengths tends to be the highest for young adults than for older age groups, implying the crucial role that early nurturance may play in the effective development of these traits (Isaacowitz, Vaillant, & Seligman, 2003).

Scholars have explored the role of early childhood environment, nature of caregivers and techniques of parenting as possible determinants of the level and nature of character strength a child will display later in life (Jach et al., 2017; Schwartz et al., 2012). According to Jiang, Huebner and Hills (2013), children's global life satisfaction is highly correlated with their character strengths that in turn are influenced by the parenting styles adopted by their prime caregivers. In a study on Indonesian parents and children, Dewanggi, Hastuti and Herawati (2015) demonstrated that attachment with the mother is a significant predictor of emergence of character strengths in a child.

How does parenting contribute to the development of character strengths? According to Govindji and Linley (2007), parenting contributes mainly by helping an individual not only to know one's strengths but also to use those strengths in specific activities. Strengths become useful only when they are used, rather than simply being recognized and identified. This makes the role of parents and caregivers crucial in the development and utilization of character strengths. They help by identifying the strengths in a child. Further, parents reiterate to the child his/her key strengths—traits where the child excels are distinguished from others, and authentic and valuable. Parents subsequently play the more crucial role of identifying the conditions that nurture and generate these strengths, and creating experiences that allow the child to practise such strengths. Researches show that knowing one's strengths versus using one's strengths may have differential effects on well-being (Govindji & Linley 2007; Jach et al., 2017; Seligman et al., 2005).

Parenting and Development of Specific Character Strengths: Hope

Hope, the character strength contributing to transcendence, has for long been in the focus of psychological research. Research on hope first gained prominence with Erik Erikson's theory about the eight developmental stages of human life cycle. According to Erikson, every stage presented an individual with a psychosocial crisis that, if resolved well, would lead to the development of a virtue, a concept closely resembling character strength (Erikson, 1963). Erikson proposed that the first such virtue that develops is hope, or a disposition to expect positive outcomes in future life endeavours. The rise of hope, according to the theory, rises from a psychosexual crisis of 'Trust versus Mistrust' that is closely dependent on parenting. The infant's early years are spent in a state of helplessness, where it is dependent on the caregivers for satisfaction of every single need. If the child gets a nurturing parent who caters to the fulfilment of the child's needs swiftly, the child develops trust in the world, whereas abandonment and neglect results in mistrust. In case the early experiences of the infant contribute to generation of trust in the world and significant others, the resulting virtue is hope, a general feeling of positivity towards future ventures and expectations from life. Erikson called hope the building block on which other virtues build, and proposed that involved parenting plays a crucial role in the earliest stages of life to build a positive, effective and resilient personality (Erikson, 1959; Wallerstein, 1998).

Snyder, Cheavens and Sympson (1997) proposed the Hope Theory that states hope has three constituents: goals thinking (the time range and the probability one estimates of achieving goals one sets for oneself), agency thinking (the extent to which one perceives oneself as being able to achieve a particular goal) and pathways thinking (one's ability to figure out ways to reach one's goals). Bowlby (1973) opined that attachment with parents encourages children to explore the environment. Further, love and attention from parents encourage children to have confidence in themselves, which in turn inspire agency thinking and pathways thinking (Rieger, 1993). Jiang et al. (2013) proposed that hopeful thinking first originates through vicarious learning from and active encouragement of parents, which in turn leads to positive behavioural outcomes such as life satisfaction, perseverance and agency. Hope has also been found to be a mediator between parental attachment and the adolescent's life satisfaction (Jiang et al., 2013).

PARENTING PRACTICES TO BUILD CHARACTER STRENGTHS

Strength-based Parenting

The concept of strength-based parenting was first forwarded by Waters (2015a), who proposed that parenting practices that seek to focus on enhancing character strengths are especially effective in increasing the intensity of character strengths in children and youth, and in identifying and cultivating positive states, positive processes and positive qualities' in children (Waters, 2015a, p. 690). Strength-based parenting is done through identification of the specific strengths that a child possesses and generation of experiences and environment that encourage display of those strengths and attitude of nurturing them. Strength-based parenting consists of two factors:

1. Developing strength awareness or the knowledge of the strengths one possesses and
2. Developing strength use, the extent to which a person can use the strengths in different settings (Govindji & Linley, 2007; Jach et al., 2017).

Thus, in strength-based parenting, the caregiver identifies for the child the strengths he/she possesses and the various contexts in which such strengths may be used. Parents also help by providing social verification for a child's understanding of his/her own strengths (Waters, 2015b). Finally, parents role model the use of strengths and thus propel children towards development of their ideal selves (Waters, 2015a).

The key component of strength-based parenting is positive feedback. Parents by giving children positive feedback on what they have done well in an occasion or tend to do well, make children repeat the same behaviour over and over again, leading to honing of strengths and their further blooming into trait-like qualities (Jach et al., 2017; Waters, 2015a). Loton and Waters (2017) demonstrated that strength-based parenting enhances self-efficacy in students, which in turn reduces depression and anxiety. It has also been associated with greater well-being among children (Waters 2015a, b).

Jach et al. (2017) demonstrated that strength-based parenting affects outcomes by creating and nurturing a growth mindset, as opposed to a fixed mindset, in children. People with a growth mindset tend to see tasks as challenges and make efforts, while people with an entity view or a fixed mindset tend to avoid challenges due to fear of failure (Biswas-Diener et al., 2011). The growth mindset makes children view their strengths and competencies as something malleable or something that can be improved, as opposed to being something stable, which can neither grow nor is needed to be honed or rehearsed, subject neither to atrophy nor to enhancement (Mangels, Butterfield, Lamb, Good, & Dweck, 2006). Such a mindset makes children appreciate that the strengths they possess require use for improvement, while strengths that they are deficient in may be built and improved with time and effort (Jack et al., 2017). Thus, it is important for parents not only to identify and encourage children to use their strengths, but also make them have a growth mindset towards it, seeing strengths as aptitudes to be polished into skills, rather than as permanent attributes of a person.

Role of Praise and Compliments

Research on character strength recognizes that the level of character strengths displayed by a person needs to be developed in order to lead a meaningful and fulfilling life (e.g., Park & Peterson, 2009). One simple way that has been found to manipulate a child's mindset towards his or her strengths is changing the type of praise given, by phrasing of language or by quasi-education (e.g., Levy et al., 1998; Mueller & Dweck, 1998). Gunderson et al. (2013) proposed that limiting praises to action words such as 'you did well' rather than descriptions such as 'you are smart' affects the child's subsequent efforts. Children who are made aware of their strengths as attributes make relatively less effort to enhance or rehearse them. On the other hand, children who are informed of their strengths in terms of actions they have committed try to repeat such actions in the future, leading to further rehearsal and enhancement of the specific strengths.

Novel Uses of Strengths

Seligman et al. (2005) reported that along with identifying and using strengths, it is important to use strengths in novel ways that enhances competencies in using the strengths and test its limits. For instance, if a child shows kindness towards pets, he/she may be encouraged to participate in charitable events, to further universalize the acts of kindness. Novel situations test the strength's scope and limitations, and allow the individual to find out in what ways it needs to be exercised for satisfaction and growth. Novel uses also let new strengths emerge, thereby letting the individual gain a clearer understanding of what attributes need to be nurtured and what need to be built further before taking up new challenges (Park, 2009; Park & Peterson, 2008).

SCOPE FOR FUTURE RESEARCH

The relationship between parenting and character strengths has been explored extensively in recent research. While the causal influence of strength-based parenting on building of character strengths has been studied, other researches have explored the mediating role of character strengths between parenting styles and positive life outcomes, such as school performance and psychological harmony in adolescents (Duan, Zhang, Li, Tang, & Duan, 2012). Strength-based parenting interventions have been found to have positive effects, and increase the self-efficacy and positive emotions of not only the children but also the parents themselves (Waters & Sun, 2016). Seligman (2002) has proposed that authentic happiness rises from identifying and using one's strengths life activities such as parenting. It might be interesting to explore the impact of the parents' character strengths on the development of character strengths of children. While parents with a clear understanding and appreciation of their own strengths are more likely to identify and encourage strengths in their children, an important question may be whether parents tend to encourage use of strengths that align with their own strengths and preferences, or if they encourage an independent emergence of character strengths in children.

The role of parenting styles in development of strengths needs to be explored. While strength-based parenting encourages emergence of strengths, it may be interesting to explore whether it would have similar effects when the parent adopts a more autocratic style over democratic or permissive parenting styles. It might also be interesting to explore the dynamics of development of character strengths in children with parents having varying levels of child centrism (Ashton-James et al., 2013), communal strengths (Le & Impett, 2016) and passion about parenting (Coulson et al., 2012).

A related question is the impact of culture on the development of specific strengths. The development of character strengths shows culture-specific variations (Banicki, 2014; Biswas-Diener, 2006). Future research may focus on how far culture-specific parenting practices and gender role orientations lead to culturally influenced emergence of character strengths in children. One may also explore ways to combat such biases, such that there is a natural development of character strengths free from limiting environmental pressures.

Research is limited on the comparative influence of the father and the mother's parenting styles on the development of character strengths in children (Day & Padilla-Walker, 2009; Williams & Kelly, 2005). For instance, Dewanggi et al. (2015) showed that maternal attachment predicts character strengths in children but reported no such correlation with paternal attachments. Again, Day and Padilla-Walker (2009) demonstrated that when one parent's connectedness and involvement with the children is low, the other parent's involvement and connectedness compensated for the loss and led to development of character strengths in the children. Hence, future research may focus on the impact parents of either sex have on the development of the child's character. Barring a few instances (Fung et al., 2011), literature is also relatively silent on the impact of other caregivers on the child's character building. While strength-based parenting, by definition, comprises practices that are likely to work when administered by any caregiver, it may be interesting to explore whether the same empowering practices have differential impacts when administered by parents, by other family members who are caregivers, or by non-related caregivers such as nurses or teachers.

CONCLUSION AND IMPLICATIONS

As opposed to the medical model, character strengths arise out of the ecological model that views individuals as potential to be unlocked rather than problems to be cured (Anderson & Heyne, 2012; Saleebey, 2006). Building strength is a positive activity that shows more results than making students work on reducing their weaknesses. This is because working on something in which a person is already proficient is motivating for the person and is more likely to show results than working on something a person is deficient (Park & Seligman, 2009). However, as Park (2009, p. 46) stated: simply saying 'do your best or be the best you can be is not an effective way to cultivate good character'. Parents play the crucial role in the development of character strengths by identifying and guiding children in developing, nurturing and enhancing their potentials in becoming individuals of worth. While many nuances of parental influence, interaction with various environmental factors and dynamics of the processes of strength-based parenting remain to be explored, the role of parenting in the development and nurturance of character strengths is undeniable. Effective interventions are the call of the day to assist parents in creating an atmosphere conducive for growing their children into effective adults, and in the process fulfilling their conjugal, familial and parental goals.

REFERENCES

Anderson, L., & Heyne, L. A. (2012). *Therapeutic recreation practice: A strengths approach*. State College, PA: Venture Publishing.

Ashton-James, C. E., Kushlev, K., & Dunn, E. W. (2013). Parents reap what they sow: Child-centrism and parental well-being. *Social Psychological and Personality Science, 4*(6), 635–642.

Banicki, K. (2014). Positive psychology on character strengths and virtues. A disquieting suggestion. *New Ideas in Psychology, 33*(1), 21–34.

Baumrind, D. (1991). Effective parenting during the early adolescent transition. *Family Transitions, 2*(1), 1.

Bennett, W. J. (Ed.). (1993). *Book of virtues.* New York, NY: Simon & Schuster.

Biswas-Diener, R. (2006). From the equator to the North Pole: A study of character strengths. *Journal of Happiness Studies, 7(3)*, 293–310.

Biswas-Diener, R., Kashdan, T. B., & Minhas, G. (2011). A dynamic approach to psychological strength development and intervention. *The Journal of Positive Psychology, 6*(2), 106–118.

Bornstein, M. H. (2001). Parenting: Science and practice. *Parenting, 1*(1–2), 1–4.

Botvin, G. J., Baker, E., Dusenbury, L., Botvin, E. M., & Diaz, T. (1995). Long-term follow-up results of a randomized drug abuse prevention trial in a white middle-class population. *Journal of the American Medical Association, 273*(14), 1106–1112.

Bowlby, J. (1973). *Attachment and loss: Vol. 2. Separation.* New York, NY: Basic Books.

Bradley, R. H., & Caldwell, B. M. (1995). Caregiving and the regulation of child growth and development: Describing proximal aspects of caregiving systems. *Developmental Review, 15*(1), 38–85.

Chand, N., Farruggia, S., Dittman, C., Sanders, M., & Ting Wai Chu, J. (2013). Promoting positive youth development: Through a brief parenting intervention program. *Youth Studies Australia, 32*(1), 29.

Coulson, J. C., Oades, L. G., & Stoyles, G. J. (2012). Parents' subjective sense of calling in childrearing: Measurement, development and initial findings. *Journal of Positive Psychology, 7*(2), 83–94.

Dahlsgaard, K., Peterson, C., & Seligman, M. E. (2005). Shared virtue: The convergence of valued human strengths across culture and history. *Review of General Psychology, 9*(3), 203.

Day, R. D., & Padilla-Walker, L. M. (2009). Mother and father connectedness and involvement during early adolescence. *Journal of Family Psychology, 23*(6), 900.

DeVore, E. R., & Ginsburg, K. R. (2005). The protective effects of good parenting on adolescents. *Current Opinion in Pediatrics, 17*(4), 460–465.

Dewanggi, M., Hastuti, D., & Herawati, T. (2015). The influence of attachment and quality of parenting and parenting environment on children's character in rural and urban areas of Bogor. *Jurnal Ilmu Keluarga & Konsumen, 8*(1), 20–27.

Duan, T. T., Zhang, W. J., Li, Y. H., Tang, T. Y., & Duan, X. Q. (2012). Influence of parenting style and character strength on psychology harmony. *Psychological Exploration, 32*(2), 183–187.

Dunn, J., & Plomin, R. (1992). *Separate lives: Why siblings are so different.* New York, NY: Basic Books.

Erikson, E. H. (1959). Identity and the life cycle: Selected papers. *Psychological Issues*, *1*, 1–171.
Erikson, E. (1963). *Childhood and society* (2nd ed.). New York, NY: W. W. Norton.
Eyberg, S. M., Nelson, M. M., & Boggs, S. R. (2008). Evidence-based treatments for child and adolescent disruptive behavior disorders. *Journal of Clinical Child and Adolescent Psychology*, *37*(1), 213–235.
Farruggia, S. P., & Bullen, P. (2010). Positive youth development in Aotearoa/ New Zealand. In J. Low & P. Jose (Eds.), *Lifespan development: New Zealand perspectives* (2nd ed., pp. 144–154). Auckland: Pearson.
Fung, B. K., Ho, S. M. Y., Fung, A. S. M, Leung, E. Y. P., Chow, S. P., Ip, W. Y.,... Barlaan, P. I. G. (2011). The development of a strength-focused mutual support group for caretakers of children with cerebral palsy. *East Asian Archives of Psychiatry*, *21*(2), 64.
Gander, F., Proyer, R. T., Ruch, W., & Wyss, T. (2013). Strength-based positive interventions: Further evidence for their potential in enhancing well-being and alleviating depression. *Journal of Happiness Studies*, *14*(4), 1241–1259.
Govindji, R., & Linley, P. A. (2007). Strengths use, self-concordance and well-being: Implications for strengths coaching and coaching psychologists. *International Coaching Psychology Review*, *2*(2), 143–153.
Grusec, J. E., & Kuczynski, L. E. (1997). *Parenting and children's internalization of values: A handbook of contemporary theory*. New York, NY: Wiley.
Gunderson, E. A., Gripshover, S. J., Romero, C., Dweck, C. S., Goldin-Meadow, S., & Levine, S. C. (2013). Parent praise to 1- to 3-year-olds predicts children's motivational frameworks 5 years later. *Child Development*, *84*(5), 1526–1541. doi:10.1111/cdev.12064.
Harzer, C., & Ruch, W. (2014). The role of character strengths for task performance, job dedication, interpersonal facilitation, and organizational support. *Human Performance*, *27*(3), 183–205.
Harzer, C., & Ruch, W. (2015). The relationships of character strengths with coping, work-related stress, and job satisfaction. *Frontiers in Psychology*, *6*, 165. doi:10.3389/fpsyg.2015.00165
Heyne, L. A., & Anderson, L. S. (2012). Theories that support strengths-based practice in therapeutic recreation. *Therapeutic Recreation Journal*, *46*(2), 106.
Irvine, A. B., Biglan, A., Smolkowski, K., & Ary, D. V. (1999). The value of the Parenting Scale for measuring the discipline practices of parents of middle school children. *Behaviour Research and Therapy*, *37*(2), 127–142.
Isaacowitz, D. M., Vaillant, G. E., & Seligman, M. E. P. (2003). Strengths and satisfaction across the adult lifespan. *International Journal of Aging and Human Development*, *57*(2), 181–201.
Jach, H. K., Sun, Loton, Chin, T. C., & Waters, L. E. (2017). Strengths and subjective wellbeing in adolescence: Strength-based parenting and the moderating effect of mindset. *Journal of Happiness Studies*, 1–20. doi:10.1007/ s10902-016-9841-y

Jiang, X., Huebner, E. S, & Hills, K. J. (2013). Parent attachment and early adolescents' life satisfaction: The mediating effect of hope. *Psychology in the Schools*, *50*(4), 340–352.

Le, B. M., & Impett, E. A. (2016). The rewards of caregiving for communally motivated parents. *Social Psychological and Personality Science*, *42*(3), 323–336.

Levy, S. R., Stroessner, S. J., & Dweck, C. S. (1998). Stereotype formation and endorsement: The role of implicit theories. *Journal of Personality and Social Psychology*, *74*(6), 1421–1436. doi:10.1037/0022-3514.74.6.1421.

Linley, P. A., Nielsen, K. M., Gillett, R., & Biswas-Diener, R. (2010). Using signature strengths in pursuit of goals: Effects on goal progress, need satisfaction, and well-being, and implications for coaching psychologists. *International Coaching Psychology Review*, *5*(1), 6–15.

Loton, D. J., & Waters, L. E. (2017). The mediating effect of self-efficacy in the connections between strength-based parenting, happiness and psychological distress in teens. *Frontiers in Psychology*, *8*, 1707. doi:10.3389/fpsyg.2017.01707

Lounsbury, J. W., Fisher, L. A., Levy, J. J., & Welsh, D. P. (2009). An investigation of character strengths in relation to the academic success of college students. *Individual Differences Research*, *7*(1), 52–69.

McElhaney, K., Allen, J., Stephenson, J., & Hare, A. (2009). Attachment and autonomy during adolescence. In R. Lerner & L. Steinberg (Eds.), *Handbook of adolescent psychology* (3rd ed., Vol. 1, pp. 358–403). New York, NY: Wiley.

Mangels, J. A., Butterfield, B., Lamb, J., Good, C., & Dweck, C. S. (2006). Why do beliefs about intelligence influence learning success? A social cognitive neuroscience model. *Social Cognitive and Affective Neuroscience*, *1*(2), 75–86. doi:10.1093/scan/nsl013.

Milevsky, A., Schlechter, M., Netter, S., & Keehn, D. (2007). Maternal and paternal parenting styles in adolescents: Associations with self-esteem, depression and life-satisfaction. *Journal of Child and Family Studies*, *16*(1), 39–47.

Mueller, C. M., & Dweck, C. S. (1998). Praise for intelligence can undermine children's motivation and performance. *Journal of Personality and Social Psychology*, *75*(1), 33–52. doi:10.1037/0022-3514.75. 1.33.

Nash, S. G., McQueen, A., & Bray, J. H. (2005). Pathways to adolescent alcohol use: Family environment, peer influence and parental expectations. *Journal of Adolescent Health*, *37*(1), 19–28.

Park, N. (2004). Character strengths and positive youth development. *The Annals of the American Academy of Political and Social Science*, *591*(1), 40–54.

———. (2009). Building strengths of character: Keys to positive youth development. *Reclaiming Children and Youth*, *18*(2), 42.

Park, N., & Peterson, C. (2006). Moral competence and character strengths among adolescents: The development and validation of the Values in Action Inventory of Strengths for Youth. *Journal of Adolescence*, *29*(6), 891–909.

———. (2008). Positive psychology and character strengths: Application to strengths-based school counseling. *Professional School Counseling*, *12*(2), 85–92.

———. (2009). Character strengths: Research and practice. *Journal of College and Character*, *10*(4), 1–10.

Park, N., Peterson, C., & Seligman, M. E. (2004). Strengths of character and well-being. *Journal of Social & Clinical Psychology, 23*(5), 603–619.

———. (2006). Character strengths in fifty-four nations and the fifty US states. *The Journal of Positive Psychology, 1*(3), 118–129.

Peterson, C. (2006). *A primer in positive psychology*. New York; NY: Oxford University Press.

Peterson, C., Park, N., Pole, N., D'Andrea, W., & Seligman, M. E. (2008). Strengths of character and posttraumatic growth. *Journal of Traumatic Stress, 21*(2), 214–217.

Peterson, C., & Seligman, M. E. (2004). *Character strengths and virtues: A handbook and classification* (Vol. 1). New York, NY: Oxford University Press.

Platt, T., Ruch, W., Gander, F., & Hofmann, J. (2017). Team roles: Their relationships to character strengths and job satisfaction. *The Journal of Positive Psychology, 13*(2), 190–199.

Poffenberger, A. T., & Carpenter, F. L. (1924). Character traits in school success. *Journal of Experimental Psychology, 7*(1), 67.

Plakun, E. M. (2017). In R. S. Wallerstein & L. Goldberger (Eds.), *Ideas and identities: The life and work of Erik Erikson*. Madison, CT: International Universities Press.

Poffenberger, A. T., & Carpenter, F. L. (1924). Character traits in school success. *Journal of Experimental Psychology, 7*(1), 67.

Rieger, E. (1993). Correlates of adult hope, including high- and low-hope adults' recollections of parents (Unpublished master's thesis). Lawrence, KS: University of Kansas.

Ruch, W., Proyer, R. T., Harzer, C., Park, N., Peterson, C., & Seligman, M. E. P. (2010). Values in Action Inventory of Strengths (VIA-IS): Adaptation and validation of the German version and the development of a peer-rating form. *Journal of Individual Differences*. doi:10.1027/1614-0001/a000022

Saleebey, D. (2006). *Power in the people*. London: Routledge.

Sanders, M. R., Markie-Dadds, C., & Turner, K. M. T. (2003). Theoretical, scientific and clinical foundations of the Triple P-Positive Parenting Program: A population approach to the promotion of parenting competence. In *Parenting research and practice* Monograph 1. Brisbane: University of Queensland.

Schwartz, O. S., Dudgeon, P., Sheeber, L. B., Yap, M. B., Simmons, J. G., & Allen, N. B. (2012). Parental behaviors during family interactions predict changes in depression and anxiety symptoms during adolescence. *Journal of Abnormal Child Psychology, 40*, 59–71. doi:10.1007/s10802-011-9542-2

Seligman, M. E. (2002). Positive psychology, positive prevention, and positive therapy. In C. R. Snyder & S. J. Lopez (Eds.), *The handbook of positive psychology* (pp. 3–12). New York, NY: Oxford University Press.

Seligman, M. E., & Csikszentmihalyi, M. (2000). Special issue on happiness, excellence, and optimal human functioning. *American Psychologist, 55*(1), 5–183.

———. (2014). Positive psychology: An introduction. In M. Csikszentmihalyi (Ed.), *Flow and the foundations of positive psychology* (pp. 279–298). Netherlands: Springer.

Seligman, M. E., Steen, T. A., Park, N., & Peterson, C. (2005). Positive psychology progress: Empirical validation of interventions. *American Psychologist, 60*(5), 410.

Shoshani, A., & Aviv, I. (2012). The pillars of strength for first-grade adjustment: Parental and children's character strengths and the transition to elementary school. *The Journal of Positive Psychology, 7*(4), 315–326.

Smith, G. M. (1967). Usefulness of peer ratings of personality in educational research. *Educational and Psychological Measurement, 27*(4), 967–984.

Snyder, C. R., Cheavens, J., & Sympson, S. C. (1997). Hope: An individual motive for social commerce. *Group Dynamics: Theory, Research, and Practice, 1*(2), 107–118.

Sprafkin, J. N., Liebert, R. M., & Poulos, R. W. (1975). Effects of a prosocial televised example on children's helping. *Journal of Experimental Child Psychology, 20*(1), 119–126.

Steger, M. F., Hicks, B. M., Kashdan, T. B., Krueger, R. F., & Bouchard, T. J., Jr. (2007). Genetic and environmental influences on the positive traits of the values in action classification, and biometric covariance with normal personality. *Journal of Research in Personality, 41*(3), 524–539.

Wallerstein, R. S. (1998). Erik H. Erikson, 1902–1994: Setting the context. In Robert S. Wallerstein & Leo Goldberger (Eds.), *Ideas and identities: The life and work of Erik Erikson*. Madison, CT: International Universities Press.

Waters, L. (2015a). The relationship between strength-based parenting with children's stress levels and strength-based coping approaches. *Psychology, 6*, 689–699. doi:10.4236/psych.2015.66067

———. (2015b). Strength-based parenting and life satisfaction in teenagers. *Advances in Social Sciences Research Journal, 2*(11), 158–173. doi:10.14738/assrj.211.1651

Waters, L., & Sun, J. (2016). Can a brief strength-based parenting intervention boost self-efficacy and positive emotions in parents? *International Journal of Applied Positive Psychology, 1*(1–3), 41–56.

Weber, M., & Ruch, W. (2012). The role of a good character in 12-year-old school children: Do character strengths matter in the classroom? *Child Indicators Research, 5*, 317–334. doi:10.1007/s12187-011-9128-0

Williams, S. K., & Kelly, F. D. (2005). Relationships among involvement, attachment, and behavioral problems in adolescence: Examining father's influence. *Journal of Early Adolescence, 25*, 168–196.

Chapter 14

The Popularization of Technology and Family
The Impacts of Family Atmosphere, Parent-Child Conflicts and Parenting Approaches on Adolescents' Digital Character*

Vincent Wan-ping Lee, Henry Wai-hang Ling and
Johnson Chun-sing Cheung

INTRODUCTION

Parent–child relationship in adolescent stage is a great challenge for both parents and children. During this period, children begin to search for their own identity and seek higher autonomy from their parents. On the other hand, parents may feel difficult to adapt to the new environment in which their children may have lower attachment with them, and what they are doing may become more and more deviant

---

*The findings of this research article are extracted from the output of a research project funded by the Hong Kong Family Welfare Society entitled 'Internet-based Family and Youth Mental Health Research: A Study on Youth's Digital Usage Habit in Relation to Family Relationships'. The researchers would like to thank Professor Wong Yu-cheung from the Chinese University of Hong Kong for giving valuable advice to the project and the approval of data usage.

from parents' expectations. Parents still intend to retain some kind of supervision in their children's daily lives. However, adolescents would spend much less time with their parents than they did during childhood, which could make parenting more challenging than before. It is common for parents and adolescents begin to have more disagreements on certain issues, and conflicts would occur particularly in incidents related to adolescents' decision-making and evolution of independent mindsets and lifestyles.

The evolution and proliferation of information and communication technology (ICT) has also nurtured a generation who were raised in the digital age and are having a distinctive culture and social norms that are quite different than the older generations. The term 'digital natives' refers to those who were all born after 1980, when social digital technologies, such as Usenet and bulletin board systems, came online (Palfrey & Gasser, 2008; Tapscott, 1998, 2009). They all have access to networked digital technologies. On the other hand, older people were there at the start, and these 'digital settlers' or 'digital immigrants'—not 'native' to the digital environment, because they grew up in an analog-only world—have helped to shape its contours.

From the three focus-group interviews for a research study funded by a social service agency with 21 parents in Hong Kong during summer 2014, we had obtained a set of qualitative data on these parents' perceptions about the usefulness of mobile devices in everyday life, their adolescent children's digital behaviour (in using mobile devices) and interpersonal and parent–child relationships. The parents had shared about which approaches were more effective or ineffective in facilitating positive use of mobile devices by their children, as well as their efforts to develop positive parent–child relationships. The objectives are listed below:

- To understand the contemporary habit of youth digital usage (especially smartphones and tablets)
- To understand parents' perspectives on their children's digital usage habit and parents' own usage
- To examine the correlation between youth's digital usage and parent–child relationship
- To explore different parenting styles and their effectiveness when guiding and educating children on using mobile Internet devices and

- To examine the effectiveness of different parenting methods (especially conflict resolution styles) on conflicts in respect of the youth's digital usage

LITERATURE REVIEW
Digital Age, Parent-Child Relationship and Mobile Devices

There is a rich body of literature about the function of parenting methods and parenting mediation—strategies to guide and correct children's behaviours, in shaping children's behaviours. Generally speaking, the researchers do not underestimate the challenges of parents in guiding and supervising adolescent children whose physical and mental needs evolve constantly during this life stage.

Good parent–child communication about what is happening on the Internet and what one is doing online should have a protective effect. Respectful and open communications could help to prevent real-life meetings with strangers, and also the quality of communication is important. A number of researchers have found that parents' active mediation and communications about media use are also good references in the digital age. Feng and Xie's results (2014) suggested that as an important socialization agent, parents could influence their children's attitudes and behaviours through parental mediation that involved monitoring and controlling their children's media consumption. van den Eijnden et al. (2010) suggested that qualitatively good communication by parents regarding Internet use could enable young people to feel more understood. Conversations about their Internet use could indeed lower the risks of developing compulsive Internet use. Wong (2010) found in Hong Kong that better-educated parents, the adoption of an authoritative parenting style, more active involvement in children's online activities and more discussions of the online experiences are factors associated with more satisfactory results in influencing children's behaviour. Wong, Ho and Chen (2015) found that in Shanghai, better Internet knowledge, an authoritative parenting style, more involvement in children's online activities and a positive attitude towards the Internet are factors which were associated with higher parenting confidence in Internet supervision.

Children's Internet use for external interactions and the family factor have also attracted the attention of a number of researchers in recent years. In a comparative study of the United Kingdom and Bahrain, Davidson and Martellozzo (2013) investigated Internet usage and online behaviours, definitions of risk, awareness of safety and use of social networking sites. The findings suggested that young people use digital media in much the same way regardless of the social and cultural contexts. Rudi et al. (2015) examined parents' use of four widely used ICTs (text message, email, social networking sites and Skype) to communicate with family. They found that children's use of various ICTs is dynamic, reflecting developmental differences in the child and relational differences in the family system. It was suggested that parents may be using new technologies to facilitate intergenerational family connections that has a positive impact on parent–child relationships.

Beginning from early 2010s, the body of literature on issues related to youth's use of mobile devices has been expanding. Researchers are beginning to touch upon this topic, and there should be more researches releasing in the upcoming years. Most studies on youth's use of smartphones at this stage, however, are mainly focusing on the problems associated with addictions, safety issues or other types of problematic use. Researches on how parents respond to the mobile trends and identifying effective parenting strategies and parental self-efficacy are not yet the common research themes.

For example, De-Miguel-Molina, Martinez-Gomez, De-Miguel-Molina and Ribes-Giner (2012) challenged the suitability of children in using mobile phone services, since everyone regardless could have easy access to a wide range of contents on the Internet via their devices. There is also a study on the use of social networking mobile applications and mobile addiction among youths (Salehan & Negahban, 2013); compulsive behaviours and 'technostress' in forming the dark side of the smartphone trend (Lee, Chang, Lin, & Cheng, 2014); comparison between Korean students' addiction in games in SNS (Jeong, Kim, Yum, & Hwang, 2015) and problematic Internet use on PC and smartphone (Kim, Nam, Oh, & Kang, 2016); as well as predictive factors of addictive behaviour in smartphone usage by different generational cohorts from a sample in Israel (Zhitomirsky-Geffet & Blau, 2016) and investigation of the relationship between risk of smartphone addiction and whether satisfaction with life mediated by stress and academic performance facilitates smartphone addiction (Samaha & Hawi, 2016).

As far as generational difference is concerned regarding the use of mobile devices, Anshari et al. (2016) found that majority of young people agreed that they could not live without smartphones; but for the older generation, majority of them reported that they could live even without smartphones. A digital divide between younger and older generations in perceiving the importance of smartphone exists.

Impacts of Parenting Methods and Approaches

Different parenting methods had significant impact on children and youth's development according to previous studies.

Parenting style (i.e., systematic and non-systematic) exerted a significant moderating effect on the expression of behavioural symptoms at home (Monastra, Monastra, & George, 2002). The behavioural symptoms included the expression of inattentive, hyperactive and impulsive behaviours. According to Steinberg, Lamborn, Dornbusch and Darling (1992), authoritative parenting has positive impact on adolescent better school performance and stronger school engagement. Non-authoritativeness had beneficial impact of parental involvement in schooling on adolescent achievement. Kordi and Baharudin (2010) revealed that authoritative parenting styles were associated with higher levels of children's school achievement. There is powerful impact from parents' attitude and style on their children. Children's achievement could be also reflected by the attitude and style of the parents.

Sanders (2008) highlighted the Triple-P parenting programme aimed to develop parents' capacity for self-regulation. It can strengthen the parenting of the parents. Five elements that had been operationalized from self-regulation were to promote self-efficacy, promote personal agency, promote problem-solving, increase parental self-efficacy and use self-management tools. Duncan, Coatsworth and Greenberg (2009) proposed that mindful parenting was important for the quality of parent–child relationships, especially when their children came across the transition stages of adolescence.

Character Strength and Young People

As foundations of positive youth development, character strengths are highly associated with academic success, life satisfaction and well-being for children and youth (Park, 2009). Correlations were identified between character strengths and positive youth development (Park & Peterson, 2008). The use of strengths is associated with the decrease of stress (Wood et al., 2011) and the improvement of depressive symptoms (Huta & Hawley, 2010). Good character is not the absence of deficits but a well-developed cluster of positive personality and morally desirable traits (Park & Peterson, 2006; Rashid et al., 2013). It is different from talent and ability. It refers to a set of distinct strengths that a person possesses and is critical for lifelong optimal human development. For Park and Peterson (2008), character strengths refer to traits that are morally valued. They manifest in one's thoughts, emotions and behaviours. It serves as a vital force for positive societal well-being and promoting a thriving and flourishing environment. Therefore, cultivating good character among youth people has been a crucial objective in parenting and education (Park, 2009; Proctor, 2013). However, many programmes in schools and other youth services have only focused on training young people's skills and abilities so as to help them pursue their life goals. As Park and Peterson (2008) remind, adolescents may not desire to do the right thing with a good character. According to Baumrind (1998), 'it takes virtuous character to will the good, and competence to do good well' (p. 13).

Park (2004) contends that character strengths can be taught, cultivated and acquired through practice. Weber, Wagner and Ruch (2016) conducted a study to examine the relationships between students' character strengths, school-related affect, positive school functioning and school achievement. They found that a number of character strengths showed positive correlations with school-related positive affect such as positive school functioning and overall school achievement. Another study (Proctor et al., 2011) revealed that working on strengths-based exercises in school enhanced life satisfaction of adolescents. Seider et al. (2013) support that character strengths help young people to regulate their thoughts and actions in a possible way. In a study of 488 early adolescents, they found that moral character strengths were predictors of students' good achievement and conduct.

Steen, Kachorek and Peterson (2003) highlight the importance of peer influence in the journey of character strengths development of young people. They interviewed 459 students from 20 different high schools and were told by the informants that strengths were not innate but largely acquired and developed through ongoing life experience. Young people can choose to develop themselves in a life-enhancing way and shape their own future if they have the opportunities to examine their character strengths. Toner et al. (2012) have examined the dimensions underlying the Values in Action (VIA) character strengths and suggest that temperance, vitality and transcendence were associated with well-being and happiness of adolescents. Tariq and Zubair (2015) argue that character strengths and learned optimism predicted social competence among university students. Yet, female students exhibited more wisdom, humanity, justice, temperance and transcendence when compared with male students. A recent study in Hong Kong conducted by Ngai (2015) supports that parental care supports the development of character strengths among Chinese adolescents in the areas of authenticity, bravery, perseverance, kindness, love, social intelligence, fairness and self-regulation. He also points out that low parental care and high parental control were negatively associated with a number of character strengths.

The present study is therefore able to expand the research area of the impact of the use of smartphones from addiction-oriented to a more familial and parental-focused one by identifying different types of parenting methods in guiding and supervising children to use mobile devices, and factors associated with parental self-efficacy in helping children to make good use of the devices. Parents' and children's background, parenting methods, parents' attitude towards the Internet and family relationship are topics to be examined.

Conceptual Framework

This study is built upon 'The Four Factor Model for Assessment and Management of Oppositional Defiant Disorder' by Barkley (2013, 2015). This framework aims to help human service professionals and parents understand the nature of defiant, oppositional or non-compliant behaviour in children, and explain the four major factors contributing to those issues associated with the children and parental factors. Children, according to Barkley, may often fail to comply with orders requested by an adult within a reasonable time limit, and show failure to sustain compliance to a command from an adult and to follow rules and protocols that have been set previously by an adult. On the other hand, Barkley (2015) also proposed the concept of 'defiance' referring to the situation when many instances of non-compliant behaviour where the child has displayed fierce verbal or physical resistance to complying with such parental guidance and supervision.

To provide better understandings of the factors behind children's non-compliance and defiance, Barkley (2013) has developed a conceptual model outlining the correlations between the four major factors of 'child oppositional behaviour', namely, (a) coercive family processes operating in the parent–child relationship, (b) predisposing child characteristics, (c) predisposing parent characteristics and (d) predisposing contextual factors. All these factors are correlated to defiant child behaviour, including both the emotional components and social components.

Coercive family processes: These refer to disruptive parenting practices and include low parental warmth and poor parental monitoring of the child activities. Under such circumstances, children would respond to those parenting approaches and methods by employing emotional coercion, non-compliance and defiance. They may consider those demands by parents as unpleasant, boring or effortful. This concept could help us to understand how parents' ways of guiding and supervising their children to use mobile devices in our study could trigger different responses from the children who might be very dependent on mobile devices and the family atmosphere—whether the parent–child relationships would be confrontational or not.

Predisposing child characteristics: These refer to issues related to children's temperament, emotional status, or whether they have mental health issues such as hyperactive-impulsive ADHD. Barkley (2013) pointed out that children having behavioural problems in the aforementioned dimensions are far more prone to experience conflicts, both verbal and physical, with their parents. In this study, the parent interviewees were asked about how the nature and characters of their children were associated with their patterns in using mobile devices, and also in their communications with parents and friends.

Predisposing parent characteristics: These refer to the fact that some parents could be more likely than others to engage in coercive parenting practices and to have more defiant children and also parent–child confrontations. From the focus group interviews for this study, we found that there were diverse types of personality and attitudes amongst the parent interviewees with regard to their perceptions of mobile devices, their children's behaviours and expectations for them. These were found to be associated with how the children responded to their parents, as well as their patterns of using mobile devices. Finally, parental behaviours and attitudes could also be affected by their socio-economic status—surrounding social ecology or family context. Marital status and family social disadvantage or social adversity could be factors associated with risks of childhood defiant behaviours. Although the parents who attended the focus group interviews were not asked to provide their marital status and information on family income and their socio-economic status, they were asked to share their level of digital proficiency, learning experiences and their own patterns of mobile use. These could be associated with parents' socio-economic status, as found by Wong (2010) and Lee (2016). Generally speaking, this 'Four Factor Model' suggested by Barkley is a logical framework to guide us in designing this study and undertaking data collection.

Research Methodology

Focus group and in-depth interviews with parents were conducted to gather information during July and August, 2014. The key informants invited to participate in the interviews were the parents with diversified background in order to ensure different opinions are being gathered. The interviews were arranged by purposive sampling method, where we selected key informants whom we perceived to be suitable to provide opinions on the subject matter with the recommendation by schools and the collaborating social service agency. A total number of three such focus group interviews with more than 20 parents present were held during data collection. The details of the focus group arrangements are listed in Table 14.1.

This study adopted a qualitative constructivist grounded theory research design. This approach aims to investigate, explain and understand the phenomenon or meanings individuals create around their perspectives, values, attitudes, experiences, life histories and ways of being. This approach moves beyond the individual to understand the meanings that groups of individuals attach to their experiences and the environment. As a study on the parenting experiences in the digital age, this approach aligns well with the research questions outlined in this proposed study. It captures the patterns of individuals' lives in conceptual categories through participants' voices, while discovering other patterns that might not be obvious to the participants (Charmaz, 2000; Mills, Bonner, & Francis, 2006).

Interviews were audio-recorded after obtaining informed consent from each informant. The recordings were transcribed verbatim, coded and analysed. A constant comparative approach will be used in data analysis, following a grounded theory coding process that involves inductive open/substantive coding followed by axial coding and selective coding. This involved coding the data line by line, then analysing the data across participants (in comparison) and identifying themes occurring across the interviews (Charmaz, 1995, 2000). Based on the transcripts of the first few interviews, an initial coding framework would be established. The resulting codes were compared to ensure that the inter-coder reliability was maintained. After thorough data analyses, three themes related to parents' perspective on guidance and children's

Table 14.1 Details of the Focus Group Interviews with the Types of Key Informants, Location and Number of People

Group (Location)	Date	Total Number of Participants
Parents (family service centre)	5 July 2014	6
Parents (school)	2 August 2014	8
Parents (school)	2 August 2014	7

use of smartphones have been extracted, and these are further divided into organizing themes and reporting themes (Table 14.2).

Major Findings

As mentioned in the section on coding, this study will focus on the three major themes with regard to parents' perceptions on their children's use of mobile devices, and what usual approaches they would adopt in guiding and supervising children to use the technology. We are particularly interested in looking at how parents perceived their adolescent children's characters and behaviours under the impact of ICTs. The basic themes to be studied in this article are (a) parents' and children's smartphone usage—what their differences in usage pattern

Table 14.2 *The Coding Frame, with the Basic Themes, Organizing Themes and Reporting Themes Extracted from Data Analyses*

Basic Themes	Organizing Themes	Reporting Themes
Parents' and children's smartphone usage	Parents' perceptions of their own and children's usage	Differences between parents and children in viewing and using smartphones from parents' perspectives
Children's interpersonal relationship after using smartphones	Parents' reports and views on children's interpersonal relationship and participation sport activities	Parents' views on whether smartphones have affected children's interpersonal relationship and sport activities—reduced or not
Parental guidance and supervision	Parents' methods and strategies in guiding and supervising children to use smartphones	What methods and strategies have the parents adopted to set rules and facilitate children to use smartphones appropriately; narratives on parent–child interactions; parents' views on mutual trust between two sides; parents' worries of the negative impacts of smartphones

and mentalities are, (b) parents' perceptions about children's interpersonal relationships with the impact of mobile devices—views on children's social life and (c) their approaches and strategies in guidance and supervision—methods in guiding and supervising children to use mobile devices, such as how to counsel and communicate with them to nurture proper behaviours in using the technology.

Differences in Usage Patterns Between Parents and Children

Overall speaking, the parents being interviewed recognized that there was a significant difference between them and their adolescent children in terms of knowledge and using patterns of smartphone. In general, parents admitted that they were less proficient and skilful than their children in using smartphones. For example, a parent reported that she tried to share her using experiences with her children, but she found that such kind of communication was not easy, as she was not quite familiar with 'this kind of knowledge' (ICT); she only knew some of the skills. Also, she had not heard of most of the apps that her children had been using. Another parent reflected that her son showed his mobile phone to her, but she only knew it was an 'object', which smartphone design looked better and so on. 'I don't know anything about which type of phone could be "intruded" [violation of privacy] and other security issues.... I'm not sure about most of the functions of a smartphone.'

In terms of the extent of children's reliance on smartphones in their daily lives, most parents in the interviews reported that the kids heavily relied on smartphone and other mobile devices. Most parts of their daily tasks and activities would involve smartphones, as they belonged to the generation of 'digital natives' as mentioned in the literature review. For the parents, since they were only 'digital migrants', and ICTs were not yet popular before they became adults, they held quite different mentalities towards mobile devices than their children, which resulted in differences in lifestyles between the two generations. As one parent pointed out, the current generation (i.e., the children) was quite different than theirs. The kids nowadays were having 'good' channels to communicate with others. However, a few parents also thought that the new technologies could also be easily abused, and the parent–child communications might not get better due to their differences in digital literacy and usage preferences. As one parent noted:

> For example, they are now used to tell me everything through WhatsApp, not by phone. I told them if the environment [the location of her child] is not favourable, it is okay for them to use WhatsApp to communicate with me, but I've told them not to type simplified Chinese. Since I'm not good in typing Chinese characters on mobile phone, I would use English to communicate with them on WhatsApp. Also, I insist that they should use proper and formal languages in writing to me. But of course, they won't do so accordingly....

As shown by the paraphrases and transcripts in this section, the disparity between parents and their adolescent children in proficiency and attitudes in using mobile devices, particularly with regard to the communication styles, is quite obvious. Many of the parents who participated in the interviews had shown a considerable degree of concern about the wellbeing of their children and parent–child relationships under the influence of popularization of mobile devices in daily lives, especially amongst the younger generations.

Children's Interpersonal Relationship from Parents' Perspectives

Parents were asked in the focus group interviews about how they viewed about their children's interpersonal relationships after using smartphones. Majority of the parents noted that their children now mainly communicated with friends through instant messaging apps and social media. Their daily lives had now been frequently engaged by online communications with friends. As one parent mentioned, now the volume of WhatsApp usage of his child had increased. Since there were more mutual communications between his child and friends, there would be so many messages that they needed to reply. Another parent said her daughter now rarely talked on the phone and preferred to record voice memos on WhatsApp. However, this parent did not prefer this new way of communication:

> I understand this is a preferable way [of communication] amongst her social circle; this is because of their culture. But since they are still kids,

they mostly use [smartphones] at school. She would also send audio memo to me in everyday life, but I told my daughter not to that to me, because I couldn't hear that all the time.

A few parents also reflected that after the proliferation of mobile devices, their children had participated less in face-to-face outdoor activities such as sports and gatherings in countryside. These parents had shown their worries about this tendency which they perceived as not beneficial to the kids. One parent pointed out that nowadays everyone only knew things related to online games. For example, her son was not quite willing to participate in BBQ gatherings or go to play in the beach: 'He only plays online games every time he gathers with his classmates, or watch movies. They seldom go to the beach or organize BBQ parties.'

Parents had reckoned the drastic change of interpersonal communications in the younger generations. The kids were more dependent on technology to stay in touch with parents and friends rather than relying on traditional modes such as telephone and outdoor activities in the past. From their testimonials, it seemed that parents had different habits than their children in interpersonal communications. Parents seemed to prefer more traditional means of communication such as face-to-face dialogues and phone calls, and did not fully appreciate the alternative communication tools provided by mobile devices in which their children were keenly engaged. This is echoing what the literature review mentioned about different norms and mentalities of the 'digital natives' and 'digital migrants'. One example was what a parent shared about her differences with children about their respective preferences in using text messages and phone calls: 'The four of us in our family always use WhatsApp to communicate, I think this is good. At the same time, I also think that it has some shortcomings to us, like they tend to inform me everything through WhatsApp, not by phone calls.'

Parental Guidance and Supervision Approaches

Parents had discussed about their approaches in guiding and supervising their adolescents to use the mobile devices. Although most parents were worried about the negative impacts of mobile devices on their children such as excessive usage, interactions with bad people and exposure to indecent materials online, some of them also understood the contemporary online culture and its importance to the kids. As long as parents could nurture in their children positive values since they were small, they should have the ability to make choices appropriately. Even though the access to smartphones had become ubiquitous and there were disparities between older and younger generations in terms of digital proficiency, these parents also found that positive understanding of the role of technology to the children and the adoption of liberal parenting approaches would help to nurture their children's appropriate behaviours and independence in using mobile devices.

A parent told the focus group that to her it was more ideal for her son to seek support from home when he had some demands or something to ask. In order to achieve that, it was more preferable for parents to adopt more liberal approaches in responding children's use of mobile devices: 'When he has some demands or something to ask, it is more ideal for him to seek help at home. If parents only enforce restrictions, such as setting limit on using time and setting passwords, he would end up going to stay in Internet bars.' Another parent further shared that it was getting challenging in enforcing strict rules about using mobile devices since the kids were growing up with new technologies, so rigid time limits and restrictions would not work, it would not help to build up trust between two sides: 'We won't understand our children's scope of study. Time limit and too many restrictions would restrain their mindsets. However, we need to build up trust ... they have been using mobile phones and computers since they were very small....'

As mentioned above by a parent, children's trust for parents was pivotal in ensuring positive parent–child relationships and interactions, especially in handling matters related to their use of mobile devices. Parents generally agreed that they should try their best to trust that the kids had been using mobile devices appropriately, and their privacy should be respected. Parents should avoid checking children's devices and reading their communication records without their consents. One parent said it was a dilemma for her to have curiosity to know what her daughter was doing online, but she had also learnt to trust her:

> As you may know, you can register for multiple accounts online at the same time. I don't quite trust my second daughter, but sometimes I

admit that this is not right.... It is a dilemma.... When she has grown up and needs to search a lot of information on the Internet, that requires compromises and agreements between the two sides in order to build up trust. How to build up trust? It is not a problem for her to use the Internet to search for information she needs, but she also needs to get other things done first.

Similar to the experience of the parent who asked his son to change clothes before using mobile devices after returning home, this parent also made agreements with her daughter about what she needed to accomplish first before picking up their mobile devices. These parents thought that trust could be built between them since there would be mutual understandings resulted from fulfilling those agreements and promises to each other. Under such circumstances, parents would be confident in children's mobile use, and children would feel respected by their parents.

Privacy in ICTs has been a growing concern for people in recent years. The parent interviewees in this study had also developed such kind of sense in guiding and supervising adolescent children to use mobile devices. A few parents had once checked their children's communication contents, but later they found it not beneficial to long-term parent–child relationships, so they now tried to avoid that.

> I once told my eldest daughter that when she used her Internet-accessible smartphone, I would check it. Of course, she rejected to comply, but overtime I also stopped checking, since the kids now needs privacy as they are growing older. They could use their phones on the way to school. It is enough for me to understand their daily behaviour.

Another parent had similar reflections, agreeing that checking was a kind of privacy violation that could affect parent–child relationship:

> The effectiveness of parenting depends on trust ... when the kids get older, it is difficult for us to guide and supervise them. For example, beginning from around age 15 or 16, I had emphasized that I won't check her mobile phone. Beginning from teenage, children usually won't listen to parents when they are asked to go to bed earlier.... There was once a scenario in which there were some problems with my daughter's phone, but she still didn't know how to fix it, so as father

I fixed it up for her. Accidentally I found that she had been chatting with an elder man online, so I questioned her about that … violation of privacy could affect our relationship.

A parent said she had developed an open mindset to trust what her children doing online are appropriate, since she understood the needs of the younger generation in using mobile devices and mobile devices to do what they needed. This mother also endorsed the thoughts and activities of her children, because she claimed that she understood their true nature, thus no strict restrictions and monitoring are needed:

> I can see they are having positive values, as I was also very 'foolish' during my teenage, so it is also normal for them to be 'foolish' too. As for my children, they are quite clever and lovable to me.… If you understand there isn't any serious problems with her nature and she has her own rights, then as parents we can't stop her from doing something. My daughter might not be very 'productive', but she is joyful in general. This is a kind of teenage experience, she deserves to enjoy that.

Another parent responded with similar thoughts about understanding and building up positive relationship with kids: 'I need to remind myself constantly: is my personal experience really suitable to her? Perhaps what I have done to her might not necessarily benefit her, even though I am attempting to help her. I might not fully understand her situation and thoughts'.

The parent interviewees generally agreed that parents nowadays should give up the past standards in evaluating children's behaviours and performance. Instead, they should take a liberal and proactive approach to interact with them with respect and care. They found that mutual trust was very important to effective guidance and supervision, and also better understanding of youths' digital cultures and needs could also help.

DISCUSSIONS

The popularization of smartphones amongst the children has brought big challenges to parents nowadays. In our focus group interviews, we found that parents and children engaged more in conflicts and confrontations over smartphone usage, and parents would feel that parenting had become more challenging than before. In parents' eyes, whenever children tended to use their phones for entertainment purposes, it was liable to affect their academic performance and health if they were not under control.

It was quite obvious that from parents' perceptions, it was generally agreed that the norms and cultures amongst the younger generations in the digital age with mobile devices accessible all the time had become divergent to what parents usually believed in the past. This echoed what Rudi et al. (2015) and Anshari et al. (2016) found about the digital divide between generations and within families. It was hence necessary for parents to understand and appreciate what the kids were interested in and what they needed to learn from new technologies. The forceful restrictions and impositions of adult values as well as violation of privacy by checking children's devices were not effective means to ensure effective parenting, children's growth and parent–child relationships, as proven by the experiences of these parents. The shortcomings of these restrictive means undertaken by parents have also been suggested by previous researches (Lee, 2016; van den Eijnden et al., 2012; Wong, 2010; Wong et al., 2015).

The parents generally agreed that their children could now develop their own characters, thoughts and survival skills through online learning and communications with friends, even though they still had some concerns about children's length of time spent online, virtual interpersonal relationships and web safety. The conflicts and quarrels always occurred when mistrusts between two sides occurred. Some parents set rules specifying the time limits in using smartphones, or they were not allowed to use outside home and during dinner times. However, quite a number of parents agreed that parental trust for children in using the Internet was very crucial to family harmony and parent–child relationship, as well as with what attitude parents responded to children's concerns over using technology.

For the social service providers, this study shall provide a comprehensive reference for them to understand how parents and adolescents think about family dynamics and relationships under the impact of technological development on individual families, so that they could consider which intervention approaches could effectively support families in managing parent–child conflicts, developing cohesiveness and facilitating adolescents' positive use of new technologies.

More importantly, they could teach the parents how to develop the character strength of their children through parenting and different technologies.

Character Strength-based Training Programme for Parents

As stated, both parents and children would face the challenges brought by technological advancement, it would be good to develop the character strength-based parents training programme. The character strengths included several elements such as self-regulation, perspective and love of learning through parenting (Park & Peterson, 2005). The core elements can be added in the outline of character strengths-based parent training programme. The overall training objective is to train the parents to try to enhance the character education of their children. For the contents, it can be developed according to the experiences of practitioners (Table 14.3).

Table 14.3 *Core Elements of Character Strengths-based Parent Training Programme Related to Technology*

	Character Strengths	Training Objective(s)
1.	Self-regulation	To enhance their children's self-control of the usage of electronic devices
2.	Judgement	To train their children with the ability of better judgement (right and wrong)
3.	Love of learning	To facilitate their children to master new knowledge with the help of technology
4.	Zest	To nurture their children to do everything with excitement and energy
5.	Decision-making	To learn how to strengthen their children in decision-making process
6.	Open-mindedness	To strengthen their children's open-mindedness and encourage them to accept different views from the others
7.	Perspective	To widen their children's perspective in daily life

For some suggested contents, the parents could learn how to set contract with their children about their usage of electronic devices under the theme of 'self-regulation'. The parents will be taught how to supervise their children about the contract in order to build up trust between both sides. If the children can observe the rules related to mutually agreed time, they could continue to enjoy the right to use the electronic devices. The parents could also learn how to select proper materials from news and pick the right timing to teach their children to make a better judgement when they may encounter threats from the Internet under the theme of 'judgement'. They could learn how to strengthen in their children the decision-making process. The parents could widen their children's perspective in daily life by widening children's exposures with their participation under the theme of 'perspective'.

Apart from the character strength's elements, the parents should also equip with the following basic components (Table 14.4) in parent training programmes.

For the suggested contents of basic parent training programmes, the parents could understand themselves through some experiential exercises. They can reflect their expectation on parenting in the group facilitated by social worker, counsellors or teachers, from which they could learn the assessment skills and methods so they can assess their developmental needs and challenges. The parents will be able to know more about technological advancement such as knowing the platforms of social media, watching videos and playing games through electronic devices. They will also be encouraged to engage their children by using mobile devices together, and learn how to appreciate their children, adopt effective guidance and to have effective communication skills from social workers, other professionals and from the other group members. The parents can also learn various ways related to relationship-building with the children by joining more family programmes and groups so as to enhance their relationship. In addition, parents can learn more about conflicts management through lectures, role-plays and sharing.

CONCLUSION

As shown in the findings of this study, majority of parents understand the unavoidable trend of using electronic advice. With the utilization

Table 14.4 Basic Components in Parent Training Programmes

Basic Components	Training Objective(s)
1. Basic understanding of self	To increase understanding of the parents on their own
2. Parenting expectation	To facilitate them to have reflection on their expectation on their children
3. Understanding children	To know and assess their children's development needs and challenges
4. Understanding technology	To understand the technology advancement and to equip basic skills in using electronic devices
5. Parenting style	To increase their understanding towards different parenting style
6. Appreciation	To encourage the parents to appreciate their children
7. Effective discipline	To teach the parents effective approaches in discipline
8. Effective communication	To teach the parents effective communication
9. Relationship-building	To share with the parents the practical skills in building relationship with their children
10. Conflict management	To equip parents with knowledge and skills in conflict management with their children

and integration of character strength elements into the parent training programme, it is important to build up the children character strength and then strengthen their positive and effective usage of electronic devices. It can also enhance the parent–child relationship under the digital era. Even though most of the 'digital migrants' today have used ICT to a certain extent, such as using the smartphones or tablets, working and communicating with others through online tools and search for information they need online as compared with the situation in the past, the digital divide between the 'digital migrants' and the 'digital natives' still exists, largely owing to their different patterns of mobile use.

The younger generations, on the other hand, are not limited to what their parents are using on mobile devices, but much of their daily lives has become highly dependent on technology. They would be more enthusiastic in staying in touch with their peers not only through emails, but also the instant messaging software and apps. They would take ICT and the gadgets as integral parts of their life rather than supplementary tools as taken by their parents. Inevitably, there would be confrontations and even quarrels between parents and adolescent children over the amount of time spent on mobile devices, online contents they read and friends they make.

As revealed by the research findings, it is now important for parents to take a proactive attitude with an open mindset to understand the norms of their children's digital lifestyle. It is recommended that there should be frequent and frank discussions between parents and children over mobile phone usage and the potential problems. Forceful and restrictive types of guidance should be avoided in supervising adolescent children since that could trigger adverse effects and harm parent–child relations. Besides, as pointed out by a number of parent interviewees in this study, mutual trust is pivotal in nurturing positive parent–child relations under the impacts of new technologies and the generational differences in usage patterns.

In response to these challenges, social support services should focus on helping parents to identify the character strengths of their children accurately and to guide them to utilize ICT for nurturing potential and positive personalities. But most importantly, parents themselves need to understand the merits of mobile devices and ICT for the developmental needs of children, and be more proficient in the skills and functions.

This research has two major limitations. First, the parents were not asked about their socio-economic status such as educational attainment and occupation, since these could be useful information for us to analyse the digital proficiency and parenting challenges of different parents. Second, there seemed to be a sampling bias in the recruitment of subjects, since the parent interviewees who attended the focus group interviews were recruited by one single agency. This might potentially affect the diversity of demographic characteristics and data. Future researches on this theme should collect some basic socio-economic information of the subjects for deeper analyses, and the recruitment of research subjects from more sources.

REFERENCES

Anshari, M., Alas, G., Hardaker, J. H., Smith, M., & Ahad, A. D. (2016). Smartphone habit and behavior in Brunei: Personalization, gender and generation gap. *Computers in Human Behavior, 64*, 719–727. doi:10.1016/j.chb.2016.07.063

Baumrind, D. (1998). Reflections on character and competence. In A. Colby, J. James, & D. Hart (Eds.), *Competence and character through life* (pp. 1–28). Chicago, IL: University of Chicago Press.

Barkley, R. A. (2013). *Defiant children: A clinician's manual for assessment and parent training* (3rd ed.). New York, NY: Guilford Press.

———. (2015). *Oppositional defiant disorder: The four factor model for assessment and management.* Retrieved from http://www.continuingedcourses.net/active/courses/course079.php

Charmaz, K. (1995). Grounded theory. In J. A. Smith, R. Harre, & L. Van Langenhove (Eds.), *Rethinking methods in psychology* (pp. 27–49). Thousand Oaks, CA: SAGE Publications.

Charmaz, K. (2000). Grounded theory: Objectivist and constructivist methods. In N. K. Denzin & Y. S. Lincoln (Eds.), *Handbook of qualitative research* (pp. 509–536). Thousand Oaks, CA: SAGE Publications.

Davidson, J., & Martellozzo, E. (2013). Exploring young people's use of social networking sites and digital media in the Internet safety context: A comparison of the UK and Bahrain. *Information, Communication & Society, 16*(9), 1456–1476.

De-Miguel-Molina, M., Martinez-Gomez, M., De-Miguel-Molina, B., & Ribes-Giner, G. (2012). A qualitative study on mobile services aimed at children and self-regulation in Spain. *Quality and Quantity, 46*, 1795–1806. doi:10.1037/10020833

Duncan, L. G., Coatsworth, J. D., & Greenberg, M. T. (2009). A model of mindful parenting: Implications for parent–child relationships and prevention research. *Clinical Child and Family Psychology Review, 12*(3), 255–270.

Feng, Y., & Xie, W. (2014). Teens' concern for privacy when using social networking sites: An analysis of socialization agents and relationships with privacy-protecting behaviors. *Computers in Human Behavior, 33*, 153–162. doi:10.1016/j.chb.2014.01.009

Huta, V., & Hawley, L. (2010). Psychological strengths and cognitive vulnerabilities: Are they two ends of the same continuum or do they have independent relationships with well-being and ill-being? *Journal of Happiness Studies, 11*, 71–93. doi:10.1007/s10902-008-9123-4

Jeong, S. H., Kim, H., Yum, J. Y., & Hwang, Y. (2016). What type of content are smartphone users addicted to? SNS vs. games. *Computers in Human Behavior, 54*, 10–17.

Kim, D., Nam, J. E. K., Oh, J. S., & Kang, M. C. (2016). A latent profile analysis of the interplay between PC and smartphone in problematic Internet use. *Computers in Human Behavior, 56*, 360–368. doi:10.1016/j.chb.2015.11.009

Kordi, A., & Baharudin, R. (2010). Parenting attitude and style and its effect on children's school achievements. *International Journal of Psychological Studies*, 2(2), 217–222.

Lee, W. P. V. (2016). *The Internet and parent-adolescent relationships: Parenting challenges and strategies in the digital age* (Doctoral thesis). Hong Kong: The University of Hong Kong.

Lee, Y. K., Chang, C. T., Lin, Y., & Cheng, Z. H. (2014). The dark side of smartphone usage: Psychological traits, compulsive behavior and technostress. *Computers in Human Behavior*, 31, 373–383.

Mills, J., Bonner, A., & Francis, K. (2006). Adopting a constructivist approach to grounded theory: Implications for research design. *International Journal of Nursing Practice*, 12(1), 5–13.

Monastra, V. J., Monastra, D. M., & George, S. (2002). The effects of stimulant therapy, EEG biofeedback, and parenting style on the primary symptoms of attention-deficit/hyperactivity disorder. *Applied Psychophysiology and Biofeedback*, 27(4), 231–249.

Ngai, S. S. (2015). Parental bonding and character strengths among Chinese adolescents in Hong Kong. *International Journal of Adolescence and Youth*, 20(3), 317–333. doi:10.1080/02673843.2015.1007879

Palfrey, J., & Gasser, U. (2008). *Born digital: Understanding the first generation of digital natives*. New York, NY: Basic Books.

Park, N. (2004). Character strengths and positive youth development. *ANNALS, AAPSS*, 591. doi:10.1177/0002716203260079

Park, N. (2009). Building strengths of character: Keys to positive youth development. *Reclaiming Children and Youth*, 18(2), 42–47.

Park, N., & Peterson, C. (2005). The Values in Action Inventory of Character Strengths for Youth. In K. A. Moore & L. H. Lippman (Eds.), *What do children need to flourish? Conceptualizing and measuring indicators of positive development* (pp. 13–24). New York, NY: Springer Science and Business Media.

———. (2006). Moral competence and character strengths among adolescents: The development and validation of the values in action inventory of strengths for youth. *Journal of Adolescence*, 29(6), 891–909. doi:10.1016/j.adolescence.2006.04.011

———. (2008). Positive psychology and character strengths: Application to strengths-based school counseling. *Professional School Counseling*, 12(2), 85–92. doi:10.5330/PSC.n.2010-12.85

Proctor, C. (2013). *The importance of good character*. doi:10.1007/978-94-007-6398-2_2

Proctor, C., Tsukayama, E., Wood, A. M., Maltby, J., Eades, J. F., & Linley, P. A. (2011). Strengths gym: The impact of a character strengths-based intervention on the life satisfaction and well-being of adolescents. *The Journal of Positive Psychology*, 6(5), 377–388. doi:10.1080/17439760.2011.594079

Rashid, T., Anjum, A., Lennox, C., Quinlan, D., Niemiec, R. M., Mayerson, D., & Kazemi, F. (2013). Assessment of character strengths in children and adolescents. In C. Proctor, P. A. Linley, C. Proctor, & P. A. Linley (Eds.), *Research,* applications, and interventions for children and adolescents (pp. 81–115). New York, NY: Springer Science + Business Media. doi:10.1007/978-94-007-6398-2_6

Rudi, J., Dworkin, J., Walker, S., & Doty, J. (2015). Parents' use of information and communications technologies for family communication: Differences by age of children. *Information, Communication & Society, 18*(1), 78–93.

Salehan, M., & Negahban, A. (2013). Social networking on smartphones: When mobile phones become addictive. *Computers in Human Behavior, 29*(6), 2632–2639.

Samaha, M., & Hawi, N. S. (2016). Relationships among smartphone addiction, stress, academic performance, and satisfaction with life. *Computers in Human Behavior, 57*, 321–325. doi: 10.1016/j.chb.2015.12.045

Sanders, M. (2008). Triple P-positive parenting program as a public health approach to strengthening parenting. *Journal of Family Psychology, 22*(3), 506–517.

Seider, S., Gilbert, J., Novick, S., & Gomez, J. (2013). The role of moral and performance character strengths in predicting achievement and conduct among urban middle school students. *Teachers College Record, 115*(8), 1–18.

Steen, T. A., Kachorek, L. V., & Peterson, C. (2003). Character strengths among youth. *Journal of Youth and Adolescence, 32*(1), 5–16.

Steinberg, L., Lamborn, S. D., Dornbusch, S. M., & Darling, N. (1992). Impact of parenting practices on adolescent achievement: Authoritative parenting, school involvement, and encouragement to succeed. *Child Development, 63*(5), 1266–1281.

Tapscott, D. (1998). *Growing up digital: The rise of the net generation.* New York, NY: McGraw-Hill.

———. (2009). *Grown up digital: How the net generation is changing your world.* New York, NY: McGraw-Hill.

Tariq, I., & Zubair, A. (2015). Character strengths, learned optimism, and social competence among university students. *Pakistan Journal of Psychology, 46*(2), 35–51.

Toner, E., Haslam, N., Robinson, J., & Williams, P. (2012). Character strengths and wellbeing in adolescence: Structure and correlates of the values in action inventory of strengths for children. *Personality and Individual Differences, 52*(5), 637–642. doi:10.1016/j.paid.2011.12.014

van den Eijnden, R. J. J. M., Spikerman, R., Vermulst, A. A., van Rooij, T. J., & Engels, R. C. M. E. (2010). Compulsive Internet use among adolescents: Bidirectional parent-child relationships. *Journal of Abnormal Child Psychology, 38*(1), 77–89.

Weber, M., Wagner, L., & Ruch, W. (2016). Positive feelings at school: On the relationships between students' character strengths, school-related affect, and school functioning. *Journal of Happiness Studies, 17*(1), 341–355. doi:10.1007/s10902-014-9597-1

Wood, A. M., Linley, P. A., Maltby, J., Kashdan, T. B., & Hurling, R. (2011). Using personal and psychological strengths leads to increases in well-being over time: A longitudinal study and the development of the strengths use questionnaire. *Personality and Individual Differences, 50,* 15–19. doi:10.1016/j.paid.2010.08.004

Wong, Y. C. (2010). Cyber-parenting: Internet benefits, risks and parenting issues. *Journal of Technology in Human Services, 28*(4), 252–273.

Wong, Y. C., Ho, K. M., & Chen, H. (2015). Internet supervision and parenting in the digital age: The case of Shanghai. *The Open Family Studies Journal,* 7(Suppl 2: M8), 112–123.

Zhitomirsky-Geffet, M., & Blau, M. (2016). Cross-generational analysis of predictive factors of addictive behavior in smartphone usage. *Computers in Human Behavior, 64,* 582–693. doi:10.1016/j.chb.2016.07.061

Chapter 15

Positivism in Relation to Signature Strengths in Educated Working Women and Housewives

S. S. Nathawat and Tanya Tripathi

Positivism in one's life is considered fundamental to good mental health, harmonious relations and desired quality of life. The factors that influence positivism include structural level (good living environment, employment and education), community level (sense of belonging and social support) and individual level (like ability to deal with thoughts, beliefs, attitudes, feelings and emotional resilience). If a man or woman is positive he or she would transmit positivism to the community. If thoughts of an individual are positive, he/she would send positive vibrations.

Martin Seligman, originator of positive psychology in 1998, holds that positive psychology is the study of how human beings prosper even in the face of adversity. Its goals are to identify and enhance the human strengths and virtues that make life worth living and allow individuals and communities to thrive. Seligman (2011) in his book *Flourish* adds that when individual flourish, health, positivity and peace follow.

Amitian[1] movement of positivism has a lot to share from positive psychology and vice versa (Chauhan & Nathawat, 2011). Positivism and positive psychology are intermixed and often confused domains but each serving its own purpose. Just as positive psychology relates to quantitative approach to study, positivism focuses on qualitative approach encompassing all strengths, values, virtues, happiness, truth, compassion, courage and acceptance. Thus, positivism is a positive consciousness/perception humans have about themselves and their values, and how they practice those sets of values in life.

Positive psychology holds that you are happiest when you are living consistently with your virtues and utilizing your signature strengths to successfully craft your life. On the other hand, when you are experiencing unpleasant emotions (about yourself) you are most likely behaving inconsistently with your virtues.

Positivism in relation to signature strength needs some elaboration. Signature strengths are positive traits that a person owns, celebrates and frequently exercises. You can identify your signature strengths through Values in Action (VIA) survey of character strengths. The survey will list your top five strengths—most will feel authentic, but one or two may not speak to you; you may be good at displaying those strengths, but you may not feel like you own those. Each person possesses several signature strengths of character that he or she self-consciously owns, celebrates and exercises every day in work, love, play and parenting and in having a meaningful life. Consider the following statements, and if one or more applied to your top five strengths these are your signature strengths:

1. a sense of ownership and authenticity ('this is the real me') vis-à-vis the strength
2. a feeling of excitement while displaying it, particularly at first
3. a fast learning curve as themes are attached to the strength and practised
4. continuous learning of new ways to enact the strength
5. a sense of craving to act in accordance with the strength

---

[1] Includes faculty and students of Amity University.

6. a feeling of inevitability in using the strength, as if one cannot be stopped
7. the discovery of the strength as a peak experience
8. positively motivated rather than exhaustion when using the strength
9. the creation and pursuit of fundamental projects that revolve around the strength
10. intrinsic motivation to use the strength

There are six virtues—admirable qualities—and they stand for moral excellence observed in the vast majority of cultures. The six virtues include (a) wisdom and knowledge, (b) courage, (c) humanity and love, (d) justice, (e) temperance and (f) transcendence.

Following are the 24 strengths as components of these six virtues:

A. Wisdom and knowledge
   1. Curiosity/Interest in the world, 2. Love of learning, 3. Judgement/Critical thinking/Open-mindedness, 4. Ingenuity/Originality/Practical intelligence/Street smartness, 5. Social intelligence/Personal intelligence/Emotional intelligence, 6. Perspective
B. Courage
   7. Valour and bravery, 8. Perseverance/Industry/Diligence, 9. Integrity/Genuineness/Honesty
C. Humanity and love
   10. Kindness and generosity, 11. Loving and allowing oneself to be loved
D. Justice
   12. Citizenship/Duty/Teamwork/Loyalty, 13. Fairness and equity, 14. Leadership
E. Temperance
   15. Self-control, 16. Prudence/Discretion/Caution, 17. Humility and modesty
F. Transcendence
   18. Appreciation of beauty and excellence, 19. Gratitude 20. Hope/Optimism/Future-mindedness, 21. Spirituality/Sense of purpose/Faith/Religiousness, 22. Forgiveness and mercy, 23. Playfulness and humour, 24. Zest/Passion/Enthusiasm

Studies on this topic in India are conspicuous by their absence. However, some observations are made in the West. Diener (2006) conducted a study to evaluate 24 character strengths, called the Values in Action (VIA) classification across cultures. The results disclosed differences between and within cultures in terms of gender, the perceived importance of specific strengths and the existence of cultural institutions that promote each strength.

Linley and his associates (2007) carried out an internet survey on character strengths in the United Kingdom employing the VIA inventory of the strengths on 17,056 respondents and found that women scored high on character strength than men. Strengths showed small but significant positive associations with age, with the strongest associations of age being with curiosity and love of learning, fairness, and forgiveness and self-regulation.

Brdar and Rijavec (2011) investigated possible gender differences in the relationship between character strengths and life satisfaction and found that zest, hope and gratitude had the strongest link to life satisfaction. Women and men differ significantly in 10 character strengths, but they did not differ in their life satisfaction. Five highest weighted strengths for women were integrity, kindness, love, gratitude and fairness, while men weighted highest in the strengths of integrity, hope, humour, gratitude and curiosity.

Proctor et al. (2011) in their study on strength used as predictors of well-being and health related quality of life found that the VIA strengths of hope and zest were significant positive predictors of life satisfaction. The most commonly endorsed VIA strengths found were love, humour, kindness, social intelligence and open mindedness, while the least-endorsed VIA strengths found were leadership, perseverance, wisdom, spirituality and self-control. Overall results suggested an important link between genetic strengths use and specific VIA strengths and their impact on subjective well-being.

None of the aforementioned studies investigated role of signature strengths in educated housewives and educated working women. It therefore occurred to us to fulfil this research gap considering new concept of positivism. More specifically, the present study was conducted on Positivism in relation to Signature Strengths in educated working women and housewives.

A 2×2 factorial design was employed on a sample of 55 educated working women and equal number of educated housewives. They were further classified as women with young and middle adulthood based on their age range 25–45 and 46–60, respectively. They were administered Signature Strength self-rating scale, adapted by Jonathan Haidt from Seligman's *Authentic Happiness* (2002).

Major findings are presented in the following six tables (viz., Tables 15.1a and 15.1b; 15.2a and 15.2b; 15.3a and 15.3b; 15.4a and 15.4b; 15.5a and 15.5b; 15.6a and 15.6b).

Tables 15.1a and 15.1b explicitly demonstrate insignificant findings on measure of wisdom on three sources: housewives–working women; women in young adulthood and middle adulthood; and joint interaction effect of the two independent variables (IVs) on the factor Wisdom.

Tables 15.2a and 15.2b show the means of housewives and working women as 0.80 and 3.50, respectively, which are significant at 0.5

Table 15.1a Means and SDs on WISDOM of Signature Strengths of Four Groups

Housewives/ Working Women	Young Adulthood		Middle Adulthood		Mean Total
	Mean	SD	Mean	SD	
Housewives	1.35	3.81	1.47	3.42	2.81
Working	1.82	4.78	0.73	4.48	2.53
Total	3.17		2.19		

Table 15.1b ANOVA for Wisdom

Source	SS	Df	Mean Square	F	Sig Level
AGE	32.52	1	32.52	1.81	n.s.
OCCUP*	16.23	1	16.23	0.90	n.s.
AGE × OCCUP	39.03	1	39.03	2.18	n.s.
ERROR	1,901.542	106	17.939		

Note: *OCCUP stands for occupation.

Table 15.2a Means and SDs on Courage of Signature Strengths of Four Groups

Housewives/ Working Women	Young Adulthood		Middle Adulthood		Mean Total
	Mean	SD	Mean	SD	
Housewives	0.80	2.85	00*	3.05	0.80
Working	1.17	3.01	2.33	2.92	3.50
Total	1.97		2.33		

Note: *Mean 00 refers to equal scores of plus and minus averaging to 00.

Table 15.2b ANOVA for Courage

Source	SS	Df	Mean Square	F	Sig Level
AGE	0.700	1	0.700	0.08	n.s.
OCCUP	40.01	1	40.01	4.61	< 0.05
AGE × OCCUP	20.919	1	20.919	2.41	n.s.
ERROR	919.508	106	8.67		

levels. It indicated that the working women are more courageous as compared to housewives. No significant difference was found on young adulthood and middle adulthood women, and same was the case in the interaction effect of age and occupation on Courage.

Tables 15.3a and 15.3b explicitly demonstrate insignificant findings on all measures of humanity on three sources: housewives–working women; women in young adulthood and middle adulthood; and joint interaction effect of the two IVs on the factor of Humanity.

Tables 15.4a and 15.4b show mean of women in young adulthood and middle adulthood as 51.8 and 55.93, respectively, which were significant at 0.5 level. However, the means of housewives and working women differ considerably but not significantly. The interaction effect of age and occupation was significant at 0.01 level on the dimension of Justice.

Tables 15.5a and 15.5b explicitly demonstrate insignificant findings on all measures of Temperance on three sources: housewives-working women; women in young adulthood and middle adulthood;

Table 15.3a Means and SDs on Humanity of Signature Strengths of Four Groups

Housewives/Working Women	Young Adulthood		Middle Adulthood		Mean Total
	Mean	SD	Mean	SD	
Housewives	2.40	2.78	2.87	2.56	5.26
Working	2.82	2.69	2.87	1.85	5.68
Total	5.22		5.72		

Table 15.3b ANOVA for Humanity

Source	SS	Df	Mean Square	F	Sig Level
AGE	1.41	1	1.41	0.21	n.s.
OCCUP	0.98	1	0.98	0.14	n.s.
AGE × OCCUP	0.98	1	0.98	0.14	n.s.
ERROR	722.84	106	6.82		

Table 15.4a Means and SDs on Justice of Signature Strengths of Four Groups

Housewives/Working Women	Young Adulthood		Middle Adulthood		Mean Total
	Mean	SD	Mean	SD	
Housewives	24.22	4.18	29.33	2.92	63.55
Working	27.58	5.028	26.60	3.901	54.18
Total	51.8		55.93		

Table 15.4b ANOVA for Justice

Source	SS	Df	Mean Square	F	Sig Level
AGE	93.19	1	93.19	4.93	<0.05
OCCUP	2.07	1	2.07	0.110	n.s.
AGE × OCCUP	201.86	1	201.86	10.69	<0.01
ERROR	2,001.68	106	18.88		

Table 15.5a *Means and SDs on Temperance of Signature Strengths of Four Groups*

Housewives/ Working Women	Young Adulthood		Middle Adulthood		Mean Total
	Mean	SD	Mean	SD	
Housewives	2.08	3.05	−2.47	3.91	4.55
Working	2.20	3.05	−2.80	2.88	5.00
Total	4.28		5.27		

Table 15.5b *ANOVA for Temperance*

Source	SS	Df	Mean Square	F	Sig Level
AGE	5.36	1	5.36	0.54	n.s.
OCCUP	1.15	1	1.15	0.12	n.s.
AGE × OCCUP	0.24	1	0.24	0.024	n.s.
ERROR	1,057.31	106	9.97		

as well as joint interaction effect of the two IVs on the factor Temperance.

Tables 15.6a and 15.6b explicitly demonstrate insignificant findings on all measures of Transcendence on three sources: housewives–working women; women in young adulthood and middle adulthood; and joint interaction effect of the two IVs on the factor Transcendence.

COMMENT

One of the significant findings emerged from this study is that educated working women were found to have significantly high scores on courage as virtue (Signature Strength) as compared to educated housewives. Nathawat and Mathur (1993) have also demonstrated that educated working women reported high scores on general health, life satisfaction and self-esteem measures and lower scores on hopelessness, insecurity and anxiety as compared to educated housewives. On the other hand, Hooda and Singh (2014) have argued that women as

Table 15.6a *Means and SDs on Transcendence of Signature Strengths of Four Groups*

Housewives/Working Women	Young Adulthood		Middle Adulthood		Mean Total
	Mean	SD	Mean	SD	
Housewives	2.10	6.27	1.80	5.12	3.90
Working	0.87	4.62	3.73	5.59	4.60
Total	2.97		5.53		

Table 15.6b *ANOVA for Transcendence*

Source	SS	Df	Mean Square	F	Sig Level
AGE	35.70	1	35.70	1.19	n.s.
OCCUP	2.74	1	2.74	0.09	n.s.
AGE × OCCUP	54.41	1	54.41	1.82	n.s.
ERROR	3,173.31	106	29.94		

homemakers had higher levels of happiness as compared to working women. Housewives along with having less work-related stress enjoy a better supportive environment and quality life which contribute to their overall health when compared to working women. Dual role of working women as homemakers and working women might add to their overall stress. There are different opinions with respect to overall stressful life of working women and housewives. But it is generally believed that educated working women might do better in every sphere of life as compared to housewives.

By and large, no significant differences were observed in most of the virtues including Wisdom, Humanity, Temperance and Transcendence in these two groups of educated women—either housewives or working ones.

Furthermore, young-aged and middle-aged women have shown significant differences on the virtue of Justice where young-aged women were found to have significantly higher scores on Justice as compared to middle-aged women. So also age and occupational status jointly affected Justice scores in this sample. We have reported elsewhere (Nathawat & Tripathi, 2017) that working educated women scored significantly higher than their counterparts who were housewives on measures of psychological well-being, happiness, meaningful life and other measures of positivism. We need to conduct further studies on bigger samples to verify these findings.

From the observations of this pilot study, it can be inferred that signature strengths or virtues play a vital role in positivism in life in educated women. More so, they may be benefited more if they are working because positivity in life is considered to be significantly related with occupational well-being.

REFERENCES

Brdar, I., Anic, P., & Rijavec, M. (2011). Character strengths and well-being: Are there gender differences? In I. Brdar (Ed.), *The human pursuit of well-being: A cultural approach* (pp. 145–156). New York, NY: Springer.

Chauhan, A. K., & Nathawat, S. S. (2011). *New facets of positivism*. New Delhi: Macmillan.

Diener, R. (2006). From the equator to the North Pole: A study of character strengths. *Journal of Happiness Studies*, 7(3), 293–310.

Hooda, S., & Singh, S. (2014). Marital adjustment, coping and happiness in carrier women. *International Journal for Research Publication and Seminar*, 5, 40–43.

Linley, P. A., Maltby, J., Wood, A. M., Joseph, S., Harrington, S., Peterson, C.,... Seligman, M. E. (2007). Character strengths in the United Kingdom: The VIA inventory of strengths. *Personality and Individual Differences*, 43(20), 341–351.

Nathawat, S. S., & Mathur, A. (1993). Marital adjustment and subjective well-being in Indian-educated housewives and working women. *The Journal of Psychology*, 127(3), 353–358.

Nathawat, S. S., & Tripathi, T. (2017). Role of positivism in life in women: Psychological well-being, happiness, meaningful life and signature strength in working and non-working women. Paper presented at the 5th Rajasthan Science Congress, held at Amity University, Rajasthan, 13–15 October 2017.

Proctor, C., Maltby, J., & Linley, P. A. (2011). Strengths use as a predictor of well-being and health-related quality of life. *Journal of Happiness Studies*, 12(1), 153–169.

Seligman, M. E. P. (2002). *Authentic happiness: Using the new positive psychology to realize your potential for lasting fulfillment*. New York: Simon and Schuster.

Seligman, M. E. P. (2011). *Flourish: A visionary new understanding of happiness and well-being*. New York, NY: Simon & Schuster.

Chapter 16

Character Strength Development
Does Family Matter?

Padmakumari P. and Dolly Jose

Character is the sum of all dispositions and habits that determine the manner in which one usually responds to opportunities, desires, challenges, fears, failures and success (Pala, 2011). Character strengths reflect one's thinking, feeling and behaving in a way that enhances optimal functioning in the achievement of valued outcomes (Linley & Harrington, 2006).

Character strengths develop from the joint activation of negative as well as positive human states and also as a result of a dialectical process involving a person's struggle with adversity. When one is able to find meaning and purpose for life's struggles and adversities, it leads to the development of character strengths (Smith, 2013). Scholars agree that the interaction between heredity and environment too play a role in character strength development (Iorg, 2007; Park, Peterson, & Seligman, 2004; Smith, 2006). Some scholars agree that people develop strengths as part of human driving force to meet basic psychological needs such as belonging and affiliation, feeling secure, competent, and finding meaning and purpose in life (Bandura, 1997; Deci & Ryan, 2000; Smith, 2006). Character strengths may be stable and enduring aspects which influence one's life, but the process through which they are developed and the manner in which they are expressed could definitely be influenced by people and things around oneself—be it parents, teachers, peers or other significant people and experiences.

While the character is formed by genetics and early environmental factors, the character continues to be developed and shaped over a lifetime, and thus can be considered as a lifelong process. Lickona (1992) adds that three important social institutions, namely, the family, the church and the school, have traditionally been responsible for shaping the character of the young. Research also shows that a person's upbringing, role models, value systems, self-discipline, relationship, church environment, personal crisis and trauma, and religion are most significant factors in character development (Braine & Verrier, 2007).

Character building is one of the most important goals of any youth development programme. Empirical research on youth development programmes indicate that one of the ways to prevent the problem behaviours is by building or optimizing the character strengths, namely, social intelligence, morality, self-control, spirituality and such others (Weissberg & O'Brien, 2003). A variety of factors definitely contribute to the development of character strengths. However, if character can be cultivated, considering the vital role of family in it, how does one go about developing such programmes for the children?

The review on character development strongly confirmed the notion that the foundation of character development starts from family background. In the given situations, most of the interactions of the developing child with the environment and parents occur at a non-conscious level and they leave their imprint on the character structure of the child and future adult (Rizzuto, 2007; Rulla, Ridick, & Imoda, 1986). Adults play the part of positive role models and mentors for their younger generation in the imitation and development of character strengths (Bandura, 1977; Sprafkin, Liebert, & Poulos, 1975).

There is unanimous agreement among researchers also that the manner in which families foster the relationships contributes powerfully to the way children grow up (Heckman, 2008; Kuczynski, 2003; Laursen & Collins, 2009; Steinberg, 2001; Syvertsen, Roehlkepartain, & Scales, 2012; Tuttle, Knudson-Martin, & Kim, 2012).

STRENGTH-BASED PARENTING

The concept of strength-based parenting talks about the healthy parenting which aims at identifying and cultivating positive states, processes and qualities in children (Waters, 2015). The empirical intervention studies done on strength-based parenting show that it predicts positive coping strategies, reduction of stress and fewer problem behaviours (Nowak & Heinrichs, 2008; Saunders et al. 2003; Sheely, Moore, & Bratton, 2015). When parents practise authoritative parenting characterized by warmth, sensitivity and support, and try to cultivate strengths in their children, they report higher level of life satisfaction (Waters, 2015). Researchers are of the opinion that parents' awareness of the importance of expressing love and emotional support (Eshel, Daelmans, de Mello, & Martines, 2006) results in positive outcomes. However, they lack the understanding that it has to be offered systematically and consistently.

Many authors have documented that when parents provide warmth, responsiveness and autonomy, children develop higher self-esteem, life satisfaction and well-being (Baumrind, 1991a; DeVore & Ginsburg, 2005; Milevsky et al., 2007; Sanders et al., 2003; Whittle et al., 2014). According to Waters (2015), strength-oriented parents not only try to acknowledge the capabilities of their children, but also encourage them to use and develop their known and unknown strengths.

Parental interaction, for example, prepares the child for cognitive inclinations for learning and being (Greenspan & Shanker, 2002). The development of character strength occurs naturally out of healthy relationships and quality of life that children experience at home. Though there are various factors of the family that make an impact on character growth, it is quite certain that interactions in the family have a strong influence on the character growth of children, and when children are well cared for and feel secure at home, they grow in character (Arthur, Powell, & Lin Chiung, 2008; Berkowitz & Grych, 2000; De Braine & Verrier, 2007; Lexmond & Reeves, 2009; Lickona, 2004). The experiences of being cared, loved and valued by parents and family members get strengthened when parents spent time with their children, and it nurtures the proper ground to cultivate character strengths in them. When children feel loved, they become emotionally attached to parents. The attachment makes them more responsive to parents' authority and receptive to parents' values (Lickona, 2004).

It is seen that when parents offer great sacrifices to keep a loving and caring environment in the family, they indirectly set the foundation for secure interactions at home where children could have their strengths enhanced. Experiences of encouragement, appreciation, correction, advice and evaluation of children's performances and character give rise to the formation of character strengths such as humility, wisdom and transcendence. When parents encourage and recognize children's performances, they convey the intrinsic value of their individual act. In parent–child interactions, this generates security, confidence, concern, gratitude and, above all, self-worth. Parental acceptance and appreciation have strong association with children's positive relationship with others. Studies (Gestwicki, 2015; Lickona, 2004) also have indicated the significance of parental appreciation towards children during decision-making in the family.

The role of another important agent for developing character strengths, namely, sibling relationships, is also documented in empirical research. During the process of learning to share with siblings, children may encounter conflicts and in the act of dealing with those, they get many opportunities to develop character strengths such as social intelligence and social problem-solving skills (Dunn, 1988). There is also evidence that the prosocial behaviour children thus learn may be generalizable to others as well (Zahn-Waxler, Robinson, & Emde, 1992). In addition to that, a concrete family structure which provides steady rules, ceremonies and customs, along with an environment of mutual respect among family members, enhances character development in children (Baumrind, 1998).

INTENTIONAL ACTIONS FOR THE FAMILY TO FOSTER CHARACTER STRENGTH DEVELOPMENT

If families are able to plan effective actions intentionally and practise those consistently, children can be motivated to cultivate the character strengths they need to become effective individuals as they grow up. The concept of developmental relationships makes us understand that the intimate connections parents develop with the children help them to identify their abilities, enhance their character strengths and use them to mould their life and to significantly interact with and contribute to others (Pekel, Eugene, Roehlkepartain, Syvertsen, & Scales, 2015). Developmental relationships are characterized by sharing power, showing care, supporting growth and increasing possibilities for survival. These developmental relationships may contribute a great deal to children's character strength development. Research also shows that when children are ably supported by effective developmental relationships across different facets of their lives, there is high likelihood of them developing character strengths (Olson, DeFrain, & Skogrand, 2008).

Developmental relationship framework suggests that there are some essential actions which should be taken up by significant others for the character strength development of children. These include establishing a caring relationship, challenging their growth for improvement, giving ample support to complete tasks, sharing power with the children in decision-making process and expanding possibilities for the children to locate available opportunities.

Establishment of a Caring Relationship

It is through caring, pleasurable and supportive relationship that parents can nurture the signature strengths of the children. A pleasurable relationship allows for open communication and for mutual enhancement. Parents should express the care by engaging in key behaviours like listening to the children actively when they are with them, expressing warmth in their interactions and thereby letting the child know that they like being with the child, investing quality time and energy to do things with the child. It is also important that parents show interest in what the child likes to do and make it a priority to know what the child cares about and ensure that the parent is there for the child to depend on whenever it is needed. Parental warmth and supportiveness yield positive outcomes in children such as an increased feeling of autonomy, high competitiveness, positive self-esteem and moral development (Baumarind, 1991b, 1996; Dusek & Danko 1994; Fletcher et al., 1995; Gray & Steinberg, 1999; Lamborn et al., 1991; Maccoby & Martin, 1983; Steinberg, 2001).

Challenging Growth for Continuous Improvement

The action steps to be followed to help the child grow in a positive direction include five essential actions. Parents are expected to inspire their children to look at future possibilities and convey their expectations that the child has to optimize his/her talents with clarity. While helping the child to strengthen the positive traits in them, parents also need to be aware of the child's specific strengths. In the process of making the child's character strong, parents also should make the child accountable for his/her boundaries and limitations. The provision of a responsive and nurturing environment makes children stronger in strengths of humanity (Smith & Allen, 2008). When parents insist on hard work, children learn to give their best.

Providing Support to Ensure Task Completion

The third essential action to be taken by the parents are concerned with providing support to ensure that the tasks taken by the child are completed successfully and thereby giving him the satisfaction of achieving goals. The plan of action to achieve this include encouraging the child by reinforcing his efforts in an appropriate and timely manner, assisting him/her when the task is at hand and give accurate feedback to improve. Parents are also required to be good role models for the child to imitate and identify with and act as advocates to show the child that they are available when the child needs them to stand up for him/her. Research supports the notion that feedback on child's 'best self' from mentors help children to recognize their character strengths and use it consistently (Spreitzer, Stephens, & Sweetman, 2009). When children's formal and informal learning is supported by parents through consistent motivation, it can bring positive outcomes in the form of enhanced competence in them.

Sharing Power in Decision-making

Respecting, negotiating, responding and collaborating are the necessary actions required to manage the power dynamics that arises in the parent–child interaction. It is very important that the parents show respect to the children to give them an understanding that they are taken seriously and fairly. There should be some amount of negotiation in the decision-making process wherein the child also is given an opportunity to take part. When parents respond to the child's needs and interests and involve them also to take proper informed decisions, they also feel empowered. It is always desirable for the parent to work collaboratively with the child in solving problems and also in making decisions. Empirical studies also support the fact that when applied effectively in the family situation, the virtues of courage and humanity, and resulting character strengths, such as modesty, integrity, responsibility, dignity and authenticity, serve as bases for the development of positive parent–child relationships that stimulate children's feelings that their rights and dignity are respected (Daly, 2004). Recognizing the child's efforts, showing interest in their world and taking into account their developing ideas for decision-making by the adult family members would aid in their understanding of problem-solving.

Expanding Possibility to Find Opportunities

Helping the child to explore, connect and navigate is the action to be taken by the parents to strengthen the child's character in this context. When the parents expose the children to new ideas, experiences and situations, they find options to explore more opportunity to optimize their talents. It is also a responsibility of a parent to introduce the child to other sources which help him/her to grow. If the parents provide assistance in navigating through the hurdles and barriers which a child encounters during any given situation, he/she would develop skills to find ways to resolve such issues.

Many empirical studies demonstrate the vital role parents play in the character development process of their offspring (Damon, 1988). Specific parenting styles, especially authoritative parenting style has shown consistent relationship with children's temperament and social intelligence skills such as sharing with others, self-regulation and confidence (Baumrind, 1998). The long-time influence of parent's childrearing practices on children's character strength development is documented in research. The nature of the child-raising practices followed by the mother and the involvement of the father in childrearing during early growing-up years may predict the empathy of the individual during adulthood (Koestner, Franz, & Weinberger, 1990).

CHALLENGES AND OPPORTUNITIES

Families definitely vary in their capacity and interest in investing time and energy in ensuring that children are given adequate support, care and opportunities to grow optimally in character strengths. But all kinds of families matter in this context as nurturing character strengths can help build the communities strong. While few families fit the expected profile to provide strength-based parenting, many lack it due to several reasons. Strengthening families and supporting positive parenting practices should aim at empowering such families in utilizing their capacity to make the children strong in character. The risk factors for family instability and poor parenting need to be identified and addressed with proper interventions. The programmes aimed at enhancing family strengths should look at building relationships within families even if there are challenges and conflicts. Attention should be paid to the strengths, encouragement should be given to families to try experimenting with new practices, and emphasis should be given on making parents understand that parenting is a relationship. Community development programmes also need to engage families in strengthening the relationships.

Different approaches to strength development may result in a fixed mindset, where one may think that strengths are inborn fixed entities instead of an expected growth mindset, where strengths are considered as dynamic entities which can be developed with practice (Biswas-Diener et al., 2011). So these ideas and views may have implications for the strength development and further use. Those with fixed mindset may stagnate in their attempt to use it, not interested in employing the existing strengths because of their strong belief that mindset cannot be altered. Families have a pivotal role to play in this regard to make the children develop a growth mindset. Research also suggests that mindset moderates the association between strength-based parenting and strength use by adolescents (Jach et al., 2017).

CONCLUSION

Parenting is critical in character strength development of children but is often neglected. The role of parents and their relationship with children predict the development of character strengths. Parents caring at home can deeply benefit children's development. Parenting based on strength-based approach undoubtedly connects children to their existing strengths, encourages them to develop those strengths further and use them significantly to enhance well-being. Family's role in children's character development will always matter. Indoctrinating the families to use strength-based parenting should be an important goal for parents, educators, communities and societies. The current family, school, religious, governmental, organizational and social systems need to rethink and reinvent ways to engage in children's character strength development.

REFERENCES

Arthur, J., Powell, S., & Lin, H. C. (2010). Foundations of character-developing character and values in the early years. University of Birmingham & Canterbury Christ University. Retrieved from http://eprints.bham.ac.uk/364/1/Foundations_of_Character_Main_Report_Final.pdf

Bandura, A. (1977). *Social learning theory*. Englewood Cliffs, NJ: Prentice Hall.

———. (1997). Editorial. *American Journal of Health Promotion, 12*(1), 8–10.

Baumrind, D. (1991a). Effective parenting during the early adolescent transition. In P. E. Cowan & E. M. Hetherington (Eds.), *Advances in family research* (Vol. 2, pp. 111–163). Hillsdale, NJ: Lawrence Erlbaum Associates.

———. (1991b). The influence of parenting style on adolescent competence and substance use. *Journal of Early Adolescence, 11*(1), 56–95.

———. (1998). Reflections on character and competence. In A. Colby, J. James, & D. Hart (Eds.), *Competence and character through life* (pp. 1–28). Chicago, IL: The University of Chicago Press.

Berkowitz, M. W., & Grych, J. H. (2000). Early character development and education. *Early Education and Development, 11*(1), 55–72.

Biswas-Diener, R., Kashdan, T. B., & Minhas, G. (2011). A dynamic approach to psychological strength development and intervention. *The Journal of Positive Psychology, 6*(2), 106–118.

Daly, M. (2004). *Developing the whole child: The importance of the emotional, social, moral and spiritual in early years education and care*. Wales: Edwin Mellen Press.

Damon, W. (1988). *The moral child: Nurturing children's natural moral growth*. New York, NY: Free Press.

De Braine, R., & Verrier, D. (2007). Leadership, character and its development: A qualitative exploration. *Journal of Human Resource Management, 5*(1), 1–10.

———. (2007). Leadership, character and its development: A qualitative exploration. *SA Journal of Human Resource Management, 5*(1). doi:10.4102/sajhrm.v5i1.102

Deci, E. L., & Ryan, R. M. (2000). The 'what' and 'why' of goal pursuits: Human needs and the self-determination of behavior. *Psychological Inquiry*, *11*(4), 227–268.

DeVore, E. R., & Ginsburg, K. R. (2005). The protective effects of good parenting on adolescents. *Current Opinion in Pediatrics*, *17*(4), 460–465. doi:10.1097/01.mop.0000170514.27649.c9

Dunn, J. (1988). *The beginnings of social understanding*. Cambridge, MA: Harvard University Press.

Dusek, J. B., & Danko, M. (1994). Adolescent coping styles and perceptions of parental child rearing. *Journal of Adolescent Research*, *9*, 412–426. doi:10.1177/074355489494002

Eshel, N., Daelmans, B., de Mello, M. C., & Martines, J. (2006). Responsive parenting: Interventions and outcomes. *Bulletin of the World Health Organization*, *84*, 991–998. doi:10.2471/BLT.06.030163

Fletcher, A. C., Darling, N. E., Steinberg, L., & Dornbusch, S. M. (1995). The company they keep: Relation of adolescents' adjustment and behavior to their friends' perceptions of authoritative parenting in the social network. *Des. Psychol.*, *31*, 300–310.

Gestwicki, C. (2015). *Home, school, and community relations* (9th ed.). Belmont, CA: Cengage Learning.

Gray, M. R., & Steinberg, L. (1999). Unpacking authoritative parenting: Reassessing a multidimensional construct. *Journal of Marriage & the Family*, *61*(3), 574–587.

Greenspan, S. I., & Shanker, S. I. (2004). *The first idea*. Cambridge, MA: Da Capo Press.

Heckman, J. J. (2008). Role of income and family influence on child outcomes. *Annals of the New York Academy of Sciences*, *1136*, 307–323. doi:10.1196/annals.1425.031

Iorg, J. (2007). *The character of leadership: Nine qualities that define great leaders*. Nashville, TN: B&H.

Jach, H. K., Sun, J., Loton, D., Chin, T.-C., & Waters, L. (2018). Strengths and subjective wellbeing in adolescence: Strength-based parenting and the moderating effect of mindset. *Journal of Happiness Studies*, *19*(2), 567–586. doi:10.1007/s10902-016-9841-y

Koestner, R., Franz, C., & Weinberger, J. (1990). The family origins of empathic concern: A 26-year longitudinal study. *Journal of Personality and Social Psychology*, *58*(4), 709–716.

Kuczynski, L. (Ed.). (2003). *Handbook of dynamics in parent-child relations*. Thousand Oaks, CA: SAGE.

Lamborn, S. D., Mounts, N. S., Steinberg, L., & Dornbusch, S. M. (1991). Patterns of competence and adjustment among adolescents from authoritative, authoritarian, indulgent, and neglectful families. *Child Development*, *62*(5), 1049–1065.

Laursen, B., & Collins, W. A. (2009). Parent–child relationships during adolescence. In R. M. Lerner & L. Steinberg (Eds.), *Handbook of adolescent psychology:*

Vol. 2. *Contextual influences on adolescent development* (pp. 3–16). Hoboken, NJ: Wiley.

Lexmond, J., & Reeves, R. (2009). *Building character*. London: Demos.

Lickona, T. (1992). Character development in the elementary school classroom. In T. Lickona & K. Ryan (Eds.), *Character development in schools and beyond* (2nd ed., pp. 141–163). Cardinal Station, Washington, DC: The Council for Research in Values and Philosophy.

———. (2004). *Character matters: How to help our children develop good judgement, integrity, and other essential virtues*. New York, NY: Simon & Schuster.

Linley, P. A., & Harrington, S. (2006). Strengths coaching: A potential-guided approach to coaching psychology. *International Coaching Psychology Review*, 1(1), 37–46.

Maccoby, E. E., & Martin, J. A. (1983). Socialization in the context of the family: Parent-child interaction. In P. H. Mussen (Ed.), *Handbook of child psychology* (Vol. 4, pp. 1–101). New York, NY: Wiley.

Milevsky, A., Schlechter, M., Netter, S., & Keehn, D. (2007). Maternal and paternal parenting styles in adolescents: Associations with self-esteem, depression and life-satisfaction. *Journal of Child and Family Studies*, 16(1), 39–47. doi:10.1007/s10826-006-9066-5

Nowak, C., & Heinrichs, N. (2008). A comprehensive meta-analysis of Triple P-Positive Parenting Program using hierarchical linear modelling: Effectiveness and moderating variables. *Clinical Child and Family Psychology Review*, 11, 114–144.

Olson, D. H., DeFrain, J., & Skogrand, L. (2008). *Marriages and families: Intimacy, diversity, and strengths*. New York, NY: McGraw-Hill.

Pala, A. (2011). The need for character education. *International Journal of Social Sciences and Humanity Studies*, 3(2), 23–32.

Park, N., Peterson, C., & Seligman, M. E. P. (2004). Strengths of character and well-being. *Journal of Social & Clinical Psychology*, 23(5), 603–619.

Pekel, K., Roehlkepartain, E. C., Syvertsen, A. K., & Scales, P. C. (2015). *Don't forget the families: The missing piece in America's effort to help all children succeed*. Minneapolis, MN: Search Institute.

Rizzuto, A. M. (2007). Development from conception to death. In A. Manenti, S. Guarinelli, & H. Zollner, H. (Eds.), *Formation and the person: Essays on theory and practice* (pp. 31–46). Leuven: Peeters.

Rulla, L. M., Ridick, J., & Imoda, F. (1986/2004). *Anthropology of the Christian vocation* (Vol. 1). Rome: Gregorian University Press.

Sanders, M. R., Markie-Dadds, C., & Turner, K. M. T. (2003). Theoretical, scientific and clinical foundations of the Triple P-Positive Parenting Program: A population approach to the promotion of parenting competence. In *Parenting Research and Practice* Monograph 1. Brisbane: University of Queensland.

Sheely-Moore, A. I., & Bratton, S. C. (2010). A strengths-based parenting intervention with low-income African American families. *Professional School Counseling*, 13, 175–183. doi:10.5330/PSC.n.2010-13.175

Smith, E. J. (2006). The strength-based counseling model. *The Counseling Psychologist, 34*(1), 13–79.

———. (2013). *Strengths-based therapy: Connecting theory, practice and skills.* SAGE Publications. New Delhi.

Smith, I. D., & Allen, G. (2008). *Early intervention: Good parents, great kids, better citizens.* London: Centre for Social Justice and the Smith Institute.

Sprafkin, J. H., Liebert, R. M., & Poulos, R. W. (1975). Effects of a prosocial televised example on children's helping. *Journal of Experimental Child Psychology, 20*(1), 119–126.

Spreitzer, G., Stephens, J. P., & Sweetman, D. (2009). The reflected best self field experiment with adolescent leaders: Exploring the psychological resources associated with feedback source and valence. *The Journal of Positive Psychology, 4*(5), 331–348. doi:10.1080/17439760902992340

Steinberg, L. (2001). We know some things: Parent adolescent relationships in retrospect and prospect. *Journal of Research on Adolescence, 11*(1), 1–19. doi:10.1111/1532-7795.00001

Syvertsen, A. K., Roehlkepartain, E. C., & Scales, P. C. (2012). *The American family assets study.* Minneapolis, MN: Search Institute. Retrieved from www.searchinstitute.org/research/family-strengths

Tuttle, A. R., Knudson-Martin, C., & Kim, L. (2012). Parenting as relationship: A framework for assessment and practice. *Family Process, 51*(1), 73–89. doi:10.1111/ j.1545-5300.2012.01383.x

Waters, L. (2015). The relationship between strength-based parenting with children's stress levels and strength based coping approaches. *Psychology, 6,* 689–699. doi:10.4236/psych.2015.66067

Weissberg, R. P., Walberg, H. J., O'Brien, M. U., & Kuster, C. B. (Eds.). (2003). *Long-term trends in the well-being of children and youth.* Washington, DC: Child Welfare League of America Press.

Whittle, S., Simmons, J. G., Dennison, M., Vijayakumar, N., Schwartz, O., Yap, M. B. H.,... Allen, N. B. (2014). Positive parenting predicts the development of adolescent brain structure: A longitudinal study. *Developmental Cognitive Neuroscience, 8,* 7–17. doi:10.1016/j.dcn.2013.10.006

Zahn-Waxler, C., Robinson, J. L., & Emde, R. N. (1992). The development of empathy in twins. *Developmental Psychology, 28*(6), 1038–1047. doi:10.1037/0012-1649.28.6.1038

Chapter 17

Psychological Trauma and Posttraumatic Growth
A Brief Introduction

Rayees Mohammad Bhat and Shoma Chakrawarty

SUMMARY

Stress, trauma and suffering constitute an inherent facet of life but seldom are we prepared to handle this fact of life, and the results of a confrontation with a traumatic stressor are immensely challenging. Trauma affects all domains of functioning through anxiety, emotional distress and deficits in adaptive functioning, and even cognitively—through a fractured worldview. Research has predominantly studied the negative sequelae of traumatic stress, often forgoing the scope to explore its more salutogenic outcomes. These outcomes—variably denoted as adversarial growth, stress-related growth, benefit-finding and, most comprehensively, posttraumatic growth (PTG)—all reflect the capability of individuals to process their trauma effectively (at emotional and cognitive levels) to arrive at a renewed understanding of life marked by a reprioritization of life goals and aspirations, stronger ties with loved ones and a search for religio-spiritual well-being. The current chapter reviews the foundational aspects of PTG along with describing its determinants and theoretical precursors. PTG has tremendous implications in clinical practice for those coping with trauma, especially considering the mounting prevalence rates of trauma across the world. Promoting an awareness of this concept and its effects among non-clinical populations and at-risk populations is imperative to promote a greater acceptance of stress and its effects, rather than an avoidant approach. In this approach, PTG can be construed as a character strength with great potential as primary prevention strategy.

OVERVIEW

History bears witness to traumatic events which are common and experienced the world over and across time. As a result, people worldwide are exposed to a diverse range of traumatic events and increasingly a greater number of people are being exposed to traumatic stressors (Bar-Tal, 2004; Rouhana & Bar-Tal, 1998). Traumatic events are inevitable and their devastating consequences consistently involve multiple psychological, social, economic and environmental challenges to the integrity of an individual and to public life (Pedersen, 2006). It also disrupts an individual's sense of identity (Das, 2007) and stifles his or her psychological integrity (Baker & Shalhoub-Kevorkkian, 1999; Giacaman et al., 2007; Punamaki, Knninen, Qouta, & Sarraj, 2004).

Trauma and its psychosocial sequelae are not new experiences; poets and novelists as far back as Homer and Shakespeare were among the first to record the profound impact of trauma and its subsequent stressors on human cognition, behaviour and emotion (Friedman, Resick, Bryant, & Brewin, 2011). Exposure to traumatic events, such as war, conflict, natural and human-made disasters, assault and life-threatening illnesses are common, with over two-thirds of the general population being likely to be exposed to a traumatic incident in their lifetime (Neria, Nandi, & Galea, 2008). Exposure to such events can consequently have a series of serious adverse psychological effects. In the last three decades, there has been an increase in the discussion of trauma and its effects, with special focus on posttraumatic stress disorder (PTSD) (Jones & Wessely, 2005). Previously published systematic reviews have documented PTSD to be the most commonly studied psychopathology in the aftermath of trauma (Breslau, 2002; Neria et al., 2008; Norris et al., 2002). Trauma and culture are intertwined because traumatic experiences are part of the life cycle, universal in manifestation and occurrence, and typically demand a response from the culture in terms of healing, treatment and interventions (Drozdek & Wilson, 2007, p. 8).

However, of late, a new trend in the form of positive psychology suggests that many survivors of traumatic events—in addition to negative repercussions—do adapt and develop positive personal changes to mitigate their impact. These positive psychological changes that become apparent during the struggle and may involve some highly challenging life circumstances are collectively termed as PTG (Tedeschi & Calhoun, 1996, 2004). PTG is an important area of current research and requires attention, especially in case of highly stressful situations.

PSYCHOLOGICAL TRAUMA

Psychological or emotional trauma is the response to an extraordinary or an unexpected stressful event (mental shock or injury) that has the potential to shatter basic assumptions of the self or the world around, thereby making the victims feel helpless and vulnerable. In any case, psychological trauma damages the usual defence mechanisms that people use and may promote strategies such as repression, rationalization and denial (Everstine & Everstine, 1993).

The word 'trauma' has been derived from the Greek word that literally means 'wound'. More specifically, it refers to a mental injury caused by an emotional shock which is often caused by a repressed or unhealed memory and which may result in behavioural disorders (*Oxford English Dictionary*, 2015). Trauma refers to either a physical harm by an external event or to a psychological wound occurring due to a distressing event. Psychological trauma is an emotional response to a stressful life event and takes place immediately after the precipitating traumatic event. In traumatized individuals, shock and rejection are typical reactions that take place immediately after the trauma. Some people experience difficulties in moving on with their lives in the aftermath of the trauma. Defining trauma has turned out to be a difficult task for the researchers; much debate has occurred around the classification of trauma in terms of its nature, severity and the individual's subjective experience of the stressful event. The American Psychiatric Association in *Diagnostic and Statistical Manual of Mental Disorders*, 5th edition (DSM-5; American Psychiatric Association [APA], 2013) defines trauma as:

Exposure to actual or threatened death, serious injury, or sexual violence in one (or more) of the following ways: directly experiencing the traumatic event(s); witnessing, in person, the traumatic event(s) as it occurred to others; learning that the traumatic event(s) occurred to a close family member or close friend (in case of actual or threatened death of a family member or friend, the event(s) must have been violent or accidental); or experiencing repeated or extreme exposure to aversive details of the traumatic event(s). (p. 271)

Thus, traumatic events or stressful life experiences create a psychological trauma which restricts an individual's ability to adjust with the event and leaves the person in a state of helplessness. The individual may feel overwhelmed physically, emotionally and cognitively. Brewin (2003) provides some examples of traumatic events which include being exposed to gunfire, being exposed to a natural disaster such as an earthquake, being exposed to a man-made disaster such as a terrorist attack, being exposed to a physical or a sexual attack, being involved in a serious accident and being witness to extreme human suffering or death (Brewin, 2003). Though the DSM-5 definition of trauma is useful, however, Briere and Scott (2015) have criticized the conception of trauma being restricted to 'serious injury or threatened death, or other threat to one's physical integrity'. This is because in a majority of the events, an event may be traumatic even when there is no threat to one's life or physical injury is not a significant issue.

Traumatic events in life can have a considerable impact on those who are exposed to them directly or indirectly. For some people, experiencing stressful life events can leave them depressed, disorganised and highly vulnerable to succeeding traumatic events. The literature on trauma has found numerous traumatic life events to be the risk factors for the development of a variety of mental disorders, such as anxiety, depression and PTSD in severe and extreme cases. However, for other individuals, a traumatic life event can serve as a catalyst for positive psychological growth, an opportunity to ruminate over the purpose of life, to develop a strong religious affiliation or a strong relationship with family and friends. The latest research on trauma has documented such positive transformations as a result of the struggle with severe life events, such as, cancer, bereavement, exposure to violence and natural disasters, and has identified the factors that seem to contribute to this process of positive growth. Thus, research on stressful life experiences has shown that both pathogenic (negative) as well as salutogenic (positive) after-effects of trauma can co-occur.

FOUNDATIONS OF POSTTRAUMATIC GROWTH (PTG)

Traditionally, literature on trauma has mainly focused on the pathogenic (negative) consequences of the stressful or traumatic life events. However, there is an increasing evidence base to suggest that individuals exposed to life-threatening traumatic events can experience salutogenic psychological changes resulting from their struggle with trauma. This concept of developing positively as a result of suffering and distress is thousands of years old and is found in the early writings of the ancient Hebrews and Greeks, and in the religious teachings of Jews, Christians, Hinduism and Islam (Tedeschi & Calhoun, 1995). For decades, philosophers and psychologists have recognized the positive psychological effects occurring after the onset of traumatic events, including natural disasters, Holocaust and serious illnesses, and a variety of traumatic events (Caplan, 1964; Chodoff, Friedman, & Hamburg, 1964; Frankl, 1963; Mechanic, 1977; Nietzsche, 1955; Tedeschi & Calhoun, 1995; Visotsky, Hamburg, Goss, & Lebovits, 1961; Yalom, 1980). Studies exploring a variety of traumatic events have found that half of the individuals exposed to trauma report some degree of positive psychological changes, such as changes in life perspectives, self-perception and social relationships (Dhooper, 1983; Taylor, 1983; Wallerstein, 1986; Yarom, 1983).

More recently, a movement known as positive psychology has begun exploring psychological strengths in order to improve psychological well-being and prevent the risk of developing mental disorders. Today, there is an overwhelming body of evidence testifying to the positive psychological changes after facing a variety of life-threatening events. These positive psychological changes are denoted by a variety of terms, such as PTG (Tedeschi & Calhoun, 1995), benefit-finding (Tomich & Helgeson, 2004), meaning-making (Park, 2010), finding meaning, positive adjustment, positive consequences, adversarial growth and stress-related growth (Linley & Joseph, 2004; Park, Cohen, & Murch, 1996). These various terminologies seem to represent a similar construct, namely, positive psychological growth.

Literature concerning PTG has recently seen an outpouring of research interest and has documented evidences of PTG in operation in a diversity of traumas, such as bereavement, illness, sexual assault, natural disasters, accidents, military combat and terrorist attacks. Furthermore, the PTG model is the most comprehensively developed when compared to other salutogenic constructs. It also has a robust standardized measure reflecting the theoretical elements of the positive psychological growth (Zoellner & Maercker, 2006).

Definition of Posttraumatic Growth

The positive psychological changes in an individual in response to trauma has been referred to as PTG, and involves changes in one's philosophy of life, a greater appreciation of life, changes in interpersonal relationships, changes in one's self-perception and recognition of new goals in life (Tedeschi & Calhoun, 1995). The term 'posttraumatic growth' was coined by Tedeschi and Calhoun who defined it as the 'positive psychological change experienced as a result of a highly challenging life circumstance' (Tedeschi & Calhoun, 2004, p. 1).

Based on reviews of the literature and interviews with people who have experienced trauma, Tedeschi and Calhoun (1995) proposed that the experience of dealing with negative events produces five types of outcomes: (a) changes in self-perception, (b) improved interpersonal relationships, (c) recognition of new goals in life, (d) a greater appreciation of life and (e) changes in one's philosophy of life. There can be collectively termed as PTG.

Domains of PTG

By means of examination of literature and interviews with people who have experienced traumatic life events, plus through anecdotal and theoretical accounts, Tedeschi and Calhoun (1995) proposed that experience of growth following a traumatic event can be reported into five domains;

Personal strength: According to Tedeschi and Calhoun (1995, 1996), experiencing a stressful life event can facilitate one to become better acquainted with one's personal strengths and the individual may perceive that they have survived the most difficult event in their life so far, and start believing that they will now be able to cope with all subsequent traumas. These changes in trauma survivors make them feel more confident and capable of dealing with any of the future challenges (Updegraff, Taylor, Kemeny, & Wyatt, 2002).

New possibilities: According to Tedeschi and Calhoun (1995), what happens often as a result of trauma is a shift in life perspectives, and thus survivors report an increased sense of priority, a development of new interests and a keener sense of the domains or goals of life that are really important in life.

Relating to others: When confronted with a traumatic event, people report an improved, meaningful and more intimate relationship with others. This is often preceded by the realization that they have a good social network on whom they could rely on and to whom they could express themselves more openly (Calhoun & Tedeschi, 1990). This positive development in relationships originates from greater compassion, self-disclosure of traumatic event, increased understanding of their necessities and emotional connectedness with other people (Collins, Taylor, & Skokan, 1990; Tedeschi & Calhoun, 1996).

Appreciation of life: Tedeschi and Calhoun (1995) suggest that a greater appreciation of life is reported by the trauma victims due to their reduced sense of invulnerability. The victims recognize the importance of time and relationships that were previously taken as for granted, thereby living each day to the fullest.

Changes in philosophy of life: Traumatic experiences can strengthen religious faith or lead to a greater engagement with fundamental existential questions (Tedeschi & Calhoun, 1995). The engagement in enhanced spiritual questions and the strengthening of religious faith can serve a variety of purposes, such as gaining a self-control, comfort or intimacy out of this spiritual or religious relationship, or an effort to find meaning following the traumatic experience (Pargament et al., 1990).

Theoretical Model of PTG

Several models based on theoretical perspectives of positive psychological growth as a result of a potentially traumatic event have been proposed, and these models contribute to the general understanding of PTG. Some of the important models are those by Schafer and Moos (1992), Aldwin (1994) and O'Leary and Ickovics (1995). However, the most comprehensive and well-developed model of PTG to date is proposed by Tedeschi and Calhoun (1995, 2004), reflecting the various theoretical elements of the growth arising as a result of cognitive process feared towards coping with a life-challenging event (Zoellner & Maercker, 2006).

This model of PTG is based on the fundamental assumption that all individuals develop and hold a set of beliefs about themselves, about others and about the world. PTG is set in process by a challenging or life-threatening traumatic event, the same event that leads to psychological distress, which in turn causes psychological difficulties (Calhoun & Tedeschi, 1998). The model of PTG, shown in Figure 17.1 (Tedeschi & Calhoun, 2004, p. 7), explains how the process of psychological growth takes place. First, based on the Janoff-Bulman (1992) model of PTSD, the traumatic event needs to shatter a person's basic assumptions of themselves and the world around them so that the world is no longer manageable, comprehensible and meaningful. The authors propose that a traumatic event requires to be severe enough to considerably overturn or challenge one's assumptive world, or their pre-trauma mental representations of self and the world.

The model states that a process of growth is triggered by a seismic event or a traumatic event (Figure 17.1) that shatters the individual's basic assumptions about themselves and about their world. Tedeschi and Calhoun (2004) highlighted that the development of PTG is not a direct result of trauma but it occurs due to the impact that the trauma has on the person's assumptive world. To understand this process, authors gave an example of an earthquake as a metaphor, which states:

> Cognitive processing and restructuring may be comparable to the physical rebuilding that occurs after an earthquake. The physical structures can be redesigned to be more resistant to shocks in the future, as the community learns from the earthquake what has withstood the shaking and what has not. (p. 5)

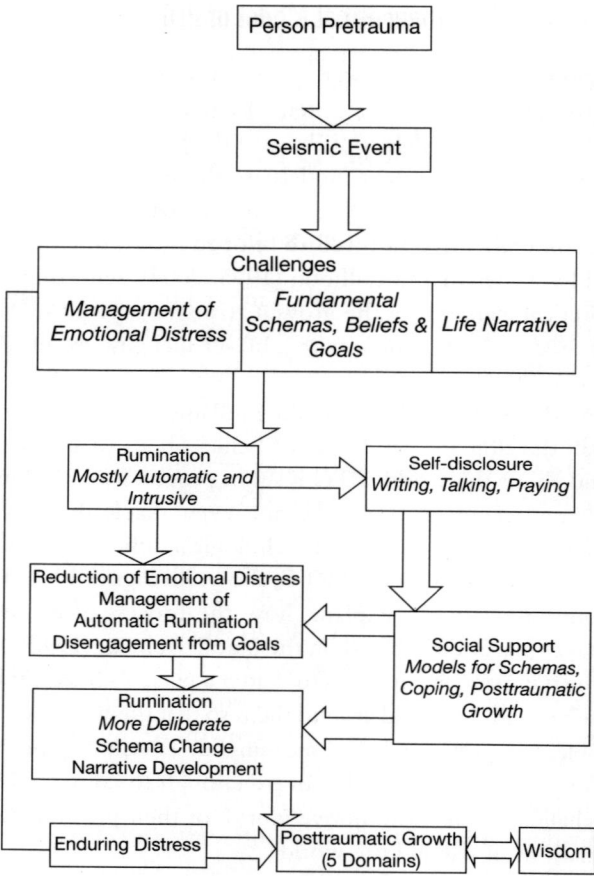

Figure 17.1 *A Model of Posttraumatic Growth*
Source: Tedeschi and Calhoun (2004, p. 7).

This shattering of mental schemas leads to psychological distress, which in turn activates cognitive processing or rumination related to the stressful event; new schemas are formed which reduce psychological distress when the ruminative thoughts are more effortful and deliberate. The cognitive processing or ruminative thought processes of developing new, deliberate and adaptive schemas forms an important intermediate component that ultimately leads to PTG.

In addition to cognitive processing, the model highlights the importance of the individual's personal characteristics, such as self-disclosure about the trauma and associated memories, talking to others about the experiences of trauma or simply addressing them into one's prayers and one's social environment in the process of growth.

Predictors of PTG

Literature on growth outcomes following trauma has suggested that a variety of factors are related to the occurrence of PTG, such as continuing existence of trauma-related distress (PTSD symptoms), trauma exposure, demographic and personality characteristics, belief systems, coping styles, rumination, self-disclosure and social support.

Since growth is considered to emerge from trauma (Tedeschi & Calhoun, 2004), it is sensible to expect that exposure to trauma is clearly related to growth. PTG has been reported in a variety of individuals exposed to a diversity of traumas, such as natural disasters, terminal illnesses, accidents and terrorist attacks (Laufer & Solomon, 2006; Mitchell, Gallaway, Millikan, & Bell, 2013).

Tedeschi and Calhoun (1995, 2004) proposed that growth and distress can coexist in traumatized individuals and that the presence of PTG does not indicate the absence of growth. A similar kind of stand is adopted by McGrath and Beehr (1990) who claim that that both positive and negative effects of psychological stress may coexist in the same individual simultaneously in a different context or in the same context with some sort of situational patterns. Though the evidences of positive and negative effects of a potentially traumatic event are common in literature, but the nature of these consequences is not empirically clear. Therefore, a variety of associations between PTG and PTSD have been reported in trauma research. Many studies on relationship between PTG and posttraumatic stress symptoms reported a positive relationship (Laufer & Solomon, 2006; Shakespeare-Finch & Lurie-Beck, 2014).

According to the PTG model, in the general process of growth, the individual's social system plays an important role in facilitating the experience of PTG by self-disclosure and looking out for support from others and to help them discover the positive aspects of trauma which they were not aware of (Tedeschi & Calhoun, 1995, 2004). Social support is defined as information conveyed to a person that he is loved, cared and valued, and that he belongs to a network based on mutual obligation (Cobb, 1976). It is suggested that social support is an important factor that encourages positive behaviours and contributes to positive growth in response to life crisis (Schaefer & Moos, 1998). Prati and Piertrantoni (2009), in a meta-analysis comprising 103 studies, found social support to be a moderate predictor of PTG in adults, and the authors credited social support to be important in the choice of effective coping strategies, thus promoting PTG. Schaefer and Moos (1998) have also suggested that individuals are likely to be involved in more active coping strategies if they enjoy good social support. Numerous studies have shown that individuals demonstrate better adjustment to traumatic events when perceived levels of social support are high (Halcomb, Daly, Davidson, Elliot, & Griffiths, 2005; Schroevers, Helgeson, Sanderman, & Ranchor, 2010; Tedeschi & Calhoun, 1996, 2004), and a number of studies have shown a positive relationship between social support and PTG (Cieslak et al., 2009; Cohen & Numa, 2011; Frazier, Tashiro, Berman, Steger, & Long, 2004; Hungerbuehler, Vollrath, & Landolt, 2011; Leung et al., 2010).

Over the past three decades, the field of psychology, in particular, and science, in general, have become more interested in the role of religion and spirituality as an essential component of psychological and physical health. Religion is a potent source of strength and it promotes sense-making in a crisis situation in a variety of ways. It gives rise to feelings such as getting closer to God and searching for the sacred. It also promotes actions such as getting involved in religious activities and finding meaning in helping others which may help channelize the negative emotions generated from the trauma into more productive avenues too. The results of several studies have demonstrated the relationship between spirituality/religion and psychological well-being and suggested that trauma may, in fact, lead to a deepening of a person's spiritual or religious beliefs (Bryant-Devis et al., 2012; Calhoun, Cann, Tedeschi, & McMillan, 2000; Pargament et al., 1990; Pargament, Ano, & Wachholtz, 2005; Tedeschi & Calhoun, 1996).

Within the field of psychology, research has tended to focus on how religion or spirituality can be used as coping skills during challenging life events and how these coping skills may be used individually (in case of personal prayers) or collectively (viz., praying in groups, religious participations and collective rituals) (Hill & Pargament, 2003; Pargament, 1997). Additionally, literature in this field has suggested that the involvement in belief system can provide an important coping mechanism against life-challenging events, help alleviate symptoms of psychopathology, lead to more positive emotions and facilitate a more adaptive adjustment process (Doolittle & Farrel, 2004; Fallot & Heckman, 2005; Moreira-Almeida, Neto, & Koeing, 2006). The link between spiritual/religious beliefs and PTG has been documented in a number of studies (Bade, 2000; Calhoun et al., 2000), and these have found that being open to religious change, connecting on a spiritual level with others, finding comfort in church and a deepening of one's spiritual beliefs and involvements are all related to reports of PTG. Several studies examining spirituality and several religious variables have been linked to increase PTG, including existential openness, intrinsic religiousness, religious participation and positive religious coping (Garcia, Paez-Rovira, Zurtia, Martel, & Reyes, 2014; Hafnidar & Lin, 2012; Laufer & Solomon, 2006; Milam, Ritt-Olson, Tan, Unger, & Nezami, 2005).

Demographic predictors of PTG have been identified in number of traumatic events, such as cancer, natural disasters and accidents, where demographic factors associated with growth have been identified. For example, marital status (Rubin & White-Means, 2009; Widows, Jacobsen, Booth-Jones, & Fields, 2005), being a minority (Helgeson, Reynolds, & Tomoich, 2006), cultural differences (Morris, Shakespeare-Finch, Rieck, & Newbery, 2005) and education and employment (Russell, White, & White, 2006) have been reported to be related to PTG. In addition, age and gender, the frequently studied demographic variables have been reported to be associated with PTG. In PTG literature, females have been shown to report more growth, when compared to their male counterparts (Linley & Joseph, 2004; Park, Cohen, & Murch, 1996; Tedeschi & Calhoun, 1996; Widows et al., 2005). However, the findings for gender are mixed (Meyerson, Grant, Carter, & Kilmer, 2011), with studies reporting no gender differences in the experience of PTG (Ho, Chan, & Ho, 2004; Widows et al., 2005) or supporting that women report higher levels of PTG than men (Hooper, 2003). However, there is enough support for females experiencing more growth than males, such as a meta-analysis carried out by Helgeson et al. (2006) which reported females experiencing small but significant amount of more growth than males. The female gender's inclination towards experiencing more growth may be attributed to their greater experience of stress as a response to stressful life event (Anderson & Manuel, 1994; Rausch, Auerbach, & Gramling, 2008) and their tendency to engage in more positive self-talk when compared to their male counterparts (Park, Cohen, & Murch, 1996; Tamres, Janicki, & Helgeson, 2002).

In addition to gender, age has also been reported to influence the experience of growth (Vishnevsky et al., 2010), but the findings concerning the relationship between PTG and age are mixed and unclear. Studies have found a positive relationship between age and PTG (Kurtz, Wyatt, & Kurtz, 1995; Milam, Ritt-Olson, Tan, & Unger, 2004), whereas several other studies have found younger adults reporting more growth (Bower et al., 2005; Cordova et al., 2007; Davis, Nolen-Hoeksema, & Larson, 1998; Evers et al., 2001; Klauer, Ferring, & Flipp, 1998; Lechner et al., 2003; Manne et al., 2004). Some studies reported no association between age and PTG (Cordova, Cunningham, Carlson, & Andrykowski, 2001; Sears, Stanton, & Danoff-Burg, 2003; Sheikh & Marotta, 2005). The higher levels of growth reported by younger individuals according to Tedeschi and Calhoun (2004) may be due to time and resources available to younger victims to acquire and incorporate into themselves what they learn from their struggle with traumatic events. In addition, the growth is questionable for children who are below the age at which cognitive abilities are developed enough to sense and understand the psychological processes which help them to identify the losses and gains (Shakespeare-Finch & de Dassel, 2009).

MAJOR THEORIES EXPLAINING POSITIVE PSYCHOLOGICAL GROWTH

Numerous theories have been proposed to explain how positive changes take place owing to trauma (for a review, see Updegraff & Taylor, 2000). These theories include Taylor's theory of cognitive adaptation (1983), Aldwin's theory of deviation amplification model of stress and coping (Aldwin, Sutton, & Lachman, 1996), Hobfoll's conservation of resources theory (1989) and Meichenbaum's stress inoculation theory (1985).

Taylor's Theory of Cognitive Adaptation (1983)

The theory of cognitive adaptation proposes that individuals are active agents and have the ability to restore or bounce back to establish psychological equilibrium after the occurrence of a traumatic event. The theory advocates that life-threatening events or traumatic events, at their onset, challenge people's self-esteem, their sense of meaning-making and their mastery about self and others. As a result of this shuffling, people are encouraged to restore what has been shattered by the traumatic event and bounce back to psychological equilibrium by construction of self-enhancing cognitions (Taylor & Brown, 1988). Constructive meaning-making can be developed by understanding the 'why' and 'what' of a traumatic event, and, similarly, a sense of mastery can be developed when individuals believe that they are able to exert control over the events. Self-esteem of an individual can be improved or kept unaffected when the victims compare themselves with others being less fortunate, thereby presenting themselves in a more positive way (Taylor & Lobel, 1989; Taylor, Wood, & Lichtman, 1983). In this way, Taylor's cognitive adaptation theory posits that positive reinterpretations of a traumatic event can help an individual regain their equilibrium and improve them in a much positive way.

Hobfoll's Conservation of Resources Theory (1989)

The conservation of resources (COR) model proposes that people tend to acquire and maintain their resources when there is a threat of loss or actual loss in resources caused as a reaction to environmental stress. Such resources include objects (e.g., house and car), conditions (e.g., job and marriage), personal characteristics (e.g., self-esteem and empathy) and energies (e.g., qualification and money). According to this model, the stress is the outcome of resource loss which takes place when people invest such resources to cope with the stress they feel when they lose their resources and develop negative state of being. In addition, they also attain future resources which buffer them against environmental stress, but are much smaller, less influential and less likely to get replaced over time (Hobfoll, 1988; Hobfoll & Lilly, 1993). Finally, this model has provided a comprehensive theoretical guide and insight for understanding the positive changes acquired while dealing with a stressful life situation.

Meichenbaum's Stress Inoculation Theory (1985)

The stress inoculation theory states that while dealing with moderate-level stressors, people may get inoculated or immunized, and prepared to withstand the pathogenic effects of stressful life situations subsequently. This theory may be compared to a kind of medical immunization to prepare individuals against the potentially traumatic events before they arise. This inoculation may arise from the understanding or use of more healthy and adaptive coping strategies, one's confidence in dealing with the stressful events or an assessment of a potentially traumatic event as less threatening (Updegraff & Taylor, 2000). According to Meichenbaum (1985), while dealing with a stressor, the best way to cope with the situation is to be prepared and ready to proactively attack the stressor with effective coping strategies and prevent its consequences. In a nutshell, stress inoculation is a kind of defence, in advance, by anticipating a stressful situation and exerting control over it before it affects a person through negative consequences.

The application of this model can be seen in stress inoculation therapy (SIT), a psychotherapy in which a therapist is preparing or inoculating patients in advance to face the stressful life event and make him handle the effects of a particular trauma or disorder. Meichenbaum (1985) describes SIT as:

> ... Analogous to the concept of medical inoculation against infectious diseases ... it is designed to build 'psychological antibodies' or coping skills, and to enhance through resistance through exposure to stimuli that are strong enough to arouse defences without being so powerful as to overcome them. (p. 21)

Aldwin's Theory of Deviation Amplification Model of Stress and Coping (1996)

Aldwin's deviation amplification theory (Aldwin et al., 1996) states that coping is 'a process that extends across situations by resulting in general changes in coping resources, such as management skills, and, as such, can affect personality processes such as mastery and self-esteem' (p. 842). According to this theory, the changes that take place as a result of traumatic event include (a) a deviation countering process which helps to decrease stress levels in order to maintain the homeostasis and (b) a deviation amplification process by which the effects of stress are magnified—either positively or negatively—and mediated by coping strategies. If the stress is processed by positive coping strategies, adaptive positive spirals (e.g., increased self-esteem) are triggered, and on the contrary, if the stress is processed by negative coping strategies, maladaptive negative spirals (e.g., depression) are much more likely to be produced. According to this theory, individuals having more effective coping resources initially can develop long-term positive effects in dealing with traumatic stress.

Aldwin's continued work on stress and coping has provided us with some interesting insights. One of the fundamental features of previous work on coping was the conceptualization of coping strategies into watertight categories (such as avoidant and active). Aldwin (2004) proposes that such an approach fails to capture the dynamic face to human coping processes; she claims that coping is a recursive process whereby individuals use different coping strategies flexibly and arrive at a strategy that works through a process of testing. Aldwin (2004) emphasized that active and avoidant forms of coping strategies are 'not mutually exclusive but can be used either simultaneously or sequentially in any given situation'. It is this choice that enables an individual to utilize his resources best in the face of a traumatic stressor.

CONCLUSION

This chapter outlines the increasing prevalence of trauma and its consequences. One of the most important consequences of trauma is the psychosocial sequelae seen in emotional distress, deficiencies in adaptive functioning and cognitive reprocessing of the traumatic event. Although the negative consequences to trauma are significant and challenging, one must take a holistic view of trauma as a human experience. Intense stress and trauma has the potentiality to give rise to PTG, a state of coming out stronger from the traumatic experience. This chapter delineates the evolution of the concept of PTG and explores it components, correlates and predictors. It also briefly reviews a host of theories exploring the same notion underlying PTG.

REFERENCES

Aldwin, C. M. (1994). *Stress, coping, and development: An integrative perspective.* New York, NY: Guilford Press.

Aldwin, C. M. (2004). Culture, coping and resilience to stress. In *Gross national happiness and development: Proceedings of the First International Conference on Operationalization of Gross National Happiness* (pp. 563–573). Thimphu: Centre for Bhutan Studies. ISBN 99936-14-22-X.

Aldwin, C. M., Sutton, K. J., & Lachman, M. (1996). The development of coping resources in adulthood. *Journal of Personality, 64*(4), 837–871.

American Psychiatric Association. (2013). *Diagnostic and statistical manual of mental disorders* (5th ed.). Washington, DC: American Psychiatric Association.

Anderson, K. M., & Manuel, G. (1994). Gender differences in reported stress response to the Loma Prieta earthquake. *Sex Roles, 30*(9/10), 725–733.

Bade, M. K. (2000). Personal growth in the midst of negative life experiences: The role of religious coping strategies and appraisals. *Dissertation Abstracts International, 61*(7), 3828. (UMINo.9980364).

Baker, A., & Shalhoub-Kevorkkian, N. (1999). Effects of political violence and military traumas on children: Palestinian case. *Clinical Psychology Review, 19*(8), 935–950.

Bar-Tal, D. (2004). The necessity of observing real life situations: Palestinian–Israeli violence as a laboratory for learning about social behaviour. *European Journal of Social Psychology, 34*(6), 677–701.

Bower, J. E., Meyerowitz, B. E., Desmond, K. A., Bernaards, C. A., Rowland, J. H., & Ganz, P. A. (2005). Perceptions of positive meaning and vulnerability following breast cancer: Predictors and outcomes among long-term breast cancer survivors. *Annals of Behavioral Medicine, 29*(3), 236–245.

Breslau, N. (2002). Epidemiologic studies of trauma, posttraumatic stress disorder, and other psychiatric disorders. *Canadian Journal of Psychiatry, 47*(10), 923–929.

Brewin, C. R. (2003). *Posttraumatic stress disorder: Malady or myth?* New Haven, CT: Yale University Press.

Briere, J. N., & Scott, C. (2015). *Principles of trauma therapy: A guide to symptoms, evaluation, and treatment* (2nd ed.). Thousand Oaks, CA: SAGE.

Bryant-Davis, T., Ellis, M. U., Burke-Maynard, E., Moon, N., Counts, P. A., & Anderson, G. (2012). Religiosity, spirituality, and trauma recovery in the lives of children and adolescents. *Professional Psychology: Research and Practice, 43*(4), 306.

Calhoun, L. G., & Tedeschi, R. G. (1990). Positive aspects of critical life problems: Recollections of grief. *Omega, 20*(4), 265–272.

———. (1998). Beyond recovery from trauma: Implications for clinical practice and research. *Journal of Social Issues, 54*(2), 357–371.

Calhoun, L. G., Cann, A., Tedeschi, R. G., & McMillan, J. (2000). A correlational test of the relationship between posttraumatic growth, religion, and cognitive processing. *Journal of Traumatic Stress, 13*(3), 521–527.

Caplan, G. (1964). *Principles of preventive psychiatry*. New York, NY: Basic Books.

Chodoff, P., Friedman, P. B., & Hamburg, D. A. (1964). Stress, defenses and coping behavior: Observations in parents of children with malignant disease. *American Journal of Psychiatry, 120*(8), 743–749.

Cieslak, R., Benight, C., Schmidt, N., Luszczynska, A., Curtin, E., Clark, R. A., & Kissinger, P. (2009). Predicting posttraumatic growth among Hurricane Katrina survivors living with HIV: The role of self-efficacy, social support, and PTSD symptoms. *Anxiety Stress Coping, 22*(4), 449–463.

Cobb, S. (1976). Social support as a moderator of life stress. *Psychosomatic Medicine, 38*(5), 300–314.

Cohen, M., & Numa, M. (2011). Posttraumatic growth in breast cancer survivors: A comparison of volunteers and non-volunteers. *Psychooncology, 20*(1), 69–76.

Collins, R. L., Taylor, S. E., & Skokan, L. A. (1990). A better world or a shattered vision? Changes in life perspectives following victimization. *Social Cognition, 8*(3), 263–285.

Cordova, M. J., Cunningham, L. L. C., Carlson, C. R., & Andrykowski, M. A. (2001). Posttraumatic growth following breast cancer: A controlled comparison study. *Health Psychology, 20*(3), 176–185.

Cordova, M. J., Giese-Davis, J., Golant, M., Kronenwetter, C., Vickie, C., & Spiegel, D. (2007). Breast cancer as trauma: Posttraumatic stress and posttraumatic growth. *Journal of Clinical Psychology in Medical Settings, 14*(4), 308–319.

Das, V. (2007). *Life and words: Violence and the descent into the ordinary*. Berkeley, CA: University of California Press.

Davis, C. G., Nolen-Hoeksema, S., & Larson, J. (1998). Making sense of loss and benefiting from the experience: Two construals of meaning. *Journal of Personality and Social Psychology, 75*(2), 561–574.

Dhooper, S. S. (1983). Family coping with the crisis of heart attack. *Social Work in Health Care, 9*(1), 15–31.

Doolittle, B. D., & Farrell, M. (2004). The association between spirituality and depression in an urban clinic. *Primary Care Companion Journal of Clinical Psychiatry, 6*(3), 114–118.

Drozdek, B., & Wilson, J. P. (Eds.). (2007). *Voices of trauma: Treating survivors across cultures*. New York: Springer Science & Business Media.

Evers, A. W., Kraaimatt, F. W., van Lankveld, W. I., Jongen, P. J., Jacobs, J. W., & Bijlsma, J. W. (2001). Beyond unfavorable thinking: The illness cognition questionnaire for chronic diseases. *Journal of Consulting and Clinical Psychology, 69*(6), 1026–1036.

Everstine, D. S., & Everstine, L. (1993). *The trauma response: Treatment for emotional injury.* New York, NY: Norton.

Fallot, R. D., & Heckman, J. P. (2005). Religious/spiritual coping among women trauma survivors with mental health and substance use disorders. *Journal of Behavioral Health Services & Research, 32*(2), 215–226.

Frankl, V. E. (1963). *Man's search for meaning.* New York, NY: Washington Square Press.

Frazier, P., Tashiro, T., Berman, M., Steger, M., & Long, J. (2004). Correlates of levels and patterns of positive life changes following sexual assault. *Journal of Consulting and Clinical Psychology, 72*(1), 19.

Friedman, M. J., Resick, P. A., Bryant, R. A., & Brewin, C. R. (2011). Considering PTSD for DSM5. *Depression and Anxiety, 28,* 750–769. doi:10.1002/da.20767

Garcia, F. E., Paez-Rovira, D., Zurtia, G. C., Martel, H. N., & Reyes, A. R. (2014). Religious coping, social support and subjective severity as predictors of posttraumatic growth in people affected by the earthquake in Chile on 27/2/2010. *Religions, 2*(5), 1132–1145. doi:10.3390/rel5041132

Giacaman, R., Mataria, A., Gillham, V. N., Safieh, R. A., Atefanini, A., & Chatterji, S. (2007). Quality of life in the Palestinian context: An inquiry in war-like conditions. *Health Policy, 81*(1), 68–84.

Hafnidar, L. C., & Lin, H. (2012). Forgiveness as a mediator for the relationship between spirituality and posttraumatic growth in Aceh conflict victims, Indonesia. *International Journal of Social Science and Humanity, 2*(3), 237–241.

Halcomb, E., Daly, J., Davidson, P., Elliott, D., & Griffiths, R. (2005). Life beyond severe traumatic injury: An integrative review of literature. *Australian Critical Care, 18*(1), 17–24.

Helgeson, V. S., Reynolds, K. A., & Tomich, P. (2006). A meta-analytic review of benefit finding and growth. *Journal of Consulting and Clinical Psychology, 74*(5), 797–816.

Hill, P. C., & Pargament, K. I. (2003). Advances in the conceptualization and measurement of religion and spirituality: Implications for physical and mental health research. *American Psychologist, 58*(1), 64–74.

Ho, S. M., Chan, C. L., & Ho, R. T. (2004). Posttraumatic growth in Chinese cancer survivors. *Psycho-Oncology, 13*(6), 377–389.

Hobfoll, S. E. (1988). *The ecology of stress.* Washington, DC: Hemisphere.

———. (1989). Conservation of resources: A new attempt at conceptualizing stress. *American Psychologist, 44*(3), 513.

Hobfoll, S. E., & Lilly, R. S. (1993). Resource conservation as a strategy for community psychology. *Journal of Community Psychology, 21*(2), 128–148.

Hooper, L. M. (2003). Parentification, resiliency, secure adult attachment style, and differentiation of self as predictors of growth among college students. *Dissertation Abstracts International: Section B: The Sciences and Engineering, 64,* 1493.

Hungerbuehler, I., Vollrath, M. E., & Landolt, M. A. (2011). Posttraumatic growth in mothers and fathers of children with severe illnesses. *Journal of Health Psychology, 16*(8), 1259–1267.

Janoff-Bulman, R. (1992). *Shattered assumptions: Toward a new psychology of trauma.* New York, NY: Free Press.

Jones, E., & Wessely, S. (2005). *Shell shock to PTSD: Military psychiatry from 1900 to the Gulf War.* Hove and New York: Psychology Press.

Klauer, T., Ferring, D., & Filipp, S. H. (1998). 'Still stable after all this...?': Temporal comparisons in coping with severe and chronic disease. *International Journal of Behavioral Development, 22*(2), 339–355.

Kurtz, M., Wyatt, G., & Kurtz, J. C. (1995). Psychological and sexual well-being, philosophical/spiritual views, and health habits of long term cancer survivors. *Health Care Women International, 16*(3), 253–262.

Laufer, A., & Solomon, Z. (2006). Posttraumatic symptoms and posttraumatic growth among Israeli youth exposed to terror incidents. *Journal of Social and Clinical Psychology, 25*(4), 229–447.

Lechner, S. C., Zakowski, S. G., Antoni, M. H., Greenhawt, M., Block, K., & Block, P. (2003). Do sociodemographic and disease-related variables influence benefit finding in cancer patients? *Psycho-Oncology, 12*(5), 491–499.

Leung, Y. W., Gravely-Witte, S., Macpherson, A., Irvine, J., Stewart, D. E., & Grace, S. L. (2010). Post-traumatic growth among cardiac outpatients: Degree comparison with other chronic illness samples and correlates. *Journal of Health Psychology, 15*(7), 1049–1063. doi:10.1177/1359105309360577

Linley, P. A., & Joseph, S. (2004). Positive change following trauma and adversity: A review. *Journal of Traumatic Stress, 17*(1), 11–21.

Manne, S., Ostroff, J., Winkel, G., Goldstein, L., Fox, K., & Grana, G. (2004). Posttraumatic growth after breast cancer: Patient, partner, and couple perspectives. *Psychosomatic Medicine, 66*(3), 442–454.

McGrath, J. E., & Beehr, T. A. (1990). Time and the stress process: Some temporal issues in the conceptualization and measurement of stress. *Stress Medicine, 6*(2), 93–104.

Mechanic, D. (1977). Illness behavior, social adaptation, and the management of illness. *Journal of Nervous and Mental Disease, 165*(2), 79–87.

Meichenbaum, D. H. (1985). *Stress inoculation training.* Elmsford, NY: Pergamon Press.

Meyerson, D. A., Grant, K. E., Carter, J. S., & Kilmer, R. P. (2011). Posttraumatic growth among children and adolescents: A systematic review. *Clinical Psychology Review, 31*(6), 949–964.

Milam, J., Ritt-Olson, A., Tan, S., Unger, J., & Nezami, E. (2005). The September 11th 2001 terrorist attacks and reports of posttraumatic growth among a multi-ethnic sample of adolescents. *Traumatology, 11*(4), 233–246.

Milam, J. E., Ritt-Olsen, A., Tan, S., & Unger, J. B. (2004). Posttraumatic growth among adolescents. *Journal of Adolescent Research, 19*(2), 192–204.

Mitchell, M. M., Gallaway, S. M., Millikan, M. A., & Bell, R. M. (2013). Combat exposure, unit cohesion, and demographic characteristics of soldiers reporting posttraumatic growth. *Journal of Loss and Trauma: International Perspectives on Stress & Coping, 18*(5), 383–395. doi:10.1080/15325024.2013.768847

Moreira-Almeida, A., Neto, F., & Koenig, H. (2006). Religiousness and mental health: A review. *Revista Brasileira De Psiquiatria* (São Paulo, Brazil: 1999), *28*(3), 242–250.

Morris, B. A., Shakespeare-Finch, J., Rieck, M., & Newbury, J. (2005). Multidimensional nature of posttraumatic growth in an Australian population. *Journal of Traumatic Stress, 18*(5), 575–585.

Neria, Y., Nandi, A., & Galea, S. (2008). Post-traumatic stress disorder following disasters: A systematic review. *Psychological Medicine, 38*(4), 467–480.

Nietzsche, F. (1955). *Beyond good and evil* (M. Cowan, Trans.). Chicago, IL: Henry Regnery.

Norris, F. H., Friedman, M. J., Watson, P. J., Byrne, C. M., Diaz, E., & Kaniasty, K. (2002). 60,000 disaster victims speak: Part I. An empirical review of the empirical literature, 1981–2001. *Psychiatry, 65*(3), 207–239.

O'Leary, V. E., & Ickovics, J. R. (1995). Resilience and thriving in response to challenge: An opportunity for a paradigm shift in women's health. *Women's Health: Research on Gender Behavior and Policy, 1*(2), 121–142.

Oxford English Dictionary. Trauma. Entry 2a. (2015). Retrieved from http://www.oed.com

Pargament, K. I. (1997). *The psychology of religion and coping: Theory, practice and research.* New York, NY: Guilford Press.

Pargament, K. I., Ano, G. G., & Wachholtz, A. B. (2005). The religious dimension of coping Advances in theory, research, and practice. In R. F. Paloutzian & C. L. Park (Eds.), *Handbook of the psychology of religion and spirituality* (pp. 479–495). New York, NY: Guilford Press.

Pargament, K. I., Ensing, D. S., Falgout, K., Olsen, H., Reilly, B., Haitsma, K., & Warren, R. (1990). God help me (I): Religious coping efforts as predictors of the outcomes to significant negative life events. *American Journal of Community Psychology, 18*(6), 793–824.

Pargament, K. I., Royster, B. J. T., Albert, M., Crowe, P., Cullman, E. P., Holley, R.,...Wood, M. (1990). A qualitative approach to the study of religion and coping: Four tentative conclusions: Four tentative conclusions. Paper presented at the annual meeting of the American Psychological Association, Boston, MA.

Park, C. L. (2010). Making sense of the meaning literature: An integrative review of meaning making and its effects on adjustment to stressful life events. *Psychological Bulletin, 136*(2), 257.

Park, C. L., Cohen, L. H., & Murch, R. L. (1996). Assessment and prediction of stress-related growth. *Journal of Personality, 64*(1), 71–105.

Pedersen, D. (2006). Reframing political violence and mental health outcomes: Outlining a research and action agenda for Latin America and the Caribbean region. *Ciencia & Saude Coletiva, 11*(2), 293–302.

Prati, G., & Pietrantoni, L. (2009). Optimism, social support, and coping strategies as factors contributing to posttraumatic growth: A meta-analysis. *Journal of Loss and Trauma, 14*(5), 364–388.

Punamaki, R. L., Kanninen, K., Qouta, S., & Sarraj, E. E. (2004). The role of psychological defenses in moderating between trauma and post-traumatic symptoms among Palestinian men. *International Journal of Psychology, 37*, 286–296.
Rausch, S. M., Auerbach, S. M., & Gramling, S. E. (2008). Gender and ethnic differences in stress reduction, reactivity, and recovery. *Sex Roles, 59*(9/10), 726–737.
Rouhana, N. N., & Bar-Tal, D. (1998). Psychological dynamics of intractable ethno national conflicts: The Israeli-Palestinian case. *American Psychologist, 53*(7), 761–770.
Rubin, R. M., & White-Means, S. I. (2009). Informal caregiving: Dilemmas of sandwiched caregivers. *Journal of Family and Economic Issues, 30*(3), 252–267.
Russell, C. S., White, M. B., & White, C. P. (2006). Why me? Why now? Why multiple sclerosis? Making meaning and perceived quality of life in a Midwestern sample of patients with multiple sclerosis. *Families, Systems, & Health, 24*(1), 65–81.
Schaefer, J. A., & Moos, R. H. (1992). Life crisis and personal growth. In B. N. Carpenter (Ed.), *Personal coping: Theory, research, and application* (pp. 149–170). Westport, CT: Praeger.
Schaefer, J. A., & Moos, R. H. (1998). The context for posttraumatic growth: Life crises, individual and social resources, and coping. In R. G. Tedeschi, C. L. Park, & L. G. Calhoun (Eds.), *Posttraumatic growth: Positive changes in the aftermath of crisis* (pp. 99–126). Mahwah, NJ: Lawrence Erlbaum.
Schroevers, M. J., Helgeson, V. S., Sanderman, R., & Ranchor, A. V. (2010). Type of social support matters for prediction of posttraumatic growth among cancer survivors. *Psycho-Oncology, 19*(1), 46–53.
Sears, S. R., Stanton, A. L., & Danoff-Burg, S. (2003). The yellow brick road and the emerald city: Benefit-finding, positive reappraisal coping, and posttraumatic growth in women with early stage breast cancer. *Health Psychology, 22*(5), 487–497.
Shakespeare-Finch, J., & De Dassel, T. (2009). Exploring posttraumatic outcomes as a function of childhood sexual abuse. *Journal of Child Sexual Abuse, 18*(6), 623–640.
Shakespeare-Finch, J., & Lurie-Beck, J. (2014). A meta-analytic clarification of the relationship between posttraumatic growth and symptoms of posttraumatic distress disorder. *Journal of Anxiety Disorder, 28*(2), 223–229.
Sheikh, A. L., & Marotta, S. A. (2005). A cross-validation study of the Posttraumatic Growth Inventory. *Measurement and Evaluation in Counselling and Development, 38*(2), 66–77.
Silver, R. L., Boon, C., & Stones, M. H. (1983). Searching for meaning in misfortune: Making sense of incest. *Journal of Social Issues, 39*(2), 81–102.
Tamres, L., Janicki, D., & Helgeson, V. S. (2002). Sex differences in coping behavior: A meta-analytic review. *Personality and Social Psychology Review, 6*(1), 2–30.
Taylor, S. E. (1983). Adjustment to threatening events: A theory of cognitive adaptation. *American Psychologist, 38*(11), 1161–1173.

Taylor, S. E., & Brown, J. D. (1988). Illusion and well-being: A social psychological perspective on mental health. *Psychological Bulletin, 103*(2), 193–210.

Taylor, S. E., & Lobel, M. (1989). Social comparison activity under threat: Downward evaluations and upward contacts. *Psychological Review, 96*(4), 569–575.

Taylor, S. E., Wood, J. V., & Lichtman, R. R. (1983). It could be worse: Selective evaluation as a response to victimization. *Journal of Social Issues, 39*(2), 19–40.

Tedeschi, R. G., & Calhoun, L. G. (1995). *Trauma and transformation: Growing in the aftermath of suffering*. Thousand Oaks, CA: SAGE.

———. (1996). The posttraumatic growth inventory: Measuring the positive legacy of trauma. *Journal of Traumatic Stress, 9*(3), 455–472.

———. (2004). Posttraumatic growth: Conceptual foundations and empirical evidence. *Psychological Inquiry, 15*(1), 1–18.

Tomich, P. L., & Helgeson, V. S. (2004). Is finding something good in the bad always good? Benefit finding among women with breast cancer. *Health Psychology, 23*(1), 16–23.

Updegraff, J. A., Taylor, S. E., Kemeny, M. E., & Wyatt, G. E. (2002). Positive and negative effects of HIV infection in women with low socioeconomic resources. *Personality and Social Psychology Bulletin, 28*(3), 382–394.

Updegraff, J. A., & Taylor, S. E. (2000). From vulnerability to growth: Positive and negative effects of stressful life events. In J. Harvey & E. Miller (Eds.), *Loss and trauma: General and close relationship perspectives* (pp. 3–28). Philadelphia, PA: Brunner-Routledge.

Vishnevsky, T., Cann, A., Calhoun, L. G., Tedeschi, R. G., & Demakis, G. J. (2010). Gender differences in self-reported posttraumatic growth: A meta-analysis. *Psychology of Women Quarterly, 34*(1), 110–120.

Visotsky, H. M., Hamburg, D. A., Goss, M. E., & Lebovits, B. Z. (1961). Coping behavior under extreme stress. *Archives of General Psychiatry, 5*(5), 423–448.

Wallerstein, J. S. (1986). Women after divorce: Preliminary report from a ten-year follow-up. *American Journal of Orthopsychiatry, 56*(1), 65–77.

Widows, M. R., Jacobsen, P. B., Booth-Jones, M., & Fields, K. K. (2005). Predictors of posttraumatic growth following bone marrow transplantation for cancer. *Health Psychology, 24*(3), 266–273.

Yalom, I. D. (1980). *Existential psychotherapy*. New York, NY: Basic Books.

Yarom, N. (1983). Facing death in war: An existential crisis. In S. Breznitz (Ed.), *Stress in Israel* (pp. 3–38). New York, NY: Van Nostrand Reinhold.

Zoellner, T., & Maercker, A. (2006). Posttraumatic growth in clinical psychology: A critical review and introduction of a two component model. *Clinical Psychology Review, 26*(5), 626–653.

Chapter 18

Young Adults' Awareness and Commitment to Use of Character Strengths
An Examination of University Students in Nairobi

Beatrice W. E. Churu and Sahaya G. Selvam

INTRODUCTION

Africa in general has a predominantly young population. Demographic surveys indicate that 70 per cent of the population is aged 30 years or less (Gyimah-Brempong & Kimenyi, 2013, p. 26). Kenya is no exception to this continental trend and opportunity. In fact, in Kenyan demographics, 'youth bulge'—the phenomenon of the age group of 15 to 30 years showing a protruding graph as compared to other age groups—is recognized both as a challenge and as an opportunity (Hope, 2012). It follows then that the youthful population needs to be taken through whatever processes that can enable them become an optimum resource to themselves, their families, communities and country. Much is being carried out in this line through formal education and professional skills development (Gyimah-Brempong & Kimenyi, 2013, p. 26). However, in the largely cohort approaches to these efforts, there is very little attention paid to personalizing developmental efforts in line with the strengths of individuals. In most cases, as is the case in more developed parts of the world, no coordinated effort at helping students individualize their development options is inbuilt into the processes of education (Park, 2009). Individualized career guidance in secondary and tertiary institutions is rare and deficient (Gacohi, Sindabi, & Chepchieng, 2017; Wambu & Fischer, 2015).

Positive psychology offers a perspective of personal development that focuses on the strengths of the individual as a springboard for overcoming challenges, and for developing competencies, knowledge, identity and virtue (Lounsbury, Fisher, Levy, & Welsh, 2009; Park, 2009). This chapter uses the approach of positive psychology that suggests that character development is necessary for positive personal development (Park & Peterson, 2008). Here, being consistent with positive psychology, character strengths are understood to be morally oriented, trait-like, measurable qualities of individuals that are expressed in their cognitive, affective and behavioural patterns (Park, 2009; Selvam, 2015). Humanity has traditionally recognized and propagated virtues across cultural, religious and philosophical traditions (Dahlsgaard, Peterson, & Seligman, 2005; Peterson & Seligman, 2004, pp. 33–52; Snyder & Lopez, 2007, pp. 23–50). Character strengths are perceivable in a person's interactions, be it in the family, school, work or other relationships (Choudhury & Barooah, 2016).

The relationship between virtue and happiness also has been of interest to scholars and philosophers in all ages and across cultures (Kesebir & Diener, 2014; Park & Peterson, 2008). There are those who emphasize that virtue leads to promotion of happiness, while others focus on the preventive power of virtues against what leads to unhappiness (see, e.g., Selvam, 2015). In any case, the symbiotic relationship between virtue and well-being is largely agreed upon. Character strengths are particularly evident when an individual is left feeling energized, invigorated and happy after a certain activity; it shows that in that activity, the person is engaging one or more of his or her strengths and this builds him or her up (Shaw, 2015). The benefits of cultivating character strengths extend to achievement, positive self-concept and life satisfaction (Lounsbury et al., 2009; Park, 2009). These strengths are the ingredients for displaying human goodness (Choudhury & Barooah, 2016), which come almost naturally to a person, habitually and consistently. But this does not mean that they are static or unchanging. Character strengths are malleable; they can be developed through practise. The lack of exercise, on the contrary, can lead to their diminishment, as argued by Baumeister and colleagues in the case of self-control (Muraven & Baumeister, 2000).

Often, particularly in traditional societies, the emphasis in educational and counselling settings is to consider a good person as one who displays the absence of problem behaviour, pathology or destructive habits. Children are assessed in school to be of good character if they do not get into trouble, or if they present no major challenges to the teachers and parents. Few educational settings, families, schools or colleges have invested in imparting how to develop even such 'good character'. Positive psychologists have helped to sharpen awareness that character development is a process of growing in a composite of character traits that are positive in themselves and contribute to thriving of individuals (Park, 2009). There is an increasing interest in some settings on the role of strengths approach to human development accompanied by scientific studies and intervention (Park, 2009; Quinlan, 2012). This may not be the case in the developing world, and particularly in Africa, as alluded to by the gap in literature. The focus in youth development in Africa has been on life skills. Life skills are psychosocial abilities that one acquires to help deal effectively with daily challenges (Selvam, 2008). Character strengths are mental and moral habits that form the framework for individual's thoughts, motivation and behaviour. Therefore, training in character development could include, and be more fundamental to, life skills training.

Based on observation of the accompaniment processes towards personal development offered to youth in secondary schools and institutions of tertiary education in Kenya, the present study assumes that young adults are largely unaware of their character strengths. Even when they may be aware of them, they may not put much premium on these strengths as pillars of their personal development. Education systems from families to faith communities and schools have tended to focus members on overcoming their weaknesses; yet research has suggested that efforts to overcome weakness yield mediocre results while focus on cultivating strengths can lead to excellence (Shaw, 2015).

Young adulthood, which, for many, coincides with first years in college, is a particularly fertile stage for studying and cultivating character strengths (Lounsbury et al., 2009). Since the proposal of Arnett (2000) that there is a developmental stage between adolescence and adulthood, which he named 'emerging adulthood', there is a large and increasing consensus on their specific characteristics (Gibbons & Ashdown, 2006; Nelson & Barry, 2005; Swanson, 2016). The present study, while including emerging adults in the considerations of some of these characteristics, goes beyond the age limit of emerging adults (18–25 years) and uses a wider bracket (18–30 years), referring to the population of the study as, 'young adults'. This approach is much consistent with the criteria used in youth policies across Sub-Saharan Africa. In Kenya, for instance, the Ministry of Youth Affairs (2007) identifies youth to be the section of the population aged 15 to 30 years. Therefore, we consider young adults to be from 18 to 30 years of age. While it is an age of turmoil for most, young adulthood is also an age of considerable optimism (Arnett, 2014). This, in our view, makes this stage particularly well suited for harnessing the power of the character strengths-based education towards self, relationships and career development.

Several studies suggest that there is a positive correlation between character strengths and academic performance among young adults in universities (Choudhury & Barooah, 2016; Lounsbury et al., 2009). Studies in China and elsewhere also demonstrate the possibility of scaffolding the development of character strengths of young adults (Duan, Ho, Tang, Li, & Zhang, 2014). These interventions necessarily involve heightening awareness of the subjects about their strengths; and the impact of such an exercise is well documented (Fredrickson & Joiner, 2002; Kruger & Prinsloo, 2008). The current study aimed at replicating such interventions in Kenya.

Despite that authors such as Biswas-Diener (2006) and Selvam and Collicutt (2013) have demonstrated ample parallels between the character strengths of the Values in Action (VIA) and African values to which African youth should presumably be socialized, there has not been much effort yet on carrying out interventions to enhance character strengths among youth in Africa, particularly in Kenya. The present study aimed at filling this gap. Furthermore, such a study might increase the efforts put into character strengths education in Kenya.

OBJECTIVES OF THE STUDY

The general aim of the present study was to explore in detail, through a five-step assessment, the sampled young adults' self-perception in terms of character strengths and the potential use of the strengths in the development of the self, relationship with others, and their career prospects.

The specific objectives of the study were to:

1. establish the level of the young adults' awareness of their own character strengths in comparison to the results of a standardized test;
2. observe individual participant's reaction to the improved awareness of their strengths;
3. examine the association between knowledge of their own strengths and commitment to their corresponding use; and
4. explore how the new awareness of the strengths impacts a change in the way young adults may perceive the use of the strengths to promote development of the self, relationship with others, and their career prospects.

Method

The study adopted a qualitative approach, using interview method of data collection. Twenty young adults were sampled through a snowball process of recruitment from the Faculty of Education of Tangaza University College in Nairobi. Since the aim of the study was to explore in detail, through a five-step interview, the level of awareness of and the openness to use character strengths, a sample size of 20 was thought to be justified. The criteria for choice of the candidates for the study included the following: they were within the age range of 18 to 30; they were willing to voluntarily participate in the interview and to be able to take the online test of Values in Action Inventory of Strengths (VIA-IS) and they were open to share the results with the researchers.

Procedure

The study was carried out over a period of one week, during which the primary researcher met personally each of the sampled participants and explained to them the purpose of the study as well as the meaning of character strengths, using the VIA breakdown developed by positive psychologists in the last two decades (Park, 2009). The need for the explanation of the character strengths became evident when the first few participants showed no knowledge of distinction between character strengths and values, skills, talents and other characteristics. To facilitate a shared understanding and greater coherence in the work, this preliminary discussion using the VIA character strengths became invaluable.

Then the interview followed. This had five steps:

Step 1. Based on the explanation of the VIA catalogue, the young adult participants were required to spontaneously name their top four character strengths and to give an explanation on how they know they have these strengths.

Step 2. They were required to explain how they are using these strengths in their personal, family, careers and other development.

Step 3. This step involved having them take the VIA-IS inventory test online, and compare the results with their list of the top four strengths that they had mentioned spontaneously to the researcher. The VIA-IS inventory has 120 items, each of the 24 character strengths being tested by five items as per the dimensions described in the VIA catalogue of strengths (Peterson & Seligman, 2004).

Step 4. At this step, they described their reaction to the results and to comment on how they felt when they compared their earlier perception of their own strengths and the outcome of the online test.

Step 5. The final step was, for the participants, to project how they will use their awareness of their strengths in the future in the development of the self, their relationships with others, especially the family, and their careers.

These steps were captured in an interview protocol that the primary researcher used throughout the process of data collection. For each participant, the whole process took about 60 to 75 minutes.

Data Handling and Analysis

The data was captured on worksheets that had open-ended questions that the participants themselves filled up during the interview as the researcher asked them the questions. The answers from the open-ended questions have been summarized or enumerated in the results section further. The reliability of the interpretations of the answers was improved by the involvement of the two researchers in the final process of summarizing.

Results

The present section reports the findings of the study, following an outline that is based on the four objectives of the study.

Young adults' awareness of their own character strengths: The respondents were required to spontaneously identify four of their top character strengths from the VIA list. All participants could do this with some relative ease. Most of these young adults could speak about their own positive qualities with fluency. They could articulate that they are good at one thing or another, mentioning a range of intellectual abilities as well as personality traits. This was an interesting and consistent experience with all the 20 participants. One of the 20, however, could not raise a fourth top strength, in spite of being given the VIA list.

To demonstrate their conviction of their strength: In Step 2 of the interview, they were required to give an illustration of how they see these strengths operating in their lives, or to explain why they think they have this strength. Most of the participants could not give the reasons in their own terms and had to resort to the definitions or explanations given in the VIA catalogue. In any case, most could identify with these definitions and explanations, even if they appeared new to them. The inability of the participants to demonstrate their strengths in their own words is perhaps more indicative of the little value placed by the young people on their character strengths. They have little day-to-day awareness of the usefulness of these strengths.

In terms of agreement between their self-perceived, four top strengths and those discovered after the online VIA inventory, 12 participants had only one strength matching among the top four in the two lists, three had two of four strengths concur, and only one had three similarities. Four had none of the strengths matching between the two lists. Taken together, it could indicate that the young adults are aware of their strengths only to a limited level. This conclusion has to be considered also together with the possibility that the participants may not be familiar with the nuances around the vocabulary used to refer to the character strengths in common parlance and in the VIA online test.

Energy and enthusiasm generated by new self-knowledge: The respondents took delight in their strengths as they discovered them particularly after the online VIA test. The most frequently reported feeling was 'good'. Only one participant reported being disappointed. Ironically, this is the one who had three concurrent strengths between their own estimation and the VIA-IS generated results. Asked how they felt about the comparison of their two lists, most reported feeling affirmed and/or 'pleasantly surprised'. Generally, the exercise generated energy and excitement for most, with one participant explicitly reporting an increase in self-appreciation.

Coherence between knowledge of strengths and their use: Asked how they use these strengths in daily lives for the development of their own self, relationships with others and career prospects, most had rather generic descriptions of how they use their strengths. Some direct quotations from the section on how they use their strengths for self-development can shed clear light on the general perception of the participants. What follows is a collation of statements that participants made:

> My strengths help me to be a more responsible person, by always trying to be conscious of my situation and trying to be as human as possible with everyone; I use my strengths to help me be true to myself and be able to create healthy relationships with those around me; I am able to live a happy life, to accept people as they are; I do not live a fake life; I have used my strengths to make myself grow into a trustworthy person; I use my strengths to ensure I portray a good

image of myself to future generations; I have always used fairness when dealing with a group and especially if I realise there are those who are seeking favours; my strengths have helped me to achieve more skills and abilities and build me as a strong person and of what I want in life.

About how they use the strengths at present in their relationship with the family and significant others, the participants had this to say:

These strengths have helped me bring my family together; I pray for my family every day and hope for them the best in their endeavours; Having forgiveness has made me and my family and friends understand each other characters well; I make sure that people are in a good mood most of the time if not all the time; knowing my strength will help me know others also; if I lose my temper I know how to cool down; my family is happier I attend most family occasions thus showing teamwork.

About career development, the participants had the following expressions:

I feel my career is in the right path and more challenges are coming than I am ready to handle; learn and adapt to changes in my career; working on a social business idea; being courageous is making me to meet or able to handle hard issues in different places, especially at school hence am able to do it; I teach the young ones on how to be creative, particularly in developing themselves; I can express myself confidently based on my knowledge and can know if my output was understood; taking risk is a matter or enhances ones career development and unearths the potentials one has; for any career development to be a team-builder, kind and honest to grow in all dimensions being a team-player has helped me work great in organisations; since I'll be a teacher, these strengths will enable me to touch the hearts of my students for them to be transformed which is my aim in life; my strengths help in creating unity and a peaceful environment for my family members and friends

The aforementioned responses seem to be generic in scope and show certain ordinariness, thereby lacking precision and excitement about their strengths. The new discovery has not stimulated them to use these strengths in specific and distinguishing ways. One senses a need to galvanize that new enthusiasm into action plans for self-improvement and engagement.

New Self-knowledge and Prospects into Future

Though the awareness of the strengths of the students brought enthusiasm and joy, it was noted to have little impact on the way the participants projected themselves into the future. It was surprising to note that hardly any of the participants gave much energy to what they could do with the new discovery. In the interviews, it almost looked as if the discovery of the strengths was the trophy, the confirmation of their greatness. They did not see it as a springboard for more or different kinds of engagement. There was a general sense of complacency. Though the respondents are hope-filled for the future, their responses were rather generic, such as 'I think I will achieve my dreams; I will make my family proud of me, I will teach my family many things; I will build on my strengths; I will have to grow more deeply'. One exception to this was when a participant mentioned that she will engage in artistic programmes to develop her strength of creativity. Such particular focus was lacking among the other participants.

However, the complacent spirit was less visible when it came to the use of strengths for career development as compared to their concern about self and relationship with others. Evidently, the participants have a grip on the potential to use these strengths more to their career advantage. One participant said that the VIA-IS test results opened his eyes more to why he is interested in certain careers. Another, the same one who was enthused by her creative strength, reported that she will follow 'my one-time aspiration to be an author'. Three others were excited about their strengths in team work and expressed that they will use this in their career front to enhance success.

The seeming inability or lack of interest of the participants to imagine ways in which they could use newly discovered strengths may be a factor of the interview setting which may have not given enough time and, especially, not enough accompaniment to engage one's imagination. The female participant who spoke about being an author in using her strength of creativity, might have been struggling with this career option for some time as she implied in the interview. Now she found herself happily surprised to discover that she has ample resources for taking it up again. Other participants, in spite of their evident excitement, did not show concern to explore more deeply how their new awareness might impact their life plans. They behaved as if the discovery of their strengths was a reward in itself!

DISCUSSION AND CONCLUSION

The present study began with the aim of exploring young adults' self-assessment of character strengths and the potential use of the strengths in the development of the self, relationship with others, and their career prospects. The results have shown very mixed findings. On the one hand, the whole discourse of character strengths and their discovery excites young adults. And they also report using these strengths in their daily lives. On the other hand, the participants are not articulate enough about the use of specific character strengths, and they do not appear enthused about their use for future development.

This reality may be a product of the socialization that has not much invested in developing strengths as investments for personal progress. Strengths can appear to them as a victory against the possible negative challenges in their behaviour that they may have spent their life's energy fighting against, instead of viewing them as potential foundational pillars for great careers and relationships.

What potential might there be in a more conscious accompaniment of young adults to acknowledge and exercise own strengths in their daily lives, relationships and career developments? Young adulthood is a stage where goal and direction setting is crucial for individuals in their social milieu. It follows that taking into account one's own strengths can be a positive boost to success in achieving such goals. Expectations of young adults from family and society can be experienced as pressure. Shulman and Nurmi (2010) observe that many young adults fail to accomplish their goals because the goals are unrealistic. It may be that such goals have no connection to the strengths of the individual. There are still many who fail to accomplish their goals even though these seem quite reasonable.

Character Strengths, Goal-setting and Well-being

In the view of Shulman and Nurmi (2010), the determining factors for a sense of goal attainment includes the kind of goals set—broad and adaptive or narrow and definite. Broader goals allow for a greater sense of attainment as they offer a wider range of possible measures of achievement. Setting adaptive goals contributes to a more favourable assessment of goal attainment and therefore more sense of success. The ability to set adaptive goals is associated with ability to mobilize inner strength (Shulman & Nurmi, 2010). Given that self-efficacy is a strong predictor of goal achievement and self-criticism is detrimental to the self-regulation necessary especially in overcoming obstacles (Shulman & Nurmi, 2010), it follows that the awareness and cultivation of character strengths is crucial for increasing self-efficacy, goal-setting, goal adaptability and, ultimately, the sense of achievement and success that in turn propels the individual to greater heights. The importance of accompaniment for young adults towards raising the profile of their character strengths, therefore, is indisputable.

In a study, reported by Park (2009), it was found that adults who were encouraged to deliberately use their signature strengths in new ways as they go forward in life became significantly happier—more satisfied with their lives—than those who were not given this guidance and encouragement. Kesebir and Diener (2014), in their survey of empirical research between virtue and happiness, tender that it is impossible to conceive of a happy life, characterized, as it might be, by better social relationships, higher productivity, more prosocial behaviour and physical health without the exercise of virtue. Diener and Seligman (2002) found that the only variable that consistently corresponded with happiness was positive social relationships. Being consistent with the African worldview (Magesa, 1998; Selvam & Collicutt, 2013), it is our view that social relationships have much to do with character strengths. Yet, as Kesebir and Diener (2014) also point out, most people are unable to make the direct link between virtue and happiness, especially in a long-term integration, though immediate gratification from the exercise of virtue is sometimes recognized.

Based on the findings of the present study, as also supported by literature, our proposal is that adults and educators need to encourage young adults, even as they experiment much with their lives at this stage (Arnett, 2000), to harness the use of their strengths in new ways. This can result in discovering surprising new resources and possibilities. This is particularly important in situations such as in Kenya where opportunities are not always easily accessible to young adults on account of 'the youth bulge', which we referred to in the introduction. It cannot be taken for granted that knowing one's signature strengths results in increasing their use and in creating opportunities for themselves. In a similar vein, in a population such as the Kenyan young adults who have been subjected more to education towards eradication of negative traits rather than to strengthening of positive strengths, this is even more important. Experts in positive psychology encourage actionable and measurable ways of exercising one's own strengths with clear targets (Park, 2009).

Young adulthood is also an age where most people experience fresh freedom from stringent parental and teacher supervision while they are not yet encumbered by the demands of parenthood themselves. It is therefore a window period during which development of strengths, especially in college, can take priority (Lounsbury et al., 2009). In the college setting, the focus is already on the development of the students and so a very small crossover is needed to add the dimension of emphasis on own strengths to maximize students' preparedness for life and its many faces.

Facilitating Young Adults Towards Growth in Character

Lounsbury and colleagues (2009) refer to many possibilities of interventions, some of which have been empirically tested, that help people develop character strengths effectively. These can be studied and modified as necessary to devise ways of assisting Kenyan young adults. Even a once only character-strengths-based intervention has been found to have considerable impact on the well-being of young adults (Duan & Bu, 2017); this means that systematic and repeated interventions can go much further. The college setting is particularly appropriate for simple but constant interventions that can also become new habits for the participants.

Perhaps the fact of their proximity to their imminent parenthood means that it can ultimately translate into a change of culture towards positive ways of raising their own children. Creating a virtue-salient culture, mindful that virtues are effected through character strengths, is essential to increasing the possibility for young adults to flourish (Kesebir & Diener, 2014), and this is ultimately the desire of every young adult. Accordingly, there is an increasing recognition that working on the character strengths of children and young people is a necessity, not a luxury (Park, 2009), and that character strengths contribute to mental health and academic performance (Lounsbury et al., 2009). In particular, the presence of negative affect such as depression among children and youth can be given a big and effective antidote. Specific character strengths have been found to be effective in mitigating against risky behaviour such as drug abuse and suicide ideation, while helping youth to thrive (Park & Peterson, 2008).

There is much scope for development of this and similar studies in the Kenyan context. For example, it would be beneficial to explore which strengths are supportive of specific careers, which may foster relationships and which of the strengths may correlate more strongly with identity confirmation that is a major concern in young adulthood within the African cultural setting. Of particular interest is the role that character strengths play in the achievement of psychosocial developmental targets during young adulthood; for example, in which way do specific strengths correlate with the individual person's development from a sense of isolation to intimacy and social integration?

In the areas of therapy and accompaniment, studies could be carried out exploring how far therapeutic settings for young adults are cognizant of the opportunity of cultivating character strengths during this life stage, and what approaches are in use in this setting to support clients. There is certainly much scope for and promise in the fruitful use of a strengths approach to therapy (Magyar-Moe, Rhea, Owens, & Conoley, 2015; Scheel, Davis, & Henderson, 2013), particularly with children, adolescents and young adults. In the college/university settings, exploring the particular relationship between achievement of academic goals and the priming of character strengths can be of special interest.

REFERENCES

Arnett, J. J. (2000). Emerging adulthood: A theory of development from the late teens through the twenties. *American Psychologist, 55*(5), 469–480.

———. (2014). Presidential address: The emergence of emerging adulthood: A personal history. *Emerging Adulthood, 2*(3), 155–162. doi:10.1177/2167696814541096

Biswas-Diener, R. (2006). From the equator to the north polo: A study of character strengths. *Journal of Happiness Studies, 7*(3), 293–310.

Biswas-Diener, R., Todd, B. K., & King, L. A. (2009). Two traditions of happiness research, not two distinct types of happiness. *The Journal of Positive Psychology, 4*(3), 208–211.

Choudhury, S. A., & Barooah, I. P. (2016). Character strength and academic achievement in undergraduate college students. *Indian Journal of Positive Psychology, 7*(1), 76–81.

Dahlsgaard, K., Peterson, C., & Seligman, M. E. (2005). Shared virtue: The convergence of valued human strengths across culture and history. *Review of General Psychology, 9*(3), 203–213.

Diener, E., & Seligman, M. E. P. (2002). Very happy people. *Psychological Science, 13*(1), 80–83.

Duan, W., & Bu, H. (2017). Randomised trail investigating of a single-session character-strength-based intervention on freshman's adaptability. *Research on Social Work Practice, 20*(10), 1–11.

Duan, W., Ho, S. M. Y., Tang, X., Li, T. & Zhang, Y. (2014). Character strength-based intervention to promote satisfaction with life in the Chinese university context. *Journal of Happiness Studies, 15*, 1347–1361. doi:10.1007/s10902-013-9479-y

Fredrickson, B. L., & Joiner, T. (2002). Positive emotions trigger upward spirals toward emotional well-being. *Psychological Science, 13*(2), 172–175.

Gacohi, J. N., Sindabi, A. M., & Chepchieng, M. C. (2017). Influence of career information on choice of degree programme among regular and self-sponsored students in public universities, Kenya. *Journal of Education and Practice, 8*(11), 38–47.

Gibbons, J. L., & Ashdown, B. K. (2006). Emerging adulthood: The dawning of a new age. A review of J. J. Jensen Arnett & J. L. Lynn Tanner (Eds.), *Emerging adults in America: Coming of age in the 21st century.* Washington, DC: American Psychological Association. doi:10.1037/a0003504

Gyimah-Brempong, K., & Kimenyi, M. S. (2013). *Youth policy and the future of African development*, Africa Growth Initiative. Washington, DC: Brookings Institution.

Hope, K. R., Sr. (2012). Engaging the youth in Kenya: Empowerment, education, and employment. *International Journal of Adolescence and Youth, 17*(4), 221–236.

Kesebir, P., & Diener, E. (2014). A virtuous cycle: The relationship between happiness and virtue. In N. Snow & F. Trivigno (Eds.), *The philosophy and psychology of character and happiness* (pp. 287–306). New York, NY: Routledge.

Kruger, L., & Prinsloo, H. (2008). The appraisal and enhancement of resilience modalities in middle adolescents within the school context. *South African Journal of Education, 28*(2), 241–259.

Lounsbury, J. W., Fisher, L. A., Levy, J. J., & Welsh, D. P. (2009). An investigation of character strengths in relation to the academic success of college students. *Individual Differences Research, 7*(1), 52–69.

Magesa, L. (1998). *African religion: The moral traditions of abundant life.* Nairobi: Paulines Publications.

Magyar-Moe, J. L., Owens, R. L., & Conoley, C. W. (2015). Positive psychological interventions in counseling: What every counseling psychologist should know. *The Counseling Psychologist, 43*(4), 508–557.

Ministry of Youth Affairs (2007). Kenya National Youth Policy. Sessional Paper No. 3.

Muraven, M., & Baumeister, R. F. (2000). Self-regulation and depletion of limited resources: Does self-control resemble a muscle? *Psychological Bulletin, 126*(2), 247–259.

Nelson, L. J., & Barry, C. M. (2005). Distinguishing features of emerging adulthood: The role of self-classification as an adult. *Journal of Adolescent Research, 20*(2), 242–262. doi: 10.1177/0743558404273074

Park, N., & Peterson, C. (2008). Positive psychology and character strengths: Application to strengths-based school counseling. *Professional School Counseling, 12*(2), 85–92.

Park, N. (2009). Building strengths for character: Keys to positive youth development. *Reclaiming Children and Youth, 18*(2), 47–57.

Peterson, C., & Seligman, M. E. P. (2004). *Character strengths and virtues: A handbook and classifications*. New York, NY: Oxford University Press.

Quinlan, D., Swain, N., & Vella-Brodrick, D. A. (2012). Character strengths interventions: Building on what we know for improved outcomes. *Journal of Happiness Studies, 13*(6), 1145–1163.

Scheel, M. J., Davis, C. K., & Henderson, J. D. (2013). Therapist use of client strengths: A qualitative study of positive processes. *The Counseling Psychologist, 41*(3), 392–427.

Selvam, S. G. (2008). *Scaffoldings: Training young people in Christian life skills*. Nairobi: Paulines Publications Africa.

Selvam, S. G. (2015). Character strengths in the context of Christian contemplative practice facilitating recovery from alcohol misuse: Two case studies. *Journal of Spirituality in Mental Health, 17*(3), 190–211.

Selvam, S. G., & Collicutt, J. (2013). The ubiquity of the character strengths in African traditional religion: A thematic analysis. In H. H. Knoop & A. Delle Fave (Eds.), *Well-being and cultures: A positive psychology perspective* (pp. 83–102). Heidelberg: Springer.

Shaw, B. (2015). *10 ways to improve well-being*. Retrieved from http://thepositivepsychologypeople.com/wp-content/uploads/2015/03/PDF-Final-1.pdf

Shulman, S., & Nurmi, J. E. (2010). Dynamics of goal pursuit and personality make-up among emerging adults: Typology, change over time, and adaptation. *New Directions for Child and Adolescent Development, 130*, 57–70. doi:10.1002/cd.281

Snyder, C. R., &. Lopez, S. J. (2007). *Positive psychology: The scientific and practical explorations of human strength*. Thousand Oaks, CA: SAGE Publications.

Swanson, J. A. (2016). Trends in literature about emerging adulthood: Review of empirical studies. *Emerging Adulthood, 4*(6), 391–402.

Wambu, G. W., & Fischer, T. A. (2015). School guidance and counselling in Kenya: Historical development, current status and future prospects. *Journal of Education and Practice, 16*(11), 93–102.

Chapter 19

From Deficit to a Strength Model
Character Strength Interventions for Children with Disabilities

Jessline Williams and Aneesh Kumar P.

INTRODUCTION

The introduction of character strengths in the realm of positive psychology revealed the presence of certain positive traits that existed universally within every human being. This insight led to the understanding that all individuals across time and cultures possessed innate attributes that can promote their moral and general well-being (Park, Peterson, & Seligman, 2004). However, in the disability field, promotion of well-being has repeatedly been associated with the elimination of disorder-related deficiencies. Such a deficit-oriented approach towards enhancing human excellency has often been adopted by researchers and practitioners while dealing with individuals with various forms of disability (Niemiec, Shrogen, & Wehmeyer, 2017).

The World Health Organization (WHO, 2011) defines disability as impairments or restrictions caused to the normal functioning of individuals as a result of complex interactions between personal, environmental and health factors that cause hindrance to the person's optimal development. Disabilities can be in various forms such as congenital conditions like Down syndrome, mental health problems like depression, neurodevelopmental disorders like specific learning disorder, intellectual disability, visual–hearing impairments and even physical disabilities such as arthritis. A disability can be visible or invisible, temporary or long term. However, irrespective of its nature or degree of severity, a disability impacts the individual's overall development and functioning.

According to WHO's Global Burden of Disease Study (2004), 0.7 per cent to 5.1 per cent of children, between the age groups of 0 to 14 years, had moderate to severe disability, whereas for adolescents above the ages of 15 years, the worldwide prevalence of disability ranged between 3.8 per cent and 19.4 per cent (as cited in WHO, 2011). The 2011 census in India reported that out of 121 crore population, 2.21 per cent of individuals have some form of disability. Children between the age groups of 0 to 9 years constituted 12 per cent of the total disabled population. Whereas adolescents disabled between the age groups of 10 to 19 years constituted 17 per cent of nationwide disabled population (as cited in *Disabled Persons in India: A Statistical Profile*, 2016).

Children and adolescents with disabilities often experience exclusion in various spheres of life. The lack of awareness, negative social perceptions and attitudes towards disability make them victims of social rejection, stigma and stereotypes that adversely affect their general well-being, leading to mental health problems. Society views and judges these children based on their deficits rather than their existing strengths, which causes everyone to treat them as vulnerable individuals rather than regarding them as individuals who are capable of thriving despite their disability (Emerson & Hatton, 2007; UNICEF, 2013).

Bringing up a child with disability can also be equally stressful for the parents and family members. They are required to make difficult adjustments, deal with financial strains, face the lack of support and negative societal attitudes of significant others and even that of professionals (Jones & Passey, 2005). However, there is growing empirical evidence that indicates how parents can remain resilient despite these challenges. The disability of the child instead of having a negative impact can rather have a positive effect on the family in terms of improving harmony and communication among family members and so on. But this has been found to depend on other important factors such as degree of the child's disability, family structure and financial status, to highlight a few (Ferguson, 2002).

Parents play a vital role in helping children with a disability to enhance their psychosocial functioning and helping them gain confidence to reach sufficient independence. This however also depends on internal child factors such as their level of cognitive abilities that enable them to function more independently (Holmbeck et al., 2002). Therefore, if parents could enable children with higher cognitive abilities to understand and build their lives on their strengths rather than their deficits, these children would learn to thrive despite all their disorder-related challenges and difficulties. Apart from children with certain physical impairments, few of the childhood neurodevelopmental disorders such as specific learning disorder, high functioning autism and mild intellectual disabilities include children who possess the required cognitive abilities that would enable them to act as active agents of change in their own lives.

The National Center for Learning Disabilities (2014) stated that in America among 5.7 million children diagnosed with all kinds of disorders, 42 per cent of them were found to have learning disorders. They also constituted the largest group of students who received special education services, followed by children with speech or language impairment, health problems, intellectual disabilities, autism and emotional disturbance (as cited in Cortiella & Horowitz, 2014).

In India, however, factual data concerning the prevalence of learning disorder, unlike other disabilities, remain limited. Conducting national-level longitudinal studies in the Indian context was found to be challenging due to widespread lack of awareness about the disorder, multilingualism, stigmatization associated with labelling, difficulty is identification of the disorder especially in rural areas due to environmental, economic and educational disadvantages (John et al., 2013).

It was only recently in 2016 that the Parliament of India included specific learning disability as one of the conditions that come under the Rights of Persons with Disabilities Act which now ensures equal opportunities for people with the disability (Narayan & John, 2017). There clearly exists an urgent need for further study in understanding the lives of children with learning disabilities and other neurodevelopmental disorders in India about which there still exists limited social awareness.

DEFICIT-BASED PERSPECTIVE OF DISABILITY

In the Indian society, parents focus on academic achievement of their children from the day they start school. With the increasing cut-throat competition, the actual abilities of children go unnoticed. The effect-oriented theorists stress on the discrepancy between intellectual ability and actual ability when talking about learning disorders or other mild developmental disorders. This discrepancy can create a lot of tension in a family where the parents' expectations are not met by the children. The availability and understanding of special education is not as widespread in our country. Due to the lack of awareness, many children with the disabilities are pushed to achieve what other children of the same age can. Such pressure may cause high level of anxiety in these children while completing a task. Failure to fulfil the demands leads to low self-esteem and low self-confidence in such children.

Childhood neurodevelopmental disorders like learning disability and ADHD wherein the child has the required cognitive capacity to understand the discrepancy between one's endeavours and actual academic achievement can leave them feeling incompetent. Academic failures lead to development of negative academic self-perception. This further hinders the individual from believing in one's ability to overcome obstacles thereby they lack the needed motivation and determination to strive harder towards reaching their goals. Damaged self-esteem causes the individual to attribute all failures to oneself which prevents them from acknowledging their other non-academic strengths (Tabassam & Grainger, 2002). Further, unfavourable feedbacks and lack of support from significant others at home and school, aggravate their hardships. Hence, negative self-views that are developed out of experiences with constant personal failures and social rejections, lower their self-esteem causing many to socially withdraw (Raskind, Margalit, & Higgins, 2006).

In a study conducted by Caroll and Iles in 2006, it was found that students with learning disability experienced higher levels of stress compared to those without a learning disability. Erikson had theorized that children need to acquire a balance between a positive self-image and feelings of inferiority for healthy development which such children fail to achieve. Children with dyslexia also have problems with oral language even in their adolescence. This may cause difficulty in forming new relationships with peers (Elksnin & Elksnin, 2004). Inability to form and maintain social relationships adds to their social immaturity. Clinical observations reveal that children with learning disability may exhibit the same kind of difficulty in remembering sequence of events. This may hinder the child's ability to learn from previous experiences and mature over time (Social and Emotional Problems Related to Dyslexia, 2004). Many of the emotional problems caused by learning disorder occur out of frustration with school or social situations. Discrepancy between the expectation of independence and the child's learned dependence causes an internal conflict. The adolescent then uses his anger to break away from those people on whom he feels so dependent (Social and Emotional Problems Related to Dyslexia, 2004). Little emphasis is given to understanding the causal factors of failure or inability to achieve what is expected in our society.

Research conducted by Gitanjali Sharma (2004) also found a significant difference between children with learning disabilities and those without learning disabilities on certain personality factors (Sharma, 2004). This study also indicated certain maladaptive tendencies in the personality dispositions of those with learning disorders which may worsen with age (Sharma, 2004). This reiterates the importance of screening children for dyslexia or other learning disorders at an early age.

Therefore, children and adolescents with physical or developmental disabilities are found to report greater mental health problems than those without disorder. Constant exposure to stressful life challenges at home and school lead to mental health problems. These products of social and academic inadequacies, further attenuate their general functioning and well-being (Emerson & Hatton, 2007; Herring et al., 2006; Wilson, Armstrong, Furrie, & Walnut, 2009). Hence, the disorder-related deficits account for innumerable psychosocial and academic difficulties that children with disabilities need to encounter on daily basis.

CAN ERADICATION OF DEFICITS ALONE PROMOTE WELL-BEING?

In the past, studies and interventions on children and adolescents with disabilities like specific learning disability and intellectual disability, focused primarily on correcting unfavourable environmental influences and disorder related deficits of individuals in order to promote their well-being (Niemiec et al., 2017; Ramaa, 2007). A positive and nurturing environment of growth is often created by the child's larger community which includes his parents, teachers and peers. Support from their significant others develop the necessary environmental and internal assets that promote general well-being (Damon, 2004). Environmental assets include those facilities and skills that are provided by the society to the young people in the form of support, empowerment, programmes and communities that contribute towards their development. Whereas internal assets include personal values, learning styles, social competencies, positive identity and attributes which also equally help young people to reach their highest potentials (CORE, 2018). Hence, though external factors play an important role in the development of children and adolescents. Several internal attributes and strengths of the child can also function as a buffer against stressors of life. According to Carl Rogers (as cited in Ismail & Turkey, 2015) development of an individual greatly depended on his sense of self. He emphasized on an innate tendency found in every human being that causes him to strive towards achieving his highest potentials.

However, this aspect is often undermined and ignored while dealing with individuals with a disability. Their well-being and level of functioning is usually measured according to the extent to which disorder related difficulties and unfavourable environmental support is rectified. This deficit-oriented approach towards individuals with disability overemphasizes the role of external factor and disregards the strengths of the individuals' personal attributes. Individuals are appeared to play a passive rather than an active role in their development.

However, in reality it may not be possible to eradicate all difficulties to create a completely positive environment for these children to develop. It may not be possible to ensure these children receive unconditional support and encouragement from their significant others. There also may be no possibility of overcoming their academic related deficits too. It is a known fact that individuals with any form of disability must continually struggle with their social/academic competencies and their associated psychosocial challenges through life. Hence, it is of greater importance to help these children identify other non-academic strengths and personal assets. Awareness of these could compensate for their academic incompetence which is often overemphasized in Indian societies. This would enable them to maintain a positive self-concept despite their daily challenges and struggles (Bear & Minke, 1996).

ROLE OF CHARACTER STRENGTHS IN POSITIVE DEVELOPMENT

Research literature have indicated instances wherein children and adolescents who have a disability with average cognitive abilities such as visual disability/learning disorder were aware of their disorders but were still able to selectively focus their attention on their non- academic competencies and encouraging feedbacks which helped them maintain positive feelings towards oneself and their challenging environment. These children were also found to maintain a positive self-concept by comparing oneself to similar peers. They viewed themselves as active agents of change and remain resilient (Bear & Minke, 1996; Lifshitz, Hen, & Weisse, 2007).

This ideology was highlighted and proposed by Garmezy and colleagues (as cited in Shean, 2015) in their works on resilience. Their works indicated that individuals possess personal attributes or strengths that can coexist with external stressors, enabling them to remain resilient. Though stress lowers competence, the presence of character strengths or attributes could reduce the degree of effect stress has on the individual, thereby enabling them to thrive despite all challenges and difficulties.

Individuals with disabilities are also exposed to innumerable stressors at home and school due to their condition-related deficit. These often cause psychosocial problems, increase stress levels and lead to negative self-views that adversely impact their overall well-being. However, as stated in the model, if the adolescents are aware and make use of their innate character strengths or personal attributes, the negative impact of all these stressors could be recompensed by their strengths, enabling them to remain resilient and thereby improving their well-being.

EMPIRICAL EVIDENCE

Though studies examining the role of character strengths among children with disabilities still remain an under-researched area. There has been considerable empirical evidence regarding the positive impact character strengths have on academic functioning and general well-being of children and adolescents who have no special needs. Character strengths were found to predominantly help in the development of positive attitudes towards academics, reduce stress and improve well-being of these children and adolescents.

Examining the benefits brought about by character strength use, Shoshani and Slone (2012) carried out a study to understand the school adjustment of adolescents during their transition to middle school which is marked by several stressful changes. The aim of the study was to analyse the association between strength use, subjective well-being and adjustment in school. The results of the regression analysis showed that character strengths significantly predicted achievement, improvement in academic performance and overall well-being. Therefore, despite all the challenges and difficulties adolescents encounter during the phase of transition to middle school, character strengths helped them to cope successfully and thereby protect their well-being.

In 2015, a study conducted by Li and Liu also showed how character strengths enabled adolescents to withstand several stressors. This study examined a sample of adolescents character strengths related to three domains namely relationship, conscientiousness and vitality. It attempted to analyse if there existed a relationship between strengths, psychological stress and psychological symptoms. The results of the study indicated that character strengths use differed between males and females, urban and rural setting, and among different types of family. Results of the regression analysis indicated that character strengths moderated the relationship between psychological stress and symptoms. Therefore, according to this study, greater usage of character strengths lead to reduced stress in the domains of study, family and social life, and development, whereas psychological symptoms were found to be negatively correlated with stress.

Abed (2016) conducted a strength-based intervention study to examine the role of character strengths in improving the self-concept of children with learning disorders. The sample of the study comprised of children belonging to the age groups of 12 to 15 years. During the pretest, the self-concept of participants of both control and intervention groups were assessed by the administration of a self-report scale. This provided information regarding the degree to which the child perceived himself having problems in the domains of emotional, behavioural and social functioning. The strength-based intervention was provided to the experimental group in an attempt to improve their self-concepts through the awareness of their character strengths. The results of the posttest indicated there was no significant difference in the overall self-concept of the two groups. However, the intervention was found to bring about an improvement in the self-concept of the children only with regard to how competent they felt while dealing with problems related to their emotions and peers. It changed their perceptions regarding their difficulties, making them more resilient. They reported experiencing reduced distress, and their difficulties caused no perceived hindrance to their daily functioning.

Emphasizing on the positive impact of character strength use on life satisfaction, Douglass and Duffy (2014) conducted a study on 224 undergraduate participants. The results of the study indicated that greater strength use was significantly associated with higher levels of life satisfaction. Self-esteem was found to mediate this relationship partially thereby implying higher self-esteem strengthens the link between strength use and life satisfaction. Finally, positive affect was found to function as a significant moderator to the association between self-esteem and life satisfaction.

Addressing the influence character strengths have on school-related performance and feelings, a study was carried out on a sample of adolescents between the age groups of 10 to 14 years. Weber, Wagner and Ruch (2014) based this study on a theoretical model of well-being called the engine model of well-being which emphasized that well-being was enhanced through the interaction between inputs (characteristic traits), process (emotional reactions) and output (accomplishments). The aim of this study was to examine the interaction between character strengths, feelings related to school and school-related performance and accomplishments. The results of the study indicated that character strengths were significantly associated with positive school-related feelings. Zest, perseverance, social intelligence and love for learning were strongly associated with positive school-related feelings. Therefore, character strength use is likely to reduce negative feeling related to school. Further, the study also showed that positive school-related affect was significantly associated with better school functioning and achievement which was assessed by teachers and self-ratings.

The results of studies that examined the impact of character strengths on children and adolescents verified the positive influence it had on their self-perceptions, ability to withstand stress, attitude towards academic struggles and general well-being. Children with academic difficulties were found to maintain a positive attitude towards themselves and their lives by focusing more on their non-academic strengths. Though most of these studies involved typical children, the results indicate that character strengths serve as a protective factor for children while encountering stressful challenges. It enabled them to remain resilient thereby promoting their well-being in the midst of life struggles.

SIGNIFICANCE OF ADOPTING A STRENGTH-BASED PERSPECTIVE

Adoption of a strength-based perspective towards children and adolescents with various forms of disability could help them perceive themselves in a positive light despite their incompetencies in certain domains. Teaching these individuals to focus on their strengths rather than their deficits could protect their self-concept and thereby enhance their general well-being (Abed, 2016). The findings of strength-based intervention studies also echo the tremendous benefits the awareness and use of character strengths have on the overall functioning of the child (Proctora et al., 2011).

Therefore, by adopting a strength-based approach towards helping children with a disorder, both parents and teachers could support them towards achieving their highest potential. Hence, it is important for parents and teachers to first correct faulty attitudes and perceptions they hold about the disabilities, so that they can provide the needed assistance for the development of strengths in these children.

The science of character strengths could bring about change in the current intervention programmes that often limit themselves towards eliminating academic difficulties of the child rather than focusing on his overall development. For children with learning disabilities for instance, the early identification and awareness of their non-academic strengths plays a crucial role in helping them overcome the negative effects of their disorder-related challenges. This insight enables them to attribute their academic difficulties solely to their condition thereby helping them maintain a positive self-image (Bear & Minke, 1996). Therefore, there is an urgent requirement for more strength-based interventions as this has a positive impact on the feelings, thoughts and behaviours of the child. Positive self-views enable him also develop a more positive approach towards learning which motivate him to thrive and function more efficiently in school (Weber et al., 2014).

Creating positive classroom environment where teachers constantly work towards building character strengths of children along with their academic learning could greatly benefit children who are struggling with disabilities. Helping these children to measure their self-worth based on their character strengths, rather than just their academic achievement and perceived social approval, could make them more resilient. It would enable the individual to perceive himself as an active agent of change who is capable of shaping his own development. This feeling of independence could motivate them and give them the needed confidence to thrive despite unfavourable life circumstances.

Therefore, the emergence of the study of character strengths in the field of positive psychology are creating ripples of change in the approaches that have been adopted by researchers and practitioners in understanding the life experiences of individuals with disabilities. Providing them the needed insight and opportunity towards becoming self-actualized individuals who are able to thrive independently despite challenges and difficulties.

SUMMARY

This chapter highlights the need for adopting a strength-based approach towards children and adolescents with disabilities. Previous research focused on improving their level of functioning and well-being only through the elimination of their disorder-related deficits rather than developing their existing strengths. Many disabilities like visual/hearing impairment or learning disorders are conditions that cause lifelong difficulties wherein despite every intervention, social and academic excellence always remain challenging to achieve. This discrepancy between one's efforts and achievement can affect the child's self-confidence if sufficient support and feedbacks are not provided by parents, teachers and peers. However, most often children are not provided all the necessary help from their significant others at home and school. In such a circumstance where it is not possible to eradicate unfavourable external factors, building the innate strengths of these children could help them withstand all stressful challenges. Although there is strong empirical evidence on the role of character strengths in the positive development of typical children, there is limited work done on children with disabilities. By shifting the focus from deficits towards development of character strengths, researchers and practitioners can create a more positive environment of growth for these children. Helping the children to look beyond their inadequacies could enable them to base their self-worth on their innate strengths rather than external support. This self-awareness would help them strive towards reaching their highest potentials in the midst of challenges and struggles thereby protecting their general well-being.

RECOMMENDATIONS

The review of evidences indicate that the non-academic strengths of children with disabilities are neglected. The paper highlights the strengths of positive psychology specifically character strength-based interventions in working with children and adolescents with disabilities. These strengths or assets if nurtured from a very early age could help the individual to overcome the challenges of the disability he/she has. School-based interventions both at macro and micro levels could enhance children's experiences. The reflections from the paper could be applied to general population where the individual faces challenges in day-to-day life.

REFERENCES

Abed, G. M. (2016). Inculcating positive thinking in the self-concept of children with learning difficulties. *i-manager's Journal on Educational Psychology, 101*(31).

American Psychiatric Association. (2013). *Diagnostic and statistical manual of mental disorders* (5th ed.). Washington, DC: American Psychiatric Association. Retrieved from https://www.psychiatry.org/File%20Library/About-APA/Organization-Documents-Policies/APA-Annual-Report-2011.pdf

Bear, G., & Minke, M. K. (1996). Positive bias in maintenance of self-worth among children with LD. *Learning Disability Quarterly, 19*(1), 23–32. Retrieved from http://www.jstor.org/stable/1511050

Carroll, J. M., & Iles, J. E. (2006). An assessment of anxiety levels in dyslexic students in higher education. *British Journal of Educational Psychology, 76*(3), 651–662.

Connors, C., & Stalker, K. (2007). Children's experiences of disability: Pointers to a social model of childhood disability. *Disability & Society, 22*(1), 19–33.

Core, S. H. S. (2018, May 21). *40 Developmental Assets*. Retrieved from http://www.youtherie.com/the-assets

Cortiella, C., & Horowitz, S. (2014). The state of learning disabilities: Facts, trends and issues. Retrieved from https://www.ncld.org/wp-content/uploads/2014/11/2014-State-of-LD.pdf

Damon, W. (2004). What is positive youth development? *The Annals of the American Academy of Political and Social Science*, *591*, 13–24. Retrieved from http://www.jstor.org/stable/4127632

Douglass, P. R., & Duffy, D. R. (2014). Strengths use and life satisfaction: A moderated mediation approach. *Journal of Happiness Studies*, *16*, 619–632. doi:10.1007/s10902-014-9525-4

Emerson, E., & Hatton, C. (2007). Mental health of children and adolescents with intellectual disabilities in Britain. *The British Journal of Psychiatry*, *191*(6), 493–499.

Ferguson, P. M. (2002). A place in the family: An historical interpretation of research on parental reactions to having a child with a disability. *The Journal of Special Education*, *36*(3), 124–131.

Herring, S., Gray, K., Taffe, J., Tonge, B., Sweeney, D., & Einfeld, S. (2006). Behaviour and emotional problems in toddlers with pervasive developmental disorders and developmental delay: Associations with parental mental health and family functioning. *Journal of Intellectual Disability Research*, *50*(12), 874–882.

Holmbeck, G. N., Johnson, S. Z., Wills, K. E., McKernon, W., Rose, B., Erklin, S., & Kemper, T. (2002). Observed and perceived parental overprotection in relation to psychosocial adjustment in preadolescents with a physical disability: The mediational role of behavioral autonomy. *Journal of Consulting and Clinical Psychology*, *70*(1), 96.

Ismail, H. A. N., & Turkey, T. M. (2015). Rediscovering Rogers's self theory and personality. *Journal of Educational, Health and Community Psychology*, *4*(3). Retrieved from https://www.researchgate.net/.../286456614

John, A., Sadasivan, A., Sukumaran, B., Bhola, P., David, N. J., & Manickam, L. S. S. (2013). Practice guidelines: Learning disability. *Indian Journal of Clinical Psychology*, *40*(1), 65–88. Retrieved from https://www.researchgate.net/profile/Poornima_Bhola/publication/259445180_Practice_Guidelines_Learning_Disability/links/00b4952fccb6e34be1000000/Practice-Guidelines-Learning-Disability.pdf

Jones, J., & Passey, J. (2005). Family adaptation, coping and resources: Parents of children with developmental disabilities and behaviour problems. *Journal on Developmental Disabilities*, *11*(1), 31–46.

Li, T. T., & Liu, X. M. (2016). Role of character strengths and stress in psychological symptoms among Chinese secondary vocational school students. *Psychology*, *7*, 52–61. Retrieved from http://dx.doi.org/10.4236/psych.2016.71007

Lifshitz, H., Hen, I., & Weisse, I. (2007). Self-concept, adjustment to blindness, and quality of friendship among adolescents with visual impairments. *Journal of Visual Impairment & Blindness*, *101*(2), 96.

Ministry of Statistics and Programme Implementation, Government of India. *Disabled persons in India: A statistical profile 2016*. Retrieved from http://mospi.nic.in/sites/default/files/publication_reports/Disabled_persons_in_India_2016.pdf

Narayan, L. C., & John, T. (2017). The Rights of Persons with Disabilities Act, 2016: Does it address the needs of the persons with mental illness and their families. *Indian Journal of Psychiatry, 59*, 17–20. Retrieved from https://www.ncbi.nlm.nih.gov/pmc/articles/PMC5419007/

National Center for Learning Disabilities. (2014). The state of learning disabilities: Emerging issues. Retrieved from https://www.ncld.org/wp-content/uploads/2014/11/2014-State-of-LD.pdf

Niemiec, M. R., Shrogen, A. K., & Wehmeyer, M. L. (2017). Character strengths and intellectual and developmental disability: A strengths-based approach from positive psychology. Retrieved from https://www.viacharacter.org/www/LinkClick.aspx?fileticket=GSd9m1ic80E%3D&portalid=0

Park, N., Peterson, C., & Seligman, M. E. (2004). Strengths of character and well-being. *Journal of Social and Clinical Psychology, 23*, 603–619. Retrieved from http://www.viacharacter.org/blog/wp-content/uploads/2013/12/Character-strengths-well-being-Park-Peterson-Seligman-2004.pdf

Proctora, C., Tsukayamab, E., Woodc, M. A., Maltbyd, J., Eadese, F. J., & Linleyf, A. P. (2011). Strengths gym: The impact of a character strengths-based intervention on the life satisfaction and well-being of adolescents. *The Journal of Positive Psychology, 6*(5), 377–388. doi:10.1080/17439760.2011.594079

Ramaa, S. (2000). Two decades of research on learning disabilities in India. *Dyslexia, 6*(4), 268–283. Retrieved from www.readcube.com

Raskind, H. M., Margalit, M., & Higgins, L. E. (2006). 'MY LD': Children's voices on the Internet. *Learning Disability Quarterly, 29*(4), 253–268. Retrieved from http://www.jstor.org/stable/30035553

Sharma, G. (2004). A comparative study of the personality characteristics of primary-school students with learning disabilities and their nonlearning disabled peers. *Learning Disability Quarterly, 27*(3), 127–140.

Shean, M. (2015). *Current theories relating to resilience and young people: A literature review*. Melbourne: Victorian Health Promotion Foundation. Retrieved from http://evidenceforlearning.org.au/assets/Grant-Round-II-Resilience/Current-theories-relating-to-resilience-and-young-people.pdf

Shoshani, A., & Slone, M. (2012). Middle school transition from the strengths perspective: Young adolescents' character strengths, subjective well-being, and school adjustment. *Journal of Happiness Studies, 14*, 1163–1181. doi:10.1007/s10902-012-9374-y

Tabassam, W., & Grainger, J. (2002). Self-concept, attributional style and self-efficacy beliefs of students with learning disabilities with and without attention deficit hyperactivity disorder. *Learning Disability Quarterly, 25*(2), 141–151. Retrieved from http://www.jstor.org/stable/1511280

UNICEF. (2013). *Children and young people with disabilities fact sheet*. Retrieved from https://www.unicef.org/disabilities/files/Factsheet_A5__Web_NEW.pdf

Weber, M., Wagner, L., & Ruch, W. (2014). Positive feelings at school: On the relationships between students' character strengths, school-related affect, and school functioning. *Journal of Happiness Studies, 17,* 341–355. doi:10.1007/s10902-014-9597-1

Wilson, A., Armstrong, C., Furrie, A., & Walnut, E. (2009). The mental health of Canadians with self-reported learning disabilities. *Journal of Learning Disabilities, 42*(1). doi:10.1177/0022219408326216

World Health Organization. (2011). *World report on disability*. Retrieved from https://www.unicef.org/protection/World_report_on_disability_eng.pdf

Chapter 20

Character Strengths and Virtues
Manifestation and Links with Positive Youth Development in Greece

Sophie Leontopoulou*

INTRODUCTION

This study, embedded in the tradition of positive developmental psychology, set out to examine the scope and impact of character strengths and virtues, and other emotional and cognitive assets on positive youth development. In particular, it sought to fathom the interplay between character strengths and virtues, creativity, optimism and self-efficacy in Greek children. Positive education and, in particular, character strengths and virtues research in education is still in its infancy in Greece and much is needed in the way of understanding the factors that

---

* This chapter builds on the work of D. Brasinika, E. Xenitidou and L. Sidiropoulou, students at the University of Ioannina, to whom many thanks are extended. Their undergraduate thesis was completed under the supervision of the author, and informed parts of this work (data collection and input). All statistical analyses were reworked by the author for the purposes of this study.

foster character strengths development, their interconnections and the pathways linking individual character strengths and virtues to specific positive developmental outcomes.

There are different ways to look at the relations between character strengths and virtues, and other psychosocial and emotional developmental assets. Optimism and self-efficacy can be conceptualized as assets or resources, linking character strengths to psychosocial outcomes, such as creativity. Alternatively, along with creativity, they can be seen as positive developmental outcomes themselves. More broadly, optimism, self-efficacy and creativity can also be considered personal strengths. This is why a discussion of the theoretical origins and empirical measurement of character strengths, virtues and other individual assets is critical in order to clarify the concepts and demonstrate the importance of understanding them.

Strengths, Virtues and Other Assets: Links with Positive Psychological Functioning

The construct of character strengths was developed within the paradigm of positive psychology by Peterson and Seligman (2004). The authors proposed the Values in Action (VIA) classification, which organizes 24 distinct character strengths under six virtues: wisdom and knowledge (curiosity, love of learning, judgement, creativity, perspective), courage (bravery, industry, integrity, zest), humanity (love, kindness, social intelligence); justice (citizenship, fairness, leadership), temperance (forgiveness, modesty, prudence, self-control), and transcendence (appreciation of beauty, gratitude, hope, humour, spirituality). They are thought to represent positive characteristics that go beyond the Big Five personality traits (Haslam, Bain, & Neal, 2004). Researchers claim that they allow persons to function optimally and pursue valued outcomes (Linley, Joseph, Harrington, & Wood, 2006); yet others suggest that they are intrinsically valued (Peterson & Seligman, 2004). They were found to relate to a wide array of positive psychosocial outcomes, such as happiness and life satisfaction, positive emotions, subjective well-being and resilience (Hutchinson, Stuart, & Pretorius, 2011; Lee, Foo, Adams, Morgan, & Frewen, 2015; Leontopoulou &

Triliva, 2012; Peterson, Ruch, Beermann, Park, & Seligman, 2007; Wood, Linley, Maltby, Kashdan, & Hurling, 2011). Demographic differences in character strengths, including gender, age and nationality, are beginning to be explored. A recent meta-analysis (Heintz, Kramm, & Ruch, 2017) suggests that only small gender differences in character strengths exist, including higher scores for females in appreciation of beauty, excellence, kindness, love and gratitude.

Although creativity, one's ability to have novel, surprising and useful ideas or practical inventions (Boden, 2004), is included in the VIA as one of the character strengths that comprise the virtue of wisdom and knowledge, it has long been investigated independently as a positive personal characteristic/asset, either leading to or exemplifying positive psychosocial functioning. Recent research has identified pathways linking creative self-efficacy, optimism and original behaviour (Michael, Hou, & Fan, 2011) and creative self-efficacy and creative performance (Tierney & Farmer, 2011), also between creativity, optimism and different types of motivation (Icekson, Roskes, & Moran, 2014). Other studies discovered significant interaction effects between others' smiles and nodding and avoidance orientation (Fujiwara, Takemura, & Suzuki, 2017), while positive affect was found to mediate the relation between creativity and optimism (Rego, Sousa, Marques, & Cunha, 2012).

The concept of optimism has received a lot of research attention over the years. It is generally conceived as a generalized expectation that one's life experiences will have positive outcomes (Carver & Scheier, 1987). Optimism is thought to bear similarities to the character strength of hope and as such was found to relate to well-being (Magaletta & Oliver, 1999). Research has identified optimism's many benefits for individuals; in particular, optimistic children are better able to handle difficulties and to adapt, have higher school performance and a healthy social life, are better protected from risks, have better physical and mental health and tend to set targets for their life, which they try to achieve by different types of strategies (Μπούτρη, 2011). Furthermore, optimism is also known to relate to self-efficacy, a cognitive personal characteristic linked to positive psychological functioning and resilience (Karademas, 2006; Luszczynska, Gutiérrez-Doña, & Schwarzer, 2005; Μόττη-Στεφανίδη, Ντάλλα, Παπαθανασίου, Παυλόπ ουλος, & Τάκης, 2005).

Cultural and Demographic Issues

There are arguments for the cultural variability of many mental health variables, as culture likely influences the type and frequency of stressors and risks facing individuals, the acceptability of various responses to them, the availability and type of resources used to counter them and the expressions of positive outcomes (Calvete & Connor-Smith, 2006; Kitayama & Markus, 1999). Even in European societies, differences exist between northern and southern countries, such as the Mediterranean Greece, in an array of psychosocial variables with mental health implications (Petrogiannis, 2011). Such differences are exacerbated in situations of economic crises, such as the current severe crisis facing Greece since 2008. The effects of poverty and socio-economic disadvantage harshly impact children and adolescents, especially those from low and middle socio-economic backgrounds (Papanastasiou, Ntafouli, & Kourtidou, 2016), by undermining the protective factors that can lead to healthy physical and psychological development and by enhancing the risk factors that facilitate the emergence of mental disorders (Anagnostopoulos & Soumaki, 2012). Thus, a culturally embedded view of character strengths and virtues and other psychosocial assets, as well as positive psychological outcomes, is required in order to further understand the complex constellations of pathways leading to positive youth development.

Character strengths are conceptualized as being universally recognized and valued (Park & Peterson, 2006). Cross-cultural research seems to support the existence of character strengths and their prevalence in many countries, with kindness, honesty, gratitude and judgement prevailing, and prudence, modesty and self-regulation being the least prevalent character strengths in human beings (Park, Peterson, & Seligman, 2006). More recently, in a study of 10- to 12-year-olds in Argentina, the most commonly reported strengths were honesty/integrity and kindness/goodness, while love of learning, spirituality and prudence were least reported (Grinhauz & Castro Solano, 2015). Indian youths were found to consider love, gratitude, kindness, fairness and honesty as their highest strengths, with social responsibility (teamwork), perseverance, prudence and self-regulation as their lowest (Tripathi, Banu, & Mehrotra, 2015).

In terms of gender differences in character strengths, women's highest scores appear to lie on the strengths of honesty, kindness, love, gratitude and fairness, while men's on honesty, hope, humour, gratitude and curiosity. For women, life satisfaction seems to be best predicted by zest, gratitude, hope, appreciation of beauty/excellence and love, and by creativity, perspective, fairness, and humour for men (Brdar, Anic, & Rijavec, 2011). Women were also found to be higher on gratitude than men (Mann, 2014). Indian male youths scored higher on social strengths, while females scored higher on relational strengths (Tripathi et al., 2015). Similar findings were rendered by a study of 500+ Spanish adolescents, where females showed more prominent strengths relating to prosocial behaviour and peer relationships (Ferragut, 2014). In a different study of character strengths in youths, females typically scored higher on character strengths than males, while personality factors such as Big Five traits of agreeableness and openness were consistently more predictive of character strengths than demographic or well-being measures (Neto, Neto, & Furnham, 2014). In Greece, female university students scored higher in love than males; also, for both genders, higher scores on the virtues of wisdom, courage, temperance and transcendence were significantly associated with good mental health and well-being, while courage and justice were positively associated with physical health (Leontopoulou & Triliva, 2012). Overall, wisdom, courage and transcendence appeared to be the most salient among Greek youths' virtues, since these strengths were highly and positively correlated with the well-being subscales of environmental mastery, purpose in life and self-acceptance.

Current Study

This study aimed to document the ways character strengths and virtues are manifested (i.e., their prevalence and relations with other emotional and cognitive assets) in Greek children, in order to highlight how these are related and can lead to positive psychosocial and emotional youth development. It also sought to explore socio-demographic differences in an effort to map the ways gender, age and socio-economic factors relate to character strengths and virtues, and to other youth developmental assets. Finally, addressing cultural differences and assessing their potential impact on development was important for this study, since the identification of best practices and approaches for nurturing character strengths in children needs to be culturally relevant in order to be sustainable, impactful and resource effective.

Method

Sample and Procedure

About 282 students at the last three grades of primary schools at the Prefecture of Ioannina, a city in northwestern Greece, participated in this study. The sample was equally distributed for gender— 29.8 per cent studied at the 4th grade, 31.6 per cent at the 5th grade and 22.5 per cent at the 6th grade. About 22.5 per cent originated from lower socio-economic status (SES) families, 28.2 per cent from middle SES families and 49.3% from higher SES families. About 86.1 per cent had at least one sibling.

Primary school principals and class teachers were briefed on the aims, materials and procedures of the study. Once school involvement was secured, parental consent forms were distributed to students during class. After all signed consent forms were returned, students completed a questionnaire battery during two class periods. Teachers were not present at completion, but researchers were available for clarifications.

Materials

The questionnaire battery compiled for this study consisted of two parts. The first one included questions on participants' demographic characteristics, such as age, gender and SES. The second part comprised the four questionnaires mentioned in the following paragraphs.

Measurement of *character strengths* was based on the widely used VIA instrument (VIA Children's Strengths Survey [VIA-CSS]; Seligman, 2002). The scale consists of 48 positively and negatively phrased items, two for each signature strength, which they fall into six subscales (wisdom and knowledge, courage, humanity, justice, temperance and transcendence). This 5-point Likert-type scale (from 'very much like me' to 'very much unlike me') suggests that high scores indicate higher levels of each strength. Cronbach's α for this study was $\alpha = 0.70$.

Creativity was measured using the Kogan and Wallach (1965) Creativity Test. The test comprises two parts, a verbal and a visual one. The verbal part consists of three sub-tests, namely naming objects, alternative uses and similarities between objects. The visual part consists of two sub-tests, lines and patterns. Each correct answer in the verbal part receives one point, while each answer in the visual part receives three points. Higher scores on the test suggest higher creativity. Cronbach's α for the study was $\alpha = 0.90$.

Optimism levels of students were measured using the The Youth Life Orientation Test - YLOT (Ey et al., 2005). The scale consists of 19 items scored on a 4-point Likert-type scale (from 'true for me' to 'not true for me'). A low score suggests high optimism. Cronbach's α for this study was $\alpha = 0.80$.

Self-efficacy was measured with the Children's Self-Efficacy for Peer Interaction Scale (Wheeler & Ladd, 1982). The scale includes 20 items, scored on a 4-point Likert-type scale (from 'very difficult' to 'very easy'). Self-efficacy is measured for two types of situations, namely, conflict and non-conflict ones. Higher scores on the scale indicate higher self-efficacy. The study's Cronbach's α was $\alpha = 0.81$.

RESULTS

The Manifestation of Character Strengths and Virtues in Greek Children

Table 20.1 shows the means and standard deviations (SDs) for character strengths and virtues for the total sample and also for, gender, age and SES. As regards the prevalence of character strengths and virtues in the total sample, the top five strengths were creativity, love of learning, kindness, judgement and zest, while modesty, curiosity, forgiveness, love and hope were the bottom five strengths. In terms of virtues, courage was highest, followed by humanity, transcendence, wisdom and knowledge, justice, with temperance being the least prevalent virtue in the total sample. When considering gender differences, for females the five highest character strengths were kindness, love of learning, creativity, zest and prudence, with love, forgiveness, hope, curiosity and modesty being the lowest strengths. For males, creativity, love of learning, judgement, kindness and gratitude were most prominent, with love,

Table 20.1 Means and Standard Deviations (SDs) for Character Strengths and Virtues and for Creativity, Optimism and Self-efficacy for the Total Sample, for Gender, Grade and SES

Character Strengths	Total		Gender				Grade						SES					
			Females		Males		4th		5th		6th		Lower		Middle		Higher	
	Mean	SD	Mean	SD	Mean	SD	Mean	SD	Mean	SD	Mean	SD	Mean	SD	Mean	SD	Mean	SD
Curiosity	3.09	0.90	4.30	0.83	4.11	1.01	4.16	0.92	4.21	0.83	4.32	0.65	3.19	0.89	2.98	0.96	3.10	0.87
Love of learning	4.15	0.93	4.27	0.88	4.02	0.97	4.14	0.90	4.16	0.87	4.17	0.83	3.88	1.12	4.24	0.86	4.21	0.86
Judgement	4.05	0.85	4.23	0.76	3.99	0.90	4.14	0.95	4.13	1.04	4.11	0.95	4.00	0.81	4.10	0.95	4.05	0.82
Creativity	4.17	0.89	4.17	0.95	3.97	0.96	4.09	0.82	4.11	1.10	4.05	0.95	3.96	1.07	4.26	0.89	4.22	0.79
Perspective	3.77	0.98	4.17	0.94	3.96	1.09	4.06	1.09	4.00	1.07	4.03	0.87	3.48	1.07	3.99	0.93	3.77	0.94
Bravery	3.59	1.06	4.13	0.96	3.92	1.16	4.02	1.04	3.91	1.03	4.00	1.06	3.42	1.06	3.75	1.01	3.58	1.09
Industry	3.90	1.03	4.12	0.69	3.87	1.02	4.02	0.99	3.91	1.11	3.99	1.03	3.61	1.11	3.88	1.12	4.03	0.92
Integrity	3.91	1.19	4.12	0.80	3.86	0.98	3.94	0.88	3.90	1.00	3.98	0.70	3.78	1.32	3.85	1.19	4.01	1.14
Zest	4.05	1.07	4.10	0.93	3.80	1.17	3.90	0.93	3.87	0.96	3.98	1.05	4.00	1.14	4.08	1.05	4.05	1.05
Love	3.50	1.06	4.08	0.95	3.79	1.11	3.89	1.23	3.84	0.91	3.97	0.81	3.23	0.97	3.59	1.02	3.57	1.11
Kindness	4.14	0.91	4.06	0.93	3.78	1.00	3.88	1.09	3.83	1.12	3.96	0.91	3.89	0.96	4.17	.89	4.22	0.88

(Continued)

Table 20.1 (Continued)

Character Strengths	Total		Gender				Grade						SES					
			Females		Males		4th		5th		6th		Lower		Middle		Higher	
	Mean	SD	Mean	SD	Mean	SD	Mean	SD	Mean	SD	Mean	SD	Mean	SD	Mean	SD	Mean	SD
Social intelligence	3.61	1.04	3.92	0.96	3.78	1.02	3.85	0.94	3.78	1.02	3.92	1.15	3.41	1.16	3.51	1.09	3.75	0.94
Citizenship	3.66	1.16	3.90	0.89	3.77	0.97	3.83	1.16	3.77	0.61	3.91	0.84	3.60	1.16	3.66	1.20	3.68	1.14
Fairness	3.70	1.04	3.89	0.86	3.76	0.51	3.83	0.93	3.76	1.40	3.90	0.88	3.68	1.10	3.62	1.07	3.76	1.00
Leadership	3.87	0.92	3.88	0.50	3.75	0.94	3.80	0.79	3.76	0.61	3.86	0.87	3.72	0.95	3.94	0.95	3.91	0.89
Forgiveness	3.38	1.12	3.88	0.80	3.75	0.77	3.80	0.58	3.76	1.16	3.85	0.82	3.35	1.06	3.41	1.19	3.37	1.12
Modesty	2.75	1.07	3.83	0.614	3.71	1.08	3.80	0.57	3.71	0.72	3.83	1.00	2.70	1.10	2.94	1.08	2.66	1.04
Prudence	3.98	1.04	3.80	1.01	3.70	0.56	3.74	0.99	3.70	1.13	3.81	0.51	3.80	1.05	3.85	1.14	4.13	0.97
Self-control	3.92	0.98	3.77	1.01	3.70	1.36	3.69	1.09	3.69	1.18	3.80	0.46	3.69	0.99	3.96	1.06	4.00	0.92
Appreciation of beauty	3.84	0.95	3.73	1.20	3.66	1.16	3.67	1.10	3.69	1.16	3.71	0.69	3.72	0.91	3.91	1.02	3.85	0.93
Gratitude	3.84	1.15	3.62	0.72	3.64	0.78	3.65	1.16	3.69	1.09	3.71	0.96	3.69	1.15	3.87	1.15	3.90	1.16
Hope	3.54	1.01	3.60	0.91	3.63	1.05	3.63	1.03	3.53	0.80	3.70	1.01	3.55	1.07	3.56	1.02	3.52	0.99

Humour	3.61	1.18	3.56	1.20	3.63	1.07	3.62	0.77	3.53	1.11	3.67	1.16	3.61	1.20	3.52	1.29	3.66	1.10
Spirituality	3.99	0.98	3.52	1.14	3.62	1.16	3.61	1.17	3.52	1.20	3.58	0.92	3.86	1.00	3.87	1.09	4.11	0.90
Virtues																		
Wisdom/Knowledge	3.79	0.54	3.44	1.15	3.56	0.97	3.50	1.04	3.47	1.08	3.51	1.23	3.63	.61	3.87	0.53	3.81	0.50
Courage	3.94	0.86	3.43	1.15	3.39	1.08	3.48	1.10	3.42	1.07	3.44	0.93	3.79	1.00	3.94	0.86	4.01	0.78
Humanity	3.81	0.79	3.36	0.51	3.34	0.61	3.41	1.12	3.31	0.56	3.40	0.58	3.56	0.75	3.88	0.77	3.89	0.79
Justice	3.63	0.75	3.30	0.98	3.32	1.10	3.33	0.54	3.26	1.10	3.31	1.17	3.54	0.79	3.57	0.78	3.71	0.71
Temperance	3.35	0.56	3.07	0.87	3.10	0.94	3.10	0.95	2.99	0.98	3.15	0.79	3.25	0.59	3.44	0.55	3.34	0.56
Transcendence	3.79	0.56	2.69	1.11	2.80	1.03	2.6845	1.06	2.75	1.09	2.80	1.07	3.67	0.56	3.77	0.55	3.86	0.56
Variables																		
Creativity	3.05	0.88	3.28	0.96	2.81	0.73	2.84	0.75	3.2	0.86	3.02	0.96	2.88	0.59	3.12	0.99	3.08	0.93
Optimism	1.86	0.45	1.77	0.42	1.95	0.47	1.91	0.37	1.7	0.42	1.91	0.53	1.99	0.42	1.92	0.46	1.78	0.45
Self-efficacy–Conflict	3.11	0.51	3.13	0.51	3.09	0.51	3.05	0.50	3.10	0.49	3.17	0.53	3.01	0.52	3.07	0.53	3.18	0.48
Self-efficacy–Non-conflict	3.06	0.60	3.09	0.50	3.04	0.69	3.06	0.79	3.03	0.47	3.09	0.53	2.92	0.51	2.99	0.47	3.16	0.68

bravery, forgiveness, curiosity and modesty the least prominent. The ordering of the virtues for females was courage, wisdom/knowledge, humanity, transcendence, justice and temperance. For males, courage remained first in order, followed by transcendence, humanity, wisdom/ knowledge, justice and temperance. Few age differences, as portrayed by differences in the configuration of strengths and virtues in students at the 4th, 5th and 6th grades were found. In particular, while creativity, love of learning and kindness all featured in the top five character strengths for all grades, judgement and zest which were included in the top five strengths in the 4th and 5th grade were replaced by integrity and spirituality in the 6th grade, indicating a developmental change in children at the onset of adolescence. As regards virtues, courage was first for all grades and temperance last. With respect to socio-economic class differences, creativity, love of learning and kindness were among the top five strengths for all participants; however, judgement and zest were replaced by prudence and spirituality for students from the highest SES backgrounds. In the lowest places for all SES groups were modesty, curiosity, forgiveness, love and social intelligence, with the exception of hope, instead of social intelligence being in the bottom five strengths for children from the highest SES backgrounds. As far as virtues were concerned, courage was highest, and justice and temperance lowest for participants from all SES backgrounds (for more details, see Table 20.1).

Relations Between the Study Variables

Means and SDs for creativity, optimism and self-efficacy, both in conflict and non-conflict situations are shown in Table 20.1. Correlations for the total sample between these variables and character strengths are shown in Table 20.2, and between these and virtues in Table 20.3. Character strengths appeared significantly correlated with each other, especially within each virtue (for details, see Table 20.2). Virtues were all significantly correlated with each other, with wisdom/knowledge in particular showing high correlations with other virtues and as high as 0.62 with humanity (see Table 20.3). To illustrate certain significant correlations between character strengths and virtues and the other study variables, creativity as measured with the Kogan and Wallach (1965) Creativity Test was significantly related to the character strength of

Table 20.2 Correlations Between Character Strengths and Creativity, Optimism and Self-efficacy for the Total Sample

	2	3	4	5	6	7	8	9	10	11	12	13	14	15	16	17	18	19	20	21	22	23	24	25	26	27	28
1. Curiosity	−.23c	0.06	0.27c	0.06	0.17a	0.12a	0.26c	0.21c	0.12a	0.30c	0.07	0.16b	0.19c	0.22c	−0.02	−0.26c	0.33c	0.07	−0.00	0.07	0.12a	0.10	0.07	−0.02	0.04	0.05	−0.01
2. Love of learning		0.39c	0.17a	0.16a	0.18b	0.26c	0.41c	0.23c	0.26c	0.23c	0.11a	0.20c	0.18c	0.14a	0.27c	−0.07	0.24c	0.04	0.11	0.19c	0.12a	0.11	0.25c	0.07	−0.01	0.09	0.04
3. Judgement			0.13a	0.15a	0.28c	0.37c	0.29c	0.31c	0.10	0.36c	−0.02	0.22c	0.27c	0.14a	0.27c	−0.07	0.24c	0.04	0.11	0.19c	0.12a	.11	0.25c	.07	−0.01	0.09	0.06
4. Creativity				0.33c	0.24c	0.33c	0.34c	0.41c	0.31c	0.29c	0.34c	0.12a	0.19b	0.30c	0.09	−0.03	0.21c	0.24c	0.03	0.06	0.07	−0.02	0.01	0.12c	0.01	0.08	0.00
5. Perspective					0.21c	0.17b	0.13c	0.22c	0.26c	0.40c	0.23c	0.38c	0.33c	0.27c	0.07	0.22c	0.15a	0.09	0.14a	0.00	0.15a	0.04	0.13a	0.11	−0.03	0.12a	0.14a
6. Bravery						0.34c	0.21c	0.21c	0.18b	0.32c	0.32c	0.26c	0.25c	0.38c	0.27c	0.10	−0.11	0.21c	0.06	0.44c	0.10	0.17b	0.02	0.29c	0.12a	−0.12a	0.04	0.09
7. Industry							0.47c	0.35c	0.10	0.36c	0.26c	0.15b	0.32c	0.28c	0.22c	−0.11	0.22c	0.29c	0.17c	0.16b	−0.15a	0.13c	0.33c	0.11	−0.04	−0.03	−0.03
8. Integrity								0.44c	0.17b	0.35c	0.26c	0.20c	0.32c	0.33c	.31c	−0.12a	0.31c	0.15c	0.24c	0.21c	0.11	0.01	0.32c	0.14c	0.00	0.03	−0.07
9. Zest									0.13c	0.31c	0.16b	0.094	0.27c	0.18c	0.17a	0.00	0.12b	0.17b	0.14a	0.05	0.01	0.00	0.09	0.05	0.03	0.12a	0.15a
10. Love										0.27c	0.19c	0.18c	0.16b	0.25c	−0.05	0.00	0.24c	0.05	0.15b	0.19c	0.12c	0.25c	0.18b	0.09	−0.02	0.04	0.00
11. Kindness											0.27c	0.36c	0.31c	0.44c	0.10	−0.18c	0.30c	0.27c	0.29c	0.25c	0.13c	0.24c	0.26v	0.14c	−0.12c	0.08	0.14a
12. Social intelligence												0.16b	0.26c	0.31c	0.12c	0.01	0.21c	0.06	0.17c	0.02	0.00	0.11	0.13c	0.06	−0.11	0.02	−0.04
13. Citizenship													0.24c	0.24c	0.20b	−0.10	0.19b	0.05	0.08	0.15c	0.42c	0.10	0.20c	0.04	−0.03	0.05	0.12a
14. Fairness														0.19b	0.100	0.01	0.38c	.05	0.28c	0.23c	0.22c	0.06	0.41c	0.05	−0.04	0.05	0.02
15. Leadership															−0.019	0.01	0.37c	0.13c	0.23c	0.38c	0.13c	0.10	0.24c	0.08	−0.05	0.03	0.09

(Continued)

Table 20.2 (Continued)

	2	3	4	5	6	7	8	9	10	11	12	13	14	15	16	17	18	19	20	21	22	23	24	25	26	27	28
16. Forgiveness															—	−0.17[b]	−0.07	0.01	0.16[b]	0.05	−0.01	−0.19[c]	0.14[a]	0.05	−0.04	0.02	−0.03
17. Modesty																—	−0.10	−0.10	−0.20[b]	−0.06	−0.02	−0.12[a]	−0.04	−0.07	−0.01	0.04	−0.04
18. Prudence																	—	0.09	0.13[a]	0.36[c]	0.14[a]	0.07	0.31[c]	0.14[a]	−0.11	0.10	0.05
19. Self-control																		—	0.15[a]	0.13[a]	0.04	0.21[c]	0.04	0.08	−0.09	−0.06	−0.04
20. Appreciation of beauty																			—	0.14[a]	0.13[a]	0.00	0.23[c]	0.09	−0.12[a]	0.07	0.13[a]
21. Gratitude																				—	0.35[c]	0.23[c]	0.38[c]	0.11[a]	0.02	0.02	0.03
22. Hope																					—	0.02	0.19[c]	0.05	0.01	0.07	0.02
23. Humour																						—	0.12[a]	0.06	−0.03	−0.03	0.04
24. Spirituality																							—	0.09	−0.03	0.03	−0.00
25. Creativity																								—	−0.17[b]	0.04	0.02
26. Optimism																									—	−0.33[c]	−0.32[c]
27. Self-efficacy–Conflict																										—	0.55[c]
28. Self-efficacy–Non-conflict																											—

Notes: [a] $p < 0.05$, [b] $p < 0.01$, [c] $p < 0.001$.

Table 20.3 Correlations Between Virtues and Creativity, Optimism and Self-efficacy for the Total Sample

	Courage	Humanity	Justice	Temperance	Transcendence	Creativity	Optimism	Self-efficacy – Conflict	Self-efficacy – Non-Conflict
Wisdom/Knowledge	0.61***	0.62***	0.58***	0.31***	0.51***	0.15**	−0.04	0.12*	0.10
Courage		0.42***	0.45***	0.34***	0.38***	0.13*	−0.04	0.12*	0.10
Humanity			0.47***	0.25***	0.49***	0.16**	−0.07	0.08	0.06
Justice				0.41***	0.47***	0.08	−0.08	0.06	0.03
Temperance					0.19***	0.05	−0.09	0.07	−0.00
Transcendence						0.18**	−0.09	0.05	0.08
Creativity							−0.17**	0.04	0.02
Optimism								−0.33***	−0.32***
Self-efficacy–Conflict									0.55***

Notes: * $p < 0.05$, ** $p < 0.01$, *** $p < 0.001$.

creativity ($r=0.12$, $p<0.05$). Creativity was also related to bravery ($r=0.12$, $p<0.05$), integrity, kindness and prudence (for all correlations, $r=0.14$, $p<0.05$) and gratitude ($r=0.11$, $p<0.05$). Finally, creativity was related to optimism ($r=0.17$, $p<0.01$). Optimism was significantly correlated with bravery, kindness and appreciation of beauty (in all cases, $r=0.12$, $p<0.05$). Optimism was significantly, albeit modestly, with self-efficacy in conflict ($r=0.33$, $p<0.001$) and non-conflict ($r=0.32$, $p<0.001$) situations. Self-confidence in conflict situations was significantly correlated with perspective and zest (in both cases, $r=0.12$, $p<0.05$), while self-efficacy in non-conflict situations was significantly correlated with perspective and kindness (for both, $r=0.14$, $p<0.05$), zest ($r=0.15$, $p<0.05$), citizenship ($r=0.12$, $p<0.05$) and appreciation of beauty ($r=0.13$, $p<0.05$). The two self-efficacy scales were significantly correlated with each other ($r=0.55$, $p<0.001$). As far as correlations between virtues and the other study variables are concerned, creativity (Kogan and Wallach Creativity Test, 1965) was correlated significantly with wisdom/knowledge ($r=0.15$, $p<0.01$), courage ($r=0.13$, $p<0.05$), humanity ($r=0.16$, $p<0.01$) and transcendence ($r=0.18$, $p<0.01$). Optimism was not related to any of the virtues. Self-efficacy in conflict situations was significantly correlated with wisdom/knowledge and courage (in both cases, $r=0.12$, $p<0.05$), while self-efficacy in non-conflict situations was not related to any virtue.

Demographic Differences

Analyses carried out to explore any demographic differences between the study variables revealed the following patterning. In terms of gender differences in character strengths, females scored significantly higher than males in love of learning (t(280)=2.26, $p<0.05$), perspective (t(280)=2.31, $p<0.05$), bravery (t(280)=3.28, $p<0.001$), industry (t(280)=3.08, $p<0.01$), integrity (t(280)=3.07, $p<0.01$), zest (t(280)=1.98, $p<0.05$), kindness (t(279)=3.35, $p<0.001$), prudence (t(280)=3.08, $p<0.01$) and self-control (t(280)=2.46, p<0.01). Males scored higher than females only in citizenship (t(280)=−2.03, $p<0.05$) and hope (t(280)=−4.11, $p<0.001$). With respect to virtues, females exhibited less wisdom/knowledge and courage than males (t(280)=2.78, $p<0.01$ and (t(280)=3.45, $p<0.001$ respectively). Finally, females were significantly more creative (Kogan and Wallach Creativity Test, 1965) than males (t(280) = 4.52, $p < 0.001$), but also less optimistic (t(279) = −3.35, $p < 0.001$). Figure 20.1(a) displays selected gender differences in character strengths.

As far as age (grade) differences are concerned, differences were observed in the character strengths of judgement ($F(2, 279) = 3.36$, $p < 0.05$), where 5th graders scored highest, followed by 4th and 6th graders; creativity ($F(2, 279) = 3.19$, $p < 0.05$), where 6th graders scored highest, followed by 4th and 5th graders; and love ($F(2, 279) = 4.52$, $p < 0.01$), where 6th graders scored highest, followed by 4th and 5th graders. A single age difference was found for creativity (Kogan and Wallach Creativity Test, 1965. ($F(2, 279) = 5.24$, $p < 0.01$), where 5th graders scored highest, followed by 6th and 4th graders. See Figure 20.1(b) for selected age (grade) differences in character strengths.

The effects of any SES differences on the study variables were also explored. SES differences were revealed for the character strengths of love of learning ($F(2, 279) = 3.23$, $p < 0.05$), with children from middle and higher SES scoring higher than children from lower SES backgrounds, even though post-hoc tests failed to reveal any significant differences between children from any two types of SES backgrounds; perspective ($F(2, 279) = 4.55$, $p < 0.01$), where children from lower SES families scored significantly lower than those from middle SES families; industry ($F(2, 279) = 3.57$, $p < 0.05$), where children from higher SES families scored significantly higher than those from lower SES families; kindness ($F(2, 279) = 2.99$, $p < 0.05$), where children from higher SES families scored significantly higher than those from lower SES families; and social intelligence ($F(2, 279) = 2.88$, $p < 0.05$), with children from middle and lower SES scoring higher than children from higher SES backgrounds, even though post-hoc tests failed to reveal any significant differences between children from any two types of SES family backgrounds. SES differences were also revealed for the virtues of wisdom/knowledge ($F(2, 279) = 3.72$, $p < 0.05$), where children from middle SES families scored significantly higher than those from lower SES families; and humanity ($F(2, 279) = 4.20$, $p < 0.01$), where children from middle and higher SES families scored significantly higher than those from lower SES families. Finally, SES differences were revealed for optimism ($F(2, 279) = 5.73$, $p < 0.01$), where children from lower SES families scored significantly higher than those from higher SES

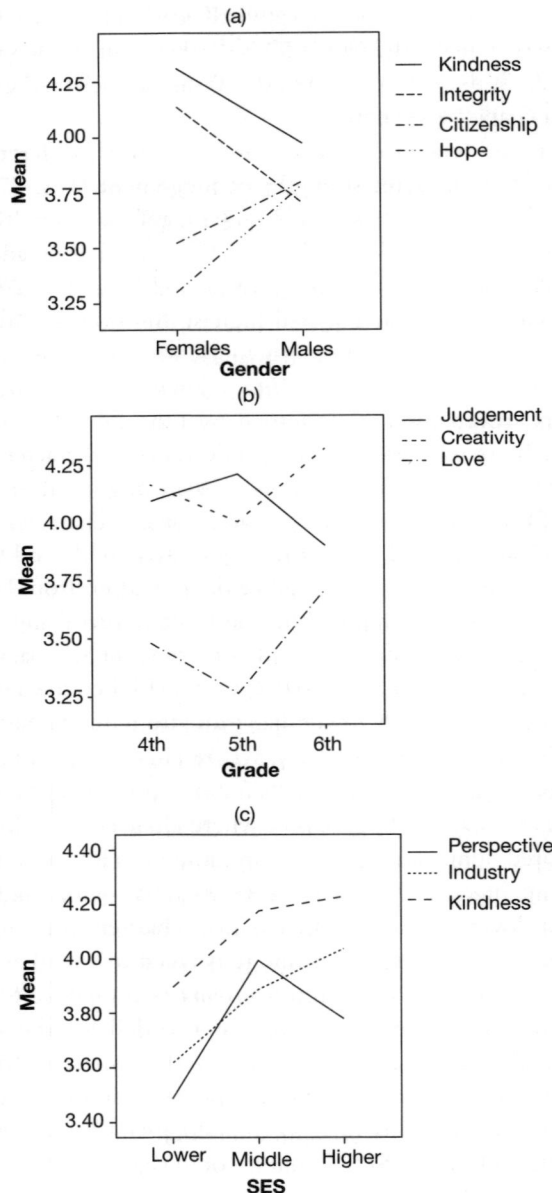

Figure 20.1 Gender (a), Grade (age, b) and SES (c) Differences in Character Strengths

families; and self-efficacy in non-conflict situations ($F(2, 279) = 4.20$, $p < 0.01$), where children from higher SES families scored significantly higher than those from lower SES families. Figure 20.1(c) portrays selected SES differences in character strengths.

RELATIONS BETWEEN VIRTUES AND CREATIVITY, OPTIMISM AND SELF-EFFICACY

In an effort to examine the pattern of possible relations between the study variables, a set of one-way analyses of variance (ANOVAs) were carried out. The results indicated that levels of participants' virtues[1] of (a) courage were dependent on their levels of self-efficacy in non-conflict situations ($F(31, 247) = 1.61$, $p < 0.05$) and (b) temperance differed according to their levels of both types of self-efficacy ($F(26, 252) = 1.53$, $p < 0.05$) for conflict situations and $F(26, 252) = 2.46$, $p < 0.001$ for non-conflict situations). As far as the other study variables were concerned, the level of (c) optimism exhibited by children differed significantly according to their levels of both self-efficacy types (i.e., conflict and non-conflict. $F(62, 216) = 2.00$, $p < 0.001$, and ($F(62, 216) = 1.65$, $p < 0.01$, respectively); (d) self-efficacy in conflict situations differed depending on creativity ($F(49, 229) = 1.62$, $p < 0.01$), optimism ($F(49, 229) = 1.17$, $p < 0.01$) and self-efficacy in non-conflict situations ($F(49, 229) = 3.09$, $p < 0.001$) and (e) self-efficacy in non-conflict situations differed by levels of optimism ($F(31, 247) = 3.50$, $p < 0.001$) and self-efficacy in conflict situations ($F(31, 247) = 8.18$, $p < 0.001$).

In a series of hierarchical linear regressions an attempt was made to examine whether virtues could be reliably predicted by demographics (gender, age/grade and SES were entered in the equation first) and the other study variables, namely, creativity (Kogan and Wallach Creativity Test, 1965), optimism and self-efficacy. Humanity was predicted by creativity and also by SES. In particular, students from lower SES backgrounds seemed to exhibit higher levels of creativity. Creativity remained a strong predictor of humanity even when optimism and self-efficacy entered the regression equation. Transcendence was also

---

[1] In the interest of brevity and simplicity, further analyses were carried out only for virtues, since virtues capitulate and encompass character strengths.

predicted by creativity, which remained a strong predictor even after the inclusion of optimism and self-efficacy. Finally, creativity was only predicted by gender (females more creative than males) and grade (6th graders the most creative students), but not by virtues or the other study variables. However, the link between optimism and self-efficacy identified earlier was corroborated by the regression analysis, which indicated that optimism, apart from demographics (females were more optimistic than males, 6th graders were the most optimistic participants and children from higher SES families the most optimistic of all) was also predicted by self-efficacy in both conflict and non-conflict situations. Details for all regression analyses are shown in Table 20.4.

Discussion

The results from this study seem to confirm a recognizable finding in many other studies across the globe, namely that psycho-socio-emotional development is closely related to the development of character strengths and virtues (Park, Peterson, & Seligman, 2006). Human strengths and virtues can be confidently understood as developmental assets that aid children in their route towards positive development. The next sections offer an overview of the scope of character strengths and virtues as connected to the positive psychological outcomes of creativity, optimism and self-efficacy, thus highlighting the importance of understanding the interconnections between these concepts.

THE SCOPE OF CHARACTER STRENGTHS AND VIRTUES

The most prominent character strengths in Greek children, namely, creativity, love of learning, kindness, judgement and zest, and virtues bore some resemblance to those found in different countries, since kindness and judgement seem to prevail elsewhere as well (Grinhauz & Castro Solano, 2015; Park et al., 2006; Tripathi et al., 2015). As far as the least prevalent strengths in Greece, namely, modesty, curiosity, forgiveness, love and hope are concerned, only modesty was similar with children elsewhere. Some of the study findings contradict those found in Argentina and India, in particular, since love of learning was among the least reported strengths in the former, and love was among

Table 20.4 Hierarchical Regression Analyses for Virtues, Creativity and Optimism

			β	T	SigT	R²	ΔR²	ΔF
Humanity	Demographics					0.04	0.04*	2.33
		SES	−0.15	−2.21	0.02*			
	Creativity		0.15	2.48	0.01**	0.06	0.02**	6.18
Transcendence	Creativity		0.18	2.99	0.00**	0.05	0.03**	8.97
Creativity	Demographics					0.11	0.11***	7.26
		Gender	−0.26	−4.63	0.00***			
		Grade	0.26	2.17	0.03*			
Optimism	Demographics					0.09	0.09***	5.74
		Gender	0.20	3.45***	0.001			
		Grade	−0.12	−1.97	0.05*			
		SES	−0.16	−2.45	0.01**			
	Self-efficacy					0.24	0.00***	20.59
		Conflict	−0.20	−3.20	0.00**			
		Non-conflict	−0.19	−2.97	0.00**			

Notes: * $p < 0.05$, ** $p < 0.01$, *** $p < 0.001$.

the most frequently reported in India (Grinhauz & Castro Solano, 2015; Tripathi et al., 2015). The prominence of love of learning in the study sample can be attributed to cultural reasons. Traditionally, Greek society has always valued education highly, not only for its intrinsic value, but also as a means of attaining higher social and economic status and quality of life (Tsakloglou & Cholezas, 2005). Greek parents are known to go to great lengths to afford their children the best education possible. This has created a strong culture of positive orientation towards learning, as mirrored in the results presented here. The inclusion of zest among the most prevalent strengths for Greece can also be a cultural characteristic. Greece, as indeed other Mediterranean countries, is characterized by heightened and expressive sociability, by family solidarity (Tamis-LeMonda, Wang, Koutsouvanou, & Albright, 2002), as well as by warmth and pathos. Resonances of the famous Greek creativity in general and as a problem-solving mechanism are transmitted throughout the ages, Homer's Ulysses being a prototype of inventiveness and creativity under difficulty. In a study of basic human values in Europe, Davidov, Schmidt and Schwartz (2008) identified five core values for Greece, including hedonism and stimulation, stimulation and self-direction, universalism and benevolence, power and achievement, and conformity and tradition. Hence, the findings that want Greek students exhibiting the strengths of kindness, creativity and zest seem to indicate that the prevalent cultural values in Greece are translated and evident in children's character strengths. Overall, only partial support is offered towards the universality of character strengths, as suggested by Park and Peterson (2006). Finally, as research in virtues is sparse, the study finding that courage was the most prevalent one, with humanity, transcendence, wisdom and knowledge, justice and temperance following suit is informative and novel. It corroborates findings with a Greek sample of university students where courage, transcendence and wisdom were the most salient virtues, and points to the developmental continuity of virtues (Leontopoulou & Triliva, 2012).

THE IMPACT OF DEMOGRAPHICS

A number of demographic differences in character strengths and virtues were unearthed in this study. Both genders appeared to exhibit creativity, kindness and love of learning, offering support to findings that want gender differences in character strengths minimized (Heintz et al., 2017). Females scored higher only on zest and prudence, typical values associated with feminine gender roles: women are thought to be more emotionally expressive than men, hence the manifestation of zest; and also, as they are considered primarily as caregivers, they exhibit prudence as part of their caring role in society (Fischer & Manstead, 2000). Males scored higher on gratitude and judgement, the latter falling under the more typical set of masculine gender roles that want males more rational than females (ibid). This patterning of character strengths appear to differ somewhat from that found in other countries, where kindness was associated with females, but not with males, and gratitude was exhibited by both genders (Brdar et al., 2011). In fact, in this study a reverse finding was found for gratitude, as elsewhere females were found to score higher on gratitude than men (Mann, 2014). Here, both genders scored low in love, forgiveness, curiosity and modesty, with males being less brave and females less hopeful. For both genders, the virtue of courage was most prominent and temperance least prominent. This result agrees with that of a different study with Greek university students and especially women exhibiting high levels of courage and wisdom/knowledge (Leontopoulou & Triliva, 2012). Finally, females appeared to be more creative (as measured by the Kogan and Wallach Creativity Test, 1965) and less optimistic than males. This finding partly supports the outcome of a review of gender differences in creativity, which suggested that, if anything, test scores in creativity and creative accomplishments tend to favour females, although, in general, a consistent lack of gender differences emerge (Baer & Kaufman, 2008). In Greece, however, females were found to be more creative than males (Νημά, 1999). In terms of the higher optimism levels for males found in this study, there is some research evidence indicating that males are more optimistic than females regarding a broad range of issues, including expectations about the future, and economic and financial decision-making (Jacobsen, Lee, Marquering, & Zhang, 2014). All of the aforementioned findings need replication to ascertain their validity.

As regards the influence of age on character strengths, only few differences were found, including judgement, creativity and love, where, in general, older students at the verge of adolescence scored higher than younger children. The same picture emerged for creativity, as measured by the Kogan and Wallach Creativity Test (1965). In a Hong Kong study comparisons between 6th graders and university students indicated that young adults were more creative in real problem-solving, but less so in terms of figural tasks. These results suggested that developmental influences on creativity are at work and that they can be attributed to the interaction between task structures and students' knowledge bases (Wu, Cheng, Ip, & McBride-Chang, 2005). In a Greek study, older students (6th graders) were found to be more creative than younger ones (Χάσκου, 2010). Overall, the aforementioned findings attest to the influence of developmental factors in the exhibition of character strengths. It also suggests that interventions and practices with a clear focus on strengthening character strengths can aid the overall positive developmental course in children and adolescents.

Socio-economic influences on the character strengths of love of learning, perspective, industry, kindness and social intelligence were unearthed, favouring children from middle and higher SES backgrounds. This result lends further support to those reported by Park and Patterson (2006), whereby children from lower SES families scored lower in character strengths tests. Similar differences were revealed for the virtues of wisdom/knowledge and humanity. Children from lower SES backgrounds were more optimistic than those from higher SES backgrounds. This finding is surprising, given that higher SES is usually associated with higher optimism levels and that this is a developmental trend (Carver, Scheier, & Segerstrom, 2010) and needs further exploration. Finally, higher SES students scored higher in self-efficacy in non-conflict situations, a finding that corroborates findings from a meta-analytic review indicating small but significant relations between SES and self-efficacy; the development of self-efficacy over the years follows an ascending trajectory, and is only reversed for adults over 60 years of age (Twenge & Campbell, 2002).

CONSTELLATION OF RELATIONS BETWEEN THE STUDY VARIABLES

A set of relations between virtues and creativity, optimism and self-efficacy emerged from this study, highlighting the close link between the former and aspects of positive youth development. An examination of virtues revealed that self-efficacy in non-conflict situations affected children's levels of the virtue of courage. This finding corroborates research findings that suggest a direct link between different types of self-efficacy beliefs in business students' abilities and courage and meaningfulness (May, Luth, & Schwoerer, 2014). In addition, research into courage development proposed that interpersonal and intrapersonal attribution processes can influence self-perceptions of courageous thought and action (Hannah, Sweeney, & Lester, 2007). Furthermore, in the present study, self-efficacy in both conflict and non-conflict situations also affected students' levels of temperance. This result substantiates findings which suggest that temperance predicts self-efficacy in adolescents living under challenging conditions (Weber, Ruch, Littman-Ovadia, Lavy, & Gai, 2013). With regards to the virtues of humanity and transcendence, creativity appeared to be a good predictor of them both, while SES additionally predicted humanity. While there is no research in character strengths and virtues and creativity, this finding points towards a connection between them. Craft (2003) drew links between the two concepts and suggested that 'education in the twenty-first century needs to foster creative decision making and personal autonomy alongside values of compassion and humanity' (p. xi). In terms of transcendence, Miller and Cook-Greuter (2000) argued for important connections between creativity, spirituality and transcendence. They based these on the argument that creativity and spirituality are natural aspects of self-actualization and urged for explorations of one's own creative self-expression in a quest of personal integrity and wisdom. Returning to this study, creativity and optimism were influenced by both types of self-efficacy (conflict and non-conflict); optimism was also predicted by demographics. Magaletta and Oliver already in 1999 found convincing evidence for the relation between optimism and self-efficacy. Reffel (2003) suggested that creativity is positively related to aspects of optimism and negatively to aspects of pessimism. Fredrickson (2000) ascertained that positive emotions, such as optimism, contribute to the development of original ideas that enhance creativity. It seems likely that positive characteristics of students reinforce each other and often coexist signalling positive development.

Limitations, Future Directions and Contribution of the Study

Limitations of this exploratory study include its cross-sectional nature; future studies should try to adopt a longitudinal design, if developmental changes that influence the development of character strengths are to be addressed effectively. The age range of participants could be broadened to include students in lower grades in primary school and also high school, college and university students, so that the whole spectrum of childhood, adolescence and emerging adulthood can be comprehensively studied. In addition, the complex relations between the study variables can be further examined via the prism of mediation and moderation models, and the implementation of structural equation modelling techniques that can further clarify and highlight the intricate relations between character strengths and virtues and creativity, optimism and self-efficacy, thus revealing pathways to positive youth development.

Nevertheless, this study, embedded within positive education and character strengths research in educational settings, contributes to the discipline of positive developmental psychology at theoretical, research and practice levels. The overview of the manifestation and patterning of specific character strengths and virtues and their relations to other psychological assets, such as creativity, optimism and self-efficacy, here offered go some way towards the identification of individual factors and their constellations that foster positive developmental pathways. Although exploratory in its nature, the study made some headway in understanding the scope of character strengths and virtues in Greek children. In addition, it highlighted the importance and impact of culture and demographics on positive youth development. Therefore, it can contribute towards the identification of best approaches for nurturing them, via developing and implementing targeted, sustainable and effective practices and interventions based on character strengths approaches at home, at the school and the community, and also in consulting and therapy settings.

REFERENCES

Anagnostopoulos, D. K., & Soumaki, E. (2012). The impact of socio-economic crisis on mental health of children and adolescents. *Psychiatriki*, *23*(1), 15–17.

Baer, J., & Kaufman, J. C. (2008). Gender differences in creativity. *Journal of Creative Behavior*, *42*(2), 75–105.

Boden, M. (2004). *The creative mind: Myths and mechanisms*. London: Routledge.

Brdar, I., Anic, P., & Rijavec, M. (2011). Character strengths and well-being: Are there gender differences? In I. Brdar (Ed.), *The human pursuit of well-being: A cultural approach* (145–156). Dordrecht: Springer.

Calvete, E., & Connor-Smith, J. K. (2006). Perceived social support, coping, and symptoms of distress in American and Spanish students. *Anxiety, Stress, and Coping*, *19*(1), 47–65.

Carver, C. S., & Scheier, M. F. (1987). Dispositional optimism and physical well-being: The influence of generalized outcome expectancies on health. *Journal of Personality*, *55*(2), 169–210.

Ey, S., Hadley, W., Nuttbrock Allen, D., Palmer, S., Klosky, J., Deptula, D.,… Cohen, R. (2005). A new measure of children's optimism and pessimism: The Youth Life Orientation Test. *Journal of Child Psychology and Psychiatry*, *46*(5), 548–558.

Hannah, S. T., Sweeney, P. J., & Lester, P. B. (2007). Toward a courageous mindset: The subjective act and experience of courage. *The Journal of Positive Psychology*, *2*(2), 129–135.

Haslam, N., Bain, P., & Neal, D. (2004). The implicit structure of positive characteristics. *Personality and Social Psychology Bulletin*, *30*(4), 529–541.

Heintz, S., Kramm, C., & Ruch, W. (2017). A meta-analysis of gender differences in character strengths and age, nation, and measure as moderators. *The Journal of Positive Psychology*. doi: 10.1080/17439760.2017.1414297

Carver, C. S., Scheier, M. F., & Segerstrom, S. C. (2010). Optimism. *Clinical Psychology Review*, *30*(7), 879–889.

Chang, Y., Wang, P. C., Li, H. H., & Liu, Y. C. (2011). Relations among depression, self-efficacy and optimism in a sample of nurses in Taiwan. *Journal of Nursing Management*, *19*(6), 769–776.

Craft, A. (2003). *Creativity across the primary curriculum: Framing and developing practice*. London: Routledge.

Davidov, E., Schmidt, P., & Schwartz, S. H. (2008). Bringing values back in: The adequacy of the European social survey to measure values in 20 countries. *Public Opinion Quarterly*, *72*(3), 420–445.

Ferragut, M. (2014). Analysis of adolescent profiles by gender: Strength, attitudes toward violence and sexism. *The Spanish Journal of Psychology*, *17*, Article E59.

Fischer, A. H., & Manstead, A. S. (2000). The relation between gender and emotions in different cultures. In A. H. Fischer (Ed.), *Gender and emotion: Social psychological perspectives* (pp. 71–94). Cambridge: Cambridge University Press.

Fredrickson, B. L. (2000). Cultivating positive emotions to optimize health and well-being. *Prevention & Treatment, 3*(1), Article 1a.

Fujiwara, K., Takemura, K., & Suzuki, S. (2017). When a smile does no good: Creativity reduction among avoidance-versus approach-oriented individuals in dyadic interactions. In A. Brem, R. Puente-Diaz, & M. Agogue (Eds.), *The role of creativity in the management of innovation:* State of the art and future research outlook (pp. 159–179). Retrieved from https://doi.org/10.1142/9781786342010_0009

Grinhauz, A. S., & Castro Solano, A. (2015). An exploratory study about character strengths in Argentinean children. *Avances en Psicología Latinoamericana, 33*(1), 45–56. doi:http://dx.doi.org/10.12804/apl33.01.2015.04

Hutchinson, A. K., Stuart, A. D., & Pretorius, H. G. (2011). The relationships between temperament, character strengths, and resilience. In I. Brdar (Ed.), *The human pursuit of well-being: A cultural approach* (pp. 133–144). New York, NY: Springer.

Icekson, T., Roskes, M., & Moran, S. (2014). Effects of optimism on creativity under approach and avoidance motivation. *Frontiers in Human Neuroscience, 8*, 105. doi:10.3389/fnhum.2014.00105

Jacobsen, B., Lee, J. B., Marquering, W., & Zhang, C. Y. (2014). Gender differences in optimism and asset allocation. *Journal of Economic Behavior & Organization, 107*(Part B), 630–651.

Karademas, E. C. (2006). Self-efficacy, social support and well-being: The mediating role of optimism. *Personality and Individual Differences, 40*(6), 1281–1290.

Kitayama, S., & Markus, H. (1999). The yin and yang of the Japanese self: The cultural psychology of personality coherence. In D. Servone & Y. Shoda (Eds.), *The coherence of personality: Social–cognitive bases of consistency, variability, and organization* (pp. 242–302). New York, NY: The Guildford Press.

Kogan, N., & Wallach, M. A. (1965). *Modes of creative thinking in young children: A study of the creativity-intelligence distinction.* New York, NY: Holt, Rinehart and Winston.

Lee, J. N. T., Foo, K. H., Adams, A., Morgan, R., & Frewen, A. (2015). Strengths of character, orientations to happiness, life satisfaction and purpose in Singapore. *Journal of Tropical Psychology, 5*, 1–21. doi:10.1017/jtp.2015.2

Leontopoulou, S., & Triliva, S. (2012). Explorations of subjective wellbeing and character strengths among a Greek University student sample. *International Journal of Wellbeing, 2*(3), 251–270.

Luszczynska, A., Gutiérrez-Doña, B., & Schwarzer, R. (2005). General self-efficacy in various domains of human functioning: Evidence from five countries. *International Journal of Psychology, 40*(2), 80–89.

Magaletta, P. R., & Oliver, J. M. (1999). The hope construct, will, and ways: Their relations with self-efficacy, optimism and general well-being. *Journal of Clinical Psychology, 55*(5), 539–551.

Mann, N. B. (2014). Signature strengths: Gender differences in creativity, persistence, prudence, gratitude, and hope. *Dissertation Abstracts International: Section B: The Sciences and Engineering, 74*(7-B(E)), np.

May, D. R., Luth, M. T., & Schwoerer, C. E. (2014). The influence of business ethics education on moral efficacy, moral meaningfulness, and moral courage: A quasi-experimental study. *Journal of Business Ethics, 124*(1), 67–80.

Michael, L. H., Hou, S. T., & Fan, H. L. (2011). Creative self-efficacy and innovative behavior in a service setting: Optimism as a moderator. *The Journal of Creative Behavior, 45*(4), 258–272.

Miller, M. E., & Cook-Greuter, S. R. (Eds.). (2000). *Creativity, spirituality, and transcendence: Paths to integrity and wisdom in the mature self.* Greenwich, CT: Ablex Publishing Corporation.

Μόττη-Στεφανίδη, Φ., Ντάλλα, Μ., Παπαθανασίου, Α. Χ., Παυλόπουλος, Β., & Τάκης, Ν. (2005). Ψυχική ανθεκτικότητα και προσδοκίες αυτοαποτελεσματικότητας: Μια μελέτη μεταναστών και παλιννοστούντων εφήβων (Resilience and self-efficacy expectations: A study of migrant and remigrating adolescents). *Ψυχολογία, 12*(3), 349–367.

Μπούτρη, Α. (2011). Ευτυχία, Ελπίδα-Αισιοδοξία, Περιέργεια (Happiness, hope–optimism, curiosity). Στο Σταλίκας, Α. και Μυτσκίδου, Π., *Εισαγωγή στη Θετική Ψυχολογία* (pp. 63–86). Αθήνα: Εκδόσεις Τόπος.

Neto, J., Neto, F., & Furnham, A. (2014). Gender and psychological correlates of self-rated strengths among youth. *Social Indicators Research, 118*(1), 315–327. doi:10.1007/s11205-013-0417-5

Νημά, Ε. (1999). *Δημιουργικότητα και σχολική επίδοση: Διερεύνηση των δύο μεταβλητών σε δείγμα μαθητών γυμνασίου* (Διδακτορική Διατριβή. Creativity and school performance: Exploration of the two variables in a high school student sample. Doctoral dissertation). Αριστοτέλειο Πανεπιστήμιο Θεσσαλονίκης.

Linley, P. A., Joseph, S., Harrington, S., & Wood, A. M. (2006). Positive psychology: Past, present, and (possible) future. *Journal of Positive Psychology, 1*(1), 3–16.

Papanastasiou, S., Ntafouli, M., & Kourtidou, D. (2016). The state of the children in Greece report 2016. *Hellenic National Committee for UNICEF 2016.* Retrieved from https://www.unicef.gr/uploads/filemanager/PDF/2016/children-in-greece-2016-eng.pdf

Park, N., & Peterson, C. (2006). Moral competence and character strengths among adolescents: The development and validation of the Values in Action inventory of strengths for youth. *Journal of Adolescence, 29,* 891–909. doi:10.1016/j.adolescence.2006.04.011

Park, N., Peterson, C., & Seligman, M. E. P. (2006). Character strengths in fifty-four nations and the fifty US states. *The Journal of Positive Psychology, 1*(3), 118–129.

Peterson, C., & Seligman, M. E. P. (2004). *Character strengths and virtues: A handbook and classification.* New York, NY: Oxford University Press.

Peterson, C., Ruch, W., Beermann, U., Park, N., & Seligman, M. E. (2007). Strengths of character, orientations to happiness, and life satisfaction. *The Journal of Positive Psychology, 2,* 149–156. doi:10.1080/17439760701228938

Petrogiannis, K. (2011). Conceptions of the transition to adulthood in a sample of Greek higher education students. *International Journal of Psychology and Psychological Therapy*, *11*(1), 121–137.

Reffel, J. A. (2003). Creative teachers value creative characteristics in their students. In D. Treffinger (Ed.), *Creative Learning Today Newsletter*. Sarasota, FL: Centre for Creative Learning.

Rego, A., Sousa, F., Marques, C., & Cunha, M. P. E. (2012). Optimism predicting employees' creativity: The mediating role of positive affect and the positivity ratio. *European Journal of Work and Organizational Psychology*, *21*(2), 244–270.

Seligman, M. E. P. (2002). *Authentic happiness: Using the new positive psychology to realize your potential for lasting fulfilment*. New York, NY: Free Press.

Tamis-LeMonda, C. S., Wang, S., Koutsouvanou, E., & Albright, M. (2002). Childrearing values in Greece, Taiwan, and the United States. *Parenting: Science and Practice*, *2*(3), 185–208.

Tierney, P., & Farmer, S. M. (2011). Creative self-efficacy development and creative performance over time. *Journal of Applied Psychology*, *96*(2), 277.

Tripathi, R., Banu, H., & Mehrotra, S. (2015). Self-perceived character strengths in urban Indian youth: Observations and reflections. *Journal of the Indian Academy of Applied Psychology*, *41*(3), 176–187.

Tsakloglou, P., & Cholezas, I. (2005). Education and inequality in Greece. IZA Discussion Paper No. 1582. Retrieved from https://ssrn.com/abstract=719924

Twenge, J. M., & Campbell, W. K. (2002). Self-esteem and socioeconomic status: A meta-analytic review. *Personality and Social Psychology Review*, *6*(1), 59–71.

Χάσκου, Σ. (2010). *Νοημοσύνη και δημιουργικότητα μαθητών σχολικής ηλικίας* (Διδακτορική Διατριβή. Intelligence and creativity of school-age students. Doctoral dissertation). Εθνικό και Καποδιστριακό Πανεπιστήμιο Αθηνών.

Weber, M., Ruch, W., Littman-Ovadia, H., Lavy, S., & Gai, O. (2013). Relationships among higher-order strengths factors, subjective well-being, and general self-efficacy: The case of Israeli adolescents. *Personality and Individual Differences*, *55*(3), 322–327.

Wheeler, V. A., & Ladd, G. W. (1982). Assessment of children's self-efficacy for social interaction with peers. *Developmental Psychology*, *18*, 795–805.

Wood, A. M., Linley, P. A., Maltby, J., Kashdan, T. B., & Hurling, R. (2011). Using personal and psychological strengths leads to increases in well-being over time: A longitudinal study and the development of the strengths use questionnaire. *Personality and Individual Differences*, *50*, 15–19. doi:10.1016/j.paid.2010.08.004

Wu, C. H., Cheng, Y., Ip, H. M., & McBride-Chang, C. (2005). Age differences in creativity: Task structure and knowledge base. *Creativity Research Journal*, *17*(4), 321–326.

About the Editors and Contributors

EDITORS

Aneesh Kumar P., PhD, is an Assistant Professor of Psychology at the Department of Psychology, CHRIST (Deemed to be University), Bengaluru. He is involved in various research projects including the United States–India Education Foundation project on developing culturally competent clinical psychology programmes in India, and student mental health through positive schooling model. He teaches courses in child and adolescent counselling, counselling special population, development psychology and qualitative research methods.

Tony Sam George, PhD, is the Dean of Humanities and Sciences, and the Head of the Department of Psychology, CHRIST (Deemed to be University), Bengaluru. Dr Tony's research interests are in the areas of family violence, programme planning and evaluation, policy and administration in mental health and higher education. He teaches courses in qualitative research methods, research philosophy, family therapy and counselling theories and techniques.

Sudhesh N. T. is an Assistant Professor (Psychology) at CHRIST (Deemed to be University), Bengaluru. He is the current president of IALSE (Indian Association of Life Skills Education) Bengaluru, Karnataka chapter. He has conducted several life-skills training and community intervention programmes in the last 10 years. His research interests include adolescent and youth psychology, school psychology, life skills education, social intervention, training and development and qualitative research methods.

CONTRIBUTORS

Jessica Bertolani, PhD, is Research Officer II at the Department of Counselling, University of Malta. She is an Adjunct Professor at the University of Massachusetts and collaborates with the Center for School Counseling Outcome Research. She is an executive member of the International Association for Counselling and Representative for Europe. Dr Bertolani's research interests are in social–emotional and self-directed learning programmes in school and in counselling in international contexts.

Rayees Mohammad Bhat has his primary research interests in the experience of psychological trauma and its correlates, especially in the context of traumatic experiences associated to conflict and violence. Currently, he serves as a psychology guest faculty at Government Degree College for Women, Baramulla, Jammu & Kashmir.

Vibha Bhat is a student pursuing BSc (Honours) in Psychology at CHRIST (Deemed to be University), Bengaluru. She is currently working on her dissertation which explores coping among women diagnosed with polycystic ovary syndrome. Her current areas of interest include adolescent and women's health, positive psychology, neuropsychology and forensic psychology.

Bhagyalakshmi K. C. is currently pursuing PhD in psychology, with child abuse and safety as the key area, from CHRIST (Deemed to be University), Bengaluru. Her academic profile includes teaching and guidance in neuropsychology, psychometry and environmental psychology. Her paper was presented at the international conference on 'Parental Involvement in School Counselling Programs' (InSPA, Mysore 2017).

John C. Carey, PhD, is Professor Emeritus, Director of the Center for Youth Engagement and Associate Director of the Ronald H. Fredrickson Center for School Counseling Outcome Research at the University of Massachusetts. Dr Carey's research interests are in the development and evaluation of social–emotional learning programmes in schools and in policy research related to school-based counselling.

He is the Lead Editor of the *International Handbook for Policy Research on School-based Counseling* (2017).

Shoma Chakrawarty is an assistant professor at the Department of Psychology at St Francis College for Women, Begumpet, Hyderabad. Her doctoral research is focused on the cancer caregiving experience in the Indian context. Her broad research interests revolve around chronic illnesses and their psychosocial sequelae along with exploring the stress-buffering role of various facets of the Indian social fabric.

Johnson Chun-sing Cheung is Lecturer at the Department of Social Work, the Chinese University of Hong Kong. Dr Cheung teaches social work research, program evaluation, community work and other courses at both postgraduate and undergraduate levels. He has a proven track record of successful publications in major peer-reviewed journals in social work and also of being an editorial board member and reviewer for several reputed journals.

Beatrice W. E. Churu has a PhD in religious studies, with a focus in leadership in Catholic secondary schools, from Kenyatta University in Nairobi. Her main interest and teaching area is African religion and worldview, and its contribution to restoration of Africa.

Lui Ka Ki David is a theatre and community cultural worker and a registered social worker in Hong Kong, a part-time MPhil student at Department of Applied Social Sciences, City University of Hong Kong, and the Project Officer of Centre for Community Cultural Development in Hong Kong. He is a highly experienced practitioner of people's theatre and community arts.

Sibnath Deb, PhD, DSc, is Professor at the Department of Applied Psychology, Pondicherry University, India. In addition, Professor Deb is Acting Director (I/C), Directorate of Distance Education and Dean (I/C), School of Law, Pondicherry University. Professor Deb is also attached to the School of Public Health and Social Work, Queensland University of Technology (QUT), Brisbane, Australia as an Adjunct Professor since 2014. Professor Deb's current areas of research interest include child safety, child rights, students' mental health, adolescent reproductive health and applied social psychology.

Jennifer M. Foster is an Assistant Professor in the Department of Counselor Education and Counseling Psychology at Western Michigan University. Foster joined the faculty in 2012. Before joining WMU, Foster worked as a licensed mental health counsellor as well as professional school counsellor. Foster's chief focus has been in the area of child sexual abuse, and she is a leader and major contributor to the scholarly literature in this area.

Adrian Furnham was educated at the London School of Economics and at Oxford University. Previously a lecturer in psychology at Pembroke College, Oxford, he was professor of psychology at University College London from 1992 to 2018. He has also been made adjunct professor of management at the Norwegian School of Management (2009) and honorary professor at the University of KwaZulu-Natal (2014).

Jennifer H. Green is a child clinical psychologist and a Senior Clinical Faculty member in the Department of Psychology at Miami University, USA. Her professional interests include early childhood mental health, social–emotional learning, school-based mental health and clinical interventions for children and adolescents with internalizing and externalizing disorders. She teaches courses in child developmental psychopathology, psychological assessment, evidence-based child and adolescent intervention and clinical supervision.

Mark D. Holder is an Associate Professor at the University of British Columbia, where he leads a research team that investigates the correlates of well-being, and develops and tests interventions designed to increase well-being and decrease ill-being. Dr Holder is an award-winning lecturer and is known for his engaging, funny and accessible invited talks around the world.

Nick Holton is the Director of Positive Psychology and Positive Education at Milken Community Schools in Los Angeles, California, where he works closely with national and global leaders of positive psychology to apply the principles of human flourishing to educational practice and institutional operations. Dr Holton is a member of the American Psychological Association, the International Positive Education Network and the International Positive Psychology Association.

Zohra Ihsan is a researcher based in London and has recently graduated from the University of Bath with a BSc (Honours) in Psychology. She has undertaken several roles in the field of organizational psychology, both in academic and commercial areas.

Dolly Jose (Sr. Josiya), PhD, belongs to the Franciscan Clarist Congregation and is a psychologist, especially for long-term therapies for religious persons and priests. She holds Licentiate in depth psychology from Institute of Psychology, Gregorian University Rome, and Doctorate in Positive Psychology, CHRIST (Deemed to be University), Bengaluru. She teaches in various formation institutes, novitiate houses and conducts workshops related to well-being, character strength development, leadership, group therapy and counselling practices.

Avneet Kaur is a student of Psychology (Honours) at CHRIST (Deemed to be University), Bengaluru. As a part of her dissertation, she is researching on the relationship between nature of religiosity and eating attitudes among individuals who fast. Avneet, along with Anirudh Kedia, presented a paper on the conceptual analysis of social media websites and their relationship with personality at Synthesize, a national conference held at CHRIST (Deemed to be University), Bengaluru in March 2017.

Anirudh Kedia is a third-year undergraduate Psychology (Honours) student studying in CHRIST (Deemed to be University). His areas of interest include aviation psychology, cognitive psychology, neuroscience, education psychology and positive psychology. Anirudh wishes to explore non-conventional and upcoming fields of psychology further and use research to help better people's lives.

Ranjitha Kumar is a final-year BSc Psychology (Honours) student at CHRIST (Deemed to be University), Bengaluru. As a part of her dissertation, she is constructing and validating a situational scale to measure vicarious embarrassment among university students. Her areas of interest include neuroscience, social cognition and counselling. Ranjitha presented a conceptual paper on using epigenetic biomarkers to measure the efficacy of psychotherapy at Synthesize, a national conference held at CHRIST (Deemed to be University), Bengaluru in March 2017.

Vincent Wan-ping Lee is attached to the Department of Applied Social Sciences, The Hong Kong Polytechnic University. Dr Lee is a registered social worker in Hong Kong. He has recently been working on research projects related to community inclusion and mental health facilities, and also the livelihood of ethnic minorities in Hong Kong. He has also co-authored a number of articles published in international academic journals.

Sophie Leontopoulou is Assistant Professor of Psychology at the Department of Primary Education, University of Ioannina, Greece. She is a Fulbright Fellow and former coordinator of the Division of Developmental Psychology of the Hellenic Psychological Society. Her theoretical and research interests focus on the area of positive developmental psychology. She has published and presented her work internationally on various areas related to positive psychosocial development in childhood, adolescence and emerging adulthood.

Henry Wai-hang Ling, MPhil (HKU), BSW (HKU), RSW, is a part-time Assistant Lecturer (Practice Consultant) at the Department of Social Work and Social Administration, the University of Hong Kong. His research interests are volunteering, mental health, addictive behaviours, youth issues, school social work and parenting. Henry is the co-author of several international journals and book chapters. He has several recent publications to his credit.

Bishakha Majumdar is Assistant Professor, OB & HR, FORE School of Management, New Delhi. A Fellow of IIM Indore, Bishakha Majumdar has three years of experience in teaching and research in applied psychology and organizational behaviour. She has national and international publications in the areas of human resource management, psychology and public health. She is presently also the Associate Editor of the journal *South Asian Survey*, published by SAGE.

Raseela K. N. is a postgraduate in clinical and counselling psychology. She is currently working as Assistant Professor in Psychology at

School of Behavioural Sciences, Kannur University. She has previous experience in teaching general psychology to graduate students at various nursing colleges in Kannur as guest lecturer.

S. S. Nathawat is Professor Emeritus and Director, Amity Centre for Positivism & Happiness, Amity University, Rajasthan. He has been teaching psychology and also involved in higher-level research for over four decades in India. He has taught at several universities including Jodhpur University; Kurukshetra University; University of Rajasthan, Jaipur; and presently at Amity University, Jaipur since 2009. He edited the prestigious *Indian Journal of Clinical Psychology* (IJCP) for over 6 years.

Padmakumari P., PhD, teaches students at undergraduate, postgraduate and MPhil levels as Associate Professor at the Department of Psychology, CHRIST (Deemed to be University), Bengaluru. Her academic interests include psychopathology, research methods and positive psychology. She is actively involved in research across a wide range of topics in psychopathology and positive psychology.

Ruopfuvinuo Pienyu is Research Assistant in the Department of Psychology at CHRIST (Deemed to be University), Bengaluru since May 2017. Her area of focus is positive psychology—well-being, strengths and coping, in particular. She has authored three publications.

Vijaya R. specializes in industrial and organizational psychology, currently working as Assistant Professor at CHRIST (Deemed to be University), Bengaluru. As part of her PhD work, she researched on downsizing employees. She has authored a few articles and book chapters on organizational behaviour and continues her research work in the area of downsizing organization and retrenched employees.

Santhosh Kareepadath Rajan, PhD, is Assistant Professor at the Department of Psychology, CHRIST (Deemed to be University), Bengaluru since 2016. His research interests span positive solution-focused correctional psychology, which includes resilience, strengths and *pratixas* (a newly emerging concept). He has authored 20 publications (1 book, 2 chapters and 17 journal articles). He is a member of International Positive Psychology Association and Association of Solution Focused Practices, India.

Vaishali V. Raval is Associate Professor and Associate Chair, Department of Psychology, University of Miami, Ohio. Conceptualized from an interdisciplinary perspective, her research examines parenting, emotion and emotion communication in the family context, and child health outcomes in international populations and ethnic minority groups in the United States, particularly Asians and Asian Americans.

Sahaya G. Selvam, PhD, originally from India, has been serving in religious and academic contexts in East Africa since 1992. He has separate degrees in several areas including the psychology of religion. His doctoral work examined the mediating role of character strengths in the relationship between Christian mindfulness practice and recovery from addictive behaviour.

Vijayalaya Srinivas T. is currently working as Assistant Professor of Psychology, School of Business Studies & Social Sciences, CHRIST (Deemed to be University), Bengaluru. He is interested in organizational psychology, especially entrepreneurship. He teaches papers such as history and systems of psychology, quantitative and qualitative research methodology, and consumer and industrial psychology.

Lijo Thomas has been an adjunct professor and research scientist at the University of Louisiana, Monroe, USA, and joined as a faculty at CHRIST (Deemed to be University), Bengaluru recently. He has worked in school administration, teaching, community intervention projects and professional development programmes in India and the United States. Dr Thomas has developed and implemented a community collaborative success intervention programme, DREAMS, for lower-performing/at-risk middle school students.

Tanya Tripathi completed her MPhil in Clinical Psychology from Amity University with a gold medal in 2017. She is working as a consultant clinical psychologist at Vivekanand Institute of Mental Health and Neuro Sciences, Jaipur.

Hitankshi M. Trivedi is currently a student at CHRIST (Deemed to be University), Bengaluru, pursuing her undergraduation course in BSc Psychology (Honours). She has diverse interests in clinical psychology, forensic psychology, consumer psychology and counselling.

Ritu Verma is a student currently pursuing her BSc in Psychology (Honours) degree from CHRIST (Deemed to be University), Bengaluru. Her interests lie in the fields of sports, developmental, clinical and aviation psychology. She is currently working on her undergraduate dissertation on sports and exercise psychology.

Salome Divya Vijaykumar is an Assistant Professor at CHRIST (Deemed to be University), Bengaluru. Positive psychology, counselling psychology, developmental psychology and psychotherapy are her areas of teaching and research interest. Salome has over two years' teaching experience and currently has six publications to her credit.

Marco Weber received his PhD from the University of Zurich, Switzerland. Currently he is Visiting Professor for psychological assessment, evaluation and intervention at the Technical University of Darmstadt, Germany. He is member of the International Positive Psychology Association (IPPA) and received in 2013 IPPA's 'Honorable Mention Award' in recognition of an outstanding contribution to positive psychology research.

Sarah Weissmeyer worked as a Directed Studies student as an undergraduate at the University of British Columbia and then completed her degree with a major in Psychology. In 2013, she received the Governor General's Academic Bronze Medal and currently works as a Mental Health Support Worker in Kelowna, British Columbia.

Jessline Williams is an MSc in Clinical Psychology graduate from CHRIST (Deemed to be University), Bengaluru. She is currently pursuing her MPhil in Psychology. Her current research work is 'Character Strengths, Social Concept and Well-being Among Adolescents with Specific Learning Disorder'. She also serves as a remedial and behavioural therapist for children with special needs at Parijma Medical Center, Bengaluru.

Index

caring establishment, 306
case studies
    Maple Leaf Foods, 243–244
character strengths (CSs), 45, 233, 302
    abuse and neglect
        development of survivors, 135–137
    application of theatre development, 120
        courage, 121
        humanity, 121
        justice, 122
        temperature, 122
        transcendence, 122
        wisdom, 120
    associated outcomes, 234
    big five, 102–104
    charity sport events, 236
    children, 47
        autonomy, 67–69
        excellence and beauty, appreciation, 50–51
        hope, 48
        kindness, 51–53
        spirituality, 48–50
    classification, 1–5
        life outcomes, 251–253
        signature strengths, 251
        six board virtues, 250
    constellation of relations, 391
    corporate social responsibility, 236
    creativity, 374, 385–386
    cultural and demographic issues, 371–372

demographics
    differences, 370, 383
    impact, 388–390
development, 187–189, 303
    intentional actions for family to foster, 305–306
empirical evidence, 359–361
ethical decision-making, 238
implications
    applications, 21
    educational practitioners, 24
    parents, 24
    policymakers, 22
    possession, 21
    practical implications, 22
    pre-service training, 22
    school psychologists, 24
    service teachers, 22
    students, 23
    theoretical, 21
    well-being model, 21
improvisation as challenges, 119
interventions, 53–54
    implementation, 55–57
    importance, 54–55
    strengths, 57–59
    study, 59–62
limitations and future research, 63
materials, 373
methodologies from theatre, 118
optimism, 374
    self-efficacy, 385–386
organizational-level virtues, 235
overused strengths, 107–108

people theatre, 117
positive development
  role, 359
positive psychology interventions, 65–67
positive youth development, 237
professional development in theatre, 119
sample and procedure, 373
self efficacy, 374
self-compassion and mindfulness, 190
  barriers, 194–195
  ice breaker activity, 193
  incorporation, 193
  intervention, 192
  spreading love, 196
signature strengths, 234
small and medium enterprises (SMEs), 236
socio-cultural and economic contexts
  consideration, 64
story-telling and social interaction, 118
strength development
  body to mind, 118
student-level
  love of learning, 15
  perseverance, 16
  prudence, 17
  style-relevant experiences, 18
students and teachers, 20
study, 373
teacher level
  hope, 18
  leadership, 19
theatre and flow experience, 119
theatre for development, 114–115
training program for parents, 284–285
universal virtues, 235
VBO model, 238–241
  situational pressure, 239
  strength based intervention, 242–243
  Theodora effect, 241–242
  virtuous define, 238
VIA, 233
victimized, 155–157
virtues, 102–104, 385–386
  assets, 369–370
  measurement, 93
  scope, 386–388
  studies, 94
  VIA-IS, 100–102
weaknesses among victimized, 154–155
character strengths and virtues (CSV), 45
child abuse and neglect (CAN), 132
  abuse and neglect
    CSs development of survivors, 135–137
    demographics of victims, 133–135
  applications, 138–139
  opportunities and challenges, 139–141
  strengths, 139–141
  survivor case study, 141–145
  weaknesses, 139–141
child communications, 278
child victimization
  current scenario, 153–154
childhood neurodevelopmental disorders, 356
children
  adolescents, 357
  disabilities, 354
  dyslexia, 356
  emotional competence
    parental contributions, development, 169–171
children's emotional competence
  parents and educators
    recommendations, 171–175
children's interpersonal relationship

parents' perspectives, 278–279
children's reliance on smartphones, 277
Clifton Strength Finder, 156
Collaborative for Academic, Social and Emotional Learning (CASEL), 162, 164
   model, 162
common parlance, 181
conservation of resources (COR) model, 327
constructivist grounded theory, 275
continuous improvement
   challenging growth, 306

data collection
   method, 341
      data handling and analysis, 343
      energy and enthusiasm, 344
      procedure, 342
      strengths, awareness, 346
      young adults awareness, 343
decision-making
   sharing power, 307

Eccomi Pronto (EP), 31
   character strengths (CSs)
      curricula, developing, 40–41
   curriculum, 32
      supplements, 33
      developing effective curricula, 37–39
      development, 34–35
      evaluation, 35–36
education systems, 339
emotional competence, 160
   cultural context, 165–167
   models
      CASEL, 162
      SEL, 162
eradication of deficits, 357
ethical decision-making (EDM) model, 238

eudaimonia, 80
   authentic growth, 83–85
   character strengths (CSs), 81
      empirical work, 81
      engagement, 82–83
      life-satisfaction and well-being, 81–82
   growth and eudaimonic well-being, 85–87

FM Theatre Power, 123
   community and school settings, works, 125
   international exploration, 125
   people's theatre and traditional theatre, integration, 123–124
   young people participation, 124
   youth based collective creativity, 124

individualistic and relational emotional competence, 167–169
Information and Communication Technology (ICT), 267
International Community Arts Festival (ICAF) Rotterdam, 125
interviews, 275

Journal of Happiness Studies, 92
Journal of Positive Psychology, 92

Kogan and Wallach Creativity Test (1965), 378

Making Friends with Yourself (MFY), 196
Ministry of Youth Affairs (2007), 340

National Center for Learning Disabilities (2014), 355
nurturance, 204
   character strengths (CSs)
      children, schools role, 218–221

parents, role, 213–218
peers, influence, 221–222
recommendations, 224–226
role, 222–224
socialization
agents in CS, role, 213
biological systems, 209–213
concepts and views, 205–209

parent-child relationship, 266
character strength (CSs)
young people, 271–272
coercive family processes, 273
mobile devices, 268–270
methods and approaches, impact, 270
predisposing parent characteristics, 274
parental guidance and supervision approaches, 279–282
parenting
character strengths (CSs), 254–255
development, 255–256
novel uses, 258
praise and compliments, role, 256–257
strength-based parenting, 256–257
positive psychological theatre practice, 126
community
arts training system, 127
oriented theatre centre, 127
positive psychologists, 339
positive schooling, 5–8
character strength (CSs), 8
input variables and process variables, 9, 12
outcome variables and input variables, 11
outcome variables and process variables, 12–13
teacher level, 11, 12

positivism, 292
ANOVA
courage, 1
humanity, 1
justice, 1
temperance, 1
transcendence, 1
relation to signature strength, 293
signature strength, 294
VIA, 295
virtues, 294
posttraumatic growth (PTG), 314, 318–320
historical background, 315–316
predictors, 323–326
psychological trauma, 316–318
theoretical model, 321–323

self-compassion, 180
character strengths (CSs)
foundation, 190
virtues, 189
development, 186
intimacy vs. isolation, 185–186
qualities, 181
relation to self-esteem and concept, 182
crystallization of personality, 184–185
self-pity, 183
social-emotional learning (SEL), 162
socio-economic status (SES), 374
strength based parenting, 304
experiences, 305
subjective well-being (SWB), 44–45
children, 47
excellence and beauty, appreciation, 50–51
hope, 48
kindness, 51–53
spirituality, 48–50
limitations and future research, 63

socio-cultural and economic contexts consideration, 64

the Rights of Persons with Disabilities Act, 355
theories
    Aldwin's theory of deviation amplification model of stress and coping (1996), 329
    Hobfoll's conservation of resources theory (1989), 327
    Meichenbaum's stress inoculation theory (1985), 328
    Taylor's theory of cognitive adaptation (1983), 327
Trauma-Focused Cognitive Behavioural Therapy (TF-CBT), 138

Values in Action (VIA), 1, 156, 233, 295
model, 250
Values in Action Inventory of Strengths (VIA-IS), 96–97, 341
    factor structure, 98–100
    valid measure, 100–102
Values in Action Rising to the Occasion Inventory (VIA-RTO), 98
virtue based orientation (VBO) model, 238
    leadership, 239–241
    situational pressure, 239
    strength based intervention, 242–243
    Theodora effect, 241–242
    virtuous define, 238
virtues, 378

zestful students, 20